How Canadians Communicate IV

How Canadians Communicate IV

Media and Politics

Edited by
David Taras and Christopher Waddell

AU PRESS

Copyright © 2012 David Taras and Christopher Waddell

Published by AU Press, Athabasca University
1200, 10011 – 109 Street, Edmonton, AB T5J 3S8

ISBN 978-1-926836-81-2 (print)   978-1-926836-82-9 (PDF)   978-1-926836-83-6 (epub)

Interior design by Sergiy Kozakov
Printed and bound in Canada by Marquis Book Printers

Library and Archives Canada Cataloguing in Publication
    Media and politics / edited by David Taras and Christopher Waddell.

(How Canadians communicate ; 4)
Includes bibliographical references and index.
Issued also in electronic formats.
ISBN 978-1-926836-81-2

    1. Mass media--Political aspects--Canada. 2. Social media--Political aspects--Canada.
3. Communication in politics--Canada. 4. Canada--Politics and government. I. Taras,
David, 1950- II. Waddell, Christopher Robb III. Series: How Canadians communicate ; 4

P95.82.C3M45 2012   302.230971   C2012-901951-8

We acknowledge the financial support of the Government of Canada through
the Canada Book Fund (CFB) for our publishing activities.

Assistance provided by the Government of Alberta, Alberta Multimedia
Development Fund.

Canada Council   Conseil des Arts
for the Arts   du Canada

**Government
of Alberta** ■

Canadian   Patrimoine
Heritage   canadien

Contents

PART I   THE CHANGING WORLD OF MEDIA AND POLITICS

Illustrations

Acknowledgements

This book is the result of a collaborative effort between Athabasca University and the Alberta Global Forum, now based at Mount Royal University. We are particularly grateful to Frits Pannekoek, president of Athabasca University. Without his insights, guidance, and commitment, this book would not have been possible. The book and the conference that gave life to it received generous support from a grant awarded by the Social Sciences and Humanities Research Council of Canada. We are deeply appreciative. We are also grateful to Gina Grosenick, who did a magnificent job of helping to organize the conference, and to Peter Zuurbier, whose assistance in collecting the individual essays and preparing the final manuscript was indispensable. Walter Hildebrandt, the director of Athabasca University Press, was extremely supportive and as always brought impressive ideas and good judgment. Those who worked on the volume for AU Press, Pamela MacFarland Holway, Joyce Hildebrand, Megan Hall, and Sergiy Kozakov, were all first rate. Everett Wilson helped with the original poster design for the conference and provided ideas for the book cover.

Christopher Waddell would like to thank the School of Journalism and Communication at Carleton University for giving him a wonderful vantage point over the past decade from which to watch the evolution of Canadian media, politics, and public policy. He is also grateful to his wife, Anne Waddell, and their children, Matthew and Kerry, for giving him the time to do that and to his mother, Lyn Cook Waddell, whose life as an author has had a tremendous influence on his own work. Chris adds a special thanks to Frits Pannekoek and Gina Grosenick for everything that they have done to make the conference and this volume possible.

David Taras would like to thank Chris Waddell and Frits Pannekoek for being such insightful and inspiring colleagues, Dean Marc Chikinda and Provost Robin Fisher of Mount Royal University for their faith and vision, and Greg Forrest and Jeanette Nicholls of the Alberta Global Forum for their leadership. Gina Grosenick was magnificent, as always. Claire Cummings provided excellent assistance for the AGF on a whole series of fronts, which included helping to organize the conference. David would also like to thank his wife, Joan, for her support and understanding.

David Taras

The Past and Future
of Political Communication in Canada
An Introduction

In June 1980, in the wake of the Québec referendum on sovereignty and the 1979 and 1980 federal elections, the Reader's Digest Foundation and what was then Erindale College of the University of Toronto co-sponsored a conference on politics and the media.[1] The Erindale conference brought together prominent party strategists and organizers, journalists, and scholars. Participants spoke about the power of television images, the presidentialization of Canadian politics, the concentration of media ownership, the failure of leaders to address policies in a serious way during elections, the sheer nastiness and negativity of political attacks, the power of the media to set the agenda and frame issues during elections, and the need for politicians to fit into those very media frames if they wished to be covered at all. None of these concerns have vanished with time. If anything, they have hardened into place, making them even more pervasive and intractable.

Yet even as so much has remained the same, so much has changed. When the conference "How Canadians Communicate Politically: The Next Generation" was convened in Calgary and Banff in late October 2009, the media and political terrains had been dramatically transformed. The revolution in web-based technology that had begun in the mid-1990s had hit the country with devastating force. As online media depleted the newspaper industry, TV networks, and local radio stations of a sizable portion of their audiences and advertising, the old lions of the traditional media lost some of their bite. The stark reality today is that every medium is merging with every other medium, every medium is becoming every other medium, and all media are merging on the Internet. Most critically, a new generation of digital natives, those who have grown up with web-based media, is no longer subject to a top-down, command-and-control media system in which messages flow in only one direction. Audiences now have the capacity to create their own islands of information from the endless sea of media choices that surround them, as well as to produce and circulate their own videos, photos, opinions, and products, and to attract their own advertising.

And the country has also changed. The Charter of Rights and Freedoms, the absorption of more immigrants from more countries than any other society in history, the growth of global cities, and connectivity have all produced a profoundly different society. Furthermore, years of constitutional battles and another much more desperately fought referendum in Québec in 1995 have culminated in both frustration and exhaustion. Living on the edge of a precipice could not be sustained indefinitely, even in Québec. The country has also grown proud of its accomplishments. Canada's banking system withstood the most punishing effects of the financial meltdown that ravaged the world financial system in 2008 and 2009; multicultural experiments that appear to be failing in other societies, such as France, the United Kingdom, and Germany, are succeeding in Canada; and arts and culture are burgeoning.

The "How Canadians Communicate Politically" conference, organized by Athabasca University and the Alberta Global Forum (then based at the University of Calgary and now at Mount Royal University), brought together distinguished scholars from across Canada with the intention of examining what the next generation of political communication would look like. We asked contributors to view politics and communication through a much different and more expansive lens than was the case with the 1980 Erindale conference. While much of this volume deals with media and politics in the conventional sense—examining such topics as the interplay among journalists and politicians, the future of news, and the effectiveness of negative campaigning in both online and TV advertising—we also look at politics through the frames of popular culture and everyday life: biographies, off-road politics in rural Alberta, Québec film, hotline radio, music, and Aboriginal art. The noted Swedish scholar Peter Dahlgren has observed that changes in popular culture both reflect and condition political change.[2] Once a trend or idea becomes firmly implanted within a culture, it is only a matter of time before it permeates and affects public policy. While some of these essays deal with aspects of popular culture, our search was wider—we wanted to see how politics takes shape and change occurs in places that are beyond the prescribed battlegrounds of politicians and political parties.

The 2009 conference included a session about Alberta politics, or what might be called the Alberta political mystery. The province remains the only jurisdiction in North America, and arguably Europe as well, where a single party, the Progressive Conservatives, so dominate the political landscape that elections have become non-events, with little campaigning, debate, discussion, or voter turnout. Though other provinces may have traditional leanings, the party in power typically shifts with some regularity. In almost every American state, the governorships and senate seats change hands with the political tides. In Alberta, the tides of political change never seem to arrive. One could argue that the media in the province are just as unchanging. Yet, as Roger Epp points out, beneath the surface, political battles rage, ideas are tested, and meeting places are formed. Alvin Finkel, however, contends that power in Alberta is not only self-perpetuating but brutally imposed.

This book focuses on three changes that have taken place in the nature of political communication since the Erindale conference more than thirty years ago. First, we have moved from a media landscape dominated by the traditional media to one where Facebook, Twitter, blogs, and smart phones play an increasingly important role. The future of the news industry cannot be taken for granted. Newspapers have been corroded by a steady drop in both readership and advertising. They employ fewer journalists, paying them far less than they used to, and younger readers have fled in droves. In 1980, the conventional over-the-air networks—CBC, Radio-Canada, CTV, Global, and TVA—had the capacity to set the political agenda because they had the power to attract mass audiences. While the national news shows of the main networks are still a main stage for Canadian political life, much of the action has moved from centre stage to the sidelines of cable TV, where there are a myriad of all-news channels, each with small but stable audiences. As Marcus Prior demonstrates in *Post-Broadcast Democracy*, a book that some scholars regard as a modern classic despite its relatively recent arrival, the more entertainment options available to viewers, the more likely they are to avoid news entirely, and as a consequence, the less likely they are to vote.[3]

A second change since the Erindale conference is in the nature of political life in Canada. On one hand, the party system has remained surprisingly resilient: the same three parties—the Conservatives, the New Democrats, and the Liberals—that dominated in 1980 still dominate the political landscape today, with a variety of insurgent parties such as the Créditistes, the Reform Party and then the Canadian Alliance, the Bloc Québécois, and the Greens falling more or less by the wayside. On the other hand, the rhythms of political life are now very different: a never-ending 24-hour news cycle, changes in party financing laws that demand non-stop solicitations, the development of databases that allow for the microtargeting of both supporters and swing voters, and cybercampaigns that are fought daily on party websites, Facebook, Twitter, blogs, and YouTube have meant that political parties now wage permanent campaigns. Simply put, the political cycle never stops. Parties have also learned more definitively than ever before that negative campaigning works. The need to define and therefore place question marks in voters' minds about opponents consumes Question Period, appearances by the "talking heads" that parties designate to appear on cable news channels, and the ad campaigns that are waged before and during campaigns.

Just as there are questions about the future of news, there are questions about the future of politics and whether the new political style limits debate, makes tolerance for and compromises with opponents more difficult, and delegitimizes politics as a whole. These questions are vigorously debated in this book, with contributors lined up on different sides of the arguments.

A third change in the nature of political communication is the result of changes in Canadian society. While today's digital natives are more global, multicultural, and tolerant and have a greater command of technology than previous generations, they are also "peek-a-boo" citizens, engaged at some moments, completely disengaged at others. Despite the galvanizing power of social media, fewer people under thirty join civic organizations or political parties, volunteer in their communities, donate money to causes, or vote in elections than was the case for people in the same age group in previous generations. They also know much less about the country in which they live and consume much less news. In fact, the ability of citizens generally to recall important dates in history or the names of even recent prime ministers, as well as their knowledge of basic documents such as the Charter of Rights and Freedoms, is disturbingly low.[4] Digital natives in particular view historical

Canada as a distant and, to some degree, foreign land that is barely recognizable and, for the most part, irrelevant to their lives. How to draw digital natives more fully into the Canadian political spectacle remains one of the country's great challenges.

I: THE CHANGING WORLD OF MEDIA AND POLITICS

The first part of this book open with an article by Florian Sauvageau, a former newspaper editor, TV host, and university professor who served as director of Université Laval's Centre d'étude sur les médias and recently produced a documentary on the future of news. At first glance, Sauvageau's article reads like an obituary for the news industry. While he is reluctant to administer the last rites, Sauvageau chronicles the decline of newspapers and, along with them, much of the "reliable news" on which a society depends; readers are led to conclude that even if newspapers survive in some form, they will be mere shadows of what they once were. As Sauvageau states: "Not all print newspapers will die, but they are all stricken." There are simply too many problems to overcome. Younger readers are vanishing. Classified and other ads are migrating to web-based media, where they can target younger and more specialized audiences, and to social media sites, which allow users to reach buyers and sellers without paying the costs of advertising. Newspaper websites capture only a portion of the revenue (around 20 percent, by some estimates) that print versions generate, and digital culture has created different news habits. As Sauvageau points out, consumers have become accustomed to munching on news "snacks," short bursts of information and headline news, rather than the larger and more nutritious meals provided by newspapers. The expectation among young consumers in particular is that news has to be immediate, interactive, and, most important of all—free. In fact, a survey conducted for the Canadian Media Research Consortium in 2011 found that an overwhelming 81 percent of those surveyed would refuse to pay if their favourite online news sites erected a pay wall. If their usual news sources started charging for content, they would simply go to sites where they could get their news for free.[5]

According to Sauvageau, the problem for society is that newspapers are still the main producers of news. They have the largest staffs and the most resources, and produce almost all of the investigative reporting. He quotes an American study that found that 95 percent of the news stories discussed or quoted in blogs, social media, and websites came from traditional news sources—mostly newspapers. As Sauvageau explains: "If the other media didn't have newspapers to draw on, their news menu would often be meagre indeed. If newspapers stopped publishing, radio hosts who comment on the news would have trouble finding topics, and bloggers would have precious few events to discuss. In large part, newspapers set the public affairs agenda. If the crisis gripping newspapers worsens, it will affect all media and therefore the news system that nourishes democratic life." Simply put, if newspapers die, the whole news industry won't be far behind.

Sauvageau describes various solutions to the problem—apps on mobile phones, for example, may give newspapers a second life, and in France, the government has come to the rescue by providing subsidies. In a few cases, wealthy moguls eager for prestige and power have saved newspapers from the brink, and there are innovative schemes for turning newspaper companies into charitable non-profit institutions, as is now the case with Québec's most influential newspaper, *Le Devoir*. But ultimately, he concludes that reliable news needs to rest on reliable foundations and, in the end, people have to be willing to pay for news.

The most devastating and pessimistic critique of the changing media landscape and its effects on Canadian political culture in this book is by Elly Alboim, a long-time Ottawa bureau chief for CBC television news, a professor at Carleton University, and a principal in the Earnscliffe Strategy Group in Ottawa. Alboim believes that news organizations have lost the capacity to be a "more effective link in the process of governance" and that they feel "no real attachment to or support for current institutions." Any pride in having a broader "civic mandate" has been lost in the drive to entertain audiences: when politics is covered, for instance, stories are invariably about conflict and scandal, failures and fiascos. Compromise—the life's breath of effective politics—is treated as a sign of weakness. The message to citizens is that governments are mostly ineffective and that all politics must be viewed with suspicion. In Alboim's words, media coverage is "a priori adversarial, proceeding from a presumption of manipulative practice and venal motive."

This has created an immensely destructive feedback loop. Political leaders fear being caught in the undertow of negative media coverage for whatever actions or positions they take. Rather than engage the public in discussion, the easier course is to fit the "media narrative" with attention-grabbing pictures and snappy sound bites that convey the image but not the substance of actions and policies. The lesson learned through bitter experience is that issues are to be managed, controversies suppressed, and ideas or policy initiatives rarely if ever discussed in detail. It's hardly surprising that the end product is a disengaged public. The process is circular. The public's cynicism and disinterest feeds back into and justifies media narratives that view politics with suspicion—which prompts political leaders to avoid clashes with the media and therefore serious engagement with the public.

Some observers hoped that web-based media would bring greater interaction and debate. If anything, according to Alboim, web-based media may have accelerated the "decoupling" process by allowing users to live in their own media bubbles. Alboim's worry is that "if you don't know what you don't know and are unwilling to delegate others to tell you, you begin to narrow your universe to one driven by your preconceived interests. Governments can exacerbate the problem when they determine that it is not in their interest to devote extraordinary efforts to engage the disengaged." Not everyone would agree with the portrait that Alboim draws of a closed circle in which disengagement is constantly reinforced. The distracted nature of Ottawa political reporting is not the only measure of the media's engagement in politics. In fact, one could argue that the exact opposite phenomenon is occurring—that we live in a time of political excess and hyper-partisanship, rather than the opposite. Quebecor, for instance, which dominates the Québec media landscape and owns the Sun newspaper chain and the Sun News Network, is consumed by politics. In the case of Quebecor, what is extraordinary is not the absence of politics but the naked aggression with which ideas and passions are promoted. It's also hard to argue that the media has turned its back on politics when both national newspapers, the *Globe and Mail* and the *National Post*, regional giants such as the *Toronto Star* and *La Presse*, and chains such as Postmedia take strong editorial positions, often openly displaying their politics on their front pages. At the very least, the theory of media disengagement from politics needs much greater examination.

Alboim's assertions about citizen disconnectedness on the Internet can also be disputed. Some scholars would argue that, in some ways, citizens are more connected than ever before—they are just connecting differently. One of the most contentious issues, however, is whether web-based media suppress debate and dangerously divide publics by creating media ghettos. Leading observers such as Robert Putnam, Cass Sunstein, Kathleen Hall Jamieson, Joseph Cappella, and Eli Pariser have made the case that users increasingly dwell in their own self-contained media ghettos that shield them from facts or opinions with which they disagree.[6] For instance, Jamieson and Cappella found in their 2008 study that right-wing conservatives in the United States tended to watch Fox News, read the Wall Street Journal, and listen to Rush Limbaugh. They were unlikely to venture much beyond this ideologically secure gated community and were cut off from views they found uncomfortable or inconvenient. The same closed media circle has developed among liberals in the United States, who might read the *New York Times*, watch CNBC, and read blogs such as *Talking Points Memo*. In the Canadian context, presumably viewers of the Sun News Network will also listen to talk show hosts like Charles Adler, read the *National Post*, and follow Tory bloggers.

The problem is exacerbated by the fact that the algorithms that direct search engines provide users with information based on their previous searches. As Eli Pariser points out, "There is no standard Google anymore."[7] When conducting searches, people with conservative views will be directed to different websites than people with liberal views.

But it's not clear that all of the evidence supports the "ghettoization" thesis. Marcus Prior, for instance, refutes the claim that people are becoming the equivalent of political shut-ins. His data show that people who are consumed by politics tend to go to multiple sources; they follow the journalistic action wherever it leads.[8] Researcher Cliff Lampe also found that people on social media sites were better able than others to articulate opposing viewpoints, especially as their circle of online friends widened. So it may be too soon to make sweeping judgments.[9]

The only non-Canadian scholar to speak at the "How Canadians Communicate Politically" conference was Richard Davis of Brigham Young University, a former chair of the political communication section of the American Political Science Association and a leading expert on the effects of web-based media on American politics. In his chapter on blogs, Davis argues that the blogosphere is shaped like a pyramid: a few influential bloggers dwell at the top of the pyramid and command a great deal of the traffic while the vast majority of bloggers get little, if any, attention. A-list bloggers are read by policy-makers and journalists, and are part of the opinion-making and agenda-setting elite. Most of the others write for themselves and a spoonful of friends or fans. While the blogosphere is vast, the readership for political blogs is small (only one in twenty Americans who are online regularly read blogs) and confined to a predominantly male, white, well-educated, and higher-income group. To some degree, media ghettos are built hierarchically and are based more on social class than on political or ideological views.

One is tempted to extrapolate from blogs to other parts of the Internet, including social media such as Facebook and Twitter. These are remarkable tools for those who are already active in politics, allowing them to follow politicians and journalists, organize, become informed about events, publish, and swap and redact materials as never before. But web-based media are unlikely to mobilize people who take little interest in politics to suddenly take an interest; rather, they allow the attentive to become more attentive, leaving the vast majority to remain on the sidelines, where they prefer to be. In fact, a survey conducted at the beginning of the 2011 election campaign found that only a small minority, 4 percent of those between eighteen and thirty-four, used social media to discuss political issues on a daily basis. Surprisingly, the percentage of older and middle-aged voters who turned to social media for political debate and information was substantially higher.[10]

Election campaigns are the largest canvas on which the relationship among media, politics, and publics is played out. Elections are for political journalists what the Olympics are for athletes. They test what news organizations are made of. Christopher Waddell and David Taras review the 2011 election campaign with an eye toward how the rituals of campaigning and campaign coverage might be reformed. Despite much hype about the power of social media to engage young people, voter turnout, especially among digital natives, remained low. This may have been due to an absence of galvanizing issues and big ideas. Party policies seemed little more than a hodge-podge of micro-promises aimed at mobilizing distinct categories of swing voters. Critical questions such as the future of health care, how governments would cut spending in order to balance budgets, the state of the country's cities, and the shrinking market for good jobs were avoided by the parties as if they were political kryptonite. It's hard not to conclude that by allowing political leaders to sidestep the major issues facing the country, journalists had become "enablers"—allowing these practices to take place while pretending not to notice.

Journalists covered the photo ops and daily messaging from the leaders' tours, and they were obsessed with the horse race in much the same way that journalists were in 1980. In this regard, not much has changed, and there is little indication that it will. Waddell and Taras conclude that both media and party election scripts have become strangely disconnected from the country and need to be rewritten in critical ways.

Waddell picks up the theme of disconnection again in the next chapter. A former national editor for the *Globe and Mail* and Ottawa bureau chief for CBC Television News before becoming director of the School for Journalism and Communication at Carleton University, Waddell believes that we are witnessing the "death of political journalism." In his view, political journalism did not die suddenly as the result of a single blow but succumbed to a series of blows over the last twenty years. First, there were decisions by local newspaper and owners to eliminate their Ottawa bureaus due to financial pressures. This severed a vital lifeline between the Ottawa press gallery, local communities, and their MPs. Waddell uses the following analogy: "Would as many people go to an Ottawa Senators hockey game, a Toronto Blue Jays baseball game, or a Calgary Stampeders football game if all the local radio, television, and print media in those communities simply stopped covering the sport with their own reporters, instead using occasional stories written by wire services such as Canadian Press?" The effects on the political system as a whole were quite substantial. Because they seldom made news, MPs became almost invisible in their communities. Their lack of local influence was refracted back to Ottawa, where MPs with little recognition and hence little leverage in their communities became increasingly powerless and ineffective.

But additional blows would follow. To save costs, Ottawa bureaus eliminated reporting jobs, dispensing almost entirely with specialized reporters—such as those who covered courts, foreign affairs, or the environment—in favour of general assignment reporters, who, the assumption went, could cover any story. The problem was that reporters without the time needed to develop expertise and contacts of their own fell prey to quick and easy journalistic practices, relying on Google and on party spin merchants for information and focusing on conflict and personalities. At the same time, news organizations were also slimming down the complement of reporters in provincial legislative press galleries. Young reporters once cut their teeth covering provincial politics, gaining valuable experience and local connections, before being called up to the big leagues of the Ottawa press gallery, but that career ladder has been all but removed.

To Waddell, the final blow is the rise of "BlackBerry journalism." The very devices that are meant to connect journalists to the pulse of the country have had the opposite effect—they have allowed journalists to construct an "alternate reality" based on Ottawa insider politics. Through BlackBerrys and other smart phones, as well as social media such as Twitter, reporters and party operatives trade information and gossip, discuss party strategies, and constantly react to each other. But as Waddell concludes: "Instead of using technology to bridge the communications gap between voters in their communities and the media, the media has used it to turn its back on the public, forging closer links with the people reporters cover rather than with the people who used to read, watch, and listen to their reporting."

It's interesting to view Waddell's argument against the backdrop of Davis's discussion about blogs and other web-based media. While there is great euphoria about the connected society and the ability of web-based media to mobilize and involve young people, in particular, into the nexus of politics, the evidence is that these media are being used to narrow rather than widen the gates of public connectedness. Hierarchies, A-lists, insider baseball, gated communities, and a press gallery that's been "Berry'd alive" have become metaphors for increased worry about how web-based and mobile media are being used. Waddell's article echoes a theme raised by Alboim: that the media's neglect of politics has produced a self-fulfilling prophecy. The less priority news organizations give to political reporting, the less the public becomes interested in politics, the less pressure there is on media organizations to cover politics well. The cycle feeds endlessly on itself as the bar is continually lowered.

Another development that has altered the relationship between media and politics in the last thirty years is the notion of the "permanent campaign." At the time of the 1980 Erindale conference, political campaigns took place exclusively during elections. After an election, the music more or less stopped until the next one was called. Today, campaigns are perpetual, with political parties always in motion. While the phrase "permanent campaign" was first coined by Sidney Blumenthal in 1980, the notion was refined by Norman Ornstein and Thomas Mann in a book published by the American Enterprise Institute and the Brookings Institution in 2000.[11] The term was meant to apply to American politics. Saturation polling and the ability to track the popularity of political leaders on a daily basis, the advent of cable TV channels and the 24-hour news cycle, and the huge fundraising quarries that had to be mined for campaign costs, including TV ads in particular, had risen not only dramatically but exponentially. Add in a short two-year election cycle for those in the House of Representatives, and campaigning never ceases.

Tom Flanagan, a former chief of staff to Stephen Harper and national campaign director for the Conservative Party, and a noted scholar, believes that the permanent campaign not only has taken hold but has come to dominate Canadian politics. In Flanagan's view, "the arms race" never stops. What did change were the minority governments that governed the country from 2004 to 2011, along with party fundraising laws that curtailed how much could be given by corporations and unions. From 2004 to 2011, when these subsidies were abolished, parties benefited from quarterly allowances that they received from government coffers, the amount being determined by the number of votes that the parties had received during the previous election. Having inherited extensive voter ID lists from the populist Reform and Canadian Alliance parties, the Tories were also able to create a "direct voter contact" machine that churned out money 363 days a year. These fundraising lists also became the basis for their formidable campaign contact and get-out-the-vote efforts. The Liberals failed to develop the same machinery and, as a result, lacked much of the artillery that was critical to the Tories' success.

The principal innovation however, was that the Conservatives used their fundraising advantage to launch a series of pre-writ ad campaigns. The strategy was to use these ads to define Stephen Harper before he could be defined by his opponents and to define his opponents before they could define themselves. It also needs to be pointed out that the Conservatives had received a lesson from the school of hard knocks courtesy of the Chrétien Liberals, who used negative ads against the Reform and Canadian Alliance parties with devastating results. Not mentioned by Flanagan is an ad that aired before the 2011 election showing Harper in the prime minister's office working late at night on his economic plan. The message was that Harper was the dependable man, minding the store when everyone else had gone home. But the Conservative attack ads directed first against Liberal leader Stéphane Dion and then against his successor, Michael Ignatieff, were both personal and brutal. In fact, one could argue that Ignatieff, who had been away from Canada for thirty-four years before returning to enter politics, never recovered from the downpour of ads that claimed that the Liberal leader was "just visiting" and "just in it for himself." The conventional wisdom in politics is that no attack should go unanswered for very long. Arguably, without the money needed to respond quickly to these attack ads, Dion and Ignatieff were never able to undo the damage that had been done to their images.

Numbers speak volumes. According to one estimate the Conservatives spent more than $50 million in research and advertising between 2008 and 2011.[12] In the week prior to the federal budget that was presented just before the Tories were defeated in the House of Commons and that precipitated the 2011 election, the Conservatives ran 1,600 ads compared to just 131 for the Liberals.[13]

Jonathan Rose of Queen's University agrees with Flanagan that the permanent campaign has become the "new normal." He worries that party policy-making has been taken over by strategists, pollsters, advertisers, and PR specialists to such a degree that political parties have become little more than props in a stage show managed by others. As Rose warns, they have become the tools of PR and advertising agencies: "Party members serve as a backdrop for PR firms in communicating their arguments about how best to sell the party. The purpose of the party organization is now to be a network for the dissemination of ideas that have been focus-group tested and marketed, and appropriately branded." The increasing disconnect between voters and civic life is at least partially linked to the emptying of political parties and to the fact that calculated and manufactured messages are now so blatantly false and manipulative that voters tend to view everything with suspicion.

Rose also agrees with Flanagan that TV ads have become weapons of choice in the political battlefield. They allow parties to bypass the media's filter and target specific groups of voters by advertising on certain shows or specialty channels, and their effects can be magnified through sheer repetition. Echoing a debate that has recently been joined by Ted Brader and John Geer in the United States, Rose asks whether attack ads have become destructive to the political process.[14] First, there can be no doubt about their effectiveness. Their messages tend to be remembered longer by voters than those of other ads: once questions about opponents have been placed in the voter's mind, they are difficult to erase. But according to Rose, recent studies also show that attack ads can have a positive effect: they tend to focus on policies and provide voters with real information, and they are more truthful than so-called positive ads. They are also likely to generate debate or controversy. Those who are attacked either have to disable these political explosives by responding quickly to them with facts of their own or risk suffering serious and perhaps even fatal damage.

Some analysts, however, question the value of negative ads. They believe that negative TV spots suppress voter turnout by making politics seem venal and nasty. They also note that ads can elevate false charges, appeal to fears and emotions rather than reason, and create a highly contrived and perhaps false view of the choices available to voters. Attack ads routinely depict opponents as looking foolish or sketchy, take odd or unintended remarks out of context, and dredge up unsavoury business deals or personal relationships from the distant past. Some countries are so wary of their power that they ban them entirely. Others regulate what can and cannot be shown or limit attack ads to discrete corners of the TV schedule. Canadian election law imposes no rules or limits about what can be shown or said. The notion is that the public can be trusted to discern truth from falsehood. If ads are seen as too negative or hard-hitting, or if they don't ring true, they will backfire on those who produced them.

Tamara Small of the University of Guelph, one of the leading experts in the country on online campaigning, believes that web-based media have contributed to the permanent campaign. Party websites are continually updated; some leaders tweet their followers, including reporters, almost daily and sometimes several times each day; the blogosphere is constantly massaged and monitored; and, as Small notes in her chapter, specialized websites are created as issues and needs develop.

Party websites are the very opposite of the open spaces that idealists envision. They are based entirely on one-way, top-down communication because parties fear losing control of their message by giving a platform to people with controversial views or those who want to hijack sites, turning them into platforms for issues that parties wish to avoid. Parties are so protective of their sites that, as Small points out, they set up new and different sites for negative messaging. While the main party sites are part of a party's public face and have a pristine and official look, attack sites are for mudslinging, delivering bloody noses, and mocking opponents. In the rough-edged back alleys of the Internet, political parties descend to new lows.

The remaining two articles in this section, Alvin Finkel's description of Alberta politics and Robert Bergen's analysis of the ways in which the Canadian military's media policy has evolved in wartime situations from Kosovo to Libya, are case studies in how governments have managed issues in ways that suppress public engagement.

Alberta may be the pre-eminent example of a government's ability to dominate and dictate debate and discussion. Finkel believes that the Progressive Conservatives' long rule in Alberta is the result of a confluence of factors: charismatic leaders such as Peter Lougheed and Ralph Klein, the perceived need for strong provincial governments that can defend the province against encroachments by Ottawa, the prosperity created by a burgeoning oil and gas industry, and the Conservatives' use of communication strategies that co-opted much of the media. Although Finkel's chapter doesn't deal with wider media theories, his analysis fits with the notion of "indexing" that has become popular in the communications literature. Scholars such as Daniel Hallin and Lance Bennett and his colleagues believe that media reporting mirrors the debates that take place among political elites.[15] When a consensus existed—as was the case in Alberta during the energy wars that the province waged against Ottawa in the early 1980s or when the main political parties supported dramatic budget cuts during the early to mid-1990s—government public relations strategies were remarkably successful. When this consensus broke down—as was the case with the failure of government interventions in the economy under Premier Don Getty or during the controversial royalty review initiated by Ed Stelmach—media strategies failed. In fact, press criticism during Klein's last years in power, and for most of Stelmach's reign, was often quite stinging. The key question, perhaps, is how the Conservatives remained in power even when their media strategies seemed to collapse. Finkel's analysis suggests that the answer lies in a largely compliant society that accepts Conservative ideologies and a press that gives the opposition little coverage and hence little credibility.

Robert Bergen's description of the media strategies employed by the Canadian Forces is an indication of the adept ability that governments possess in avoiding real engagement with the media and the public on critical issues. In Bergen's view, questions about war and peace—including the very reasons for Canadians being in Kosovo, Afghanistan, and Libya—were deflected by what the military saw as the need to protect operational security. Bergen, a former reporter who has been assigned to war zones, contends that the camouflage of operational security has prevented Canadians from knowing very much about what their military has done on overseas missions over the last fifteen years. His detailed analysis of military briefings during the Libya campaign of 2011 raises key questions about the limits of the "operational security" argument in a democracy. If very little can be revealed about the nature of Canadian involvements and the public is continually kept in the dark, then how can these missions be considered legitimate? On the other hand, Bergen understands the need to safeguard the troops and their families. The question is where to draw the line. Interestingly, he argues that the explosion of web-based media has made little dent in the ability of the Canadian Forces to use the media to create a single and unchallenged view of Canada's involvement in recent wars.

The themes that emerge in this first section on the changing world of media and politics are disconnection, dysfunction, and crisis. Sauvageau, Alboim, Small, Waddell, and Taras all believe that institutions and/or certain practices are in need of reform and rethinking. Flanagan believes that the instruments and rules of power have changed and that those best able to adapt to the new rules will survive. He doesn't make judgments about whether the rules are fair or in the public interest. In Rose's view, the negativity that many see also has a positive side: issues are discussed and exchanges take place. Finkel and Bergen believe that governments still have an extraordinary capacity to set the media agenda and, under the right conditions, to suppress debate and controversy.

The contrast between this section and the one that follows couldn't be greater. The next section is about creative engagement, activity, and involvement. When it comes to the spontaneous combustion of popular culture and grassroots activism, there is far more reason for optimism.

II: CITIZENS AND POLITICS IN EVERYDAY LIFE

Historian David Marshall's exploration of Canadian biography provides us with an extraordinary vantage point on Canadian political history and identity. The advantage of biography is that, as Marshall argues, "biography makes debates concrete because people can more readily identify with individuals and personalities than with abstract concepts." Yet Canadian biography has changed dramatically over the last century. Where biographies were once largely hero literature that celebrated the deeds of powerful people and thus reinforced the institutions that they represented, today's biographies expose personal flaws and magnify the errors and injustices that their subjects committed. And where biographies once focused only on the public aspects of public lives, revealing little about personal passions or demons, today's biographers take great delight in ripping away the protective masks worn by their subjects. The result is that some of the very best writing about Canada comes in biographies.

Marshall compares the recently published Extraordinary Canadians series of biographies edited by John Ralston Saul with the Makers of Canada series published over a hundred years earlier. The Great Man theory of history has clearly been overthrown since the new series includes those who lost battles— such as the Cree Chief, Big Bear; Louis Riel; and Gabriel Dumont—as well as those who fought for social change, such as Nellie McClung and Norman Bethune, but who never saw the promised land that they fought for. The new pantheon includes artists, athletes, writers, and a sports hero, Rocket Richard.

One effect of biography is that it reorders public memory. While political leaders such as Mackenzie King, John Diefenbaker, and René Lévesque may have triumphed on the political battlefield, their reputations have not survived their biographers' scalpels. Others, such as R. B. Bennett, have been resurrected, and the legacies of John A. Macdonald and Wilfrid Laurier have been resignified by recent biographies. David Marshall's pantheon of great works includes David Hackett Fischer's biography of Samuel de Champlain, in which Fischer lays out both a theory of Canada and a guide for political leadership. John English's magisterial biographies of Lester Pearson and Pierre Trudeau do the same, although the private lives and political styles of the two men couldn't have been more different.

The next chapter in this section is by Roger Epp, a political scientist at the University of Alberta. Although the article deals with grassroots politics in Alberta, the questions that he addresses resonate throughout the entire book. The most salient issue that Epp raises is how, in the absence of central meeting places and an "adequate deliberative forum," citizens can come together to test ideas and weigh solutions to problems. The "political deskilling" that Epp sees occurring in Alberta is occurring elsewhere in the country, except that in Alberta politics, the situation is more extreme. In a rural Alberta now pockmarked by transmission lines, oil and gas wells, and giant feedlots, Epp argues that a culture of "negotiating and acting together" has taken hold. The "off-road politics" of Alberta, just as much, perhaps, as the off-road politics of the Web, has produced conflicts that are typically "eruptive and short-lived" and "may generate no more than an inchoate proto-politics." But it is politics nonetheless—meaningful, authentic, and practical. As Epp observes, without these informal openings for dialogue and debate, democracy is "managed."

Teaching a class on recent Québec films at the predominantly anglophone University of Calgary, Dominique Perron finds that the old certainties about Québec identity—and, indeed, about Québec's relationship to the rest of Canada—can no longer be taken for granted. Her classes are made up of students who have come from all over the world, from global Canada, with the result that the "elements of recent Canada-Québec relations are almost completely alien to them. They might know certain facts, but they are culturally, as well as generationally, disengaged emotionally from these conflicts between the solitudes." Surprisingly, many of her students didn't view these Québec films within a Canadian context at all. Students relocated the films, fitting them into a global context. Even movies about Rocket Richard and an Inuit hunter were renegotiated so that comparisons were made with Asian or Latin American situations.

These reactions caused Perron to reflect on the transformations occurring within Québec itself. The animosity and distrust produced by generations of conflict with English Canada have given way to what can be described as a "Canadianization through globalization." The emergence of Montreal as a global city in terms of both the economy and immigration has had the effect of connecting it to Canada. There is now a cohort of highly educated, mobile, cosmopolitan Québecers whose lives and experiences are interchangeable with elites in English Canada. While they strongly identify with Québec, this technocratic group "does not consider the territory of Québec as a limitation on its goals and visions." Perron is also persuaded by Jocelyn Letourneau's thesis that there remains another Québec—a Québec that is rural, dependent on the vagaries of primary industries, more insular and traditional, and far more nationalistic.

In the wake of Québec's wholehearted embrace of Jack Layton and the NDP, and the evisceration of the sovereigntist Bloc Québécois during the 2011 federal election, there was much speculation in English Canada about the death of separatism in Québec. More than a few pundits eagerly declared victory. The reality, as Perron's discussion about the reception of Québec films by English-speaking students suggests, is far more complex. While there may be increasing interaction and comfort on some levels, the chill of isolation and mutual indifference remains. After all, it took enrolling in a class for English-speaking students to be exposed to Québec films. Although this old married couple may not be near divorce, which was certainly the issue when the Erindale conference took place in 1980, it's not clear how well English-speaking Canada and Québec know each other.

Shannon Sampert analyzes a very different aspect of media culture in her article on Canadian talk radio. Sampert, who teaches at the University of Winnipeg, focuses on Charles Adler's national radio show (Adler is also a host on Sun TV), comparing it to the spectacle of professional wrestling. Like wrestling, talk radio "has clearly defined heroes and villains, pageantry, outrageous posturing, and high drama, and it attracts fans much in the same way that wrestling does." Her main point, however, is that just as wrestling is a "morality play," Adler's show "adjudicates issues of morality." He rails against the injustices of daily life, airs popular grievances, and promotes his show as the only place where you can hear the truth. The "truth," according to Adler and his listeners, is that liberals, feminists, and special interest groups have transformed work, schools, and the broader culture in ways that are absurd and destructive to Canadian values. Adler's role is to hold "those in authority accountable." The show is a conservative counterattack, a space for venting anger against institutional and social forces that listeners often find incomprehensible and overwhelming.

Sampert points out that Adler is part of a long line of talk show personalities stretching back to such original characters as Jack Webster and Rafe Mair in Vancouver, Ron Collister and Dave Rutherford in Alberta, Ed Needham in Toronto, Lowell Green in Ottawa, and Andre Arthur in Québec City, to name but a few of Canada's radio stars. While some observers see talk radio as a media dinosaur, one of the last meeting places for an older and more conservative male audience at a time when younger listeners are increasingly going elsewhere, Sampert argues that Adler is still "an agenda setter, selecting and framing central issues of the day for other political and journalistic elites." In other words, one ignores talk radio at one's own peril.

The relationship between the majority of Canadians and First Nations peoples is haunted by a problem of "knowing." Nature guide and artist Troy Patenaude describes how this gap is being closed, at least to some degree, by the widespread acceptance of Aboriginal art. While it's important to point out that the art of the Inuit is very different from Haida art or the art produced by Native artists on the prairies, the special power of Aboriginal art, according to Patenaude, is that it is rooted in "storywork." Through storywork, artists tell stories that are rooted in the natural and the spiritual worlds, and participants are invited to share that knowledge. In this way, "contemporary Canadian Aboriginal artists are sustaining an age-old tradition of communicating with other generations, species, entities, and cultures through forms of art, or story, from the ground up." Their works are intensely political because they integrate other Canadians into Native cultures and world views while naturalizing Canadians with their own environment in doing so. Patenaude quotes George Melynk, a leading interpreter of Canadian culture, as saying that there is now a "métisization of art" that has allowed Canadians to see their history and place in the world differently.

While the article examines the storywork of a number of path-breaking Aboriginal artists including Norval Morriseau, Lawrence Paul Yuxweluptun, and Joanne Cardinal Schubert, Patenaude believes that the work of Haida artist Bill Reid deserves special reverence. Reid's majestic sculpture *The Spirit of Haida Gwaii*, whose image adorns the back of Canada's twenty-dollar bill, has come to symbolize Canada itself. A boat is occupied by thirteen mythical creatures, each representing an aspect of life on Haida Gwaii off of British Columbia's west coast, formerly the Queen Charlotte Islands. Those who view the sculpture are asked to respect the individuality and special place of each of the characters. In one sense, the sculpture is a metaphor for Canada, but in another, it brings us all "into a profound relationship with Haida Gwaii: its people, land and ecosystems."

There is, however, an ironic twist. The centrality now given to Aboriginal art also coincides with the increasing marginalization of Native peoples in Canadian life. Canada's symbolic terrain is shockingly different from the Canada that really exists. The level of neglect and destitution, as well as the violence on many First Nations reserves, is deeply disturbing. Large numbers of the homeless who wander city streets are Aboriginal, and levels of education, housing, and sanitation on reserves are often abysmal. While the majority of Canadians have been invited through storywork to enter the world of Aboriginal peoples, one could argue that everyday life holds few such encounters.

The same cannot be said about the music that is part of the everyday experience of most Canadians. While Richard Sutherland of Mount Royal University reminds us that music is overwhelmingly about entertainment and typically divorced from politics in Canada, the reasons behind this divorce tell us much about the country. Because music is "a marker of identity," Canadian music, much like the country itself, is divided by regional and linguistic identities. Nova Scotia, Newfoundland, Québec, and even Alberta, with its deep country-and-western sensibility, all have musical traditions that reflect distinct styles and passions. Not unexpectedly, the sharpest distinction is between Québec and English-speaking Canada. In Québec, popular music and politics have long nurtured each other. *Chanson* created by artists such as Felix Leclerc and Raymond Lévesque expressed the emotions and patriotism behind the sovereignty movement and became anthems sung at mass rallies. As Sutherland points out, in the rest of Canada, groups such as the Guess Who, Blue Rodeo, the Tragically Hip, or the Rheostatics often refer to Canada in their lyrics, but the message is almost never about politics. In the case of popular artists such as Bryan Adams, Sarah McLachlan, Alanis Morissette, Jean-Pierre Ferland, or Leonard Cohen, their songs "register as Canadian (at least with Canadians)— not because they offer a distinctly Canadian musical style or contain lyrical references to Canadian places or people," but simply because audiences know that they are Canadian. While Canadian politicians use music in their appearances and campaign ads, music almost never uses them.

THE CHALLENGES AHEAD

A final essay by Christopher Waddell summarizes one of the main dilemmas posed in the book: our capacity to access information and connect with each other has increased to such an extraordinary degree that in some ways, we now have less information and are less involved than in previous decades. According to Waddell, the 2011 federal election campaign was "a campaign in which everyone talked about new technology, the digital revolution, social media, and interactivity, but virtually no one used it to communicate with voters." Moreover, at the same time that the digital revolution has produced massive amounts of information about every imaginable topic, interest, or passion, the Harper government has eliminated the long census form and made access to information far more difficult, and rarely speaks candidly about issues or decisions. Waddell hopes that by 2015, the year in which the next federal election will likely be fought, our political gyroscopes will have changed—that, by 2015, Canadians will have become more involved in community and civic life, information that is so vital to people's lives and to public debate will no longer be hidden, and political parties and journalists will have broken out of the deep ruts they now find themselves in. If we fail to meet this challenge, then 2015 will look much like 2011.

One of the major changes to take place since the 1980 Erindale conference is the shrinking of our great public spaces. Much of this volume will chronicle the diminished space that Canadians have in which to communicate with each other, to deliberate, and to be informed about politics. The transition from mass media to Me-media has meant that the news organizations that the country once depended on to produce news—the old lions of the Canadian newspaper industry and the evening newscasts of the main television networks—are in retreat. While we must be careful about suggesting that we are anywhere close to holding a deathbed, candlelight vigil, traditional news media's ability to assemble a mass audience, to conduct "shoe leather" investigative journalism, and to offer journalists viable careers is evaporating. It is less clear if web-based media provide comparable meeting places. Despite the kinetic power of social media and their extraordinary ability to mobilize, inform, and create, the audience for politics appears to be sporadic, elusive, and, to some degree, highly ghettoized. While Twitter and Facebook are magnificent tools for engaging those who are already mobilized, they do little to engage a mass public. In fact, if we accept Marcus Prior's contention that the vast cornucopia of entertainment now available through web-based media and on cable TV has made it more likely that large numbers of people will avoid news entirely, then the break between large numbers of citizens and the political system may be extremely difficult to bridge.

A second loss of space has occurred as a result of the changing nature of politics. Election campaigns were as cutthroat and negative thirty years ago as they are today; politics has, after all, always been brutal and personal. But only recently has the campaign season become permanent. The combination of negative politics and the permanent campaign has created a new toxic mix. Two surveys taken during the 2011 federal election campaign show that many Canadians are deeply frustrated by the negative attacks that characterize so much of Canadian politics. An Angus Reid/*Toronto Star* poll taken at mid-campaign found that over 60 percent of those surveyed believed that Canadian democracy was in crisis, and almost 80 percent, an astonishingly high number, thought that politicians were less honest than in the past. Most expressed a mix of emotions—mistrust, cynicism, and alienation—and none of the parties were seen as a satisfactory choice by a majority of those who were asked.[16] Another Angus Reid poll, conducted after the leaders' debates, found that a majority of those who were shown clips of the debates online were "annoyed" by what they saw.[17] Respondents reacted with irritation when the leaders attacked each other but responded positively when the leaders discussed their policies. In other words, people were genuinely interested in learning about issues rather than listening to contrived messages and spitball attacks.

It's difficult not to conclude that the never-ending maelstrom of negative politics that has become one of the earmarks of the permanent campaign has produced a cancerous by-product—a strong distaste among voters for the political system. While scholars have focused their attention on why younger voters in particular have turned their backs on politics, the reality may be that the political system has turned its back on Canadians.[18] The question is also whether news organizations have added to the problem by highlighting conflict and personalities instead of changing the media script so that political leaders have to address the major issues facing the country. That health care, the future of cities, the environment, or job growth could be almost entirely ignored during the 2011 election is an example of how both politics and journalism have become smaller. Interestingly, this narrowing of the arteries has taken place at the same time that web-based media was expected by many observers to produce the opposite effect—to widen discussions and reinvigorate the public square.[19] The result, at least so far, has been to turn politics inward.

When it comes to grassroots politics and some aspects of popular culture, the country seems much more vital. While Canadian culture has always been a minority culture in Canada because of the overpowering presence of the US entertainment industry, Canadian literature, music, drama, film, and art are filling more and more of our psychic landscape. Although most of grassroots politics and popular culture has little to do with formal politics, the "story-work" of artists, writers, and filmmakers is often intensely political. Their work has entered the bloodstream of national discussion, and has altered perceptions and consciousness. Québec films, Aboriginal art, political biographies, and the off-road politics of rural protest are also part of politics.

NOTES

1   *Politics and the Media: An Examination of the Issues Raised by the Quebec Referendum and the 1979 and 1980 Federal Elections* (Toronto: Reader's Digest Foundation of Canada and Erindale College, University of Toronto, 1981).

2   Peter Dahlgren, *Media and Political Engagement* (Cambridge: Cambridge University Press, 2009), 136–48.

3   Marcus Prior, *Post-Broadcast Democracy: How Media Choice Increases Inequality in Political Involvement and Polarizes Elections* (Cambridge: Cambridge University Press, 2007).

4   See, for instance, Ipsos Reid/Dominion Institute, "National Citizen Exam: 10 Year Benchmark Study," June 2007, http://www.dominion.ca/Dominion_Institute_Press_Release_Mock_Exam.pdf.

5   Canadian Media Research Consortium, "Canadian Consumers Unwilling to Pay for News Online," March 29, 2011, http://www.cmrcccrm.ca/documents/CMRC_Paywall_Release.pdf.

6   Robert Putnam, *Bowling Alone: The Collapse and Revival of American Community* (New York: Simon and Schuster, 2000), chap. 9; Cass Sunstein, *Republic.com 2.0* (Princeton: Princeton University Press, 2007); Kathleen Jamieson and Joseph Cappella, *Echo Chamber: Rush Limbaugh and the Conservative Media Establishment* (New York: Oxford University Press, 2008); Eli Pariser, *The Filter Bubble: What the Internet Is Hiding from You* (New York: Penguin, 2011).

7   Pariser, *The Filter Bubble*, 2.

8   Prior, *Post-Broadcast Democracy*, 271–74.

9   On Lampe, see Rory O'Connor, "Word of Mouse: Credibility, Journalism and Emerging Social Media," Joan Shorenstein Center on the Press, Politics and Public Policy, Discussion Paper Series (Cambridge, MA: Harvard University, 2009), 18–19.

10 Greg Markey, "One-Fifth of Canadians Discussing Politics on Social Media," *Vancouver Sun*, April 11, 2011, http://www2.canada.com/vancouversun/news/archives/story.html?id=d8e38ac2-b13c-4df6-aacd-3d43817c7ac7.

11 Norman Ornstein and Thomas Mann, eds., *The Permanent Campaign and Its Future* (Washington: American Enterprise Institute and The Brookings Institution, 2000).

12 Robin Sears, "Quebec Storm Sweeps Canadian Electoral Landscape: The Realignment Story of Campaign 41," *Policy Options* (June–July 2011): 31.

13 Paul Wells, "The First Mistake," *Maclean's*, May 16, 2011, 16.

14 See Ted Brader, *Campaigning for the Hearts and Minds: How Emotional Appeals in Political Ads Work* (Chicago: University of Chicago Press, 2006); and John Geer, *In Defense of*

Negativity: Attack Ads in Presidential Campaigns (Chicago: University of Chicago Press, 2006).

15 Daniel Hallin, *The Uncensored War: The Media and Vietnam* (Berkeley: University of California Press, 1986); Lance Bennett, Regina Lawrence, and Steven Livingston, *When the Press Fails: Political Power and the News from Iraq to Katrina* (Chicago: University of Chicago Press, 2007).

16 Susan Delacourt, "Voters Filled with Dashed Hopes, Angus Reid-Star Poll Suggests," *Toronto Star*, April 25, 2011, http://www.thestar.com/news/canada/article/979612--voters-filled-with-dashed-hopes-angus-reid-star-poll-suggests.

17 Susan Delacourt, "TV Debates Annoyed Canadians, Poll Finds," *Toronto Star*, April 16, 2011, http://www.thestar.com/news/canada/politics/article/975746--tv-debates-annoyed-canadians-poll-finds?bn=1.

18 See Henry Milner, *The Internet Generation: Engaged Citizens or Political Dropouts* (Boston: Tufts University Press, 2010).

19 See Matthew Hindman, *The Myth of Digital Democracy* (Princeton: Princeton University Press, 2009), chap. 1.

PART I THE CHANGING WORLD OF MEDIA AND POLITICS

Florian Sauvageau

The Uncertain Future of the News

The financial crisis gripping the traditional media, especially newspapers, has put fear into the hearts of people who hold that a vibrant democracy depends on an informed citizenry and that the news function played by the media is therefore vital. In the United States, the past few years have been disastrous for newspapers, bringing closures, shifts to Internet-only publishing, and massive layoffs of journalists. The worst of the storm happened in 2008 and 2009, but the situation has continued to deteriorate, although at a slower pace (see www.newspaperlayoffs.com). Meanwhile, we have been inundated with studies, reports, conferences, and blogs on the decline of the press and its political consequences.

In his evocatively titled book *Losing the News: The Future of the News That Feeds Democracy*, Alex S. Jones, director of the Shorenstein Center on the Press, Politics, and Public Policy at Harvard University, explains that what we risk losing is not freedom of expression or opinion, which is in fact flourishing on the Web; rather, we face "a dearth of reliable, traditional news." For it is news rather than commentary that shapes opinion. In a chapter titled "Newspapers on the Brink," Jones summarizes the situation in the United States in one terse sentence: "Panic is not too strong a word for the collective mind of the newspaper industry."[1]

Even though the level of anxiety is not as high in Canada, the situation is just as worrisome. Many journalists have been laid off, in print and television alike, and the working conditions of the survivors have, in many cases, deteriorated. In English Canada, severe job cuts (six hundred, or 10 percent of the workforce) were announced at the end of 2008 at the Sun Media newspaper chain, owned by Montréal-based media giant Quebecor. Significant buyouts and layoffs, along with retraining of reporters for the digital age, have also occurred at the Postmedia newspapers, including the flagship *National Post*, since this newly formed company acquired Canwest's newspapers in 2010. (The Canwest group had entered bankruptcy protection in 2009.) More layoffs and buyouts were announced in the fall of 2011 by Postmedia and Torstar, owner of the *Toronto Star*. In Montréal, *La Presse* management threatened to close the newspaper in December 2009 if the employees did not accept major changes to their collective agreement, and in January 2009 the *Journal de Montréal*, published by Quebecor, decreed a lockout, which lasted more than two years, until February 2011. Ultimately, three-quarter's of the newspaper's employees lost their jobs, and the newsroom staff was reduced by half.[2]

My topic is the future of the news, but I shall discuss, above all, newspapers because their fates are intertwined. Newspapers play a dominant role in the gathering and dissemination of the news. Their newsrooms are far better staffed than those of the other media, and each day, in most of the communities they serve, they cover more events than their competitors do, and often in greater depth. In the United States, a study of Baltimore's news "ecosystem" by the Pew Research Center's Project for Excellence in Journalism did a fine job of demonstrating the preponderant role of newspapers. Even though the news sources available to the public have proliferated in recent years, especially on the Internet, we tend to find the same news everywhere. The study showed that 95 percent of the articles and reports that contained original information came from traditional media—most of them newspapers.[3]

The situation is somewhat different in Canada because of the presence of the public broadcaster, especially in French Canada, where it claims an outsized share of journalistic manpower. A survey conducted in 1996 showed that 31 percent of the journalists working for the country's French-language media were employed by Radio-Canada and that almost a fifth (19 percent) of all Canadian journalists were employed by CBC/Radio-Canada.[4] It is probably safe to assume that this situation has not changed much. Even so, newspapers also play a vital role in the country. If the other media didn't have newspapers to draw on, their news menu would often be meagre indeed. If newspapers stopped publishing, radio hosts who comment on the news would have trouble finding topics, and bloggers would have precious few events to discuss. In large part, newspapers set the public affairs agenda. If the crisis gripping newspapers worsens, it will affect all media and therefore the news system that nourishes democratic life.

Moreover, many studies point out that the print media foster an informed citizenry (Henry Milner provides an exhaustive review in *Civic Literacy: How Informed Citizens Make Democracy Work*). Newspaper readers, especially those who read the broadsheets, are better informed than non-readers and are more likely to be involved in the political and democratic life of their country. On the contrary, people who watch a great deal of television, especially commercial TV, are less informed about public affairs. The adage "words fly away but writings remain" appears to be true.

This brings me to the financial crisis, which is accompanied, in my opinion, by a crisis that is just as profound: namely, that of a style of journalism that is slightly dated and has difficulty adapting to technological leaps and to the behaviour of a fragmented, diversified public. In this chapter, I shall try to explain the roots and consequences of both crises.

A MULTIFACETED CRISIS

The financial crisis that the print media is experiencing is twofold: in economic parlance, it is both cyclical and structural. The recession (the cyclical aspect) and the falling advertising revenues that go hand in hand with it have accelerated the slow decline that newspapers have been experiencing for years, suddenly turning it into a freefall. But the difficulties will not magically disappear as the economy recovers. The roots of the crisis go deeper. To understand the changes that are occurring, we must look at a broader framework: that of the decline of the mass media as we knew them in the twentieth century and the rise of niche media based on digital technology. This phenomenon is similar to the decline of the department store, which offers everything for everyone, and the triumph of the specialized store, which enables shoppers to satisfy a specific need or a particular passion. Just as generalist television has seen a portion of its audience and revenues migrate to TSN and other specialty channels, daily newspapers are coming under attack from websites of every kind imaginable.

That being said, the problems that newspapers are experiencing were foreseeable long before the advent of the Internet. For decades, newspaper circulation has been out of sync with population growth and increases in the number of households (see figure 1.1). Even so, newspapers still had enough readers to continue to attract advertisers, and their profits caused owners to turn a blind eye to the public's declining interest in their product. But more recent consumer behaviour—especially that of young people, who rarely buy newspapers—as much as advertiser behaviour, has caused newspaper owners to sound the alarm.

Figure 1.1   Total daily newspaper paid circulation in Canada, 1950–2008 (percentage of households)

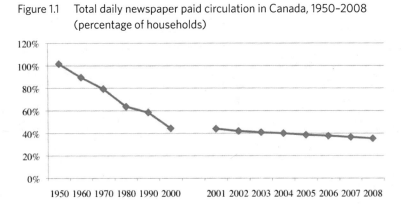

SOURCE: Adapted from Canadian Media Research Consortium, *The State of the Media in Canada: A Work in Progress*, May 2009, http://www.cmrcccrm.ca/documents/SOM_Canada_0702.pdf, 52.

It is often said that in United States, each newspaper reader who dies leaves no heir, which is not far from reality. In 2007, according to figures provided by the Newspaper Association of America, one-third of young adults (namely people aged eighteen to thirty-four) regularly read a newspaper, as opposed to two-thirds of people aged fifty-five and over.[5] The proportions are about the same in Canada (see table 1.1). Most young adults go elsewhere for the news. Unlike their parents, they are not loyal to one newspaper or newscast; instead, they nibble away at the news, whenever and wherever they feel like it. They prefer frequent news snacks to regular full meals. They take the news, shape it, comment on it, and exchange it with their "friends" on Facebook or via Twitter. Their relationship with the media is characterized by the desire for interactivity, the need for a mobile medium, and the attraction of the freebie—not to mention a dose of mistrust toward the large press groups.[6]

Table 1.1   Regular readers of a daily newspaper, 2009

Age Group	Percent
18–34	35.9
35–49	43.3
50+	58.8

SOURCE: Calculated by the Centre d'études sur les médias on the basis of NADbank data.

The freebie culture that has developed among young Internet users plays a determining role in their overall news-consumption behaviour. They willingly read a newspaper if they don't have to pay for it. In Montréal, the free newspapers *Métro* and *24 heures* are very popular with young people, so perhaps we should take their supposed rejection of printed newspapers with a grain of salt (see table 1.2). But that doesn't solve the financial problems of the traditional media. Who will pay for news gathering if the customers of tomorrow won't and if advertisers are ever more reluctant to do so? It appears that the business model is broken, and efforts to find a new model have thus far been unsuccessful.

At the same time, we must not exaggerate the current scope of the changes. Even though Canada's newspapers and other traditional media are a bit short of breath, they are by no means on their last legs. The situation is evolving slowly. Over the past twenty years, I have, on dozens of occasions, cited Vannevar Bush, a former science advisor to US President Franklin D. Roosevelt: he said we tend to exaggerate the short-term impacts of new technologies while minimizing their long-term impacts. Television isn't dead, and printed newspapers won't all disappear next year. But the general trend shows that profound changes are taking place.

Canadians are increasingly using the Internet to stay informed, but television is still the preferred media platform of the majority. In Québec, two surveys by the Centre d'études sur les médias, carried out two years apart and involving the same group of people, show that the new media's share of the time spent consuming the news increased by 3.4 percent from 2007 to 2009, rising from 12.6 percent to 16 percent of total time, but that the traditional media were still dominant. The 2009 survey obviously indicates that younger people are using the new media much more to track the news, but television remains, for them as for their elders, the main news source. Another study, focusing on heavy users of information technology, yielded additional revealing findings. Many respondents identified a combination of media (especially television and the Internet) as their main news source. Newspapers played almost no role as a news source for heavy users of the new media. This study confirms that the general trend does not bode well for printed newspapers over the long term.[7]

Table 1.2   Regular readers of Montréal daily newspapers (Monday to Friday)

Newspaper	2004	2009	Difference
Le Journal de Montréal	642,000	612,500	- 29,500
La Presse	459,200	384,600	- 75,200
The Gazette	358,100	267,300	- 90,800
Métro	260,500	337,300	76,800
24 heures	152,500	267,600	115,100
Le Devoir	77,000	54,300	- 22,700

NOTE: In Montréal, the free newspapers Métro and 24 heures, which, as the table shows, have the wind in their sails, are especially popular with the 18 to 34 age group. Regular readers of Métro are on average ten years younger than readers of the broadsheet La Presse (39 and 49 years of age, respectively). In Toronto, readers of paid newspapers are also older than readers of free newspapers. Readers of the Toronto Star are on average 51 years old, and those of the Globe and Mail are 50. Readers of the free newspapers Metro and 24 Hours have an average age of 40 and 43. These data pertain to the print editions of the newspapers in question.

SOURCE: Calculated by the Centre d'études sur les médias, on the basis of NADbank data.

In North America, advertising has traditionally provided the lion's share of newspaper revenues—from 75 to 80 percent. Montréal's *Le Devoir* is an exception: it obtains half of its revenues from newspaper sales and has therefore fared better in the difficult economic climate of recent years.

Newspapers as a group suffered the first blow when classified advertising sites appeared on the Web. Classified advertising traditionally provided about a third of the advertising revenues of Canadian newspapers. In the United States, newspapers have been hit harder by the migration of classifieds to the Internet, but the phenomenon is also prevalent in Canada, where classified ad revenues fell an estimated 25 percent from 2005 to 2009.[8]

In 1964, Marshall McLuhan wrote in his celebrated book *Understanding Media: The Extensions of Man*, "Classified ads (and stock-market quotations) are the bedrock of the press. Should an alternative source of easy access to such diverse daily information be found, the press will fold."[9] This other source of information—easy to access, faster, and more practical—exists today, not only for classified ads and stock-market quotations but also for other news of the day. Not all print newspapers will die, but they are all stricken.

Advertisers follow consumers wherever they go. If consumers switch to the Internet and to niche media, advertisers will follow, in part because specialized media enable them to target more easily and for less money consumers who are potentially interested in a given product. It is more costly to advertise in the mass media, which attract consumers with diversified interests and profiles, many of them indifferent to a given advertiser's goods. For instance, when owners of car dealerships saw that customers were showing up on their lots after spending hours on websites dedicated to cars, they realized the time had come to allocate a portion of their advertising budgets to the new media, and newspapers sustained another blow. Table 1.3 shows that printed newspapers' share of advertising spending has been dropping since the start of the decade.

A newspaper is a package of content (such as comics, political news, weather forecasts, and, of course, advertising) that consumers read for different reasons: some are interested in current events, others in the sports scores, and still others in current movies and arts events. Today, large portions of this content are migrating to the Internet, along with their audiences and revenues. Until only recently, classified advertising revenues may have paid the salaries of journalists assigned to Parliament Hill, and ads placed by car dealerships may have financed costly public affairs investigations. Content bundling and the inter-financing that it enabled are breaking down. As the Canadian Media Research Consortium notes in its 2009 report on the state of the media in Canada, "For the past 100 years, journalism has lived within a bundled product called media, and that bundle now is beginning to unravel."[10] The impact on civic life is obvious.

Table 1.3   Advertising revenues by medium

Medium	Revenue (in millions)			% growth	
	1999	2008	2009	1999–2009	2008-9
Television	$2,370	$3,393	$3,102	30.89	-8.58
Newspapers	$1,629	$1,680	$1,380	-15.29	-17.86
Radio	$953	$1,547	$1,469	54.14	-5.04
Magazines	$460	$692	$590	28.26	-14.74
Outdoor	$243	$463	$416	71.19	-10.15
Internet	$50	$1,142	$1,355	2,610.00	18.65
Total	$5,705	$8,917	$8,312	45.70	-6.78

NOTE: Between 1999 and 2008, advertising revenues rose for all media, although the growth was far less substantial for newspapers. But the economic downturn in 2008 affected all media except the Internet; print media (newspapers and magazines) were hit especially hard. Advertising revenues for newspapers were much lower in 2009 than they had been a decade earlier, or even in the previous year.

SOURCE: Calculated by the Centre d'études sur les médias on the basis of data published by the Television Bureau of Canada in Net Advertising Volume, 2009. Revenues for newspapers and the Internet do not include classified ads.

Newspapers may find themselves without enough resources to continue the news gathering they are now doing—a development that could have dramatic results: fewer journalists in the field, less investigative reporting, and a dearth of original, in-depth news. Those who disagree with this analysis will argue that newspapers are just as present on the Internet, to which advertising is shifting, and that they can benefit from the shift—but that is only partially true. The websites of large newspapers receive only a portion of the advertising that is migrating to the Internet. You can find advertising everywhere: on Google, on social-networking sites, and on every other kind of site. In the short term, Internet-only publishing would spell disaster for printed newspapers. For example, the revenues from the online version of the *New York Times* cover only 20 percent of the cost of the current editorial department.[11] Of course, things are changing, but slowly. One day, newspapers will perhaps be able to generate from their digital editions alone enough revenue to offer content comparable to that of today's print versions. But when will that day come?

Today, newspapers are pinning their hopes on mobile devices such as smart phones and reading tablets, which are quickly developing and expanding. The most optimistic publishers believe that electronic tablets, especially the iPad, can change people's news-consumption habits, just as the iPod has changed the way people consume music. And why not? Whether readers get their news from the printed page of a newspaper or from an electronic tablet doesn't really matter. What counts is the content.

Some see this development as the opportunity to correct the mistake made by newspapers, which, by offering their content free of charge on the Web, have helped create the prevailing freebie culture. "It's not much of a revolution yet," writes Curtis Brainard, "but what is increasingly apparent is that mobile devices have the potential to offer the journalism business that rare and beautiful thing: a second chance—another shot at monetizing digital content and ensuring future profitability that was missed during the advent of web 1.0."[12] Does the future of the news depend on smart phones and electronic tablets? If so, salvation won't be arriving tomorrow. The period of transition during which revenues from print editions continue to fall while those from digital publishing rise, but not enough to make up the difference, may continue for some time, with predictable consequences.

THE STATE, PHILANTHROPISTS, AND WHO ELSE?

Let's get back to the question I raised earlier: Who will pay for news gathering and distribution if customers and advertisers won't continue to do so? The state? South of the border, fears that some large cities, such as Boston and San Francisco, could find themselves without a major newspaper sparked a quick reaction from various political and administrative authorities. The US Senate held hearings and analyzed various ways of helping the press. Certain proposals deserve to be examined, such as possible joint projects by publishers and journalists to convert their newspapers into non-profit corporations to secure more favourable tax treatment.

Contrary to conventional wisdom, the public sector has always subsidized the press in the United States, albeit indirectly, but this support is declining and could be reduced further. Many states, for example, are expected to shift to the Internet their mandatory publication of public notices, which in 2000 represented 5 to 10 percent of the revenues of certain local newspapers. This development couldn't come at a worse time.[13]

Is government support for newspapers the answer? For decades, the French government has been spending a fortune (€900 million in 2010 alone) on all sorts of assistance for the print media to ensure diversity and pluralism. It is true that without government assistance, some journals of opinion—such as *l'Humanité*, a newspaper with communist leanings—would have ceased to exist long ago. Even so, as French media expert Jean-Marie Charon points out, the system has not been able to prevent the disappearance of many publications or to prevent struggling symbols of journalism's independence, such as *Le Monde* and *Libération*, from passing into the hands of financiers or large media groups.[14] It is therefore entirely legitimate to ponder, as some analysts do, whether we need to help news gathering rather than specific media.

A report that was commissioned by the journalism school at Columbia University and received a great deal of coverage in late 2009 suggests that what we must protect is independent reporting. The authors of the report, published under the challenging title "The Reconstruction of American Journalism," clearly explain that they do not recommend "a government bailout of newspapers, nor any of the various direct subsidies" found in European countries. They add: "Our recommendations are intended to support independent, original and credible news reporting, especially local and accountability reporting, across all media in communities throughout the United States." Each sizeable community should have a range of diverse sources of news reporting, commercial as well as non-profit, which "should be adapting traditional journalism forms to the multimedia, interactive, real-time capabilities of digital communication, sharing the reporting and distribution of news with citizens, bloggers and aggregators."[15] In this spirit, various journalism experiments, including investigative journalism projects, have been carried out by our neighbours to the south with the assistance of foundations, philanthropists, and other similar sources of funding. But such foreign experiments are not necessarily compatible with Canada's traditions and its social and political environments. Generally speaking, in Canada, especially in Québec, the philanthropist approach does not have the same historical base as in the United States. In the best-case scenario, it would represent only a partial solution to the media's difficulties. We also see that, in the United States, some foundations tend to emphasize specific areas, such as health coverage, and the press does not always find that such patronage offers the independence and freedom of choice that are vital to fulfill its role. There is no single answer to the difficulties of the press. The solutions will depend on the traditions and circumstances in each country.

Who will pay for news gathering and distribution in the future? No doubt, we must limit the scope of the question. We don't have to find support for all the news but only the news that feeds democracy, to use Alex Jones's expression. But a question remains unanswered: Is there a sizeable public for this type of journalism? I believe so. There will always be a role, and a demand, for journalism that tries to make sense of the news of the day, that presents the "day's events in a context which gives them meaning."[16] How can we guarantee the future of free and independent news gathering in a digital world where facts and rumours intermingle, where lies are found alongside well-founded opinions, where manipulation is widespread? In a world where citizens inform one another and often place greater trust in their "friends" on social networks than they do in the major media? What purpose do journalists serve in this universe of information overload? What is their niche? It is up to the media and journalists to demonstrate their relevance.

JOURNALISM IN CRISIS

In my opinion, it isn't just the mass media that are in a state of crisis. Journalism is too. The economist Robert Picard, who is one of the most astute observers of the print media and journalism, questions the very essence of the work done by journalists. He believes that what today's journalists produce is often of little value. In a world where we had only a few newspapers and radio stations, and only one or two TV channels, information and news were scarce commodities. Digital technology has changed all that.

In today's world of abundance, the news is covered by everyone with the same techniques, is written in the same style, is endlessly recycled from one medium to another and is remarkably similar. That is why it no longer has value. This kind of journalism, which is ubiquitous, will persist. Some people are satisfied with it, as long as it is free of charge. Those who are more demanding will be prepared to pay, provided they are offered something different. Picard stresses innovation: "Journalism must innovate and create new means of gathering, processing and distributing information so it provides content and services that readers, listeners, and viewers cannot receive elsewhere. And these must provide sufficient value so audiences and users are willing to pay a reasonable price."[17]

Standardized, formatted journalistic prose often reads like a coded message. The traditional model is based on the "lead" and the inverted-pyramid writing technique, which gives the facts in descending order of importance; this technique came about as a result of the constraints imposed by old technologies, such as the telegraph and printing, and is poorly adapted to the expectations of an audience accustomed to the new media's capabilities. Young people, especially, do not quite know what to make of a language from another era—that of the journalist often cast in the role of a quasi-oracle who selects each day from on high the facts that the public ought to know. Journalism, previously a lecture, has now become a seminar or a conversation. In this new world, shaped by the Internet and interactivity, the journalist must have a dialogue with the public, for better or for worse.

Old-fogey journalism is dead. Long live neo-journalism! So wrote Christophe Barbier, the managing editor of the French magazine L'Express, a tad excessively. In an editorial stressing the need for radical change, he wrote that journalism no longer involves the vertical soliloquy of an expert addressing the ignorant: nowadays, readers are more knowledgeable and skepticism is widespread. According to Barbier, neo-journalism is modest. It accepts and even solicits contradiction. It animates the agora without monopolizing it.[18]

Journalists have no choice but to adapt to the new hand they have been dealt. They must rethink their role and clarify their distinctiveness and their ways of doing things in this world of interactivity and overabundance of news. They must hold fast to the ideal of public service, which continues to be the purpose of their métier, but avoid nostalgia for a mythical golden age. They must respect tradition but also be able to innovate.

The "reconstruction" of journalism involves not only a profound re-examination of its practice but also, according to Picard, sustained co-operation between journalists and management. Journalists cannot be passive witnesses to the changes in progress. They need to acquire entrepreneurial and innovation skills that make it "possible for them to lead change rather than merely respond to it."[19] That also means profound changes in mindsets, the culture of journalism, and the training of future journalists. Some schools of journalism have already created courses designed to develop students' entrepreneurship and to prepare them for becoming independent suppliers of the news.

In the years to come, journalism will be practiced and financed in many ways, which could contribute to the diversity of information and opinion, and thus strengthen democracy. But the ultimate solution to the problems plaguing the print media may require an introspective effort rather than merely a quest for a magical new business model.

A KIND OF EPILOGUE

Thirty years ago, the Royal Commission on Newspapers (also called the Kent Commission, after its chairman, Tom Kent) was "born out of shock and trauma" in a context of newspaper closures and takeovers. At the time, it was the concentration of newspaper ownership in the hands of large groups and the disappearance of independent newspapers that was causing concern. The decrease in competition was creating fear that the diversity of news and opinion would be jeopardized: this was the dominant concern in the commission's report—and rightly so. It is also what retained the attention of the media's commentators at the time, but it overshadowed a fascinating portion of the report.

In a chapter titled "An Industry in Transition," the commission devoted several prescient pages to the "convergence" (don't forget that this was almost thirty years ago) of the telecommunications sector, the computer sector, and broadcasting; to the two-way nature of what was then called telematics; and to the consequences of these technological innovations for the print media. The report stressed the possible impact on the print media of the explosion of new electronic media that coveted newspaper readers' time and attention as well as advertisers' dollars.

Newspaper owners and journalists would have done well to pay close attention to this other aspect of the commision's report. The new forms of electronic media "clearly have the potential to affect newspapers, starting in the second half of this decade," wrote the commissioners. "The effect could become critical in the 1990s."[20] The shakeup came about ten years later than they predicted, but today we are starting to feel its full impact.

I would like to thank Marilyn Thomson for her help with the translation and editing of the text.

NOTES

1   Alex. S. Jones, *Losing the News: The Future of the News That Feeds Democracy* (New York: Oxford University Press, 2009), 164.

2   Stéphane Baillargeon, "L'offre patronale est acceptée à 64% au *Journal de Montréal*," *Le Devoir*, February 28, 2011.

3   Pew Research Center's Project for Excellence in Journalism, "How News Happens: A Study of the News Ecosystem of One American City," *Journalism.org*, January 11, 2010, http://www.journalism.org/analysis_report/how_news_happens.

4   David Pritchard and Florian Sauvageau, *Les journalistes canadiens: Un portrait de fin de siècle* (Québec City: Presses de l'Université Laval, 1999), 64.

5   National Newspaper Association Foundation, "Youth Media DNA: In Search of Lifelong Readers," http://www.naa.org/docs/Foundation/Research/Youthmediadna.pdf.

6   Claire Boily, *The 18–24 Age Group and the News* (Québec City: Centre d'études sur les médias and Institut national de la recherche scientifique, and Vancouver: Canadian Media Research Consortium, 2006).

7   See *How Quebecers Consume the News* (Québec City: Centre d'études sur les médias, and Vancouver: Canadian Media Research Consortium, 2010).

8   Calculated by the Centre d'études sur les médias on the basis of data furnished by the Television Bureau of Canada, *Net Advertising Volume, 2009.*

9   Quoted in Canadian Media Research Consortium, *The State of the Media in Canada: A Work in Progress,* May 2009, http://www.mediaresearch.ca/documents/SOM_Canada_0702.pdf, 40.

10 Ibid.

11 Michael Hirschorn, "End Times: Can America's Paper of Record Survive the Death of Newsprint? Can Journalism?" *The Atlantic*, January–February 2009, http://www. theatlantic.com/magazine/archive/2009/01/end-times/7220/.

12 Curtis Brainard, "A Second Chance—How Mobile Devices Can Absolve Journalism of Its Original Sin: Giving Away Online Content," *Columbia Journalism Review*, July–August 2010, http://www.cjr.org/cover_story/a_second_chance.php?page=all.

13 Geoffrey Cowan and David Westphal, "Public Policy and Funding the News," USC Annenberg School for Communications and Journalism, Center on Community Leadership and Policy Research Series, University of Southern California, January 2010, http://communicationleadership.usc.edu/pubs/Funding%20the%20News.pdf.

14 Jean-Marie Charon, "Indépendance et pluralisme de la presse—Une presse peut-elle être indépendante quand l'État lui apporte en aide 900 millions d'euros?" *Le Devoir*, March 10, 2010.

15 Leonard Downie, Jr., and Michael Schudson, "The Reconstruction of American Journalism," *Columbia Journalism Review*, October 2009, http://www.cjr.org/reconstruction/the_reconstruction_of_american.php?page=all.

16 Commission on Freedom of the Press, *A Free and Responsible Press—A General Report on Mass Communication: Newspapers, Radio, Motion Pictures, Magazines, and Books* (Chicago: University of Chicago Press, 1947), 20.

17 Robert G. Picard, "Why Journalists Deserve Low Pay," *Christian Science Monitor*, May 19, 2009, http://www.csmonitor.com/Commentary/Opinion/2009/0519/p09s02-coop.html, 1.

18 Christophe Barbier, "A Suivre ... ," *L'Express*, January 8, 2009.

19 Picard, "Why Journalists Deserve Low Pay," 3.

20 Canada, Royal Commission on Newspapers, *Report of the Royal Commission on Newspapers.* (Hull: Canadian Government Publishing Centre, Supply and Services Canada, 1981), 195.

Elly Alboim

On the Verge of Total Dysfunction:
Government, Media, and Communications

In the spirit of full disclosure, I should emphasize at the outset that my views reflect a particular set of experiences—sixteen years in television news, as a parliamentary bureau chief and national political editor, thirty years as a journalism educator, and now eighteen years as a communications strategist who is informed by public opinion research specifically designed to aid communications and media management. Over that time, my views have become less certain, less fixed, and more pessimistic. What follows is an amalgam of experience-based impressions, supplemented to some degree by the more rigorous analysis available in current literature in the field.

Any discussion like this probably needs to begin by considering the role, performance, and impact of the media with respect to government in Canada, particularly the media that report on the conduct of government. There is an obvious conundrum about chickens and eggs—but it is clear that media coverage has a profound impact on the design of government communications.

People involved in governance—whether directly or indirectly, in an effort to influence it—tend to think that the media have a responsibility to inform and educate and to act as fair witness to the process. Actually, the media have no interest in becoming a more effective link in the process of governance, nor do they currently have the ability to do so. Although journalists tend to accept their responsibility in fostering democracy and generally tilt toward support of Western political systems, they feel no real attachment to or support for current institutions themselves, and certainly not for many of the traditions and conventions of those institutions.

Media organizations are increasingly large, integrated business organizations whose objectives are far removed from the idealized professional ethic that they have traditionally romanticized in order to claim special status. In a world of brutal survival strategies, the media are rapidly stratifying and differentiating. The commoditization of journalism drives it to meet both consumer demand and consumer prejudice. Market forces are turning what was once a business with a sense of corporate responsibility, one that was providing a public good, into organizations driven by the bottom line that are providing a commodity within the context of an increasingly frail business model.

As media analysts have long noted, the editorial touchstone is no longer whether something is intrinsically important. Rather, it is whether something is sufficiently relevant and interesting to readers and viewers to attract them away from other topics and other media. The operative decision-making rules have editors deciding not what people need to know but what they want to know. There is no longer a concept of an overriding civic mandate. There are no "must-carry" stories.

MEDIA AND THE COVERAGE OF POWER

The coverage of government and power has become a crucial tool for corporate positioning and marketing. The Meech Lake process and the free trade debate taught the media that a dispassionate assessment of power, an emphasis on issues of intrinsic importance, could put them on the "wrong" side of the gulf between elites and ordinary voters and consumers. That gulf was most evident in the final rejection of the Charlottetown Accord, which had been endorsed by the broadest consensus among elites seen in Canada in decades and yet failed in a national referendum.

Journalists who work for mass media have moved from reporting and evaluating to trying to represent and empower their audience. They have understood that people are alienated and suspicious of most institutions and have begun to pander to those feelings both by reinforcing the reasons for alienation and suspicion and by acting as a voice for the alienated and suspicious. Media have found it commercially rewarding to attack the effectiveness and then the legitimacy of government and its processes. This has made members of the media a priori adversarial, proceeding from a presumption of manipulative practice and venal motive. Unfortunately, that presumption has too often been proven correct, thereby reinforcing current media practice and behaviour.

In government, this combination of factors usually leads to risk avoidance, careful communications planning, secrecy, and a hesitancy about discussing or even disclosing options. It also leads to a determination to avoid having the spotlight focus on divisive issues. Put a bit more generously, government has far more room to manoeuvre when it can sort out competing demands relatively quietly—because when the media seize on an issue, the rules change. The media tend to approach contentious issues with reactive suspicion, and an impatience with process, and to continually redefine the issues to fit media narrative or consumer models. That approach prizes conflict, short-term horizons for resolution, and clear, sympathetic "winners." It is dismissive of incremental movement and half-a-loaf compromises.

Reporters try to fit virtually everything into an ongoing evaluative context—the current level of success and viability of the government in power, particularly if it happens to be a minority government. Every issue has the potential of advancing a government's interests or setting them back, of testing a minister's competence and popularity. Sometimes, the importance of issue resolution lies not with the actual substance of the resolution but with the way in which it was accomplished and its immediate political consequences. For instance, the government's compromise in dealing with secret documents relating to the treatment of Afghan detainees is now being portrayed as a triumph of political tactics, which has served to bury the issue. Incredibly, whether there was substance to the original allegations (once the object of much reporting and analysis) now seems beside the point. In many ways, political coverage has come to resemble sports reporting. Coverage of a game is much more interesting than coverage of incremental process and arcane policy deliberations.

All of this would just be interesting anthropology if the media did not play a highly significant role in "priming" public opinion and government and public policy. As a great deal of research has shown, media emphasis—tonnage and display—establishes an issue's relative importance, creating a hierarchy for readers and viewers. In their work of priming, the media also set the agenda and the permissible limits for public discourse. They create an awareness of issues and determine the degree of urgency. There is clear evidence that having established their agenda-setting purpose, the media then influence the views of media consumers about governance and leadership by assigning responsibility to leadership for resolving the problems that the media have identified. The popularity of government and leadership, in turn, varies with the amount of attention they award to those issues and their efficacy in resolving them, even if those issues are intrinsically less important than others or less susceptible to solution. Media coverage of crime has been a classic example of this dynamic. There is little doubt that media emphasis on crime and on public fears about crime is far from congruent with the overall incidence of crime. Most experts agree that the impact of this emphasis extends to political policy, as parties jockey to avoid being tarred as "soft on crime."

WHO IS PAYING ATTENTION?

The media, surprisingly, have less to do with actually shaping opinion. They only create the precondition for shaping by putting issues on the public agenda. Other sources, including family and friends, have a more important role in shaping opinion. That's in part because most Canadians expose themselves to the news only in the most cursory of ways. Most people presume, incorrectly, that journalism reaches a wide audience of readers and viewers. What is correct is that opinion leaders watch and read the news regularly. Communications strategists usually work to create fairly focused messages aimed at influencing opinion leaders in order that their retransmission to others of both content and the hierarchy of importance is relatively consistent.

For more than a decade and half now, to aid our communications efforts for both the public and private sectors, we at the Earnscliffe Strategy Group have been conducting research into the levels of engagement among the Canadian public. It appears that about 30 percent of the population is active in social, political, and community affairs. These people, who are by far those most interested in public affairs issues, are the opinion leaders, the people who seek out others to inform and sway. They consume media in highly disproportionate numbers and generate the bulk of the letters to the editor and calls to open-line shows. They occupy virtually all voluntary agency executive positions and are the ones who speak in public and attend public meetings. And they come from all partisan tendencies.

The other 70 percent is relatively disconnected from the public affairs of the nation except at election time (and increasingly less so even then) or when some massive policy issue surfaces that has a direct impact on them. Reaching them is extraordinarily difficult. Informing them directly, let alone educating them, is even more so. Most of these people have chosen to disconnect because they have decided that most public affairs are of no practical relevance to them.

There is another point to make here. It has become increasingly hard to reach Canadians as a whole, across all the regions of the country. Because of the centrifugal forces operating in Canada, and because most journalistic operations are local and hence define their issues of interest and relevance more locally, it has become ever more difficult to assemble a daily national agenda or a daily national audience. There are few national news organizations, and, combined, they serve between three and four million people, many of whom overlap. Everything else is regionally based and, these days, is by definition idiosyncratic.

We have growing pools of people with different information bases, different sets of agendas, expectations, standards for government performance, and policy demands, and different levels of attachment to traditionally shared institutions and values. This is an immense problem for governments, particularly in their communications planning.

On the whole, on those issues of generalized interest, the various publics have a pretty good idea of what they want, but they don't know much about how to get it, and they tend not to understand and accept real-world constraints. Impediments like jurisdiction meet with angry impatience. An intellectual understanding of the difficulty in providing comprehensive quick medical care doesn't reduce the emotional angst of being on a waiting list or the tendency to blame the national government for failing to fix the problem. Nor does the inability of leaders to admit error or uncertainty inspire confidence.

The years of acrimonious public debates on a variety of critical issues involving stakeholders, interest groups, activists, and leaders have exhausted the public patience for the kinds of resolutions that are the product of loud and angry partisan and ideological debate. The public tends to withhold its consent or to become actively hostile unless it believes that government gets the basic idea—in other words, that the government includes common-sense propositions in its quest to understand and solve a particular problem. Sometimes, the common-sense solution runs against the preferred policy outcome. An example of that sort of profound gap is the expert policy consensus on the need for systemic restructuring of health care versus the public demand for funding of acute and emergency care services. The public wants evidence that government is properly motivated—that the outcome being sought is appropriate, principled, and in the greater public interest. Compromise solutions often seem to fall short. The media's insistence on absolutes tends to paint compromise, incremental initiative, and evolving positions as weakness. And finally, in a complex world of thousands of difficult issues, the public, before it engages, needs to be convinced that an issue is both truly important and truly urgent. Often those conditions are not immediately obvious.

Although members of the media understand that there actually is a public demand for solutions and quiet collaborative partnerships and that the public has lost confidence in the media because of negative tone and content, they also understand that the public likes its media to act out its generalized sense of grievance. Those involved in the media believe that those conflicting impulses may be irreconcilable, and so they opt for what they believe will entertain and sell.

COMMUNICATING DIFFERENTIALLY

As a result, and at the risk of oversimplifying far too much, there are basically two legislative systems in Canada. The first is the system that has evolved over time and functions reasonably well: the process of elite brokerage and resource allocation described in classic political science texts. The other is the system that kicks in once mass media enter the process, a system that often becomes dysfunctional and spins out of control.

These days in Ottawa, competent communications advisors try to stay away from the mass media whenever they can. Government does not have the tools, the leverage, or even the podiums to fight effectively in the mass media arena. They have learned that there is seldom a win to be had, that playing for ties is about as good as it gets. The constant and usually well-motivated quest to "educate" the public has often turned out to be counterproductive.

Governments despair of being treated fairly by the media or of being able to trust that substance will be transmitted accurately and dispassionately. From this comes a variety of tactics aimed at communicating directly to the electorate (or more accurately, segments of it), tactics honed to a high art by the current government—including grotesquely expensive and cartoonishly simple-minded advertising, cultivation of less informed regional media, and boxcar loads of publicly and party-funded direct mail. Perhaps even more disturbingly, little of this communication is about the actual substance of public policy choices. There is an obsessive fixation on message control designed to stifle policy debate and enhance partisan advantage—both of which are the antithesis of normal government communications objectives.

Nevertheless, a need for traditional information still exists among elites and issue stakeholders, and in order to serve them, the media have stratified quite significantly. Elite and specialized media organizations, many of them electronically based, tend to cover parliamentary and government processes more routinely and run into issues that other organizations do not. They operate in a manner closer to the professional model of journalism and are consumed almost entirely by the people we call the "involved Canadians." Governments often "double track" their communications efforts: they co-operate (usually indirectly) with specialized media organizations in an effort to reach stakeholders and obtain input, while they downplay or stonewall communications on the same issues with mass media organizations.

Often, government communications advisors and public affairs strategists make a point of defining issues in ways that will seem technical or marginal to non-specialized media, even the quasi-elite ones. Properly managed, issues can be raised, debated, and disposed of within this public—but still essentially closed—loop. Stakeholders obtain information, pressure is applied, political calculations are made, and decisions are influenced—all without the issue hitting the broader public agenda. Some of the fiercest lobbying campaigns in Canadian history have been managed this way. Transportation and telecom deregulation and reform of financial institutions are some that come to mind.

The centrifugal forces at work seem to be accelerating, a process that is being aided by information technologies and their application to information gathering and distribution. Digitization and the Internet—which together create a converging distribution point for content in the form of print, film, television, and multimedia—are having a profound impact on the way people gather, distribute, and consume information. Although these technologies have undeniably increased choice for the consumer (to the point of paralysis for some), as we now see in specialty TV networks, there is the clear prospect of closed-loop networks—information-gathering and information-distribution systems organized by special interest groups, religious groups, or market affinity groups who will employ their own information gatherers and processors and distribute their own material, and will incur very little cost in doing so. Political activists and managers clearly understand the utility of such systems. In the United States, right-wing loops like this have managed to increasingly isolate their consumers from contrary information, analysis, and opinion. In Canada, the federal government takes particular care to monitor and feed conservative bloggers, right-wing hotline radio programs (they are the highest priority for daily morning media reports), and the more conservative media organizations.

Factors like these have led to the current, and likely accelerating, decoupling of broad masses of electorates from particular classes of important information or even from traditional news information itself. If you don't know what you don't know and are unwilling to delegate others to tell you, you begin to narrow your universe to one driven by your preconceived interests. Governments can exacerbate the problem when they determine that it is not in their interest to devote extraordinary efforts to engage the disengaged.

When there is no civic premium paid on everyone consuming a shared information set and no practical way to encourage or enforce it—and worse still, when trying to connect demands a level of patience and commitment that people are unwilling to invest—logic says the likeliest outcome is more and more detachment from all but the most threatening or overwhelming kinds of information. That means a general fragmentation of knowledge about context, process, and even basic facts. In that context, how does a society manage decisions about the allocation of resources, determine a sense of national will, or broker resolutions? Is it any wonder that over the past decades of bewildering change, we are seeing increasing instances of the withdrawal of public consent and the refusal to delegate fundamental decision making to public and political leadership?

Lest this sound entirely pessimistic, let me acknowledge that there are countervailing influences and logics. Despite all the expressed alienation, cynicism, and suspicion of government, most Canadians still believe that government can and should be the protector of the common good and the public interest and the guarantor of personal security. Most people continue to invest in government the role of organizing and planning their economy and rules of order. And most Canadians have developed a healthy skepticism about media and its coverage of government. Part of the current growing public distaste for journalism reflects the public desire for the kind of journalism that so many practitioners have virtually abandoned: journalism that hews to the traditional professional model that people continue to believe is important.

The common-sense survival instincts of that broad middle of reasonable Canadians usually tend to prevail. For instance, local grassroots movements are operating around important local issues, as involved Canadians try to re-engage the rest of us in order to build broad-based community-driven solutions. Social media have become a potentially important tool in galvanizing public interest and awareness. They had a profound impact in Québec in the 2008 election, creating a difficult problem for the Conservatives on an issue that they—and political media—had assumed was minor. Since then, social media have twice—on prorogation and the census—provided ongoing platforms for large-scale dissent. Certainly, digitized databases and information sources have empowered individual researchers to supplement and often surpass the efforts of media professionals and then to use social media as an alternative platform for publication.

An optimist, then, might say there exists the potential over time for an interesting coincidence of trends: a combination of a more restrained approach on the part of the media (and the less pressurized environment this might bring), higher levels of civic engagement; sources of information that are more transparent and more accessible, and greater public tolerance for appropriately motivated government initiative. All of these, in turn, might reduce the political cost to government of substantive re-engagement with the Canadian public.

3

Richard Davis

Blogs and Politics

In November 2010, John Tyner went to the San Diego airport to start a vacation to South Dakota. When he was asked to go through a full-body scan, he refused. When the Transportation Security Administration (TSA) agent explained the enhanced pat-down procedure to him, which included a "groin check," Tyner said: "Don't touch my junk" and added that he would have the agent arrested. Tyner argued with a TSA supervisor, who then escorted him back to the ticket counter and had his ticket refunded. The TSA also threatened him with a $10,000 fine.[1]

Tyner recorded the incident on his cellphone and posted it on the Internet. Bloggers immediately criticized or praised Tyner's action, but some went even further. Two opponents of the scans initiated a website to urge people not to fly or to opt out of scanners on November 24. Bloggers began pushing the idea across the blogosphere. Conservative blogger and syndicated columnist Charles Krauthammer called Tyner's statement "the point at which a docile public declares that it will tolerate only so much idiocy." On an MSNBC blog, one contributor urged airline passengers not only to opt out of full body scans but also to write letters of protest and fill out forms on the TSA website.[2]

The opt-out effort never did result in major slowdowns at US airports, as had been predicted, but the bloggers' efforts did strike a chord with many travellers and caught the attention of administration officials. In an initial response to the boycott idea, TSA's director, John Pistole, declared that there would be no change to the agency's procedures. President Barack Obama stated that the new procedures were necessary. But later, Pistole pleaded with passengers not to participate in the opt-out effort, and White House press secretary Robert Gibbs said the administration was taking into consideration public reaction in assessing the TSA's procedures.[3]

The role of bloggers sometimes crosses international boundaries. An American blogger, Ed Morrissey, became famous for breaking Canadian law. Morrissey, the founder and writer for the blog *Captain's Quarters*, covered the proceedings of the sponsorship scandal investigation headed by retired Justice John Gomery when Canadian media were banned by a judicial gag order from reporting on several days of testimony at the inquiry. The blog suddenly became popular with Canadians who wanted news about the inquiry but weren't able to get it from the news media.[4]

These incidents suggest that the political blogosphere has come of age even though it is only a decade old. The use of blogs and the response to them from journalists, politicians, and the public has led to discussion of the place of blogging in politics. One area in which blogs are now used is campaigns. In an age of sound bites, blogs allow candidates and parties to bypass traditional media to reach a politically astute audience. Like talk radio or TV talk shows, blogs offer an alternative venue for getting news out that traditional media will not cover and that political activists want to read. Using blogs is another example of parties and candidates diversifying their communications effort by turning to new media forms that will carry their messages more effectively than traditional media.[5]

In the United States, blogs have become an integral part of presidential elections. Presidential candidates are quick to add political bloggers to their staffs to help them understand and relate to the blogosphere. During the 2008 presidential primaries, Governor Mike Huckabee even thanked bloggers for keeping his campaign alive when he had relatively little money.[6] Senator Hillary Clinton, however, learned about blogs the hard way. She skipped the annual YearlyKos convention of liberal bloggers in 2006, but then showed up in 2007 after she was heavily criticized by liberal bloggers for ignoring the blogging community.

With blog audiences numbering collectively in the millions and politicians and journalists paying attention to blogs, blog influence on public policy would seem to be a given. Various players in American politics seem to view blogs as potentially influential in mobilizing grassroots voters. Former Democratic presidential candidate Bill Richardson called bloggers "agents of advocacy."[7] At the 2006 YearlyKos convention, us Senator Harry Reid asked bloggers to help break the myth that Democrats don't stand for anything: "We don't have a bully pulpit, but we have you. We need you to be our megaphone."[8]

The blogosphere has carved out a niche in political life. It is a factor in public relations strategies and is catered to by national policy-makers. Blog stories break into national news media topics. Whether the blogosphere has become a permanent fixture in political life is debatable, however. Online discussion has undergone various forms in the lifespan of the Internet, and, for the most part, online forums have lacked the transformative powers once predicted for them. Bulletin boards, Usenet, and chat rooms are examples of political communication forms that were at one time touted as capable of transforming politics and reshaping the way political communication is conducted. However, each failed to develop visible roles as permanent forces on the Internet, much less the larger political environment. Email is one forum that has outlasted the others and has the strongest potential of operating as a grassroots mobilizing tool, although even it has not achieved that potential.[9] Social media may have that potential.

Blogs could be different. Their history is short, but during their brief existence, they have affected some key events and possess the potential to affect more in the future. Given that potential, it is critical to understand what effect blogs are having on the public. Who reads political blogs? Why do they do so? What impact do these blogs have on the public? These are the questions we will address in the rest of this chapter.

TYPES OF BLOG READERS

Much remains unknown about how audiences use blogs and to what extent they are affected by what they read. Relatively few surveys of blog audiences exist, and very few of those have been conducted with political blog audiences.[10] Among surveyors of blog audiences are the Institute for Politics, Democracy and the Internet, the Pew Internet and American Life Project, and Harris Interactive.[11] To answer some of the many questions still unanswered, I conducted a survey of political blog readers in April 2007. The survey sample, which was drawn from an Internet survey panel developed by Knowledge Networks, comprised 2,729 people in the United States. The primary sample consisted of 653 people who read political blogs at least several times a month.

Most of those surveyed cannot be called regular political blog readers. Although 41 percent of the survey sample of 2,729 said they read political blogs at least several times a year, nearly half of those said they read them *only* several times a year. They are very occasional readers, perhaps drawn to blogs only because they stumble on one while browsing or because someone sends them a link to a blog. Clearly, since political blogs change daily, sometimes hourly, these people are not political blog readers. Although a significant minority of the population has read political blogs at some point, the vast majority of Americans do not read political blogs.[12]

The actual political blog readers—those who read blogs with some consistency—fit into three groups. Respondents who read political blogs at least several times a month, which I refer to as "occasional" readers, constitute 23 percent of the survey sample. Nearly half of those, however, said they read blogs only several times a month. They may have blogs on their favourites; they may go to blogs when they find a story about which they want information not available in traditional media sources; or they may enjoy reading blogs but do not have time to do so on a regular basis. "Regular" readers, those who read political blogs several times a week but not daily, constitute about 7 percent of respondents: for these people, political blog reading has become a habit.

Those in the last group, who constitute 5 percent of the 2,729 people surveyed, are the "daily" readers. Having made political blog reading a part of their daily routine, they are the active audience for political blogs. Yet, extrapolating from the survey data, this reading community—the daily readers—constitutes only one in twenty of online Americans (more than 75 percent of Americans are online). Even the regular readers and the daily readers together make up only 12 percent of those online, a far cry from the claims sometimes made about the size and impact of the political blog audience. And it is a considerably smaller audience than that of traditional media: seven in ten Americans say they regularly watch local TV news, just over half say they read a daily newspaper, and nearly half say they are regular watchers of national nightly network news programs.[13]

There are important differences among the three groups of political blog readers, particularly between the daily readers and the other two groups. An obvious difference lies in the level of involvement in the blogosphere. Nearly half of the daily blog readers spend half an hour or more reading political blogs. Readers in the other two groups dedicate much less time to blog reading. Daily readers also read more blogs than other readers do, are more likely to post comments on blogs and to be bloggers themselves, place a higher priority on what they read on political blogs, and are more likely to believe that what they read on blogs is more important than what they read in the mainstream media. Of these daily readers, 29 percent felt that blog content was more important than what they read in traditional media sources. Only 11 percent of regular readers and 13 percent of occasional readers shared that view.

The daily and regular readers are the real political blog readers in terms of active interaction with the blogosphere. They pay the closest attention to the political blogosphere and connect with it. However, these readers are a small fraction of adults who are online, much less the total population.

WHO ARE THESE READERS?

Are daily political blog readers representative of the general American public? The answer is no. These blog readers are significantly different from the general public.

First, there is a profound gender gap in the political blogosphere. Men are heavily overrepresented, particularly among daily blog readers (see table 3.1). This gender discrepancy grows as the frequency of reading intensifies.[14] It also corresponds to the gender gap among top political bloggers, where men heavily predominate.[15] Matthew Hindman found that there is also a gender gap in the ideological blogospheres. Males are more likely to read conservative blogs such as *Instapundit, little green footballs,* and *Michelle Malkin.* Liberal blogs attract a roughly even percentage of men and women, although some actually attract more women than men.[16]

These findings mirror other studies of gender usage of online political discussion forums.[17] We can speculate on what it is precisely that attracts males and seems to repel females. The gender discrepancy may be related to the characteristics of online discussion. The primary traits of these forums—verbal attack, conflict, and competition—may be more attractive to male readers. Political blogging can be similar, although nothing inherent in any online discussion forum mandates that approach. Another possible cause for the gender gap is the dearth of female voices among the top political blog-gers: few of the writers on the A-list of political bloggers are women. Women may simply find few relevant voices in the political blogosphere. Whatever the reason, the political blogosphere tends to be a male-oriented forum domi-nated by male bloggers who in turn attract a largely male audience. That male dominance may affect the type of discussion as well as its style, making it diffi-cult to attract female blog readers. And it also may mean that the blogosphere as a gauge of the broader general public is flawed.

Table 3.1   Blog readers versus non-blog readers

Respondent characteristic		Frequency of blog reading (%)		
		Never[a]	Regular[b]	Daily
Gender	Male	44	54	61
	Female	56	46	39
Race	White	78	71	67
	Black	7	10	10
	Hispanic	10	9	14
	Other	6[c]	9[c]	9
Education	Less than high school	10	13	5
	High school degree	31	15	17
	Some college	28	24	28
	Bachelors or higher	32[c]	48	50
Income	Under $25,000	20	20	19
	$25,000 to $49,999	31	30	22
	$50,000 to $74,999	21	22	23
	$75,000 $99,999	14	14	22
	$100,000 and up	14	14	14

[a] This category comprises 1,550 individuals (of the original sample of 2,729 respondents) who said they had never read a political blog.
[b] This category comprises 526 individuals (of the original sample of 2,729 respondents) who said they read political blogs only several times a year.
[c] Totals of 101% or 99% are due to rounding.

Table 3.1 tells us that daily political blog readers are not, however, less likely to be minorities. In fact, they are slightly more likely to be African-American or Hispanic than the American public generally. Bloggers also tend to be more racially diverse than the general population. Since the blogosphere offers a broad array of blog choices, it could well be that racial and ethnic minorities find voices in the blogosphere that are not available in the traditional media.

Political blog readers are, on the whole, much better educated than those who do not read political blogs. Daily and regular blog readers are far more likely than non-readers to have a college education. These findings match those of other politically interested groups, including others who discuss politics online.[18] One might expect that higher educational backgrounds would mean higher income levels for political blog readers. As table 3.1 shows, that was the case for the most avid readers—the daily readers. About 36 percent of daily readers made $75,000 or more, while only 28 percent of non-readers did. Similarly, at the lower end, 51 percent of non-readers made less than $50,000, while only 41 percent of daily readers did. The gap between the non-political blog reader and the daily blog reader is thus clear. Daily blog readers are more likely to be well educated, relatively affluent, and male. But the expectation does not fit in the area of race: the daily blog reader is not more likely to be white.

The profile of the average daily political blogger as an affluent, well-educated male is one that mirrors the known political online discussion audience. The culture of political blogs may reflect the expected audience. Moreover, the more one reads, the more different political bloggers look from the general public.

USES AND GRATIFICATIONS OF POLITICAL BLOG READING

Why do people read political blogs? What do they get out of blogs that they cannot obtain from exposure to traditional media? One need of the blog audience that may not be as well met by traditional news media is access to the latest political news. Fifty-six percent of daily blog readers said they are more likely to hear about the latest news from blogs than from the mainstream media (see table 3.2). While traditional media sites update periodically throughout the day, blogs do so incessantly. Readers may perceive that it is the blog rather than the traditional media that will tell them what has happened most recently. Hence, turning to the blog satisfies a need to be up to date.

Table 3.2   Reasons given for reading political blogs

Statement[a]	Frequency of Blog Reading	
	Regular (% who agree)	Daily (% who agree)
Blogs are entertaining.	51	53
I'm more likely to hear about the latest news from blogs.	34	56
Mainstream media don't give full information.	31	42
Blogs give me information I don't get elsewhere.	43	44
Mainstream media don't give me accurate information.	19	41

[a] Respondents could list more than one reason for reading.

Another real need is accurate news and information. Two studies of blog readers found that users of political blogs rate bloggers as more credible than traditional media.[19] In our study, blog readers were similarly critical of the traditional media: 41 percent agreed that the mainstream media don't provide accurate information. Nor do they feel they are getting the whole story from traditional media sources. When asked whether they agreed with the statement that the mainstream media aren't giving them full information, 42 percent of daily blog readers said yes. Blogs, unlike traditional media, apparently fill that need for the full story, particularly for daily readers. Some 44 percent of daily readers and 43 percent of regular readers agreed that "blogs give me information I don't get elsewhere." Blog readers, particularly daily readers, seem to want more than what they receive from traditional news media.

Blog readers also seemed to enjoy the entertainment value of blogs. A majority of blog readers agreed that blogs are entertaining. Bloggers are openly biased and resort to ad hominem attacks, much like talk radio does. Moreover, traditional news media tend not to be entertaining.

Table 3.3   Blog readers' familiarity with ideological blogs

| | Title of blog | Ideology of blog reader (% who have heard of blog) | | |
		Liberal	Moderate	Conservative
Liberal blogs	Daily Kos	46	21	34
	Wonkette	50	20	30
	Eschaton	46	19	35
	Crooks and Liars	54	21	25
Conservative blogs	Instapundit	45	19	35
	Michelle Malkin	34	16	49
	Little Green Footballs	30	16	53

Is blog reading a reinforcement mechanism? Do people go to blogs to be confirmed in the opinions they already hold? Does *Daily Kos* or *Michelle Malkin* or some other blog give them reassurance that their views are correct? One measure of reinforcement is the particular blogs with which readers are familiar. We would expect that liberals would be aware of more liberal blogs and conservatives of more conservative ones, and that is exactly the pattern found in our survey (see table 3.3). This suggests that, for the most part, political blog readers are gravitating to those blogs that reinforce their views. One blogger described this phenomenon: "I have 3,000 people who listen to what I say and, judging from the posted comments, many of them pretty much agree with me."[20] Another measure of reinforcement is the level of agreement with the opinions people read on political blogs. We found that the greater the devotion to blog reading, the higher the agreement with the bloggers: one-third of daily readers said they agreed with the opinions of bloggers whose blogs they read most of the time, while only 20 percent of regular readers felt that way.

SUPPLANT OR SUPPLEMENT?

Are blog readers turning away from the traditional media? Blog rhetoric often suggests that traditional media are seriously flawed, particularly in comparison to the political blogosphere. One might assume that this rhetoric would have turned political blog readers, particularly daily readers, against the traditional media. Our findings suggest that this is not the case. It is not even true for daily blog readers. In fact, other research shows that the vast majority of blog readers—regardless of frequency—are also traditional media users.[21] Of our survey respondents, most read a local newspaper and watch television news—both local and network—and nearly two in five daily blog readers said they read a national newspaper. Rather than abandoning traditional media, political blog readers, particularly daily readers, seem to be the most media dependent. They use traditional media at rates well above those of other Americans. According to a study by the Pew Research Center, only 12 percent of Americans read the website of a national newspaper online.[22]

The explanation for media dependency, particularly the greater interest in national newspapers, undoubtedly lies with political blog readers' keen interest in politics, particularly national politics. Political blogs—with their emphasis on political issues—offer the same diet of political news as do national newspapers. It is no wonder those who are the most avid readers of political blogs are also the most likely to read a national newspaper, which provides more of the kind of news they want than any other traditional news source.

Another indication that blogs and traditional media co-exist for blog readers, even the most avid ones, is the paucity of blog readers who view blogs as their primary news source. Only 3 percent of daily blog readers said they get most of their news from blogs. Most blog readers are still using traditional media—television, newspapers, or radio—as their main news source.

CONCLUSIONS AND THE FUTURE

The influence of political blogs on the public is more limited than anecdotal evidence may indicate. First, only a small percentage of Americans are readers of political blogs. Nor are these readers typical of the general public. Policymakers and journalists should be wary of concluding that political blog posts or comments are representative of the opinions of the general public when those who are most involved in the blogosphere are so atypical. Additionally, political blogs are reinforcing rather than converting: readers seem to gravitate to the blogs with which they agree. Nor are these readers isolated in the blogosphere. Interestingly, they have not abandoned the traditional news media that bloggers so heavily criticize.

Even though our study examined American blog readers, it has implications for the role of political blogs in Canada. It is likely that the effects of political blogs are even more limited in Canada due to differences between our political systems. Like our results indicated for the United States, Canadian political blogs may be reaching a small, politically interested audience that is using blog readership for reinforcement and supplementing traditional media use. Although blogs can achieve media and policy-maker attention, Canadian political communication research may conclude that their effects on the general public are limited.

Could that influence grow in the future? The study of a phenomenon in progress makes such conclusions inherently problematic. However, it is useful to assess recent developments in the blogosphere that will impact the study of the blogosphere's political role in the near future.

Commercialization

The blogosphere began more than a decade ago as an extension of the initial aim of the Internet to provide a "Wild West" atmosphere free of government regulation, commercialization, and establishment norms. By the late 1990s, the Internet had become primarily a commercial medium, but the blogosphere was touted as an antidote to that trend. However, that much-despised commercialization has come to the blogosphere. Shoestring blog operations, such as those run by Markos Moulitsas (*Daily Kos*) and Joshua Micah Marshall (*TalkingPointsMemo*), have become business enterprises incorporating networks of bloggers. Other blogs have been initiated precisely for commercial purposes. Arianna Huffington of the *Huffington Post* began her blog with a staff and several million dollars of capital. By early 2010, her blog had more than forty million unique visitors monthly.[23] Like print newspapers, this new type of blog covers the gamut of news subjects—sports, entertainment, business, and the arts, as well as politics.[24]

The trend in blog readership has been toward blog aggregators: blogs like the *Huffington Post* and *RealClearPolitics* or *National Newswatch* in Canada that collect information for blog readers from a variety of sources. Such aggregating helps establish the blog as a one-stop source for information that appeals to a variety of tastes and ideologies. These aggregators likely will attract increasing amounts of blog traffic while independent and individual blogs may languish. A 2009 analysis of blog readership found that nearly all national political blogs, primarily run by individual bloggers, had lost readership from the previous year.[25] Commercial interests will seek to initiate, fund, or at least advertise with aggregator blogs because that is where the audiences are. The commercialization of the blogosphere will create a stark cleavage between those few commercial aggregator blogs that will dominate blog readership and the vast majority of political blogs written for limited audiences.

The Impact of Social Media

Blog growth would seem to be the most promising among younger media consumers because they are less likely than their predecessors to acquire the traditional media habit in the first place.[26] However, Facebook and other social media sites have become competitors with the blogosphere, and the social media seem to be winning. Facebook alone now has over a half billion users worldwide. While blog use among young people has declined, social media use by that same group has soared.[27] Facebook has certain advantages over blogs for young people, including creating their own online community, having more immediate interaction with others, and, most recently, using a messenger service that allows young people to combine texting, chat, and email. Facebook has also acquired a social status that few young people will avoid without social ramifications. Indeed, as the telephone was for an earlier generation, so today's youth rely on Facebook as a primary means to communicate with other young people.

Whether social media will displace political blogs in the near future is an open question, however. There are indications that it will not. First, political blog readers are older and have already acquired political news acquisition habits that make political blog reading attractive. Political blog readers would therefore be less affected by the rise of Facebook as an exclusive, or even primary, social communication mechanism. Moreover, political blogs fit within a different niche than social media. News and information is still more likely to originate on a blog than a Facebook site, and political blogs generally provide more developed news commentary and analysis than Facebook does.

Competition or Integration with Traditional Media

Initially, bloggers attempted to elbow their way into the media environment by criticizing traditional media, but, as seen above, rather than supplant traditional media, they have become a supplement. Political blog readers are also traditional news media users.

It is not only the audience that has integrated traditional news media and blogs. It is also the blogosphere. Increasingly, blogs are becoming more like the media they have criticized in the past. As mentioned above, the *Huffington Post* is competing with traditional media and becoming much like a traditional print media source in its approach to a wide variety of news. Much of it is political, as is the case with a traditional print newspaper, but other sections of the blog do not primarily appeal to those who are interested in politics. Moreover, both bloggers and traditional media are crossing each other's lines. Bloggers are joining traditional media. For example, Andrew Sullivan started a blog called *The Daily Dish* and then moved it over to *The Atlantic*, and Anna Marie Cox, the founder of *Wonkette*, later became a writer with *Time.com*. At the same time, traditional journalists are becoming bloggers. For example, Anderson Cooper (CNN) and Brian Williams (NBC News) possess their own blogs hosted by their respective news organizations. Traditional media organizations are beginning their own in-house blogs that provide insights on the news that do not necessarily appear in their traditional publications or broadcasts, or even elsewhere on the website. Examples include the *Globe and Mail's* "Ottawa Notebook" and "The Caucus" of the *New York Times*.

The lines between the blogosphere and the traditional media will become increasingly blurred over time as the blogosphere adopts traditional media structure and norms, and the traditional media adapt to the world of the blogosphere. Neither are likely to displace one another. Instead, the two will adapt to each other to provide their own respective niches within the news and information environment.

NOTES

1   Catherine Saillant, "Traveler Who Resisted TSA Pat-Down Is Glad His Moment of Fame Is Nearly Over," *Los Angeles Times*, November 19, 2010.

2   Charles Krauthammer, "Don't Touch My Junk," *National Review Online*, November 19, 2010; Helen A.S. Popkin, "Tell the TSA 'Don't Touch My Junk'—Here's How," *Technolog*, November 22, 2010, http://technolog.msnbc.msn.com/_news/2010/11/22/5510440-tell-the-tsa-dont-touch-my-junk-heres-how.

3   Brian Bennett and Jordan Steffen, "TSA Chief Defends Pat-Downs, Full-Body Scans," *Seattle Times*, November 18, 2010; Brad Knickerbocker, "Obama Notes Travelers' Plight, but Won't Change Airport Security," *Christian Science Monitor*, November 21, 2010; Ray Henry, "John Pistole, TSA Chief, Pleads with Travelers Against Full-Body Scan Boycott," *Huffington Post*, November 22, 2010, http://www.huffingtonpost.com/2010/11/22/john-pistole-tsa-chief-pl_n_787277.html.

4   Gregg Sangillo, "Bloggers: A Who's Who," *National Journal*, January 21, 2006, 37–39.

5 For previous discussion of these trends, see Richard Davis and Diana Owen, *New Media an American Politics* (New York: Oxford University Press, 1998); and Bruce Bimber and Richard Davis, *Campaigning Online* (New York: Oxford University Press, 2003).

6 Scott Helman, "Romney Connecting Quickly with Bloggers," *Boston Globe*, December 31, 2006; Joe Garofoli, "Tech-Savvy Swarm of Bloggers Boosts Candidates' Online Presence," *San Francisco Chronicle*, November 3, 2007; and Katherine Q. Seelye, "Huckabee Thanks Bloggers," *New York Times*, January 1, 2008.

7 Adam Nagourney, "Gathering Highlights Power of the Blog," *New York Times*, June 10, 2006.

8 Adam Nagourney, "A Mixed Bag of First Impressions by Democrats at Blog Rendezvous," *New York Times*, June 11, 2006.

9 See Andrew Paul Williams, "Self-Referential and Opponent-Based Framing: Candidate E-Mail Strategies in Campaign 2004," in *The Internet Election: Perspectives on the Web in Campaign 2004*, ed. Andrew Paul Williams and John C. Tedesco (Lanham: Rowman and Littlefield, 2006), 83–98.

10 Carl Stempel, Thomas Hargrove, and Guido H. Stempel III, "Media Use, Social Structure, and Belief in 9/11 Conspiracy Theories," *Journalism and Mass Communication Quarterly* 84 (November 2007): 353–72; Thomas J. Johnson et al., "Every Blog Has Its Day: Politically-Interested Internet Users' Perceptions of Blog Credibility," *Journal of Computer-Mediated Communication* 13 (October 2007): 100–122; Amanda Lenhart and Susannah Fox, "Bloggers: A Portrait of the Internet's New Storytellers," Pew Internet and American Life Project, July 19, 2006, http://www.pewinternet.org/PPF/r/186/report_display.asp; Joseph Graf, *The Audience for Political Blogs: New Research on Blog Readership* (Washington, DC: Institute for Politics, Democracy and the Internet, George Washington University, 2006); and K. D. Trammell, "Celebrity Blogs: Investigation in the Persuasive Nature of Two-Way Communication Regarding Politics" (PHD diss., University of Florida, 2004).

11 See Graf, *The Audience for Political Blogs*; Amanda Lenhart and Mary Madden, "Teen Content Creators and Consumers," Pew Internet and American Life Project, November 2005, http://www.pewinternet.org/Reports/2005/Teen-Content-Creators-and-Consumers.aspx; Lee Rainie, "The State of Blogging," Pew Internet and American Life Project, January 2005, http://www.pewinternet.org/Reports/2005/The-State-of-Blogging.aspx; Harris Interactive Inc., "More Than Half of Americans Never Read Political Blogs," Harris Poll #25, news release, March 10, 2008; Harris Interactive Inc., "Two-Fifths of U.S. Adults Who Are Online Have Read Political Blogs," Harris Poll #27, news release, April 13, 2005, formerly available at http://www.harrisinteractive.com/harris_poll/index.asp?PID=556.

12 Harris Interactive Inc., "More Than Half of Americans."

13 Pew Research Center for the People and the Press, "Public Knowledge of Current Affairs Little Changed by News and Information Revolutions," April 15, 2007, http://people-press.org/reports/display.php3?ReportID=319.

14 For similar findings, see William P. Eveland, Jr., and Ivan Dylko, "Reading Political Blogs During the 2004 Election Campaign: Correlates and Political Consequences," in *Blogging,*

Citizenship, and the Future of Media, ed. Mark Tremayne (New York: Routledge, 2007), 105–26.

15 Dustin Harp and Mark Tremayne, "The Gendered Blogosphere: Examining Inequality Using Network and Feminist Theory," *Journalism and Mass Communication Quarterly* 83 (Summer 2006): 247–64.

16 Matthew Hindman, *The Myth of Digital Democracy* (Princeton: Princeton University Press, 2008), chap. 6.

17 See, for example, Susan Herring, "Posting in a Different Voice: Voice, Gender and Ethics in Computer-Mediated Communication," in *Philosophical Perspectives in Computer-Mediated Communication*, ed. Charles Ess (Albany: SUNY Press, 1996), 115–46; Richard Davis, *Politics Online: Blogs, Chatrooms, and Discussion Groups in American Democracy* (New York: Routledge, 2005), chap. 3; Richard Davis, *The Web of Politics: The Internet's Impact on the American Political System* (New York: Oxford University Press, 1999), chap. 6.

18 See, for example, Eveland and Dylko, "Reading Political Blogs"; Davis, *Politics Online*.

19 Johnson et al., "Every Blog Has Its Day," 100–122; and Thomas J. Johnson and Barbara K. Kaye, "Wag the Blog: How Reliance on Traditional Media and the Internet Influence Credibility Perceptions of Weblogs Among Blog Users," *Journalism and Mass Communication Quarterly* 81 (Autumn 2004): 622–42.

20 David. D. Perlmutter, *Blog Wars* (New York: Oxford University Press, 2008), 32.

21 Pew Research Center, "Public Knowledge of Current Affairs Little Changed."

22 Ibid.

23 Brian Stelter, "Citizen Huff," *New York Times*, March 31, 2008; and Lauren Hatch, "Huffington Post Blasts Past 40 Million Monthly Unique Visitors," *Business Insider*, March 4, 2010, http://www.businessinsider.com/huffington-post-blasts-past-40-million-monthly-unique-visitors-2010-3.

24 Stelter, "Citizen Huff."

25 "May '09 Political Blog Readership 53% Lower Than It Was in October '08," *Bloggasm*, June 11, 2009, http://bloggasm.com/may-09-political-blog-readership-53-lower-than-it-was-in-october-08.

26 Martin P. Wattenberg, *Is Voting for Young People?* (New York: Pearson Longman, 2007), 9–16.

27 Amanda Lenhart et al., "Social Media and Young Adults," Pew Internet and American Life Project, February 3, 2010, http://pewinternet.org/Reports/2010/Social-Media-and-Young-Adults/Summary-of-Findings.aspx?r=1.

4

David Taras and Christopher Waddell

The 2011 Federal Election and the Transformation of Canadian Media and Politics

There is a formidable literature within political science on the role that "critical" elections have played in both ratifying societal changes and setting the political table in ways that are fundamentally and irrevocably different from the past.[1] The 2011 election qualifies as a critical election in every way. Indeed, it overturned most of the old assumptions and relationships in Canadian politics and, arguably, those of the media as well.

Having won a strong majority government after three previous elections in which he had increased his party's seat total each time, the 2011 campaign confirmed Stephen Harper as one of the most successful political leaders in Canadian history. By any measure, his rise from leader of the western-based Canadian Alliance Party, to his takeover of the Progressive Conservatives, to his emergence as opposition leader and then prime minister has been breathtaking. To achieve his goal, he used the instruments of political power and bent them to his will in ways that demonstrated both long-term strategic thinking and raw political toughness. The Conservatives' fundraising juggernaut; their devastating pre-writ ad campaigns that were so damaging to Liberal leaders Stéphane Dion and Michael Ignatieff; Harper's use of a Senate stacked with Tory appointments to block legislation from the House of

Commons; his tight, almost manic, control over his caucus; and his deft management of the news media and government communications are just some examples of how he shaped the instruments of power to his own purposes. What is most surprising, however, is that the Conservatives won despite glaring liabilities: a ballooning deficit; a more recent policy of budgetary secrecy that left Canadians wondering how much was being spent on jets, prisons, and the G8 and G20 summits in Ontario; charges by Elections Canada over alleged improprieties during the 2006 election; and an ideological disconnect between the party and a majority of Canadians on many social issues.

Harper's Conservatives won a strong majority by altering the chessboard of Canadian politics. According to one of the contributors to this volume, Tom Flanagan, Harper was unable to duplicate the uncomfortable and ultimately combustible alliance that had brought Brian Mulroney to power—a combination of western populists, traditional Conservatives, and Québec nationalists.[2] When this proved too difficult and dangerous, Harper pivoted toward a new strategy: that of bringing together social conservatives based mainly in western Canada and in suburban Ontario; traditional Tories, many from the old Progressive Conservative wing of the party; and the burgeoning Chinese and South Asian communities of Vancouver and Toronto, as well as Jewish voters. The end result was that after years of making slow gains in the suburban 905 area code region surrounding Toronto, the Tories cut a wide swath through north Metro Toronto in 2011, breaking what had once been an impregnable Liberal stronghold. But the Conservative victory left a startling gap. Except for a slender thread of five MPs, the Conservatives were obliterated in Québec. For the first time in history, a majority government did not have significant representation from one of Canada's two main language groups.[3] It remains to be seen whether what amounts to an anglophone-only government will be seen as legitimate in Québec.

But the Conservatives' victory would not have been possible had it not been for the *collapse* of the Liberals, and collapse is not too small a word. Having held power for sixty-nine years in the twentieth century, the party had become the country's "natural governing party." They were now reduced to the lowest number of seats in the forty-one elections since Canada was founded in 1867. Most of the MPs who survived the electoral hurricane of 2011 were veteran politicians who managed to barely hold on to what had previously been safe seats. With one or two exceptions such as Justin Trudeau and

Dominique Leblanc, the successor generation was wiped out. While hindsight is always 20/20, it is tempting to argue that had Liberal leader Michael Ignatieff embraced the idea of a coalition with the NDP, not only would the Liberals have been the senior partner but Jack Layton might have been effectively sidelined.[4] What is clear is that much like the famous Monty Python character who still thinks he's going to win the battle even as his limbs are being chopped off, the Liberals have been left with little to fight with. Once the great meeting place for English- and French-language elites and the party of national unity for most of the twentieth century, the Liberals have been reduced to a handful of mostly anglophone ridings in Québec. The party also lost support in immigrant and minority communities, a relationship that was once seen as unbreakable. It had also been the party of Bay Street—the party of top business leaders such as C. D. Howe, Walter Gordon, John Manley, and Paul Martin—but a sharp turn to the left had drained much of that support. With the termination of annual subsidies to political parties announced in the 2011 budget and the sharp reduction in parliamentary funding that comes with third-party status, they are now deeply wounded.

Perhaps the most dramatic change was the explosion of support for Jack Layton and the NDP in Québec. Much of this stratospheric rise was based on personality politics. Layton's courage in battling cancer and the pain of a recent hip surgery, and his likeability (he was, after all, the leader who most people said that they wanted to have a beer with), were important factors in his rise. Layton's fine performance during the French-language leader's debate and, later, on a popular TV show, *Tout le monde en parle*, proved to be decisive turning points. But most critical was the NDP's embrace of progressive social programs and its willingness to give Québec greater powers, including giving Québec's language legislation primacy in federal workplaces in the province and reopening the constitution to obtain Québec's signature. These were positions that reflected much of what the Bloc Québécois had stood for. The NDP's strongest card was the disenchantment of Québec voters with the other parties. The Harper government had become exceedingly unpopular in Québec, and the Liberal party had been unable to win a majority among francophone voters since the "night of the long knives" in 1981, when Trudeau outmaneuvered Premier René Lévesque, moving ahead with the repatriation of the constitution and creating the Charter of Rights and Freedoms without Québec's approval. Voters had also soured on what they saw as the tired and unproductive politics of the Bloc Québécois. While an official NDP presence was virtually non-existent in most Québec ridings, a wave of popularity for "Le Bon Jack" carried a wave of surprised and, in many cases, totally inexperienced candidates into the House of Commons. The "orange crush" that was sweeping Québec was soon felt in English-speaking Canada as close to 300,000 voters left the Liberals to vote for the NDP in the closing days of the campaign.

Not only did the 2011 federal election redraw the political map in dramatic ways; it also raised questions about how elections are fought in Canada. The election followed the same script that has been in place since at least the 1970s: the media covered the leaders as they hopscotched across the country; the media's reliance on polls had become compulsive and addictive, making the horse race the focus of almost all coverage; there were only two leaders' debates, one in English and one in French; and negative attack ads had become the weapons of choice for the political parties. While news organizations and political parties had constructed a system that seemed to fit their needs, the question is whether these practices and assumptions still serve Canadians well or whether they are outdated, increasingly disconnected from any larger realities, and harmful to democracy. We believe that both the parties and the news media have created a kind of alternate universe whose values and objectives need to be rethought in fundamental ways.

At least two concerns emerged out of the 2011 election. First, political leaders, with the aide of journalists, were able to sidestep any real discussion of the issues facing the country. Whether it was health care, the future of cities, how the deficit was going to be reduced, immigration, environmental policies, or the jobs crisis facing young people, leaders were free to spin their political cloths without having to supply details or even defend their positions. Second, the increasing disengagement that Elly Alboim discusses in his article continued to be evident in this campaign. Voter turnout, at just over 61 percent, was close to a record low. Polls also found that the vast majority of Canadians viewed politicians with a combination of mistrust, suspicion, and alienation, and found none of the parties satisfying. These two concerns are undoubtedly linked: arguably, in the absence of a discussion by political leaders of the issues that touch their lives and the courage to tackle them, voters become increasingly cynical and disengaged.

While there was much hoopla in the media about the magic of social media and pundits gushed about the 2011 election being the Twitter campaign, only a very small percentage of those under thirty used social media to follow the election, and voter turnout among younger Canadians remained modest.

One of the oldest election rituals is the leader's tour. The tour was originally devised so that voters could see and hear the leaders first hand. Campaigning meant meeting as many people as possible. At the same time, the leaders were supposed to experience and learn about the country in order to understand its problems. Clearly, these original intentions have long been twisted out of shape. Harper's tightly controlled appearances, where he repeated the same message about the dangers of a Liberal-NDP coalition endlessly in front of cheering supporters and took only five questions a day from reporters, amounted to a moving film set, with cities, streets, and voters used as props. With journalists unable to penetrate the tour's "bubble" and Harper shielded from ordinary citizens, the tour served journalists, who needed colourful pictures and announcements to report on, and the Tories, who knew that their images and messages would make it onto the evening news. The other parties practiced the same rituals—Ignatieff poorly, but Layton with a sophisticated mastery of visual politics, using his cane as a campaign symbol, wearing a Canadiens hockey uniform while serving beer to hockey fans, and strumming a guitar at thirty thousand feet. The fact that very few of Layton's policies had been properly costed didn't seem to interest reporters on the campaign trail.

A second concern is the media's continuing obsession with the horse race—with who's ahead, who's behind, and who's gaining and why. These are easy stories to report. They allow news organizations to appear neutral and authoritative and absolve them of the responsibility to probe deeper, explore issues more thoroughly, and describe the consequences of party positions for the country. Polls are particularly irresistible because they create headlines and allow news organizations both to create and to control the news. In 2011, however, there was a fly in the ointment. None of the major polling organizations predicted a Conservative majority. For a variety of reasons that we will discuss later in this chapter, the polling industry is going through a crisis of identity and accuracy. This raises the question of how news organizations can make the horse race the main "peg" of their election coverage if they encounter increasing difficulty knowing where the horses really are in the race.

The conventional wisdom going into the 2011 election was that leaders' debates count for very little because leaders repeat the same mantras that they use on the campaign trail and have little opportunity to confront each other directly. Debates were also seen as boring television with audiences largely disappearing after the first fifteen minutes or half an hour. Most important, studies show that unless something surprising occurs, debates tend to reinforce the choices that voters have already made. Hence, few votes change hands. While polls taken immediately after the 2011 English-language debate showed no clear winner, journalists speculated that Harper won because he didn't lose and Ignatieff lost because he had to win big and didn't. Surveys taken after the French debate indicated that Bloc Québécois leader Gilles Duceppe had scored a resounding victory and that NDP leader Jack Layton had finished third. Nothing could have been further from the truth. The debates had what Robin Sears called a "delayed time-bomb effect"—with Jack Layton the clear winner.[5] Given the importance that debates can have in altering public perceptions, it's surprising that debate formats, as well as the decision about who participates in them, are still left to a consortium of broadcasters rather than to a neutral commission. One also has to wonder why we don't have more debates or why we don't have debates among finance, defence, or environment critics so that policy positions can be more fully aired.

In the wake of the 2011 election, analysts claimed that the Conservative attack ads that aired in several bursts prior to the election had been so successful in defining Liberal leader Michael Ignatieff that he couldn't recover. There is much discussion in this book about how negative ads, both on TV and online, have become the new normal. They reach voters directly, bypassing journalist's interpretation and framing; they can be repeated until the repetition itself has an effect; and if voters see them as true, they are likely to be exceedingly sticky, difficult to get off. But the airwaves are not equally available to all parties. The Tories had a sizable spending advantage in the pre-writ period and used it with devastating force. There are also, as discussed in the introduction to this volume, questions about the nature of campaign ads. Outrageous claims are sometimes believed and the images conveyed in ads are contrived and often not true. The question of whether these ads and the attack culture that they reflect and perpetuate are healthy for the political system is discussed by Jonathan Rose later in this volume.

In campaign lore, much credence is given to the importance of parties having a strong "ground game." Winning supposedly depends on developing databases that help parties identify their voters and on having the machinery needed to get them to the polls. Yet in Québec, the NDP won with virtually no ground game at all. Attending all-candidates meetings, mounting sign campaigns, developing sophisticated databases, and motivating volunteers seemed to be largely irrelevant. The old saying credited to American congressman Tip O'Neill that all politics is local seemed to be reversed. Very little politics is local.

This article will probe more deeply into the communication structures and practices of Canadian elections, including polls, the leader's tour, debates, and the effects of web-based media. (Campaign ads are discussed in Jonathan Rose's contribution to this volume so we have chosen not to deal with ads in our review of the election.) In each case, we will ask whether it's time to rethink the old rules so that the major challenges facing the country are not ignored by both politicians and the media, and the cycle of disengagement discussed so often in this book can be broken.

THE LEADER'S TOUR

As it has been for decades, the leader's tour in 2011 was the focus of each party's national campaign, and as has also occurred for decades, the media tagged along with Stephen Harper, Michael Ignatieff, and Jack Layton as they criss-crossed the country for thirty-six days. Following the leaders this time was more expensive than ever for news organizations (at least $45,000 per seat on each leader's tour, not including hotels, per diems, and food costs). That meant, as in every campaign since 1997, that TV networks pooled their coverage. One crew was on each leader's plane providing identical video to CBC, Radio-Canada, TVA, Global, and CTV of the day's events, the leaders' speeches, scrums, and anything else interesting that happened. TV and print reporters jumped on and off tours, and despite 2010 rumours that media cost-cutting would mean that some media would only cover the NDP sporadically, that didn't happen. In retrospect, that was a wise decision.

The first week proved a good example of how each party campaigned. Stephen Harper visited fourteen cities, Michael Ignatieff thirteen, and Jack Layton twelve, but it was where they went that was telling.[6] After the traditional Ottawa kickoff on Saturday morning, March 26, Harper went directly to Québec City and finished that day in Brampton for the first of many visits to the Greater Toronto Area. The rest of the week he was in Montreal, each of the Atlantic provinces, Winnipeg, Edmonton, Regina, and Vancouver Island. Each visit was to a constituency that the campaign had identified as one Conservatives needed to win to turn Harper's daily stump request for "a strong, stable, majority national government" into a reality. That approach continued right to the campaign's last day, which held a coast-to-coast blast that dropped Harper into selected spots such as the London North Centre riding, which the Conservatives took from the Liberals, before finishing late at night in Calgary.

Liberal ambitions were less lofty as Ignatieff initially concentrated on southern Ontario and the Montreal region, with quick visits to Winnipeg and Vancouver. Even this early in the campaign, the Liberals appeared to be using a defensive strategy, trying to hold the seats Liberals had won in 2008 and maybe take some from the NDP rather than going after Conservative-held ridings. Ignatieff's tour became much more defensive as the campaign unfolded, and polls showed the Liberals being in more and more trouble. Unlike past elections with a national wrap-up to the tour, the Liberals spent the last five days only in southern Ontario and Toronto in an increasingly desperate yet failing effort to hold seats that had been Liberal for decades.

On day one, the NDP headed to Edmonton from Ottawa to try (as it turned out, successfully) to keep the only non-Conservative seat in Alberta. Like the other leaders, Layton spent a lot of time in Toronto and southern Ontario, but in that first week, he was also in Regina, Vancouver, northern Ontario, Québec City, and Montreal. Even before the campaign had started, the NDP had plastered downtown Montreal with billboards featuring Jack Layton, suggesting that the party thought gains could be made in Québec, which turned out to be correct. He finished the campaign's last days going from coast to coast, met by large crowds of enthusiastic supporters, giving television great images of campaign momentum, creating a sharp visual contrast to the Liberals' last days on the campaign trail, and giving viewers an accurate preview of the election-night fates of the two parties. Layton began May 1 in Montreal, then took his campaign bus down Highway 401 to Toronto, stopping in Kingston for an event where police had to close streets as the crowd was so large.

Bloc Québécois leader Gilles Duceppe initially didn't venture beyond Montreal and Québec City. Even when he moved into other regions of the province, reporters started noticing and reporting that crowds were small and events were listless. It was a campaign without direction or focus, which showed in the party's election day decimation. It also received only sporadic coverage outside Québec.

There was no national train tour like the one in 2008 for Green Party leader Elizabeth May. She spent most of the campaign in her Saanich-Gulf Islands riding determined to win the Green Party's first seat, which she did. However, she still had the distinction of being the first national party leader to visit Calgary when she stopped there on April 19—three weeks into the campaign. That was another sign of how selectively the tours made stops. It was no surprise on election night when Conservatives in the Calgary area racked up margins of victory of more than thirty thousand. That's why the leaders hadn't wasted time with campaign visits.

Campaign days on all tours were similar, with leaders visiting locales that would highlight whatever issue the party wanted to address that day to give broadcast journalists and photographers audio and visuals, hopefully persuasive ones, for that day's stories. The leaders scrummed daily (although Harper's dictate that he would take only five media questions a day became a story in itself). All three leaders of the main parties usually had daily rallies that almost always featured the leader surrounded by an audience, usually of partisans, with the leader patrolling the stage like a TV host, speaking and answering questions extemporaneously.

Although a spring 2011 election had been widely anticipated, none of the parties had much new to say to voters. The Conservatives spent the first half of the campaign reannouncing spending plans first revealed in the March 22 budget that helped trigger their defeat in the Commons three days later. The Liberals released their platform in Ottawa on Sunday morning, April 3, but much of it was repackaged promises from previous campaigns, including child care and support for post-secondary students and for low-income seniors. Reporters on Layton's tour noted correctly that the NDP was largely reannouncing proposals from its 2008 campaign.

For a media culture that believes that if something has been reported previously there is no need to report it again in depth, the lack of anything "new" from the leaders created space for other issues to dominate daily coverage of leaders. The parties assisted that process on occasion by feeding reporters with negative stories about their opponents.[7]

As Harper daily mixed his calls for a majority with the threat that otherwise the other three parties would form a coalition to take power by defeating a Conservative minority, the other leaders had to respond, but other issues, not always ones the parties wanted covered, captured daily attention as well. They included the restriction on the media during the Conservative campaign and the equally rigid control of who could get into Conservative rallies and who was thrown out; a Conservative attempt to stop an advance poll at the University of Guelph; the past fraud convictions of a former Harper senior advisor; questionable comments made by Liberal candidates that led to demands for Ignatieff to respond; a leaked tentative Auditor-General report suggesting that the Conservatives had illegally spent money allocated to the 2010 G8 and G20 summits on a series of unrelated pork-barrel projects throughout the riding of Industry Minister Tony Clement; an email from Conservative organizers inviting supporters to dress in ethnic costumes to attend a Harper Toronto-area rally; the possible release of a report about how Canadians treated Afghan detainees; and the fate of Helena Guergis, who was seeking re-election in Ontario after Harper had fired her from a junior ministry in his cabinet.

Most of these stories came and went within a day or two, but the supposed importance and significance of each individually along with their cumulative negative impact on the Conservatives was heightened by the world of instant communications. The latest details, comments, and reaction dominated minute-by-minute discussion on social networks such as Twitter and were used extensively by journalists. That created the impression that there was much more engagement and interest in the issues among the public beyond the media covering the campaign than turned out to be the case. While most of these stories from the tours placed the Conservatives in a bad light (as the governing party, they were already the focus of daily attacks from the opposition parties), none of the criticisms seemed to count on election day.

So what happened? Why did reporters' stories from the tours have so little impact? Former *Globe and Mail* columnist and reporter Hugh Winsor offered an explanation by citing a post-election study done by Toronto communications consultants Ensight Canada:[8]

One of the themes in the election coverage was how the prime minister seemed to be "Teflon coated" because none of the various scandals or dictatorial heavy-handedness seemed to stick because the polls didn't show his support was declining.

As the Ensight post-election focus groups showed, there was an explanation for the phenomenon but the media did not search for it or find it during the campaign. Journalists didn't talk to enough people to learn that electors were dismissing all of this flurry as political games.[9]

Voters were tired of the infighting and nastiness in Parliament, which had increased with the series of minority governments, and they were also worried about their own financial circumstances and the state of the Canadian economy. This being so, they proved reluctant to change governments. Harper's daily responses to concerns about stability and the economy received little sustained coverage from reporters on the tours. As Winsor suggests, voters didn't find the stories from the tours important and so paid no attention.

This raises the obvious question of why the media should spend so much reporter time and energy on the tours at all. Journalists travelling with a leader are in a bubble that, as much as possible, is controlled by their party minders. Then they rush off to file their stories or to move to the next location and event. The travel time under party control was even more pronounced in 2011 as the tours each descended on a narrower range of communities than in the past, often great distances apart. As the campaign revealed, because leaders were more selective in their visits, the media missed opportunities to speak to non-partisan voters. Had they been interviewing voters on the ground rather than travelling with leaders, readers, listeners, and viewers would have had more insight into public attitudes about the parties and their policies, and the May 2 result might not have been so surprising.

Had news organizations allocated the people and money spent on the tours to coverage on the ground, journalists might have answered many questions never adequately addressed in their coverage. These include:

- Were the Conservative pre-election ads against Ignatieff as
  effective as has been claimed, and if so, with whom and why?

What grains of truth did voters see in the ads?

- What was it about the Conservative pitch on the economy and a majority government that struck home with voters? What were their concerns about the economy?
- How important was the Conservative budget and its myriad small tax breaks for specific groups in getting support for Harper in the campaign?
- How were the Conservatives doing on the ground in those ridings noted by the media at the campaign's outset as ones that the party needed to win? What happened in the ridings the Liberals thought they could take from an NDP campaign that most agreed was initially lacklustre? Why couldn't the Liberals exploit that?
- What NDP policies proved most attractive to voters, or did they even know what they were? Why did policies apparently not matter when voters decided to support Jack Layton?
- What weaknesses did the Bloc Québécois have that no media outlets identified prior to the leaders' debates, and why was the NDP the mass alternative for Bloc voters?
- What were the messages that Conservatives, led by Jason Kenney, delivered to immigrant communities, and how positively were they received?
- Why was Ontario largely a holdout in what pollsters and the media described as an NDP surge in the campaign's final week?
- Were socially liberal, fiscally conservative Liberals, primarily in Ontario, frightened enough by the prospect of a strong NDP result and possible victory in the campaign's final week that they abandoned their party and voted Conservative?
- Why—despite all the media noise about engagement of young people, vote mobs, social media, and so on—was turnout among young people little changed from their very limited level of interest in 2008?

None of these can be answered from the leaders' tours, yet the answers aren't that hard to find, and collectively, they determined the election's outcome.

Of course, the media shouldn't abandon covering the leaders as they campaign. What leaders have to say is important, but so is how communities and voters react to the presence and policies of leaders. To find that out, reporters need to be on the ground in locations before a leader arrives and after he or she goes, not pulling out of town as part of the leader's entourage. At one point, travelling with leaders was essential: otherwise reporters couldn't feed their stories back to their newsrooms. The parties set up filing rooms daily, including phone lines, and stopped tours at local TV stations to let reporters feed stories and pictures by satellite. Television edit suites weighing several hundred pounds were transported in several large boxes and had to be set up and dismantled each time a reporter wanted to do a story. The digital world has changed all that. Today an edit suite can be a laptop and reporters are in constant touch with editors by cellphone.

So the infrastructure rationale for the need to be on a leader's tour no longer exists. Reporters can report from anywhere simply and easily. As this election demonstrated, neither is there any editorial rationale for being on leaders' tours. If journalists are not on the tour, each news organization can still decide to send reporters to some, but not necessarily all, events that leaders stage during a campaign. That lets reporters get a better sense of what's happening by being outside the cocoon and experiencing a campaign as the public experiences it, not in the prefabricated travelling circus created by the parties.

The May 2 results surprised almost everyone by producing a comfortable majority Conservative government. The four years before the next vote now gives news organizations the time to plan future coverage that finally acknowledges how communications and technology have changed in the past thirty years. It is long past time to abandon travelling with the leaders. Giving up that safety blanket of having daily party-designed images and an accompanying "story" served up for reporters forces news organizations and journalists to think harder about how and what to cover. Some will succeed and some will struggle, but news organizations facing challenges from social media, citizen journalists, and anyone with a camera, a computer, and a cellphone need to break away from the old ways and the conformity that once again characterized election coverage in 2011. For those with the imagination and willingness to do it differently in 2015, there are both risks and rewards.

The leaders' debates are the only time during the campaign when Canadians see and judge the party leaders for themselves unhindered by the filter of media reporting. In news reports, a leader's words are relegated to short sound bites, clips that reporters choose because they fit their narratives but that may be out of context with what the leaders are trying to say. In fact, sound bites are now so abbreviated that one rarely hears leaders expressing a full thought or even completing a sentence. In debates, leaders are given the oxygen supply that is so vital to campaigns—direct access to the Canadian public. It is also the time during the campaign when leaders are the most vulnerable and exposed. They are forced out of the protected bubble of scripted appearances, cheering supporters, and carefully orchestrated photo ops and face the other leaders and the public directly. Their actions or policies can be challenged or ridiculed, and under pressure, they can appear shaken or may say the wrong things in the wrong way. The debates provide a level playing field in which leaders are measured against their opponents in a kind of comparison shopping that doesn't occur at other times in the campaign. Intangibles such as the ability to project confidence or composure, to hit just the right tone in terms of authority and folksiness, or the instinctive capacity to reach across the screen and connect with viewers—to have, in effect, a high TV IQ—can be decisive.

The 2011 English-language debate was watched by 3.85 million viewers, with as many as 10.65 million people watching some part of the debate. This was a record number of viewers, an increase of 26 percent from the 2008 debate and a million more viewers than had watched the English-language debate in 2000. Although exact numbers were not readily available, the audience for the French-language debate probably exceeded the 1.4 million viewers who watched the debate in 2008, a huge audience in Québec. These audience numbers rival or surpass virtually anything else broadcast on Canadian TV: top entertainment shows, the Grey Cup, and even the hockey playoffs. Because debates are a major TV event, they are one of the few times when Canadians gather together to watch politics and talk about political issues. Studies show that debates provide a learning experience for most voters.[10] Viewers inevitably learn something about either the leaders or party positions that they did not know before, and debates often bring issues to the forefront that were previously ignored or underreported.

Surprisingly, then, leaders' debates are not an officially acknowledged part of Canadian elections. They are not governed by set rules or scheduled at set times, and they do not have a set number of participants. Nor are they run by a neutral body. They are controlled by a consortium of the major broadcasters—CBC, CTV, Radio-Canada, Global, and TVA—who, every time an election takes place, negotiate with the political parties about the rules that will govern the debates in that campaign. As a result, formats and participants change with each election. In 2008, Green Party leader Elizabeth May was initially excluded by the consortium after the Conservatives and the NDP refused to participate if she was included. After a public protest, the parties and the broadcasters backed down and she was allowed to participate. In 2011, she was denied entry into the inner circle because the party had no seats in the House of Commons despite winning almost 7 percent of the vote in 2008 and receiving per-vote subsidies from the federal government like the other parties in the debate. In some debates, a panel of journalists has posed questions. In others, questions have come from selected citizens. In 2011, a handful of people were chosen to ask questions from more than four thousand who had applied. They were videotaped in their own communities, and one or two became local stars, at least for a day or two.

Whether leaders stand behind podiums or sit around a table, whether they have a chance to respond to each other, whether they are paired off into smaller one-on-one debates, or whether all four or five leaders are expected to join in a rough-and-tumble exchange—all of these details of a debate are negotiated among the parties and the networks every time an election occurs. Most crucially, because prime time shows are the principal moneymakers for the TV networks, the consortium has been reluctant to cut any further into prime time schedules than they have to or to provide time for multiple debates. The agreed-upon tradition is a single English-language debate and a single French-language debate. In 2011, the French-language debate was rescheduled so as not to conflict with a Montreal Canadiens–Boston Bruins playoff game.

The conventional literature suggests that in most circumstances, debates merely reinforce the preconceptions that voters already have. Kathleen Hall Jamieson describes the research findings with regard to American debates: "Since exposure to extended forms of communication reinforces existing predispositions, those who favored the front-runner are likely to judge the person the winner. Those favoring the person behind in the polls are likely to feel that their candidate has 'won' as well. In practice, this means that the process is rigged to favor a supposed 'victory' by the person ahead in the polls before the debate even airs."[11] Votes can shift, however, if debates reveal something new or unexpected, if leaders are being seen or evaluated for the first time so that preconceptions haven't formed, or if a leader gives a stellar performance or commits a fundamental error.

Leaders come to the debates heavily armed. They usually take time off from the campaign trail to prepare and hold rehearsals, and they are surrounded by teams of advisors who work on opening and closing statements, witty comebacks, and "memorable" lines. In some cases, party election scripts have been focus-group tested so that leaders know which words or narratives will be most effective. The goal is to get the better of the other leaders in one or two high-voltage exchanges that will be replayed in the highlight packages that appear on TV newscasts. Sometimes, there are rare but decisive moments that capture a mood or that signify an entire campaign. Perhaps the classic American example is when Ronald Reagan asked Americans in 1980, "Are you better off today than you were four years ago?" The question reminded voters that Jimmy Carter's presidency had been marred by domestic and foreign policy failures and that voting for Reagan was a safer choice. Another good example was the stern lecture that Brian Mulroney delivered about patronage appointments to Prime Minister John Turner during the 1984 English-language debate: "Sir, you had an option. You could have said no." Equally devastating was Bloc Québécois leader Lucien Bouchard's pummelling of Prime Minister Kim Campbell during the 1992 debate when he asked her repeatedly whether she knew the size of the government's deficit: she didn't. During the 2000 debate, Canadian Alliance leader Stockwell Day held up a sign that said "No 2-Tier Health Care." Aside from appearing silly, the gesture reminded voters that Day had changed policies and perhaps couldn't be trusted. His wounds were largely self-inflicted.

But usually victories and defeats are more difficult to read, and it often takes time for words and gestures to sink in. During the 2000 English-language debate, the opposition leaders took turns attacking Prime Minister Jean Chrétien for being arrogant and dictatorial, and were so anxious to score points that they gave him few opportunities to speak. Chrétien had no glittering moments, but his dignity and folksy charm seemed to refute what the other leaders were saying. The 2011 debates were particularly difficult to read. At least one poll taken after the French-language debate showed that Bloc Québécois leader Gilles Duceppe had won an overwhelming victory, with NDP leader Jack Layton finishing third behind Stephen Harper.[12] This poll, like so many others during the campaign, couldn't have been further off the mark. It was "Le Bon Jack" who had made the biggest impression and for whom support began to climb almost immediately after the debate while support for Duceppe quickly plummeted.

In the 2011 English-language debate, Liberal leader Michael Ignatieff's most formidable opponent may have been the high expectations placed on him by the media. With *Maclean's* having declared Ignatieff the winner of the campaign's opening rounds and with reporters also sensing that his fortunes were turning, the Liberals appeared to have considerable momentum going into the debate. But as the insurgent, Ignatieff not only had to win but win big. He wasn't helped by the luck of the draw that positioned Stephen Harper off to one side so that it seemed that the prime minister was facing the very coalition that he had been warning voters about and that placed Layton between Harper and Ignatieff so that he appeared to be Ignatieff's equal. But Ignatieff also made two fundamental errors. Rather than focus on jobs and economic management issues, he directed his attacks against what he saw as Harper's abuse of Parliament, forgetting, perhaps, that most Canadians blamed all of the parties, not just the Conservatives, for creating the deadlock and frenzied partisanship that had gripped Parliament. This gave Jack Layton his moment. The knife thrust was quickly administered: if Ignatieff cared so much about Parliament, then why, Layton asked, did he have the poorest attendance record of anyone in the House of Commons? "You know," Layton intoned, "most Canadians, if they don't show up for work, they don't get a promotion." Ignatieff couldn't muster a response.

The Liberal leader also spent so much time attacking Harper that he never got around to telling voters, many of whom were probably tuning into the election for the first time, what he would do if the Liberals formed a government. He made virtually no mention in the whole two-hour debate of any of the main selling points in the Liberal platform. In contrast, Harper hammered away incessantly, staring right into the camera, about the need for a Conservative majority to ensure continued economic growth. To some degree, Ignatieff rectified the situation in the French-language debate, which took place the following evening, when he referred to his proposed policies at some length. But the damage had been done. After the debates, the Liberal train never got back on track.

Even before the debates ended, party operatives via Twitter began spinning reporters. They pointed to key moments, gaffes made by the other leaders, or the importance of exchanges on issues that they saw as important. The parties understand that winning the media's coverage of the debate may be as important as winning the debate itself. Journalists have the power not only to select the exchanges that will make it onto TV newscasts, exchanges that are likely to be repeated again and again, but to point out mistakes or gaffes that leaders make. Perhaps the classic example is the first debate between Al Gore and George W. Bush during the 2000 US presidential election. While polls showed that Al Gore had easily defeated Bush, media reporting focused on two instances in which Gore seemed to inflate or invent stories, and his "know-it-all" demeanour was lampooned on late night talk shows. Gore's clear victory was "reinterpreted" as a defeat by journalists. Strangely, Bush's erroneous claim that Gore was outspending his campaign received little attention from reporters.

Reporters know that declaring winners and losers can be dangerous territory. Conscious of their professional integrity, Canadian reporters and pundits tend to be exceedingly cautious. Even so, a small army of pundits, including Robert Fife and Craig Oliver of CTV and CBC At Issue panelists Andrew Coyne and Chantal Hébert, were quick to point out that Ignatieff had not performed well.

In the aftermath of the 2011 debates, Globe and Mail writer Tabatha Southey wrote a column titled "Why Did They Can My Favourite Election Show After Only Two Episodes?"[13] Southey argued that given the mammoth audiences for the debates and the amount of discussion about politics that they generate, there should be four ninety-minute bilingual debates using simultaneous translation. A case can also be made for additional debates among party critics on subjects such as economic policy, the environment, or foreign policy. These additional debates could adopt different formats and would ensure that important issues that might otherwise be ignored by the parties and journalists could be aired more fully. More debates would also minimize the all-or-nothing risk that comes with just one encounter. Southey also thought that the questions asked by ordinary voters during the 2011 debates had not been particularly effective. As she put it, "I'm not convinced that anxious-looking people standing outside wearing parkas have any particular monopoly on curiosity or moral authority. Without specific questions on policy and vital follow-up questions, a debate is going to be pretty superficial."

While extending the debate season within the campaign might make a great deal of sense in terms of engaging Canadians, it's not clear that such changes would be supported by the political parties or by the TV networks. Presumably, parties that are in the lead or feel that they have the advantage will be reluctant to give their opponents additional openings. Debates can create new and unpredictable dynamics that can disrupt even the best-planned campaigns. And while—theoretically, at least—it's the people of Canada rather than the TV networks who own the airwaves, broadcasters will resist any further incursions into their prime-time schedules. With control over the debates now resting with the broadcasting consortium, reforms are unlikely to come any time soon. A first step would be to give power over the leaders' debates to an independent body, perhaps somewhat similar to the Commission on Presidential Debates in the United States. That commission's authority is accepted by all parties in the electoral process and organizes three presidential debates and one vice-presidential debate during every presidential election. While many politicians and journalists lament the increasing disengagement of so many Canadians from public affairs, when it comes to debates, they have been unwilling to give up control or think imaginatively about the one event that attracts the most voter attention during the campaign.

THE ADDICTION TO POLLS

Six weeks before the start of the 2011 federal election, a prescient story by Canadian Press reporter Joan Bryden predicted that a hooked media would overdose on polls during the upcoming campaign, turning small changes in party support into dramatic events. "You should really consider what is the basis for your addiction and maybe enter a ten-step program" was the recommendation in the story to news organizations from Carleton University Communications professor and pollster André Turcotte. He was equally harsh on polling firms for a predicted flood of the market, adding, "I think pollsters should reflect on what this does to our industry. It cheapens it."[14]

Bryden's prediction was a safe bet, given the way the media had covered campaigns in the previous decade. Not surprisingly, though, Turcotte's advice was ignored completely by both pollsters and the media. The 2011 election established a new high-water mark in the volume of polls, the range of methodologies and polling techniques employed, the extent of contradictory poll results, voter confusion, and the media's focus on horse-race numbers to the exclusion of everything else.

In mid-campaign, Bryden returned to the same theme, referring to the blunt critique of Allan Gregg, perhaps Canada's best-known pollster: "As far as Gregg is concerned, the election campaign has magnified problems with political polling: methodological issues that are skewing the results of both telephone and online surveys; commercial pressures that are prompting pollsters to overhype their surveys; and an unholy alliance with journalists who routinely misconstrue data and ignore margins of error."[15] The media had arrived at this point through the usual means. As in past campaigns, news organizations in 2011 aligned themselves with individual polling firms. For example, the Globe and Mail and CTV worked with Nanos Research, while Global Television relied on Ipsos Reid. Working with a specific firm gives the news organization first call on daily poll results, particularly since nightly tracking polls now dominate campaign polling activity. For pollsters, the media visibility that comes with the partnerships and frequent interviews helps establish their credibility, which in turn they exploit to win commercial business based on their political polling "success." That success is measured in only one way—how close the polling firm comes in its last reported result to the actual results on election night.

The risks in this symbiotic relationship between media and pollsters have been evident and appropriately criticized for some time, but addictions are hard to break. On the one hand, the pollsters need the exposure, particularly now that their current business model based on telephone polling has virtually collapsed in the face of answering machines, telemarketer fatigue by homeowners, and cellphones. Its chosen replacement, online polling, remains fraught with methodological challenges and doubts about its accuracy. On the other hand, the media needs a storyline and polls provide it since they are simple to follow and they now have the added benefit of potentially changing every day. Having struck a deal with one polling company, each news organization then has a vested interest in authenticating that partner's results, sometimes to the exclusion of all others. So polls drive stories, and little time or effort is spent looking for stories that may challenge or undercut how poll results frame the campaign.

In 2011, other developments pushed these trends to new heights, damaging the credibility of both the media and pollsters. The growing switch to online polling dramatically reduced entry costs for anyone who wanted to use political polls to establish a market research business. New pollsters popped up, each choosing its own methodologies and all lobbing results into the open media maw.[16] Frequently during this campaign, as in the past, news organizations and bloggers lumped a handful of different company results together for comparison, ignoring differences in methodologies, margins of errors, sample sizes, dates at which the surveys were taken, and the track record of the individual polling firms. This became easy to present to audiences as news because the media bought in to Stephen Harper's contention from the campaign's opening day that this election was solely about whether the electorate would give his Conservative party the "strong, stable, majority national government" that was the centrepiece of his every campaign appearance. If that is the campaign's overriding issue, polls are important, but the media attention was on more than just poll results.

The simplicity of computer modelling, a proliferation of pollsters, and a media seeing the election in unidimensional terms was fertile ground for the blossoming of seat projections, translating individual poll results into a virtual House of Commons on an almost daily basis to answer the majority-minority question.[17] Such projections gained some attention in previous campaigns, but 2011 was a new peak, with pollsters, media outlets, and even individuals with their own websites all playing the game from the first day of campaigning. For example, the daily Nanos tracking poll reported by the *Globe and Mail* included not only vote share percentages but also seat projections that moved up and down with vote share and a leadership index designed to highlight how the public rated the party leaders. A popular privately run website, ThreeHundredEight.com, aggregated all poll results and produced daily seat projections throughout the campaign, shifting each party's seat numbers by as little as one or two seats daily while predicting to the tenth of a percentage point the share of the overall vote each party would receive.[18] That site became a popular spot for campaign reporters to get their daily poll fix.

News organizations reported the shifts in voting intention and seat projection as fact or near fact, not pausing to explain why changes took place from day to day (probably because they couldn't do it). The result was as predicted in the Canadian Press pre-election story. As Jennifer Espey, David Herle, and Alex Swann noted in a post-election analysis in *Policy Options*, "Public opinion research turned the election into just another sporting event during the NHL playoffs."[19] It also undermined the credibility of the polling firm–news organization partnerships to the point where, as Espey, Herle, and Swann comment, "while the 'horse race' or daily standing of the parties in the election was a focus of media coverage, a secondary story was the discrepancy between polls. Polls published in the third week of April had a nine-point discrepancy among the Conservative vote numbers of one polling firm and the Conservative numbers of another, leading media commentators to begin questioning the methodologies of the various polling firms."[20] Some of that questioning took place on blogs and other new media sites, independent of mainstream news organizations. The result was an undermining of media credibility for publishing such widely divergent polling results as well as the forcing of pollsters to be on the defensive.

That was not a surprise to anyone who had followed the degree to which strategy, tactics and leaders' images now dominate media election coverage. The media viewed, packaged, and reported the 2011 campaign to Canadians through the lens of daily poll fluctuations accompanied by seat projections. That began on the campaign's opening day and picked up steam with poll results on the winners and losers in the two leaders' debates, and polling results were part of stories in almost every nightly newscast on the major English-language TV networks. CBC, Global, and CTV all referred to poll results in the campaign's final days as their coverage focused on whether the Liberals or New Democrats would be the Official Opposition to a Conservative minority or majority.

Who is to blame for the media covering the campaign like a sporting event? David Herle, a pollster himself, and his colleagues point one finger at Herle's own industry:

> Public opinion research didn't just allow that dynamic, it created it. The election turned from what do we want government to do to who is going to win the game. By focusing solely on vote intention and impressions of the leaders,

it limited the electorate's input to the grand narrative to who they liked and didn't like. It was a long, drawn out reality show. And following the main story—the running scoreboard—the pundits critiqued the performance of the leaders and the campaign tactics. In any competition, the most tantalizing unknown is who will win. When we have a tool that gives us daily updates on this unknown, the entire election becomes focused on the latest standings in the contest and what happened yesterday to cause that. The electorate's role is reduced to picking a winner.[21]

While polling captured—and, as it was reported, probably helped amplify—the extent to which Québecers switched allegiances to the NDP from the Bloc Québécois, the presence and size of the Conservative majority surprised virtually everyone. Although individual polling companies compare their final vote-share polling numbers with actual results to highlight how close each came to predicting the outcome, no one is talking much about their collective failures on the minority-majority question.

The pollsters' ultimate inability to answer the majority-minority question also undermines the whole approach to the campaign taken by the media. Their devotion to polling and the accompanying instant analysis of ups and downs, all of which can be easily digested and regurgitated on the new media platforms that are available to today's journalists, left the media with lots of egg on their collective face. As former *Globe and Mail* reporter and columnist Hugh Winsor noted in *iPolitics* after the campaign, "The media largely abandoned some of the basic journalistic mainstays of the past, like getting out and talking to many ordinary voters or extensively crunching policy options. Instead large amounts of journalistic resources were invested in blogging, Twittering and polling all in pursuit of immediacy." As he wisely added, "While the polls had been showing for months that jobs and the economy was a top-of-mind concern, there was little media investigation of how that was being translated into voting intention. If there had been, linked to an exploration of the 'strong, stable, majority government' mantra, there would have been far less 'surprise' when the votes were tallied."[22]

That majority government now provides the media and pollsters with a four-year window in which to develop a new approach to polling and campaign coverage that better serves Canadians and helps them with vote choices. There are encouraging early signs that some pollsters want to learn from what went wrong. Frank Graves of Ekos Research underestimated Conservative vote share by almost six percentage points and concludes that one failure was his attempt to include cellphone users in his overall telephone sample, which distorted the results since he discovered that cellphone users (disproportionately young people) were much less likely to be Conservative supporters. For the longer term, Graves raises an alarm about what happens when this group of the politically disinterested age and become the mainstream yet "have systematically opted out of the electoral process. This may be a far greater challenge to polling and democracy than the somewhat suspect polling sweepstakes of who came closest to the final vote outcome."[23]

Graves also notes something that has seemed obvious but unacknowledged by the polling industry for several campaigns: that sampling the general public is problematic when only 60 percent of them are voting. As his post-campaign research discovered: "The incidence of Conservative supporters is higher in the population of actual voters than it is in the population of all voters. These patterns also apply in weaker terms to those of lower socioeconomic status who were both less likely to vote and less likely to support the Conservatives and weaker still to women."[24] Espey, Herle, and Swann concur, suggesting that the failure to identify and poll only those who were intending to vote was a critical methodological flaw exposed by 2011 polling results. McGill political scientists Stuart Sirocco, Fred Cutler, Dietland Stolle, and Patrick Fournier highlighted another flaw in 2011 media polling after reviewing some of the initial results from the 2011 Canadian Election Survey. They noted that "the place to look for clues to Conservative success is among nonpartisans. Fifty-six percent of them described the Conservatives as the party best able to manage the economy, while the NDP and Liberals attracted only 20 percent each on this score. This gives the Conservatives a huge advantage on what is typically an influential issue in nonpartisans' decisions."[25] Yet in media coverage, there was little or no attempt to probe the attitudes of non-partisans to determine whether they could be crucial in producing the Conservative majority.

Highlighting all these errors is essential to preventing a repeat in 2015. The four-year hiatus also allows the media to rethink how, why, and where they should be using public-opinion polling in covering future campaigns. The focus on vote intention in polling might be a result of a series of minority

Parliaments, but even so, that is a conscious decision by the media to avoid asking about a broader range of issues.

News organizations would be wise to recall why they got into polling in the first place and chart a course back in that direction. Polls were one of several tools to help editors shape news coverage. Asking questions helped identify what issues reporters should pursue, highlighted the contrasts in what concerned Canadians in different regions of a very diverse country, and tested public reaction to party policy proposals. News organizations have abandoned all of that. Espey, Hurle, and Swann reject the suggestion that the media focuses on vote choice due to the lack of money to fund larger surveys about public attitudes to issues. They note: "The sheer survey space given to decided vote intention, leaning vote intention, second-choice vote intention, commitment of vote intention, enthusiasm for vote intention, likelihood of changing vote, past vote choice and strategic vote intention makes it clear that organizations are making conscious choices to focus solely on the daily party standings and likely winner."[26] The 2011 election demonstrated conclusively that it is past time to change how the media use polls in campaign coverage. Polling should be one element in coverage, not the core and foundation of how media report elections. Reporters, as Hugh Winsor suggests, do need to get out and talk to voters. That element of coverage has disappeared and the public has suffered as a result. As Espey, Hurle, and Swann suggest, "Public opinion research can be an effective, powerful way for the electorate to contribute to the narrative of the campaign by allowing the public to define the issues of importance and thus requiring that parties respond as to how those issues might be resolved."[27] The media is the perfect intermediary in overseeing that process, but that requires a change of attitude and approach, and a willingness to take risks.

SOCIAL MEDIA

Facebook and similar social media existed in the 2008 election, but it was early days for these new means of instant communication between individuals and to the broader world. By 2011, all that had changed. Facebook had been joined by Twitter and other social media sites and tools that were in much more widespread use, allowing individuals to talk with their friends, to promote what they liked and didn't like to that circle and beyond, and to broadcast their lives and impressions of whatever caught their interest. In the world of political communication, these are tools with obvious potential. Initial impressions, though, suggest that not much of that potential was realized in the 2011 campaign.

These new social media gave journalists and political junkies new tools with which to follow election campaigns closely and offer their instant comments on what is happening. That led to debate among the media about whether this was the first social media election. The evidence, while not easy to gather, suggests that, despite mainstream media enthusiasm for Twitter and other social media tools, the answer is no. Social media did not figure prominently in the campaign or its outcome. Available data supports such a conclusion on four grounds—the limited number of people who are active social media participants, the narrow range of issues those people highlighted during the campaign, the lack of impact on the issues they raised, and the paucity of uses that were found for social media during the campaign. Social media such as Facebook, Twitter, and their successors, as well as YouTube and other video-sharing sites may figure more prominently in the 2015 campaign, but that will depend on introducing more imaginative uses for social media than was the case in 2011.

This time, most of the campaign media attention focused on Twitter, the 140-character instant-messaging system that allows individuals to distribute their thoughts to lists of their followers and more broadly to whoever wants to read them. To judge Twitter's impact on the 2011 election requires a sense of who was using it, how they were using it, and what they were saying. Ottawa social media consultant Mark Blevis watched Twitter for Canadian Press and blogged about Twitter statistics throughout the campaign. He found, on average, that there were about 16,000 election-related tweets every day of the campaign, rising to almost 25,000 daily during the week of the debates and roughly 18,000 a day during the campaign's last week.[28] That may sound like a lot, but almost 24 million Canadians were eligible to vote and 14,720,580 did cast ballots. In that context, 16,000 comments a day is not much, nor is it very influential, particularly if those tweeters are spread across the country's 308 constituencies.

Perhaps a good comparison is with Sun TV, the much-hyped all-news specialty channel that came on the air in mid-campaign on April 18. Although its prime-time programming had almost 40,000 viewers on its first day, by late

April, less than 20,000 per hour were watching in the evening and sometimes as few as 4,000 during the day.[29] While Twitter was the campaign's media darling with 16,000 tweets a day, the same media described Sun TV with its up to 20,000 viewers as having almost no impact in a world where nightly main channel TV newscasts in Canada get up to 1.2 million viewers. But comparing tweeters with TV viewers is not completely fair. On the one hand, tweeters are active whereas television viewers are passive, so those who tweet, one could argue, are more engaged in the campaign than those who simply watch. On the other hand, although tweets are broadcast to others, Blevis's research discovered that many of the most active tweeters had under a thousand followers, so the breadth of the retweeting network may not be that significant.[30] As well, many tweeters tweet a lot, so the 16,000 average number of tweets a day during the campaign means that considerably less than 16,000 individuals were actually generating content.

What is clear, though, is that the media covering the campaign have chosen Twitter as the logical next step in the media's turning inwards, a phenomenon described by contributor Christopher Waddell elsewhere in this book. Among insiders, tweets largely replaced BlackBerry messages in this campaign; although shorter and more to the point, they still largely dealt with issues of interest to those campaign insiders and political junkies who were primarily following the campaign's micro-moves without stepping back to put things in any overall electoral context. Within the media, a clear group of leading campaign tweeters included Andrew Coyne from *Maclean's*, David Akin from Sun Media, CBC's Rosemary Barton and Kady O'Malley, and Susan Delacourt from the *Toronto Star*. They dominated tweeting and, to some degree, set the media agenda and established the framework for viewing individual issues—a form of electronic pack journalism. Sometimes, tweeting helped in a collective research exercise, spreading specific details about a policy or issue. Much of it, though, was impressionistic rather than substantive, focusing on the same perspectives of horse race, strategy, and tactics, as well as the themes of conflict and personality that, sadly, has dominated media coverage of politics and public policy in recent years. While commentary often passed back and forth among the group (and a surprising degree, for reporters, of their own opinion was mixed into their tweets), little back-and-forth tweeting occurred with those outside their circle and with the broader collective of other journalists who followed the leading tweeters. While the media used Twitter to communicate among themselves, however, they didn't use it to bring the Canadian public into the discussion. It was also used by reporters to get instant responses (in 140 characters or less) from politicians or their spokespeople on individual issues or to try to goad them into commenting when no one would reply to emails or phone messages—again, a 2011 extension of the insider network described by Waddell.

More generally, there are the questions about the content being produced by election tweeters. Mark Blevis found that early on election day, half of the tweets were original content while 39 percent were simply retweets of comments from others and only 11 percent were replies to comments filed by someone else. By 10:45 a.m. on that day, he had already recorded 15,701 tweets from 11,512 different Canadian Twitter profiles.[31] The ratio of original content to retweets to replies was fairly constant throughout the campaign, although on the heaviest day of tweeting—April 13, the day after the English-language debate and also the day of the French-language debate—there was more action and more conversation. There were 30,712 election tweets that day, with about 10 percent in French; 53 percent of 11,814 debate-related tweets contained original content.[32] In other words, those using Twitter were writing down their thoughts, others were retransmitting those thoughts more broadly, but not many were actually engaging in back-and-forth conversations. It seems that, for most people involved in the campaign, Twitter was more one-way broadcasting, even for reporters, than two-way communication with those outside the campaign.

What were tweeters commenting on? In week four, Blevis identified the top five issues for tweets as taxes; Harper's limit of five questions a day from the media; a possible coalition among the Liberals, NDP, and Bloc; the Conservative Party's use of Facebook to screen those who wanted to come to its rallies; and health care. As Blevis noted: "Each of coalition, Facebook screening, taxes and Harper's question limit has held the weekly pole position only once. Taxes held the number two spot two weeks in a row. G8 has only been in the top five once. Elizabeth May's exclusion from the debates earned her the number four position in the first week. The launch of the Liberal platform held down the number four spot during week two."[33] Blevis didn't measure positive or negative sentiment on the issues mentioned in the tweets he captured, but an informal sampling suggests that few tweets were supporting these policies. Most were attacking or ridiculing them. In this election, Twitter seemed to be used for attacking policies much more than for defending or promoting them, although there is no obvious reason why this form of social media works better to frame issues negatively than to frame them positively. The major subjects for tweeters closely paralleled the issues and stories that came daily from the leaders' tours, where each day is almost a self-contained unit and the next day, everyone moves on to something else. Those issues may captivate and engage hard-core campaign watchers, but the great mass of voters perceive a campaign differently. Nor, in this campaign, were the issues that dominated the tweetosphere the issues upon which Canadians made their vote choices. Had the apparent sentiment of tweets accurately reflected the opinion of the electorate, the Conservatives would likely be sitting on the opposition benches looking across the floor at a coalition government.

Some candidates jumped on the tweeting bandwagon while others, including Conservatives Tony Clement and James Moore, had been active tweeters for some time although they toned down their tweeting during the campaign. Probably the most memorable example of political tweeting came from the prime minister (although it is difficult to believe he was tweeting it himself) challenging Liberal leader Michael Ignatieff to a one-on-one debate. Ignatieff accepted almost immediately, tweeting back "any time, any place." That forced the Conservative leader to back down in response to reporters' questions about when the debate would take place. It was embarrassing, but it did Harper no lasting damage. It was a good lesson, though, for all politicians to think before tweeting.

Some hoped that the power and breadth of social media would finally undermine the anachronistic laws, enforced by Elections Canada, that establish media blackouts on election results until polls close in that region. Parliament has not changed the law, although it was not in force during the 2004 election. It had, at the time, been overturned by a lower court, and the decision was waiting to be heard by the Supreme Court of Canada, which ultimately endorsed the constitutionality of the blackout. Thus, in 2011 (as in the 2006 and 2008 elections), the results in Atlantic Canada—where polls closed at 7:00 p.m. EDT in Newfoundland and 7:30 p.m. EDT in the Maritimes—could not be broadcast until polls closed at 9:30 p.m. EDT everywhere west of New Brunswick to the BC border or until 10:00 p.m. in BC. An attempt to organize a protest by tweeting Atlantic results under the Twitter hashtag #tweettheresults largely fizzled. Few complied, and those who were watching for results found the site taken over by people tweeting everything from local soccer scores to the results of exams or pregnancy tests.

Facebook didn't attract nearly the same amount of media attention as Twitter, perhaps because parties and candidates used it mostly like any other one-way means of communication. Candidate and party Facebook sites were used primarily to distribute messages to voters but generated almost no debate and interaction with them about policies even though Facebook has much more potential than Twitter as a campaign tool. In urban communities, where people hardly know their neighbours and may be afraid to offend them by engaging in political discussion, Facebook can bring like-minded people together. A campaign organizer can then ask them to organize a local event or spread the word more widely for a candidate or party. Social media can also be a fundraising tool, yet there is little evidence of it being used for that in Canada.

Both the Liberals and New Democrats tried to be a bit more imaginative. For the NDP, Jack Layton's Facebook page became a way to circulate photos and videos from campaign stops while also promoting the leader's upcoming events. The NDP also developed an iPhone application that listed upcoming events, with pictures and links to other campaign documents, allowing supporters to follow Layton's tour on a daily basis. The Green Party introduced a similar app but neither the Conservatives nor Liberals tried anything like this. The Liberals, though, linked Ignatieff's Facebook page with discussion groups and also offered readers the chance to ask questions, which few seemed interested in doing. The Facebook sites for Stephen Harper and Gilles Duceppe were unimaginative static sites displaying information.

Facebook was, however, effective for parties as a free means of distributing and highlighting party election advertising. A party would post new ads on its Facebook and websites, which were picked up and redistributed by others on Facebook, and the media then wrote about them, giving the ads even more publicity and visibility—all without the party paying a cent to buy time or space on television, radio, or websites. In the 2011 campaign, Facebook was even used as the basis for a clever Liberal ad—only online—that ridiculed the Conservatives for trolling through Facebook sites to find evidence of what Conservatives viewed as Liberal connections in order to evict two young people from a Harper rally in London, Ontario.

Social media did demonstrate some potential for independent organizing through vote mobs, a student phenomenon whereby a message would spread to organize a spontaneous demonstration—in this case, to encourage young people to vote. Comedian Rick Mercer was front and centre in this campaign and campus groups organized many vote mobs with the imaginative video results easily found on YouTube.[34] For some, vote mobs became the way to participate in the campaign and would not have happened without social media, used both to call the mob together and to share the video of their experience. That, in turn, encouraged copycat mobs on campuses across the country. In the end, though, since voter turnout among young people changed little from the low levels of previous campaigns, the exercise may have been mostly a way to get outside for a break for students otherwise closeted and studying for final exams.

What was surprising was how little YouTube was used in the campaign as a stage for political satire. While some efforts were made, nothing caught on like the hilarious 2008 video *Culture en péril*, produced by Québec musician Michel Rivard. It ridiculed both federal bureaucrats for their lack of French and the Conservative government's cuts to culture and the arts. Some suggest that it played a significant role in giving the Bloc Québécois an issue around which to rally Québecers in that campaign. In a 2011 campaign that, in general, lacked humour and satire, this was an obvious opportunity lost. In a world of cellphone videos and the increasing ease of uploading material to sites such as YouTube, online video offers great potential for public comment and satirical interventions in the future.

The possibilities for social media to drive political communication and influence decision-makers are huge, but, as the 2011 election demonstrated, they remain little realized to date. Candidates, political parties, the media, and even social media devotees all seem most interested in using the technology as a new, instantaneous way to tell people what they think or what they should think. In the election, it was sometimes used to offer live tweeting play-by-play of speeches or events such as the leaders' debates. It is not clear, though, that such stenography, with no context or analysis, serves any broad purpose in enhancing the public's understanding of events or positions taken by politicians and parties.

To date, social media sites have been used very infrequently as a collective tool to develop policy, gather responses and critiques, or build networks for advocacy, or for supporting existing political parties or candidates. Equally important, the media don't know how to treat or interpret what they find on social media sites. Stories note when issues emerge on Twitter or the number of friends someone has on Facebook, or they quote the content of tweets from individuals but rarely with any context or indication of why certain tweets are chosen over others. Do the choices reflect anything more than the biases of whoever is making those choices? This is just one of the questions that news organizations need to consider as they prepare their coverage approach for the next campaign. All the players in the 2011 election realized that social media are important, but none of them had a clear strategy for how to deal with them or how to use social media to their advantage. This new technology has potential that they can't continue to ignore.

CONCLUSIONS

Journalism professor Jay Rosen once wrote that the primary mission of the communications media and, indeed, of journalism should be to "make politics 'go well' so that it produces a discussion in which the polity learns more about itself, its current problems, its real divisions, its place in time, its prospects for the future."[35] If this is the standard by which media coverage of the 2011 federal election should be judged, than there are reasons for concern.

Disturbing trends were present and noted in the past few elections but reached disquieting new heights in 2011. There was little coverage of the major issues facing the country or of the prospective solutions offered by the parties, voter turnout remained low, and the media was fixated on campaign rituals that are increasingly dysfunctional and out of date. In all of the media routines and assumptions addressed in this chapter, there was a large and increasing gap between media performance and the needs of the public. Breaking old habits and seeking new solutions will be difficult. News organizations and political parties are enmeshed in a tangled web of relationships that feed off of each other and have become deeply ingrained in the political culture. But unless the media-political system as a whole is rethought and reimagined, it will become increasingly disengaged from the citizens on which it ultimately depends for its survival.

The first issue that we addressed was the media's obsession with the horse race. While the horse race is likely to remain an essential element of coverage because there will always be a fascination with the drama of the race, it is clear that polls now take up an extraordinary amount of journalistic space and that they have displaced other kinds of reporting such as examining party positions on issues or talking to voters. The original intention behind the use of polls was to gauge the public mood not only about the leaders and the parties but also about the issues facing the country. The results helped journalists organize coverage and bring voters' concerns to the forefront of campaign reporting. That objective seems to have been almost entirely lost. To a certain degree, polls have become the political equivalent of junk bonds: some are reliable and others are shaky and problematic, yet all are treated equally by the media. The polling industry was deeply shaken by the results of the 2011 election and will have to deal with methodological problems that are not necessarily easy to solve. News organizations need to ask whether they should risk not only damaging their own reputations but also losing contact with Main Street Canada by continuing to rely on what has become an addiction.

The leaders' tours have also reached a point where they now appear to be rusted out vestiges from the past that no longer serve the country well. While it is crucial for leaders to travel across the country to address supporters and meet voters, the tours have become a kind of rolling movie set with leaders going from photo op to photo op, unveiling policies that are sometimes of little importance or are rehashed policies presented for the second or third time, and often being shielded from unexpected or uncomfortable meetings with voters. The problem is that reporters risk becoming actors in a play written and produced by the political parties. After all, TV reports that invariably showed Stephen Harper being cheered by supporters as he warned about the supposed dangers of a coalition demonstrated that little thinking went into how the tour would be covered. The dilemma for news organizations is that if they don't cover the leaders' tours, they are likely to miss critical moments, but if do, they may miss the larger picture. As we have demonstrated, the list of issues not covered and the questions not answered is painfully and unacceptably long. The problem is compounded by the expense required to place reporters on planes and buses. Having invested so much in the tours, news organizations felt compelled to use the stories that reporters produced. But the costs of being used as a prop by the parties may be even higher.

The leaders' televised debates provided the one opportunity during the campaign for leaders to step out from the protective cover of their campaigns to face the other leaders and the public directly. While this is the time of greatest exposure, and hence danger, for the leaders, debates also provide voters with a unique opportunity to learn about the parties and the issues. While debates sometimes have little impact, in 2011, they were pivotal in the campaign. Ignatieff's failure in the English-language debate and Layton's triumph in the French debate changed the course of the campaign, literally rewriting the election script. The inevitable question is why there aren't both more and different kinds of debates. While both the broadcast consortium and the political parties are likely to resist making changes, journalists can do a great deal to push for changes. Moving responsibility for organizing debates to a neutral body would be a first step in rethinking the role that debates might play in elections.

While there was a great deal of media buzz during the 2011 election about the power of social media, hype seemed to trump a more realistic assessment about the limits of their influence. In fact, part of the backdrop in recent campaigns is the degree to which journalists have become enthralled by the latest media technology so that 2000 was the first Web election; 2004, the great blog election; 2008, the YouTube election; and 2011, the Twitter election. While Twitter and Facebook are extraordinary tools for involving those who are already involved, online activity during the election was confined to a relatively small host of already active citizens. This means that reporters have to be cautious in leaping to conclusions about a citizen revolution in cyberspace, and particularly in assessing the potential of social media as a tool for mobilizing young voters. In using social media as a stand-in for the electorate, reporters can misjudge the moods of the wider public, which is made up of many people who normally take little interest in politics. Christopher Waddell also reminds us in his chapter, "Berried Alive," that web-based media can narrow rather than expand the information and perspectives available to journalists. Reporters become so preoccupied with the latest tweets from politicians and from each other that they lose sight of what's taking place beyond their own gated media community. Despite these cautions, the opportunities for social media in particular to transform the next generation of Canadian politics is extraordinary.

If Canada continues on the path of increased citizen disengagement from politics—with lower levels of voting, joining, volunteering, donating to causes, and basic knowledge about Canadian history and political institutions—then the loss to the country could be considerable. But so also is the potential loss to journalism. Without engaged citizens, audiences for TV news shows and certainly for newspapers will dry up, with enormous consequences for the survival of the traditional media. While a rethinking of the media's role in how elections are fought in Canada is critical for the health of the political system, it's also critical for the future of Canadian journalism. The greatest casualty of inaction may be journalism itself.

NOTES

1   See Walter Dean Burnham, *Critical Elections and the Mainsprings of American Politics* (New York: Norton, 1971); and Allan Cairns, "An Election to Be Remembered: Canada 1993," *Canadian Public Policy* 20 (1994): 219–34.

2   Tom Flanagan, "The Emerging Conservative Coalition," *Policy Options* 32 (June–July 2011): 104–8.

3   It should be noted that the Conservatives won several seats in Acadian New Brunswick.

4   See Warren Kinsella, "The Biggest Losers," *The Walrus* (July–August 2011): 31.

5   Robin Sears, "Quebec Storm Sweeps Canadian Electoral Landscape: The Realignment Story of Campaign 41," *Policy Options* 32 (June–July 2011): 18–36.

6   Election 2011, "Graphic: The Leader Locator for the First Week of the Campaign," *National Post*, April 1, 2011, http://news.nationalpost.com/photo_gallery/graphic-the-leader-locator-for-the-first-week-of-the-campaign/.

7   For example, CBC, CTV, and Global all cited the NDP as the source for an April 6 story about alleged racist comments made in the past by a Liberal candidate in Québec that led the party to dump him. The next day, Global pinpointed the Conservatives for having distributed to the media some controversial past comments of a Liberal candidate and former Alberta judge, who had suggested that not all sexual assaults should be treated equally by the courts. That was timed to put Ignatieff on the defensive as Harper visited the Toronto-area riding of a cabinet minister and former police chief, Julian Fantino, to talk about the need to be tough on crime. In another example, on April 24, CTV reported that the Liberals had made available a 500-page binder of damaging Harper quotations from his career in politics, supposedly compiled by Conservatives.

8   Ensight Canada, "Mind Your Majority, Eh! 2011—A Report Based on Canada's Only Genuine Exit Poll," 2011, http://ensightcanada.com/en/wp-content/uploads/2011/05/ENS.06_PostElect2011ReportWeb_F.pdf.

9   Hugh Winsor, "Media, Polls in the Election," *iPolitics*, June 13, 2011, http://ipolitics.ca/2011/06/13/winsor-election-proved-a-new-low-for-pollsters-and-media/

10 Kathleen Hall Jamieson, *Everything You Think You Know About Politics ... And Why You're Wrong* (New York: Basic Books, 2000), 163–64.

11 Ibid., 161.

12 "Duceppe Shines During French Debate, Harper Falters: Poll," *Global News*, April 14, 2011, http://www.globalnews.ca/decisioncanada/Duceppe+shines+during+French+debate+Harper+falters+poll/4615457/story.html.

13 Tabatha Southey, "Why Did They Can My Favourite Election Show After Only Two Episodes?" *Globe and Mail*, April 15, 2011, http://www.theglobeandmail.com/news/opinions/tabatha-southey/why-did-they-can-my-favourite-election-show-after-only-two-episodes/article1987332/.

14 "Pollsters Advise Voters to Be Wary of Polls Ahead of Possible Spring Vote," Canadian Press, February 13, 2011.

15 "Up, Down, No Change? Conflicting Election Polls Confusing, Headache-Inducing," Canadian Press, April 20, 2011.

16 The website ThreeHundredEight.com identified forty-eight national polls released in the twenty-seven days between April 5 and election eve, May 1. Winsor, "Media, Polls in the Election."

17 For example, seven polls were published in the final weekend of the campaign using interviews and online surveys done during the preceding four days. In 2008, five polls were published on the final weekend. Jennifer Espey, David Herle, and Alex Swann, "The Blurred Snapshot of the Election Polls," *Policy Options* 32 (June–July 2011): 86–90.

18 Éric Grenier, "Tory Majority Still Out of Reach Despite First Week Gains," *Globe and Mail*, April 3, 2011, http://www.theglobeandmail.com/news/politics/tory-majority-still-out-of-reach-despite-first-week-gains-polls-suggest/article1968806/.

19 Espey, Herle and Swann, "The Blurred Snapshot of the Election Polls," 89.

20 Ibid., 87.

21 Ibid., 89.

22 Winsor, "Media, Polls in the Election."

23 Frank Graves, "Accurate Polling, Flawed Forecast: An Empirical Retrospective on Election 41," 17–18, Ekos Politics, 2011, http://www.ekos.com/admin/articles/FG-2011-06-17.pdf.

24 Ibid., 13.

25 Stuart Soroka et al., "Capturing Change (And Stability) in the 2011 Campaign," *Policy Options* 32 (June–July 2011): 70–77.

26 Espey, Herle and Swann, "The Blurred Snapshot of the Election Polls," 90.

27 Ibid., 89.

28 Mark Blevis, "The Increasing Depth of Twitter in #elxn41," *Mark Blevis* (blog), 24 April 2011, http://www.markblevis.com/the-increasing-depth-of-twitter-in-elxn41/; Mark Blevis, "Election Twitter Traffic on a Steep Incline," *Mark Blevis* (blog), 1 May 2011, http://www.markblevis.com/election-twitter-traffic-on-a-steep-incline/.

29 "Sun News Drawing as Little as 4,000 Viewers During Some Time Slots," Canadian Press, April 27, 2011.

30 Mark Blevis, "Meet Some of the Most Active #elxn41 Tweeters and Their Networks," *Mark Blevis* (blog), 30 April 2011, http://www.markblevis.com/meet-some-of-the-most-active-elxn41-tweeters-and-their-networks/.

31 Mark Blevis, "15,701 Election Tweets by 11,512 Unique Canadian Tweeters," *Mark Blevis*

(blog), 2 May 2011, http://www.markblevis.com/15701-election-tweets-by-11512-unique-canadian-tweeters/.

32 Mark Blevis, "Traffic Lower, Engagement Higher in French Debates," *Mark Blevis* (blog), 14 April 2011, http://www.markblevis.com/traffic-lower-engagement-higher-in-french-debates/.

33 Mark Blevis, "The Five Most Tweeted Election Issues," *Mark Blevis* (blog), 24 April 2011, http://www.markblevis.com/the-five-most-tweeted-election-issues/.

34 "Federal Election 2011 – Student Vote MOB Mashup," YouTube, http://www.youtube.com/watch?v=mLvSbr_-v8Q.

35 Jay Rosen, "Politics, Vision and the Press: Towards a Public Agenda for Journalism," in *The New News v. the Old News: The Press and Politics in the 1990s*, by Jay Rosen and Paul Taylor. Perspectives on the News Series (New York: Twentieth Century Fund, 1992), 10.

5

Christopher Waddell

Berry'd Alive: The Media, Technology, and the Death of Political Coverage

In the first few days of September 2009, it seemed clear that Canadians would soon be voting in a federal election for the fourth time in five years. Opposition leader Michael Ignatieff's bellicose statement "Mr. Harper, your time is up" upon emerging from a September 1 Liberal caucus meeting in Sudbury seemed to make an election inevitable.[1]

Certainly that was what the national media wanted. Since the Harper Conservatives were first elected in a minority in January 2006, the default question for political reporters seeking a story has always been, When is the next election? They framed every issue around that question, and, time after time, coverage pumped up the prospect of a vote only to have an event deflate it just as quickly. This time, though, they thought it would be different.

Media planning for the campaign was in full swing, but it was a very different sort of planning since the media in 2009 was in the midst of a recession and an existential crisis. A dramatic fall in advertising across print and television; declining audiences and circulation; and the rising influence of the Internet as an alternative for readers, listeners, and viewers had placed a financial squeeze on news organizations so serious that, for example, by October, CanWest Global would file for bankruptcy protection for its TV operations, with its newspapers following before year-end. In the face of such losses, rumours circulated that some news organizations would not spend the money to cover the NDP's campaign, focusing only on the Liberals and Conservatives—a major departure from past campaign coverage of the three "major" parties that, had it happened, would certainly have generated controversy about the role of the media in election campaigns.

Within days of Ignatieff's announcement, however, opinion polls showed Liberal support sliding in response to the Liberal leader's suggestion that he would force an election.[2] Suddenly, the public had woken up and realized that there might actually be yet another vote. Their reaction was a resounding "No way!" accompanied by a sense that politicians and the national media had somehow lost touch with reality in thinking that anyone outside that group wanted yet another chance to vote. The reaction caught the Liberals off guard, and the media was equally surprised that its beating of the election drums for weeks had apparently gone completely unnoticed by the public. It was an example of the gulf that has emerged between Canadians on one side and the politicians and the media in Ottawa on the other as the media have come to identify more closely with the politicians than with the public. The public's waning attachment to and interest in politics had become clear a year earlier when only 59 percent of eligible voters cast ballots in the 2008 election—the lowest turnout in a federal election in Canadian history. A vote in 2009 seemed sure to break that record.

The split between the public and the media had been more than a quarter century in coming. A series of decisions over the years by news organizations to reduce coverage of politics and pubic policy was followed by the elimination of bureaus in Ottawa and cuts to reporting staff. By 2009, there were almost no reporters in the parliamentary press gallery representing individual news organizations from across the country. It had become a gallery comprising almost exclusively reporters for national news organizations.

It wasn't like that through much of the 1980s. In those days, the parliamentary press gallery included reporters from individual newspapers across the country, from several radio and TV networks, and even from individual television stations. By the end of that decade, though, closures and cutbacks had started that would shrink political coverage. English-language radio as a medium for reporting on national politics, with the exception of CBC and Broadcast News (the broadcast arm of the Canadian Press), essentially died with the closure of all-news national radio network CKO and Newsradio network operations in Ottawa. That was followed, in the early 1990s, by the shrinkage and then closure of the Standard Broadcasting radio news bureau in Ottawa. There was a similar decline in the number of francophone radio reporters in Ottawa over the same period.

Similar cuts had not yet happened in television, but they were coming later in the 1990s. In 1988, the year before CBC's all-news channel, Newsworld, went on the air, CBC Television News had sixteen reporters in its Ottawa bureau, including two who exclusively provided reports to supper-hour newscasts in eastern Canada and another two doing the same for supper-hour newscasts in the west. (By comparison, in 2011, CBC Television News had only five reporters in its Ottawa bureau who had to file for supper-hour newscasts across the country, the flagship newscast *The National*, and the network's all-news channel.)

The early 1990s was an era of print retreat in coverage of national politics and public policy as a series of newspapers from major centres shut down the Ottawa bureaus they had maintained through more than a decade. The list of closed bureaus included the *Hamilton Spectator, Windsor Star, London Free Press, Regina Leader-Post*, and *Saskatoon Star-Phoenix*. By the middle of the decade, these newspapers were all covering national politics and public policy with reporters working from their home newsrooms. This was supplemented by national news service coverage from Ottawa provided by news services such as Southam News and Canadian Press.

There were changes there as well, most noticeably at Canadian Press. An Ottawa CP bureau of approximately thirty in 1990 (from a high of thirty-four in the mid-1980s) was cut in half to about fifteen by 1997. Some of that has subsequently been rebuilt, but even so, CP is today producing fewer stories and covering fewer issues than it covered in the 1980s.

Declining numbers tell only part of the story. Just as important is the changing nature of the coverage provided by the remaining reporters and news organizations. National news services do not have the ability to inject local examples or context into national political stories. They look for stories with national appeal and cover them with broad brush strokes so that readers all across the country can understand the stories. Reporters working for these organizations are writing for a national, not a regional or local audience. They are not looking for the specific stories or issues that may have an impact primarily in one city—in Hamilton, Windsor, London, Regina, or Saskatoon.

The national news services do not pay much attention to individual members of Parliament, but the activities of local MPs had been a prime concern for reporters for the individual papers. When newspapers shut their bureaus, the direct link between individual MPs and coverage in their communities was broken. But closing bureaus did save money. One national story for all the papers in a newspaper chain replaced separate stories done by each paper's reporter, uniquely tailored to the community the newspaper served. One size would fit all regardless of the resulting compromises in content.

In addition to cost savings, there was some logic to the decision by news organizations to reduce political coverage. By the time the Charlottetown referendum was defeated in 1992, the country had been tearing itself apart for the preceding twenty-five years through almost non-stop crises and battles that too often pitted region against region, increasingly alienating the public from politics in the process. It started with the original FLQ crisis of the 1960s, followed by the rise of the Parti Québécois and its election as the governing party of Québec in 1976; two oil price shocks and inflation in the 1970s; the 1980 Québec referendum; the National Energy Program in October 1980; more inflation, unemployment, and deficit upon deficit in the 1980s; free trade negotiations with the United States starting in 1985; the Meech Lake Accord in 1987; the free trade election in 1988; the contentious collapse of the Meech Lake Accord in 1990; the rise of the Bloc Québécois and the Reform Party after Meech's failure; and the 1992 Charlottetown referendum campaign.

It was no surprise that the 1993 election produced a five-party Parliament. National politics had fractured along regional lines to such a degree that by sweeping a province, the Bloc Québécois became the Official Opposition in the House of Commons. That election also produced a Liberal majority government led by Jean Chrétien, who was determined to lower the country's political temperature by staying out of the spotlight, avoiding anything dramatic, and concentrating on fixing problems as they emerged. His comment on the constitutional paralysis created by the debate about the Meech Lake Accord, made as he announced his bid for the Liberal leadership in January 1990, perfectly captured his approach to government: "'Don't get excited. We're stuck in the snow,' he told a crowd of about 1,000 at Ottawa's Chateau Laurier hotel. 'We Canadians know what to do when we're stuck in the snow. You don't get excited, you don't spin your wheels. You just go forward, backward, forward, backward, and eventually you're back on the road.'"[3] It was an attitude that almost led to defeat for the federalist side in the 1995 Québec referendum. Despite that close call and the decision in 1995 to cut federal spending dramatically to try to balance the federal budget, Chrétien generally stuck to his low-key approach and enough Canadians agreed with that approach to re-elect him with majorities in 1997 and 2000. For news organizations, Chrétien's invisibility was the perfect cover to reduce coverage. Canadians weren't interested in politics and public policy, news managers explained as they closed Ottawa bureaus in the midst of an early 1990s recession during which advertising revenues fell and costs had to be cut to try to maintain profit margins.

It is difficult to reach definitive conclusions about the impact of the loss of Ottawa reporters in the communities their newspapers served. As noted earlier, without a reporter in Ottawa, there is less coverage of local MPs in those newspapers. With less coverage, it seems reasonable to assume, fewer people in those communities would know the name of their MP or what he or she does. It seems equally logical to assume that lack of knowledge and information may translate into less interest in voting, if for no other reason than that without coverage, it is harder to make a connection between individual MPs and their impact on the decisions made collectively by a government in Ottawa.

In fact, a fall in voter turnout is exactly what happened, as demonstrated by election results in six Ontario communities over the seven federal elections from 1979 through 2000. Newspapers in three of those communities—Windsor, Hamilton, and London—had their own reporters in the parliamentary press gallery in Ottawa through the 1980s but withdrew their reporters and closed their bureaus in the period between 1993 and 1996. Newspapers in the other three communities—Niagara Falls, St. Catharines, and Sault Ste. Marie—did not have their own reporters in Ottawa at any point in this period. As table 5.1 highlights, voter turnout in the three communities with newspapers that shut their Ottawa bureaus fell more quickly than the provincial average in the elections after their bureaus closed. The three communities whose newspapers had never had Ottawa bureaus did not see the same sort of decline in voter turnout throughout the 1990s.

People decide not to vote for many reasons. It is impossible to be definitive, but declining coverage of national politics appears likely as one explanation. An analogy helps to demonstrate the link. Would as many people go to an Ottawa Senators hockey game, a Toronto Blue Jays baseball game, or a Calgary Stampeders football game if all the local radio, television, and print media in those communities simply stopped covering the sport with their own reporters, instead using occasional stories written by wire services such as Canadian Press? Almost certainly not, so the same principle should apply, at least to some degree, in the relationship between how politics is covered and interest in voting.

Table 5.1   Voter turnout in Ontario communities, 1979–2000

		1979	1980	1984	1988	1993	1997	2000
Canada		76	69.3	75.3	75.3	69.6	67	61.2
Ontario		**78**	**71.8**	**75.8**	**74.6**	**67.7**	**65.6**	**58**
Communities with reporters in Ottawa until mid-1990s	Hamilton average	77.3	71.5	77.0	73.8	66.1	62.4	54.2
	London average	74.7	68.7	73.7	73.7	64.7	62.4	54.7
	Windsor average	72.0	68.0	68.7	72.3	62.8	59.2	54.0
Communities with no reporters in Ottawa	St. Catharines	75	70	75	74	68.4	65.5	60
	Sault Ste. Marie	77	74	76	78	71.6	66.6	63.8
	Niagara Falls	74	69	71	72	68.8	63.6	57.1

SOURCE: Compiled on the basis of Elections Canada data.

The trend toward reduced political coverage from Ottawa and cost cutting by newspapers was not universal, as is illustrated by a newspaper war that broke out in the second half of the 1990s. That war between the *Globe and Mail* and its new national challenger, the *National Post*, saw the two national newspapers significantly increase staff and spending on covering Parliament, national politics, and public policy. They focused on stories that were national in scope and wrote them from a national perspective. As a result, the stories in the *Globe and Mail* and *National Post*, just like those written by Canadian Press and Southam News, were unlikely to contain the local references about national issues that might make a connection for those living in the communities that had lost their reporters in Ottawa.

Shrinking television coverage matched the closing of newspaper bureaus during the 1990s. CBC implemented a series of budget cuts that reduced the size of its bureau, significantly ending the ability to do specific stories for eastern or western supper-hour audiences. Stations such as CJOH in Ottawa, CFTO in Toronto, and BCTV in Vancouver all eliminated their reporters in the press gallery. As with newspapers, national TV news bureaus for CBC, CTV, and Global would turn out standardized stories for all supper-hour newscasts, no longer with any local or regional distinctiveness.

Television coverage of politics and elections also changed in the 1990s in response to the proliferation of political parties on the national scene. Beginning in the 1970s, TV networks covered campaigns by putting a five-person crew (reporter, producer, camera, sound, and editor) on the national tours of the leaders of the major political parties—the Liberals, the Progressive Conservatives, and the New Democrats. Using that model for the 1997 campaign meant that five networks—CBC, CTV, Global, Radio-Canada, and TVA—would have to put five people on each of five tours (including the Bloc Québécois and Reform Party) for a month and a half, a very expensive proposition.

Instead, the networks decided to pool coverage. Each network would cover one leader with a five-person team—two cameras, a producer, an editor, and a sound person. Everything shot by each pool crew would be shared by all five networks. The pool crew would also shoot stand-ups for each network that chose to have a reporter on that leader's tour, and everything including pictures and reporters' scripts would be fed to the appropriate network's newsroom to be assembled as stories. Even without a reporter on a leader's tour, each network would be guaranteed basic coverage—video and clips every day from each of the five leaders' tours. Each network would decide what additional coverage, if any, it wanted to provide its audiences.

For CBC, it was an opportunity to try a different approach to covering a campaign. Instead of putting reporters on leaders' planes, the network placed a campaign reporter in each of the country's six regions: the reporters saw leaders as they arrived in each region and only joined the leaders' tours for the final few days. Supplementing that, CBC's all-news channel, Newsworld, offered each of the five parties a fifteen-minute window each weekday morning during the campaign for a candidate (CBC hoped it would be leaders) to speak for five minutes live on any subject and then respond to ten minutes of questions from any reporters who chose to come to the mini–news conferences at CBC stations across the country.

Pooling the coverage of leaders' tours worked and quickly became standard operating procedure for the networks for all subsequent elections. It would have happened again had there been an election in 2009. In 2000, CTV Newsnet joined Newsworld in jointly presenting the morning news conferences for all five parties on their all-news channels, but that innovation died after that election. Similarly, CBC's decision to stay away from leaders' tours lasted only through the 1997 campaign. Three years later the public broadcaster's reporters were back on the leaders' planes but were filing using pool crews. By that point, major changes were underway in the ownership of the media, which also played a role in shaping and further changing coverage of politics and public policy.

The Liberal government, in the late 1990s, eliminated restrictions that had prevented the same organization from owning newspapers and TV stations in the same market. That produced further concentration of ownership in pursuit of the latest media management fad—convergence. In 2000, TV network CanWest Global paid $3.2 billion to buy the *National Post* and the former Southam newspaper chain from Conrad Black and Hollinger Inc. That same year, CanWest became a national television network, buying a series of TV stations owned by Western International Communications. In 2007, CanWest added a series of specialty channels to its existing holdings in a $2.3 billion purchase from Alliance Atlantis. In 2000, Bell Canada Enterprises (BCE) bought the country's largest private television network, CTV, and a series of specialty channels for $2.3 billion and then joined with the Thomson family to create Bell Globemedia, bringing together CTV and the *Globe and Mail*; this was followed by further expansion as a provider of satellite TV service, as well as mobile phone and Internet service. Cable TV, mobile phone, and Internet service provider Rogers Inc. added specialty channels to its community TV broadcasting activities. The *Toronto Star* tried unsuccessfully to get a TV broadcasting license for southern Ontario after buying the *Hamilton Spectator* in 1999 and the *Kitchener-Waterloo Record* in 1998. After BCE decided in 2005 that its convergence strategy had been the conglomerate's latest expensive mistake, it sold a 20 percent interest in what was renamed ctvglobemedia to Torstar. (Five years later, in 2010, BCE became the sole owner of CTV and its specialty channels as ctvglobemedia split up, with the Thomson family taking 85 percent interest in the *Globe and Mail*.)

The belief in the first years of the decade that the media's future lay in convergence drove this frantic debt-driven consolidation. Mergers and conglomerates made sense, convergence proponents argued, when a news organization could take the work of the same group of reporters and put it in their newspapers, on their TV stations, and on the Internet, supported by advertising sold on all platforms. The key for media owners was that this could be accomplished with fewer journalists than if each media organization was separate. The same reporters could work for print, television or radio, and online. That allowed news organizations to cut the overall number of reporters they employed, in the belief that fewer reporters producing the same amount of content as before layoffs and placed across a broader spectrum of media, all supported by advertising, would increase profits. It was an accountant's view of the world that assumed that the same person could file for broadcast and print, frequently even on the same day.

It took no account of two key points. First, all reporters are not alike and most cannot transcend the medium in which they have been trained to work. Some similar skills are required to do television, print, radio, or online, but just as many skills are different. A few can manage the adjustments required to work in each medium, but as many or more simply cannot do it. It is difficult enough to change media on different days. Asking someone to file for print, television, and online all on the same day leaves little or no time for reporting and produces simplistic stories that may contain the minimum in terms of facts but virtually nothing in the way of the background or context that is essential for understanding what any story means.

Second, journalists and newsrooms are inherently competitive. They compete not just within but also across media. Newspapers compete with television, radio competes with print and TV, and everyone is competing with everyone else on the Web to get stories first and to do a better job than anyone else. Advocates of convergence within the management of news conglomerates did not understand this. They naïvely believed that suddenly sharing a common parent would, for instance, make reporters at the *Globe and Mail* willing to give up their exclusive stories to their new best friends at CTV so that the television network could run the *Globe* story on CTV National News the night before it appeared in the next morning's *Globe and Mail*. That concept produced tremendous newsroom resistance, but it didn't stop conglomerates from cutting staff in the confident belief that ultimately, it would work.

Convergence was a management theory that dealt a blow to the coverage of Parliament, politics, and public policy, but it had a much broader negative impact across the Canadian media landscape. In newspaper and TV newsrooms across the country, conglomerates shared content across their media outlets and eliminated local distinctiveness in standardizing the look and presentation of newspapers and TV newscasts across all members of their conglomerates. That allowed for further cuts in staff in both newspaper and TV newsrooms. For instance, multiple movie reviewers at different newspapers could be replaced by one reviewer writing for the entire chain, saving the conglomerate a lot of salaries.

After losing reporters, yet having to produce as much or more copy, news managers responded by consolidating and ultimately eliminating beat reporter positions, turning those specialists into general assignment reporters covering a different issue every day. Part of that cutback included eliminating reporters and coverage at provincial legislatures across the country. The parliamentary press gallery in Ottawa wasn't the only one to shrink. Provincial galleries also lost members as newspapers, radio, and TV broadcasters pulled out or cut back, closing bureaus or consolidating so that one reporter now provided provincial political news to all the newspapers or stations in a chain.

The shrinkage of provincial press galleries was another step in the general reduction in the coverage of politics and public policy across the media in Canada, but it had another, more subtle impact as well. Provincial press galleries served as training grounds for political reporters, who would then go on to cover national politics in Ottawa or work overseas. It was a place to learn the ropes in either print or broadcast, and to build political and bureaucratic contacts that would remain important if you moved to the national scene. It also gave reporters a first-hand understanding of how politics and public policy affect communities and the public since provincial governments and legislatures, with their focus on social issues such as health care and education, are closer to the public than the legislators in the House of Commons. The loss of that training ground meant that reporters in future would be assigned to Ottawa with little background or political reporting experience.

In newsrooms on Parliament Hill, the elimination of beat reporters also meant that everyone was now a general assignment reporter expected to file every day on whatever was happening. Individual reporters no longer had the time to do beat research, talk to contacts in a beat area, go to a Commons committee meeting, or read background documents. As a result, reporters would no longer meet or talk to the expert contacts they needed to check rumours and to interpret stories. They lost the ability to break stories since they were not talking to the range of people involved in an issue who can each provide a piece of a puzzle that contributes to a news story. With fewer contacts of their own, reporters are much more vulnerable to political parties, communications staff for ministers, and the legions of lobbyists and private sector communications people each pushing their own employer's point of view.

The result was a slow stripping away of the knowledge, history, experience, and context required by political reporters to provide coverage of complex issues. Now a reporter on Parliament Hill might be covering Canadian defence policy concerning Afghanistan one day, Canada's position on climate change the next day, and the federal deficit the day after that. There was no time to watch developments in Parliament and its committees, and within the political parties. Part of that time crunch came from the growing power of the Internet, which had become a larger and larger element of every news organization's coverage strategy although it was not making money for any of them. Reporters now faced several, if not hourly, deadlines, with the same person sometimes filing for websites, print, and all-news channels in the same day, whereas in the past, they had had only one deadline a day. They now first had to file for the Web and then work on their stories for newscast or newspaper deadlines later in the day.

That pressure to produce stories on issues they often knew little about or had only been covering for weeks rather than years left parliamentary reporters increasingly vulnerable to two external forces that undermined their reporting. One is the vagaries of instant research produced through Internet searches, which has become the way research is conducted for many stories. An assignment in the morning is followed by an Internet search and a rush out the door clutching the top half dozen stories about the issue found on the Web. There is often no time to check sources or confirm material found in those stories. As a result, any errors are repeated, sometimes turning fiction into fact. There is no time for an independent assessment of the issues involved in a story, which is needed to reach defensible conclusions for an audience. It is much easier and faster to recycle the framework and interpretation of the issue found in the previous stories taken off the Web.

It is also easier and faster to rely on comments from the legions of communications people working for government, corporations, and non-governmental organizations who are readily available—either in person, on the phone, or, increasingly, through email exchanges—than to look for new or different voices to comment. These insiders have become a mainstay for reporters who need people who will say something, or anything, to fill out stories written against numerous and tight deadlines. The Harper government's rigid control of communications and frequent refusal to comment since 2006 is all the more shortsighted and hard to fathom, considering the ease with which it could get its message out consistently merely by talking regularly to reporters who are facing deadline pressures and are desperate for quotes.

These changes in working conditions and demands placed on reporters led to deterioration in the nature and quality of the coverage of politics, Parliament, and public policy that they provide to Canadians. When a reporter doesn't have the time, knowledge, or background to deal with the complexity of an issue, there are still two ways he or she can tell the story—by focusing on conflict or personality. Assisted by new technology, these two approaches have become the staple of political reporting and that has helped to alienate the public from politics and public policy.

By the time Paul Martin called a federal election on May 23, 2004, the transformation of the parliamentary press gallery was almost complete. Reporters from individual TV stations across the country had long since disappeared, as had virtually all the reporters from individual newspapers. Even the major metropolitan dailies like the *Vancouver Sun* and the *Edmonton Journal* no longer had their own reporters on Parliament Hill. The former Southam chain purchased by Conrad Black in the late 1990s had been bought by CanWest Global, which was trying to integrate the newspapers with its TV network. The *National Post* remained in business but had been cut and constrained in an attempt to reduce losses. What had started seven years earlier as a battle between two national newspapers had by 2004 been won by the *Globe and Mail* although the *Post* showed no signs of disappearing despite its print and broadcast competitors regularly predicting its demise. CBC TV had cut its supper-hour newscasts to half an hour and replaced the other half hour with a common national program—*Canada Now*—produced from Vancouver and seen coast to coast in time zones across the country, and usually containing one common national story from Ottawa. CBC Newsworld and CTV Newsnet continued their competition for all-news viewers while CBC Radio and Canadian Press's Broadcast News remained the only English-language radio voices watching politics and government from the press gallery. National news organizations now produced all the stories coming from Ottawa, focusing on national issues with no mandate or interest in reporting on individual MPs and their activities. While the *Toronto Star* remained an exception in terms of a single newspaper with an Ottawa bureau, its readership area was larger in terms of number of MPs and population than every province except Ontario and Québec, so it could hardly be considered a local paper.

Not only are readers, listeners, and viewers denied the coverage of issues in Ottawa in a way that incorporates its effect on their communities; information does not flow the other way either. No information comes to the national news bureaus from newsrooms across the country as happened when newspapers and TV stations had their own reporters in Ottawa and their editors, to help shape coverage, would daily tell their Ottawa-based reporters what was important in their own communities. Decisions about what is and is not covered in Ottawa are now made without any perspective from those a long way from Parliament Hill. The isolation of the parliamentary press gallery is compounded by the fact that with the abandonment of provincial political coverage as well, few parliamentary reporters have a provincial grounding to fall back on in assessing what is worth covering in Ottawa and what it means. The key determinant now is how the issue plays among the insiders in Ottawa and what they consider important. The result is the narrow focus on what is going to trigger the next election and when it will happen.

Technology, specifically the BlackBerry as the dominant means of instant information and reaction, has played a critical role here—not in broadening political communication among Canadians but in isolating the media from Canadians in an Ottawa-insider bubble in which the political parties and their focus on strategies and tactics is the dominant theme.

The BlackBerry first appeared in national political reporting in the 2000 election, a year after Research in Motion (RIM) released the first generation of what was then primarily a two-way pager. For that campaign, CBC struck a deal with RIM to provide BlackBerrys for about sixteen key reporters, field producers, and campaign coverage managers in exchange for an assessment of how the device performed under the pressures of a campaign. The first generation BlackBerry was a small email device with a keyboard and a green and grey screen that could display a few lines of text at a time. Its coverage range rarely extended beyond major cities, yet it was still a huge advance in managing a team of reporters and producers scattered across the country. It could send a message not just to one person but to as many as were included in the address line: all recipients would get the same message at the same time. Most important, everyone would get it immediately. There was no need to connect a computer to a telephone line to receive it. Whatever was sent could be instantly translated into scripts or adjustments to campaign coverage—inspiring a question to a leader, inserting a fact or a comment someone else had made into a script or live talk with an anchor, or allowing a reporter to put a background question to the campaign team travelling on one of the tours and then circulate the answer to everyone involved in the coverage.

The BlackBerry improved the network's reporting. It kept the coverage team aware of what was happening all across the country on all the leaders' campaigns and in the newsroom, where overall campaign coverage was managed and directed. CBC did not publicize the email addresses of those with BlackBerrys since senior campaign managers had no interest in external interference in dealing with their reporters. It was a device for internal communication and campaign management only. It worked extremely well and the reporters and producers were reluctant to surrender their BlackBerrys at the end of the campaign.

They did not have to wait long for a replacement that could do even more in communication terms. In 2002, RIM introduced a second-generation BlackBerry with an upgraded instant messaging capability as well as email, a calendar, the ability to add contacts, and other business tools. It was still short of current smart phone models but was a major advancement on the original BlackBerry and an instant hit among the media.

By the time of the 2004 election, standard equipment for parliamentary and campaign reporters from all news organizations included BlackBerrys, but they were being used differently than they had been used by CBC in the 2000 campaign. Communication with editors in the newsroom and between reporters and producers working for the same organization was still important. However, reporters had given their addresses to all the political parties. Opening up their BlackBerry systems to the parties' media message control managers and communications assistants was a fateful decision since it meant that collectively, the media had handed over its communications tool to the political parties, who had both the people and incentive to figure out how to use instant communications to their partisan advantage. A device originally used for internal communication within news organizations had become a way for the parties to shape their messages and attacks on their competitors by bombarding reporters with emails at any time of the day or night.

There was a positive side to it for reporters. The pressure to file regularly for the Web required reporters to come up with something new several times a day to update their stories by at least creating the illusion that something new had happened as each campaign day went on. The answer was the "reaction" story—building a new top to a story based on a reaction to almost anything: a campaign development, an announcement from a leader, a misstep from a candidate, a damaging revelation about a candidate's past, or an external news event. All that was needed was how a leader, a party, or a candidate reacted to a particular issue or event, and a new story could be filed. The BlackBerry was the perfect tool to distribute the initial news story and then gather the reaction, and reporters were not the only ones who figured that out. The parties quickly realized the ease with which reporters who lacked context and background in many campaign issues could be manipulated and hooked on BlackBerry journalism. Their campaign offices were only too happy to bombard reporters with BlackBerry messages containing background, comments, and news releases, particularly focusing on trying to persuade reporters of the hypocrisy of their opponents by pulling past quotations from parties and their leaders that contradicted current statements and policy positions.

This all came together in the 2004 campaign. An analysis of coverage of recent election campaigns demonstrates that the media focus relatively little time and attention on policies. Campaign coverage is overwhelmingly about leaders, strategy, and tactics, and increasingly about public opinion polling results, particularly in the last four campaigns through 2011, where the nightly tracking polls have dominated opinion poll coverage.[4] Personality and conflict also dominate election campaigns, replicating the content of much of the media coverage of politics and public policy leading up to the campaign. Partisan blogs also assumed a greater importance in these four campaigns, not among the general public but within the media, which followed them closely and reported on their content when they deemed it significant. All of this is ideal material to be distributed, debated, and chewed over endlessly through BlackBerry messages, instantly spreading news and rumours across a broad cross-section of reporters and back and forth between party media managers and journalists. Adding to that is the media's fascination with and considerable coverage of the inner workings of campaigns and party "war rooms" (despite no evidence that the interest is shared by the public). That appears to be a result of the continuing influence on the media, even more than a decade after it was released, of the film *The War Room* about the 1992 Clinton presidential campaigns—in part, because its focus on strategy and tactics added credence to the sort of coverage the Canadian media already provided on its elections.

Capturing and holding the media's attention is vitally important for all the political parties in every campaign. If they can persuade the media of the importance of their messages, they might prevent negative coverage or a focus on specific issues, or a comparison of party positions on those issues. It is always better to give the media the message and help them run with it than to have to respond to unexpected and disruptive stories that might emerge if the media are not kept occupied. The parties discovered that the BlackBerry was the perfect vehicle to do that. Ideally, it supplemented the degree to which parties already managed the media agenda by having reporters on leaders' tours, moving them around the country in a bubble, and feeding them daily announcements and stories isolated from voters and what was happening in the campaigns in individual communities. Cutbacks by news organizations meant that they devoted fewer reporters and less coverage to the campaign with each election, but they still staffed the leaders' planes, giving the parties the upper hand in shaping media coverage, which they skillfully exploited, supplemented by BlackBerrys.

The 2004 election produced a minority government, the first in Ottawa since 1979, and the uncertainty surrounding its lifespan meant no let-up on the media's focus on strategy, tactics, and opinion polling. Who was up, who was down, and who would force the next election and when continued to be the dominant themes for reporting from Ottawa. Through two subsequent elections, each of which produced a Conservative minority, that emphasis did not change. Nor did it change in the 2011 campaign as the story was again whether the Conservatives would get the majority that, this time, leader Stephen Harper explicitly requested from voters on an almost daily basis.

What has continued to change is the technology. As Blackberrys have become more sophisticated, with new generations that include Web browsers, social media sites such as Facebook and Twitter have emerged and been incorporated into the parties' efforts to control the media and shape the media's coverage of politics and Parliament to their advantage, even as blogs have faded in significance. Some regard the 2011 election as the first social media campaign, but despite that label, there is little evidence that social media have either captured the attention of or engaged the general public. As social media analyst Mark Blevis wrote in the *Ottawa Citizen* on March 29, 2011, "anecdotally, the political discussion on Twitter is still taking place within an echo chamber. That is, most of the political discussion involves journalists, pundits, interest groups, the politically engaged, and—yes—even politicians. The average Canadian? Not so much." That conclusion was largely reinforced by his analysis of Twitter activity during the campaign. While there was a daily average of about sixteen thousand tweets related to the campaign, generally little more than one-third each day was new content. Almost half involved someone resending (retweeting) what someone else had sent without modification, while only between 10 and 15 percent of the tweets were commenting on someone else's message.

Toronto digital communications consultant Meghan Warby makes a similar point in her analysis of the impact of social media on the campaign. Writing during the campaign on the *Globe and Mail* website, she noted:

> Political parties are using digital channels primarily as new funnels, within which they pour talking points from speeches, sound bites from media appearances, cut-and-pasted bullets from press releases and after-the-fact event updates. This isn't unacceptable—more dangerously for our democracy, it's uninteresting....
>
> ... In the same way that advertisers and public-relations industries flaunt circulation numbers and "impressions," digital data needs to be taken with a grain of salt. Too often, frequency and "output" is confused with actual conversations and interaction between candidates and citizens.[6]

For all the enthusiastic talk about the revolution in communications that social media would bring, media coverage of the 2011 federal election was not noticeably different from that of the 2004, 2006, and 2008 elections. There remained virtually no contact or communication between the journalists writing about the election and the public. The media's emphasis remained firmly on strategy and tactics, personality and conflict. The parties created an alternate reality with the media as willing accomplices through joint participation on Blackberrys and other smart phones, exchanging information, rumours, and gossip that mean little to those outside Ottawa. Frequently, they result in stories about party strategy, insider political personalities, conflicts within parties, and other largely trivial issues within an environment in which how quickly or cleverly someone "reacts," regardless of what is said, becomes, in the media's eyes, a key determinant of competence. Interestingly, in the 2011 election, some media outlets actually told their audiences the source of these stories. For example, when Liberal leader Michael Ignatieff was caught off guard when reporters in Québec on April 6 asked him about apparently racist comments by one of his Québec candidates, CBC, CTV, and Global all stated that the candidate's comments had been given to the media by the NDP. The next day, when another Liberal candidate in Alberta, a former judge, got into hot water over past comments suggesting that not all sexual assaults should be treated equally by the courts, Global told its viewers that the comments had been given to the network by the Conservatives. The party gave the reporters the tip timed to a "tough on crime" appearance by leader Stephen Harper in the Toronto area riding of Cabinet Minister Julian Fantino, a former chief of the Toronto Police Service and the Ontario Provincial Police. Details about the comments, and then the chase for reaction, dominated BlackBerry and Twitter activity for reporters that day, resulting in Ignatieff firing his Québec candidate while retaining the Alberta candidate.

These are some of the many examples of how the political parties and the media have created a world in Ottawa in which voters have become outsiders and cannot relate to what is being reported. Too much political coverage means nothing to them and has no impact on their lives. As a result, Canadians tune out until something happens, such as the prospect of an unwanted election that temporarily forces them to pay attention and respond.

Instead of the reality check that used to be produced by newsrooms across the country telling their Ottawa reporters what did and did not play at home, the parliamentary press gallery now relies on news aggregators such as nationalnewswatch.com—a site that collects headlines and story links from across the country—for a sense of how Canadians think. Aggregators, though, simply provide lists, not a sense of what is important or why in communities from coast to coast. There are no conversations between reporters and editors scattered across the country to provide feedback about what has been reported and to highlight what needs to be covered.

The narrow personality- and conflict-driven media coverage was piled on top of a political environment through the 2011 election campaign of hyper-partisanship, total unwillingness to recognize that anyone else with a different perspective has a valid point of view, and immediately jumping to the worst and most sinister and derogatory conclusions about anyone's comments or actions—all reinforced by media coverage. This kind of coverage produces a world that people across the country can't comprehend. Canadians don't act that way when they deal with their neighbours, when they are out in the grocery store or riding a bus to work. They do not see any of it as relevant, so increasingly, they ignore it and the national political media as well.

Decisions to cut back on reporting staff, close bureaus, and replace reporters from local newspapers and TV stations with national news bureaus and national network reporters have broken the link between the public and the media that has been at the core of political communication. As a result, the media now plays a shrinking role in informing Canadians about politics and public policy. It has replaced its traditional role with an inward-looking, narrowly focused coverage that concentrates on the issues defined by the parties through their joint sharing with the media of technological tools and their ability to engage reporters in concentrating on the artificial world they have collectively created. Instead of using technology to bridge the communications gap between voters in their communities and the media, the media has used it to turn its back on the public, forging closer links with the people reporters cover rather than with the people who used to read, watch, and listen to their reporting.

NOTES

1   Steven Chase et al., "Ignatieff Throws Down the Election Gauntlet," Globe and Mail, September 2, 2009.
2   "Tories Open Up Small Lead on Liberal Election Talk," Ekos Politics, http://www.ekos.com/admin/articles/cbc-2009-09-10.pdf.
3   Susan Delacourt, "Chrétien Bids for Leadership with Promise to Rout Tories," Globe and Mail, January 24, 1990.
4   See Christopher Waddell, "The Campaign in the Media 2008," in The Canadian Federal Election of 2008, ed. Jon H. Pammett and Christopher Dornan (Toronto: Dundurn Press,

2009); Christopher Waddell and Christopher Dornan, "The Media and the Campaign," in *The Canadian Federal Election of 2006*, ed. Jon H. Pammett and Christopher Dornan (Toronto: Dundurn Press, 2006).

5   Mark Blevis, "The Five Most Tweeted Election Issues," *Mark Blevis* (blog), 24 April 2011, http://www.markblevis.com/the-five-most-tweeted-election-issues/; Mark Blevis, "#elxn41 Online Engagement Driven by Action and Participation," *Mark Blevis* (blog), 3 April 2011, http://www.markblevis.com/elxn41-online-engagement-driven-by-action-and-participation/.

6   Meghan Warby, "The Election's Digital Static," *Globe and Mail*, April 7, 2011.

6

Tom Flanagan

Political Communication and the "Permanent Campaign"

One of the most interesting developments in Canadian politics in recent years is the rise of the "permanent campaign," in which political parties seem at all times to be as much preoccupied with campaigning as with government and opposition. The most visible aspect of the permanent campaign is the growth of pre-writ advertising, emphasized by the Conservatives but also practiced by the other parties. In this chapter, I chronicle the growth of pre-writ advertising and then seek to explain the phenomenon of the permanent campaign with respect to the minority governments that existed in Canada from 2004 to 2011, as well as the public funding regime introduced in 2004 (Bill C-24), which made much more money available to political parties. It remains to be seen to what extent the practice of permanent campaigning will be affected by the election of a majority Conservative government in May 2011 and that government's abolition of quarterly allowances to federal parties.

THE GROWTH OF PRE-WRIT ADVERTISING

Advertising is an essential and usually the most expensive part of any political campaign run by a major Canadian political party. Historically, most of the media buy for advertising was concentrated during the writ period, lasting from five to eight weeks. Pre-writ advertising also took place, but it was usually confined to the weeks just before the election was expected to be called because conventional wisdom holds that advertising that occurs too long before the actual campaign will be forgotten and lose its impact. Thus, shortly before the 2004 election campaign began, the Liberals put up an attack website, titled "Stephen Harper Said," and ran ads to steer voters to the Internet site. The Conservatives responded as quickly as they could with their own website about Paul Martin.[1] After that, pre-writ advertising grew enormously in size and scope. The Conservatives led the way, and other parties tried to follow suit, albeit within the constraints of their much more limited financial means.

The first Conservative experiment in pre-writ advertising came in early 2005, when the party ran print ads in ethnic and rural newspapers opposing gay marriage. The campaign lasted several weeks and cost about $300,000. The goal was to use the debate over gay marriage, then in full swing in Parliament, to attract socially conservative ethnic voters, Roman Catholics, and rural residents in ridings the Conservatives hoped to win in the next election.[2] The Conservatives subsequently made considerable progress with all these targeted groups. One cannot ascribe causation to the ads alone, but they were the start of a long-term recruiting process.

The second Conservative experiment with pre-writ ads came at the end of summer 2005, when the party spent about $1 million to run a suite of television ads featuring the leader and other caucus members talking about Conservative policy. These ads had been produced in the spring of 2005 when the Conservatives were trying to trigger an election by defeating Paul Martin's Liberal government in the House of Commons. After spending half a million dollars on "creative" and production, the party didn't want to waste its investment and so ran the ads in the late summer.[3] It was more a display of determination and financial muscle designed to shore up the base than a serious attempt to attract voters; indeed, at that time, no one had any idea that Paul Martin's government would be defeated in November 2005.

Conservative pre-writ advertising increased in scale and became demonstrably more effective with several waves directed against Stéphane Dion, starting almost as soon as he became Liberal leader in December 2006 and continuing right up to the eve of the 2008 election.[4] On January 28, 2007, the Conservatives rolled out three ads ridiculing Dion and paid for them to run on Canadian TV networks when they were broadcasting the Super Bowl. The most effective of the three ads—titled "What Kind of Leader is Stéphane Dion?"—used footage from the Liberal leadership candidate debates. It showed Michael Ignatieff at his most professorial, saying, "Stéphane, we didn't get it done" (referring to the Liberals' commitment to cut greenhouse gas emissions under the Kyoto Protocol), and Dion replying in high-pitched, heavily accented English, "This is unfair! You don't know what you speak about. Do you think it's easy to make priorities?"[5] Just by letting the Liberals speak, the ad brilliantly showcased the divisions within the party as well as Dion's prickly personality and his difficulty in communicating in English.

The ads received a lot of free publicity and repetition in the news media precisely because it was so unusual for a party to purchase paid advertising outside the campaign period. Indeed, amplification in the news media may have had more impact than the paid media buy as the notion that Dion was "Not a Leader" worked its way into the standard narrative, becoming a fixture in stories about Dion and the Liberals. Although most people, when asked by pollsters, denied that the ads would influence their vote, the ads, and the news narrative they helped create, almost certainly contributed to the dismal leadership rankings that Dion quickly started to gather in polls.[6] By early April 2007, Dion was seen as the best leader by only 17 percent of respondents in a Nanos poll, compared to 42 percent for Stephen Harper.[7]

On May 29, 2007, the Conservatives launched another flurry of radio and TV ads targeted at Dion, this time over the Liberal-dominated Senate's holdup of the government's bill to limit senatorial terms to eight years. The theme was "Stéphane Dion is (once again) not a leader." These ads could hardly have depressed Dion's leadership numbers lower than they already were, but they may have helped keep them low.

The third cycle of Conservative ads was a pre-emptive strike against Stéphane Dion's "Green Shift," which he was planning to unveil in June 2008. The Tories beat him to the punch with radio and TV ads labelling it "Dion's tax trick" and "Dion's tax on everything."[8] Running all summer, mostly on radio in battleground ridings, the ads contributed to the Green Shift's loss of popularity during the summer. Supported by a majority of respondents when it was unveiled in June, the Green Shift was opposed by a majority in an Ipsos Reid poll when the writ was dropped in September 2008.[9]

Ten days before the writ was dropped, the Conservatives launched a new series of six positive ads about Stephen Harper. Apparently designed to rub the sharp edges off the prime minister's personality, they showed him dressed in a casual blue sweater, talking about sentimental topics such as his family, immigrants, and veterans. The background music was somewhat schmaltzy, but the ads fit with the Conservative campaign strategy of portraying Harper as the safe choice and Dion as risky. They may have contributed to the surge in polling numbers with which the Conservative campaign began: five polls released between September 7 and September 10, 2008, showed an average Conservative lead over the Liberals of 12.8 percentage points.[10] A Harris/Decima poll taken during the first week of the campaign showed that far more people had seen Conservative ads than those of the other parties, a result that certainly owed something to the jump that the Conservatives got on the other parties through their pre-writ campaign.[11]

Conservatives resorted to advertising again in December 2008 to attack the Liberal-NDP coalition. One radio spot ran as follows:

> In the last election, Stéphane Dion gave his word. He said his Liberals would never form a coalition with the NDP.
>
> "We cannot have a coalition with a party that has a platform that would be damaging for the economy. Period."
>
> But now he's cut a deal with the NDP. And he's working with the separatists to make it happen. He even thinks he can take power without asking you, the voter. This is Canada. Power must be earned, not taken.[12]

That the coalition proved to be highly unpopular with voters outside Québec was not due entirely, or even mainly, to these ads, but they played their role as part of an all-out media onslaught by the Tories, who used all the resources available to them, including speeches in Parliament and public statements by the prime minister. The ads gave the media one more thing to report within this overall game plan.

Shell-shocked by the success of Conservative advertising, a Liberal strategist predicted in 2007 that the Conservatives would again go negative as soon as the Liberals picked a new leader to replace Stéphane Dion: "Within minutes of the new leader winning in Vancouver, the Conservative party will have TV commercials on the air branding the new leader as elitist/weak/a socialist/ left-handed/a Leafs fan/or some other equally silly label. The new leader will want to strike back but will be told there is no money for competing ads and that he/she needs to still raise $1-million to pay off the leadership debt."[13] In fact, the Conservatives waited until June 2009 to unleash a barrage of ads against Michael Ignatieff. The theme of the new ads, supported by a dedicated website, was "Just Visiting."[14] According to the ads, Ignatieff's 34-year absence showed that he did not really care about Canada. He had come back only to lead the Liberal Party and thus get a quick ticket to 24 Sussex Drive. He was "just in it for himself," in the words of one ad: that is, it was all about Ignatieff's ambitious drive for power, and not about the welfare of Canadians.

The ads ran all summer without seeming to hurt Ignatieff, but the notion that he was "just visiting" was working its way into the narrative about him in the news. Then, Ignatieff announced on September 1 that he was going to trigger an election at the earliest opportunity, saying to a Liberal caucus meeting, "Mr. Harper, your time is up."[15] That move backfired because it seemed to confirm what the ads said—that Ignatieff cared only about his own advantage and would force an election that most Canadians did not want. At that point, Liberal polling numbers started to fall precipitously, until by October, they were ten to fifteen points behind the Conservatives in all polls. In an early November Nanos poll, only 18 percent of respondents thought that Ignatieff would make the best prime minister—numbers similar to those garnered by Stéphane Dion in spring 2007.[16] The fall was not due to the ads alone, but the ads had given voters a way to interpret Ignatieff's behaviour and thus helped grease the skids for the Liberals' slide.

In fall 2009, the Conservatives for the first time resorted to pre-writ advertising in an attempt to pass legislation. In order to build support for Manitoba MP Candice Hoeppner's private member's bill to abolish the long-gun registry, the party ran radio ads in rural ridings held by the Liberals and NDP. The ads encouraged listeners to call their MPs and express support for Hoeppner's bill.[17] MPs generally deny that they can be influenced by such tactics, but the bill passed second reading by a much larger margin than anyone anticipated, 164 to 137, as twelve NDP members, eight Liberals, and one independent supported it. The Conservatives repeated some of their advertising and campaign tactics when the bill came up for third reading, but this time the bill failed after Liberal leader Michael Ignatieff required all his caucus members to vote against it.[18] Advertising in support of bills can be useful, but it cannot work miracles if the numbers are just not there.

Finally, pre-writ advertising seems to have been quite important to the Conservative election victory of 2011. In December 2010, Michael Ignatieff announced that the Liberals would not support the Conservatives' next budget, expected for February or March 2011.[19] Whatever good reasons Ignatieff may have had to make this statement, it gave the Conservatives lots of time to respond. Starting in early January 2011, they rolled out a new suite of anti-Ignatieff TV attack ads and played them in heavy rotation until the government fell in late March. The ads highlighted Ignatieff's supposed ambition for power and willingness to make a coalition with the NDP and Bloc Québécois. The Liberals, without money to pay for a response, had to absorb this punishment for almost three months.[20] Their polling numbers, which had been not far from the Conservatives' in December, fell precipitously once the ads began to work. By the time the writ was dropped, the Conservatives had built up a double-digit lead and Ignatieff's leadership evaluations were down in the same territory as Dion's had been in 2008.[21] The Conservatives had opened up such a big lead in the pre-writ period that they could then get away with playing it safe in a classic frontrunner writ-period campaign.

Estimating the effect of political advertising is notoriously difficult because so many things are happening at the same time. But it is fair to say that every time the Conservatives have run a series of ads in the extended pre-writ period, things have moved in the desired direction—winning over the support of ethnic, Catholic, and rural voters; driving Stéphane Dion's leadership ratings down and keeping them down; making voters skeptical of the Green Shift; making them feel better about supporting Stephen Harper; encouraging them to dislike Dion's coalition with the NDP; driving down Michael Ignatieff's rankings after he became Liberal leader; helping pass Candice Hoeppner's long-gun registry bill on second (though not on third) reading; and softening up the Liberals in preparation for the 2011 election campaign.

Although no quantitative studies have been done on this point, I believe the ads may have worked their effect as much through news coverage as through the actual media buy. Political advertising often works that way. For example, the famous 1964 "Daisy" ad, in which Lyndon Johnson implied that Barry Goldwater was too reckless to be trusted with his finger on the nuclear trigger, played only once.[22] That single exposure set off a firestorm of discussion in the media and permanently sealed Goldwater's fate in the 1964 election. Similarly, though not so dramatically, the pre-writ Conservative ads were extensively discussed in the media, and their message worked its way into the day-to-day narrative of news coverage. I would propose as a hypothesis for future testing that the target of pre-writ advertising is the media, which can make ads affect public opinion by integrating their messages into news coverage, as much as it is the voters. In this tableau, the size of the media buy may not be critical although it has to be large enough to convince media observers that the ad campaign is real. The media won't spend much time discussing Internet ads because they understand that such ads can be produced by a teenager at home, but they will pay attention if they believe a party is investing serious resources into an ad campaign.

The success of Conservative pre-writ advertising has led other parties to compete in this realm. In January 2009, as soon as Michael Ignatieff announced that he would support the Conservative government's budget, the NDP took out radio ads to condemn him: "He's propping up Stephen Harper. Michael Ignatieff failed his first test as Liberal leader. Jack Layton is the only leader strong enough to stand up to Harper and get us through this economic crisis."[23]

For their part, the Liberals reportedly spent $2 million on TV ads in late summer 2009 to introduce Michael Ignatieff's campaign slogan, "We Can Do Better."[24] The English ad, officially known as "Worldview" but widely derided as the "Enchanted Forest" or "Magic Forest," showed Ignatieff in a woodsy setting (actually a Toronto park) explaining how Canada should "think big" and "take on the world."[25] Released in anticipation of a fall election, the ads failed to stop the slide in the polls that the Liberals endured following Ignatieff's announcement on September 1 that he would try to force an election as soon as possible.

The Liberals resorted to advertising again in January 2010 as part of their campaign against Stephen Harper's prorogation of Parliament. They posted on their website three radio ads titled "Cover Up," "Present," and "Fermeture."[26] Consisting of thirty-second soundtracks plus simple visuals for the Internet, the ads argued that Harper had "shut down Parliament" because he had "something to hide" about the torture of Afghan detainees, climate change, and so on. The messaging and tone were similar in spirit to many past Liberal ads about Harper's alleged "hidden agenda."

When they released the ads on January 10, the Liberals said they would run radio and print versions in the coming days, but it is unclear how large the media buy was or if there was any media buy at all. I never heard the ads on radio or saw them in any newspaper, nor have I met anyone who has heard or seen them except on the Internet. Be that as it may, the Liberals did spark some media commentary just by posting them on their website. The effect can't be measured directly, but Conservative polling numbers were in free fall throughout January 2010, until they had reached a virtual tie with the Liberals by the end of the month—quite a drop from the fifteen-point lead the Conservatives had enjoyed in November 2009.

With a Conservative majority government having been elected in 2011, pre-writ advertising may not be used as much. But the Conservatives will probably resort to it at some point before the 2015 election, once it becomes clear who the new Liberal leader will be and whether the NDP has maintained the unprecedented level of support it received in the 2011 election, especially in Québec. The opposition parties will also probably continue to try, within their budgetary limits, to compete with the Conservatives. Advertising may fail in specific cases, but it works in general, which is why business spends billions of dollars a year on it. If one major party resorts to pre-writ advertising, the others will be hurt if they stand idly by.

MINORITY GOVERNMENT AND THE PERMANENT CAMPAIGN

Canada has seen an extraordinary amount of campaigning in the first decade of this century, as shown in table 6.1. In fact, campaigning has been even more prevalent than the bare facts of the table indicate, for the minority governments elected from 2004 onwards were liable to be defeated at any time. Thus, federal parties had to maintain non-stop election readiness from early 2004, when Paul Martin became Liberal prime minister and indicated he would soon be asking for an election.

The last ten years deeply affected Canadian government and political culture. After so many years of continuous campaigning, federal politicians became almost like child soldiers in a war-torn African country: all they know how to do was to fire their AK-47s. In short, we were living in a period of "permanent campaign," to borrow the phrase first coined in the United States to describe the continuous interweaving of politics and government.[27] The permanent campaign goes far beyond pre-writ advertising, as described in the previous section, to include a number of other organizational initiatives. I will describe some of what the Conservatives did in this regard because I am most familiar with them, but the implications are the same for all parties.

Table 6.1   Canadian national political campaigns, 2000-2009

National election campaigns	
Year	**Winner**
2000	Liberals
2004	Liberals
2005-6	Conservatives
2008	Conservatives
2011	Conservatives
Leadership campaigns	
Year	**Winner**
2000 (Canadian Alliance)	Stockwell Day
2001-2 (Canadian Alliance)	Stephen Harper
2003 (NDP)	Jack Layton
2003 (Greens)	Jim Harris
2003 (Progressive Conservatives)	Peter MacKay
2003 (Liberals)	Paul Martin
2004 (Conservatives)	Stephen Harper
2004 (Greens)	Jim Harris
2006 (Greens)	Elizabeth May
2006 (Liberals)	Stéphane Dion
2009 (Liberals)	Michael Ignatieff

The "Fear Factory"

Early in 2007, the Conservatives rented state-of-the-art premises in Ottawa for a "war room"—the command-and-control centre of a national campaign. Dubbed the "fear factory" by a Liberal wag, the war room was quickly leased, furnished, and wired, including a TV studio so the party could stage its own press conferences.[28] It was kept continually available until the 2008 election was finally called on September 7. The cost would have been considerable— hundreds of thousands of dollars a year—but it was a great convenience for a campaign manager not to have to scramble for space and furnishings on short notice. As a signal to the other parties that they were in for a fight if they toppled the government, the normally secretive Conservatives granted the media a tour of the "fear factory."[29]

A Jet for the Leader's Tour

The centrepiece of a campaign for a national party is the leader's tour, in which the leader travels around Canada by airplane and bus, making announcements and staging events.[30] Having a jet to move the leader, his staff, and accompanying media representatives is essential because of Canada's size. The Conservatives, having leased their campaign jet from Air Canada in previous elections, quickly made a deal with Air Canada after the 2006 election to get a jet whenever they might need it. Such deals are expensive—again, hundreds of thousands of dollars a year—but they are necessary if you want a jet on short notice. Having a campaign jet in place allowed the Conservatives to play brinksmanship games in Parliament without worrying about being defeated. In contrast, the Liberals, whether from organizational problems or financial difficulties, did not lock up a jet until the last minute, when Air Inuit leased them a twenty-nine-year-old Boeing 737, which the Conservatives claimed was 20 percent less fuel efficient than their own Airbus C-319. Moreover, the Liberal jet was not ready until day four of the campaign, and then suffered a mechanical breakdown that caused it to be grounded in Montreal on September 16.[31] The Liberals may have saved money by not leasing a jet in advance, but they paid a high price in terms of bad publicity directly contrary to the environmental theme of their Green Shift campaign platform.

Direct Voter Contact

Conservative campaign doctrine emphasizes Voter Identification and GOTV (Get Out the Vote) programs, collectively referred to as Direct Voter Contact (DVC), in targeted swing ridings. In simplest terms, this means contacting voters by mail, telephone, or door-knocking; asking them about their political concerns and preferences; and recontacting identified supporters at the close of the campaign to encourage them to vote.[32] Ongoing grassroots fundraising helps to build a base for writ-period DVC because it builds supporter lists and keeps contact information up to date. The Conservatives had not been able to use their DVC program in Québec in the past, but they did start grassroots fundraising in *la belle province* after the 2006 election, thus laying the groundwork for DVC in Québec swing ridings in 2008 and afterwards.

By-Elections

An effective DVC program is particularly useful in by-elections because turnout is always low. Using DVC to get supporters to the polls while others are staying home can lead to striking upset victories. The Conservatives did this in four by-elections in the pre-writ period before the 2008 election, winning two new ridings and coming close in two others where they had been given little chance.

They pulled off a similar coup in the by-elections of November 9, 2009, winning back Bill Casey's Nova Scotia riding and taking a seat away from the Bloc Québécois in rural Québec. This later achievement touched off another round of stories about how the Conservatives were back in the game in Québec and might be able to win enough seats there in the next election to finally earn a majority government. Media commentators, however, have little understanding of how campaigns are actually conducted and hence tend to overinterpret by-election results as representing broader trends in public opinion. In fact, the Conservative by-election victory in Québec was due mainly to its aggressive DVC campaign in a race where the Bloc Québécois no longer had the advantage of incumbency. With a turnout of only 36 percent, it was possible to win by mobilizing existing supporters rather than winning over a lot of new voters.

The Conservatives pulled off another by-election coup in November 2010, when they narrowly elected Julian Fantino in the suburban Toronto riding of Vaughan.[33] Their close victory in this heavily Italian and historically Liberal riding was the harbinger for the Conservatives' success with Toronto-area ethnic voters in the 2011 general election, which provided the additional seats necessary for a majority government. Voter identification and GOTV helped to eke out the by-election victory, showing again the importance of keeping one's campaign machine tuned up and ready to go.

The point is that every opportunity counts in a period of minority government. The party that keeps its campaign weapons sharp at all times and uses them strategically when the occasion arises is more likely to build an advantage over its opponents than a party that sleepwalks its way through the pre-writ period. Harper's team never rests. A campaign manager reporting directly to the Conservative leader, not to a committee, is always on the job. Voter identification linked to fundraising goes on 363 days a year (Christmas and Easter excepted). With the cash flow from such aggressive fundraising, the party can afford to spend millions on advertising, even years in advance of the writ, and to train candidates and workers, especially in the use of the potent Direct Voter Contact program and the Constituent Information Management System (CIMS) database. Activities funded by the House of Commons can also be channelled to political purposes—travel to targeted ridings and ethnic communities, mailouts with a response coupon for voter identification, public opinion research to find policies that will resonate with target demographic groups. All parties do some of these things some of the time, but the Conservatives are unique in the scale on which they operate and the degree to which everything is coordinated. They have produced a campaign equivalent of Colin Powell's doctrine of "overwhelming force," applying all possible resources to the battleground ridings where the election will be won or lost.

THE INFLUENCE OF MONEY

Another important factor in the rise of the permanent campaign was the availability of money.[34] Just as Canada was entering a period of minority government, Jean Chrétien's Bill C-24, which was passed in 2003 and took effect at the beginning of 2004, approximately doubled the amount of money available to parties. According to Chrétien's policy advisor, Eddie Goldenberg, the intent of C-24 was to leave parties approximately where they had been by replacing the revenue from union, corporate, and high-end personal contributions with other provisions.[35] In the end, however, C-24 turned out to be much more generous than the status quo ante. Below are the main provisions of C-24 and their real-world effects upon the finances of Canadian political parties.

Grassroots Fundraising

Bill C-24 increased tax credits for political contributions. In particular, the amount of political contribution eligible for a 75 percent tax credit was raised to $400: that is, starting in 2004, the true cost for a taxpayer to give $400 to a federal party was reduced to $100. No quantitative study of the impact has been published, but it must have increased the productivity of the grassroots fundraising at which the Conservatives—and, to a lesser extent, the NDP— excel. Generous tax credits are known to be an important motivating factor to low-end contributors. At the same time, C-24 increased the relative importance of low-end contributions by capping personal contributions at $5,000 (annually adjusted for inflation), later reduced to $1,000 by Stephen Harper's *Accountability Act*, passed in 2006 and effective in 2007.

Campaign Rebates

Bill C-24 dramatically reduced the real cost of political campaigning by raising the campaign rebate from 22.5 percent to 50 percent (60 percent in the 2004 election). With the current spending limit of about $20 million, that means the true cost of running a fully funded national campaign is only about $10 million, whereas it would have been about $15.5 million under the old rules. The amount returned to parties through the increased rebate can be invested in maintaining continual election readiness.

For local candidates, C-24 raised the rebate from 50 percent to 60 percent and reduced the threshold for reimbursement from 15 percent to 10 percent of the popular vote. An unknown but significant portion of this increased money at the local level is bound to end up supporting national campaigns because parties levy general campaign fees on electoral district associations (Liberals) or specific fees for participating in programs such as Direct Voter Contact (Conservatives). Well-to-do Electoral District Associations also sometimes voluntarily transfer cash to less well-off associations, which may save the national party the need to subsidize such ridings.

Quarterly Allowances

Bill C-24 created a system of quarterly allowances for parties getting over 2 percent of the popular vote in the preceding election. The annual amount of the allowance was set at $1.75 per vote received in the last election, adjusted annually for inflation. The annual amount of the subsidies in the wake of the 2008 election was about $26.7 million for all parties taken together.

David Coletto and I have shown that the amount of quarterly allowances paid in the four years from 2004 to 2007 ($105 million) was about $37 million greater than the total of corporate, union, and associational contributions to federal parties in the four years from 2000 to 2003 ($66 million) plus the amount foregone by reducing the personal contribution limit to $5,000 ($2 million)—all amounts standardized in 2007 dollars.[36] Table 6.2 shows total contributions from corporations, unions, and associations for the years 2000 to 2003; table 6.3 shows the amount of high-end personal contributions for those same years; and table 6.4 shows the amount of quarterly allowances for the years 2004 to 2007. These tables show that the quarterly allowances *by themselves* increased the amount of money available to parties over a four-year cycle by about $37 million, or 54 percent, even after subtracting the revenue lost by limiting personal and outlawing corporate contributions.

Table 6.2   Total contributions from corporations, associations, and trade unions

	2000	2001	2002	2003	2000-2003
Liberal	13,101,019	6,691,023	5,448,848	11,339,963	36,580,853
Canadian Alliance	7,686,049	873,989	1,121,519	1,530,311	11,211,868
PC	2,843,576	1,478,274	1,076,865	1,168,986	6,567,701
NDP	3,225,986	1,511,464	1,121,680	5,308,675	11,167,805
BQ	595,785	70,605	105,450	87,509	859,349
Green	0	1,075	1,600	63,300	65,975
Total	27,452,415	10,626,430	8,875,962	19,498,744	66,453,551

NOTE: Figures are 2007 dollars.

SOURCE: Elections Canada, "Political Fundraising," http://www.elections.ca/content.aspx?section=fin&lang=e; Tom Flanagan and David Coletto, "Replacing Allowances for Canada's National Political Parties?" University of Calgary, *The School of Public Policy SPP Briefing Papers* 3, no. 1 (January 2010): 3, http://policyschool.ucalgary.ca/sites/default/files/research/flanagan-coletto-online-3.pdf.

Table 6.3   Financial impact of proposed $5,000 limit, 2000–2003

	2000	2001	2002	2003	Total revenue lost (2000–2003)	% lost
Liberal	139,052.28	92,306.30	102,700.95	313,559.41	647,618.95	3.08
Canadian Alliance	564,508.11	12,329.62	27,280.29	18,352.78	622,470.79	2.10
PC	221,981.87	108,131.75	101,882.98	17,430.06	490,518.32	4.21
NDP	48,432.43	27,820.02	142,974.65	73,605.13	292,832.24	1.43
BQ	480.73	—	—	—	480.73	0.02
Green	0	—	—	17,986.66	17,986.66	3.62
Total	974,455.42	240,587.69	374,838.87	440,934.04	2,071,907.69	2.40

NOTE: Figures are 2007 dollars.

SOURCE: Elections Canada, "Political Fundraising," http://www.elections.ca/content. aspx?section=fin&lang=e; Tom Flanagan and David Coletto, "Replacing Allowances for Canada's National Political Parties?" University of Calgary, *The School of Public Policy SPP Briefing Papers* 3, no. 1 (January 2010): 4, http://policyschool.ucalgary.ca/sites/default/files/ research/flanagan-coletto-online-3.pdf.

Table 6.4   Quarterly allowances paid to political parties, 2004–7

	2004	2005	2006	2007	2004–2007
Liberal	9,774,907	9,498,080	8,770,143	8,517,049	36,560,179
Conservative	8,461,918	7,662,540	9,604,289	10,218,123	35,946,870
NDP	3,083,774	4,055,184	4,717,196	4,923,795	16,779,949
BQ	2,923,325	3,203,395	3,018,856	2,953,218	12,098,794
Green	523,694	1,061,905	1,199,287	1,262,641	4,047,527
Total	24,767,618	25,481,104	27,309,771	27,874,826	105,433,319

NOTE: Figures are 2007 dollars.

SOURCE: Elections Canada, "Political Fundraising," http://www.elections.ca/content. aspx?section=fin&lang=e; Tom Flanagan and David Coletto, "Replacing Allowances for Canada's National Political Parties?" University of Calgary, *The School of Public Policy SPP Briefing Papers* 3, no. 1 (January 2010): 5, http://policyschool.ucalgary.ca/sites/default/files/ research/flanagan-coletto-online-3.pdf.

Of course, the impact of all these changes has been uneven across the parties. The rebates affect all parties in the same way, but the change to tax credits has disproportionately helped the Conservatives, and to a lesser extent the NDP, because they have more effective machinery for grassroots fundraising. The Liberals, on the other hand, have struggled mightily with grassroots fundraising and, even with some improvement after Michael Ignatieff became leader, raised only about half of the amount that the Conservatives raised in 2009. The quarterly allowances also helped the Conservatives because their vote share rose in this period from 30 percent in 2004 to 38 percent in 2008, as well as the NDP, who went from 16 percent to 18 percent. The Liberals, in contrast, lost vote share, dropping from 36 percent to 26 percent over the same period, so their share of the quarterly allowances was correspondingly reduced.

Not surprisingly, then, the Conservatives took the lead in shifting to a permanent campaign model because they had more money than they could spend on national campaigns. Consider that, because of 50 percent rebates, the true cost of a national campaign is now about $10 million. In 2009–10, the Conservatives were getting a little over $10 million a year in quarterly subsidies and collecting about $17 million from donors in a typical year ($21 million in the last election year, 2008). With revenues of that magnitude, they could pay normal party expenses (perhaps $8 million a year), run a national campaign every year ($10 million), and still have money left over for pre-writ political activities. Political parties are not investment clubs. If they have extra money, they won't buy stocks, bonds, or gold; they will spend it to enhance their prospects of winning elections and controlling the government.

After winning a majority government in May 2011, the new Conservative government brought in legislation to end party subsidies over a three-year transitional period. It is too early to be certain about the impact of the new legislation except to say that if parties have less money to spend, they will have to cut back on permanent campaign activities. Whether they will actually have less money will depend on how well they fundraise in the future. With the next election not expected until October 2015, parties will have three years to build up a pre-writ war chest that they might spend in the year leading up to the election. If that proves to be true, the permanent campaign will return after a temporary suspension.

The Canadian permanent campaign model, with its new emphasis on pre-writ advertising, was born of minority government, with public money serving as the midwife. Will it continue now that we have returned to the historical norm of majority government?

My tentative answer to that question is yes, although the pace will undoubtedly slow down in periods of majority government. The permanent campaign, including pre-writ advertising, has shown itself to be potent political weaponry, useful for attracting new support groups, passing legislation, questioning the opposition's policies, and undermining the image of the opposition leader—in short, for winning and holding on to power. It is a political arms race in which competitors will have to adopt new generations of weaponry or fall irretrievably behind. As long as they can find the money to pay for it, parties will be forced to keep up in order to compete.

Reducing the amount of public money flowing to political parties might reduce their permanent campaigning and pre-writ advertising. Another approach to achieving such a reduction would be to legislate spending limits for the pre-writ period, which presently is entirely unregulated. Such limits, however, arguably benefit the party in power because it can manipulate government advertising and other forms of communication for its own advantage, while spending limits prevent opposition parties from fighting back. Manitoba has tried to evade this dilemma by legislating an advertising limit of $250,000 in the year in which an election is called, in addition to what is spent in the writ period.[37] This prevents high levels of expenditure on advertising in the immediate run-up to the writ period but leaves parties free to advertise in the years between elections. Such legislation might reduce the volume of pre-writ advertising that now exists at the federal level but would not remove it altogether.

It might also induce parties to start seeking third-party surrogates to do their pre-writ work for them, as commonly happens in the United States. The Swift Boat Veterans were able to do enormous damage to John Kerry in 2004 even though they were not officially part of the Republican campaign. So-called Super PACs, which can draw on unlimited donations from corporations and other high-end donors, are playing a major role in the 2012 Republican primaries. On a smaller scale, organized labour in Canada is already using similar methods to assist the NDP, spending money both before and during the writ period to run "issue-based campaigns" that don't mention the NDP specifically but urge voters to support policies on which the NDP is running.[38] To limit such developments, some might want to extend Canada's present ban on third-party advertising during the writ period to cover the pre-writ period as well, but such regulatory creep might be seen as posing a danger to freedom of speech.

In sum, I suspect that the permanent campaign, including pre-writ advertising, is here to stay at some level, even though many observers profess not to like it. Regardless of likes and dislikes, legislative remedies seem politically difficult to enact and may be loaded with unintended consequences worse than the alleged evil they are supposed to ameliorate.

NOTE

1   See Bill Curry, "Attack Ads Signal Campaign Start," *Windsor Star*, May 19, 2004.

2   Tom Flanagan, *Harper's Team: Behind the Scenes in the Conservative Rise to Power* (Montreal: McGill-Queen's University Press, 2009), 201–2.

3   Ibid., 222–23.

4   The following five paragraphs draw from my contribution to Tom Flanagan and Harold J. Jansen, "Election Campaigns Under Canada's Party Finance Laws," in *The Canadian Federal Election of 2008*, ed. Jon H. Pammett and Christopher Dorman (Toronto: Dundurn Press, 2009), 210–11.

5   Flanagan, *Harper's Team*, 229.

6   "Anti-Dion Ads Producing Laughs, Not Votes; Poll Shows Majority Believe Conservative TV Advertisements Attacking Liberal Leader Are Unfair," Canadian Press, February 8, 2007.

7   "Harper Towers over Other Leaders in New Poll," *CTV News*, April 10, 2007, http://www.ctv.ca/CTVNews/QPeriod/20070410/ses_poll_070410/.

8   "Liberals, Tories Trade Shots over Carbon Tax," *CTV News*, June 9, 2008, http://www.ctv.ca/servlet/ArticleNews/story/CTVNews/20080609/carbon_plan_080609?s_name=&no_ads=.

9   Juliet O'Neill, "Green Shift Support Declining, Poll Shows Liberals' Carbon Tax Proposal Not Enough to Beat Tories: Pollster," *Ottawa Citizen*, September 2, 2008.

10 Fleishman Hilliard Poll Tracker, http://election08.fleishman.ca (the URL is password protected).

11 Joan Bryden, "Tory TV Ads a Success, Poll Shows: Barrage of Sweater-Clad Harper Ads Help Tories Win Air War," Canadian Press, September 13, 2008.

12 "Tories Begin Battle Against Coalition," *CBC News*, December 2, 2008, http://www.cbc.ca/canada/story/2008/12/02/harper-coalition.html.

13 Rob Silver, "The Future of the Liberal Party: E-mail Exchange with Scott Reid," *Globe and Mail*, October 17, 2008.

14 The ads were once available for viewing at http://ignatieff.me, but the site has been taken down.

15 Juliet O'Neill and Janice Tibbets, "Ignatieff to Harper: Time Is Up," *National Post*, September 2, 2009.

16 Andrew Potter, "It's the Stupid Leadership Stupid," *Maclean's*, November 14, 2009, http://www2.macleans.ca/2009/11/14/its-the-stupid-leadership-stupid-nanos-poll.

17 "MP Niki Ashton: Vote to Scrap the Long-Gun Registry," Conservative Party website, October 26, 2009, http://www.conservative.ca/EN/5439/111099.

18 Jane Taber, "Ignatieff Cracks Whip on Gun Registry," *Globe and Mail*, April 19, 2010.

19 "Ignatieff Threatening to Roll Dice?" *Winnipeg Free Press*, December 20, 2010.

20 Jane Taber, "Ignatieff's Numbers Plummet as Tories Unleash Another Attack Ad," *Globe and Mail*, March 10, 2011.

21 See, for example, the time series in the Ekos poll of April 27, 2011: "Electorate Firming Up in Strange New Normal," *Ekos Politics*, April 27, 2011, http://www.ekospolitics.com/wp-content/uploads/full_report_april_27_2011.pdf. All published polls showed the same tendency for Conservative numbers to rise and Liberal numbers to drop in the first quarter of 2011.

22 Warren Kinsella, *The War Room: Political Strategies for Business, NGOs, and Anyone Who Wants to Win* (Toronto: Dundurn Press, 2007), 111.

23 Meagan Fitzpatrick, "NDP Unveils Radio Ads Decrying Ignatieff," Canwest News Service, January 29, 2009, http://www.freedominion.ca/phpBB2/viewtopic.php?t=129636.

24 Les Whittington, "Liberals' Soft Ad Approach Questioned," *Toronto Star*, September 26, 2009.

25 "Worldview," YouTube, September 6, 2009, http://www.youtube.com/watch?v=NZ2ixKkwljI.

26 "Cover Up," "Present," and "Fermeture," Liberal Party website, posted January 10, 2010, http://www.liberal.ca/newsroom/party-news/liberals-launch-radio-and-print-ads/.

27 See Norman Ornstein and Thomas Mann, eds., *The Permanent Campaign and Its Future* (Washington: American Enterprise Institute and Brookings Institute, 2000); Corey Cook, "The Contemporary Presidency: The Permanence of 'The Permanent Campaign': George W. Bush's Public Presidency," *Presidential Studies Quarterly* 32 (2002): 753–64; Catherine Needham, "Brand Leaders: Clinton, Blair and the Limitations of the Permanent Campaign," *Political Studies* 53 (2005): 343–61; Peter van Onselen and Wayne Errington, "The Democratic State as a Marketing Tool: The Permanent Campaign in Australia," *Commonwealth and Comparative Politics* 45 (2007): 78–94.

28 Fear Factory is a heavy-metal rock group (http://www.fearfactory.com)—not to be confused with *Fear Factor*, an NBC TV show about overcoming scary challenges.

29 "Conservatives Show Off Election War Room," *Guelph Mercury*, April 3, 2007.

30 This and the following two subsections are drawn from my contribution to Flanagan and Jansen, "Election Campaigns Under Canada's Party Finance Laws," 208–9.

31 Peter Kuitenbrouwer, "Fuel Use of Liberal Campaign Jet Under Attack," *National Post*, September 8, 2008; Campbell Clark and Josh Wingrove, "Liberals Left in Dark as Plane Grounded in Montreal," *Globe and Mail*, September 17, 2008.

32 On DVC, see Flanagan, *Harper's Team*, 153–54, 267–71.

33 Tamsin McMahon, "Fantino Wins in Vaughan While Liberals and Tories Split Manitoba Ridings," *National Post*, November 29, 2010.

34 For further discussion, see Flanagan and Jansen, "Election Campaigns Under Canada's Party Finance Laws."

35 Eddie Goldenberg, *The Way It Works* (Toronto: McClelland and Stewart, 2006), 382–84.

36 Tom Flanagan and David Coletto, "Replacing Allowances for Canada's National Political Parties?" University of Calgary, *The School of Public Policy SPP Briefing Papers* 3 (January 2010): 1–13.

37 "Annual Advertising Expense Limit," Elections Manitoba website, http://www.electionsmanitoba.ca/en/Political_Financing/annual_limit.html.

38 Harold J. Jansen and Lisa Young, "Solidarity Forever? The NDP, Organized Labour, and the Changing Face of Party Finance in Canada," *Canadian Journal of Political Science* 42 (2009): 672–74.

7

Jonathan Rose

Are Negative Ads Positive? Political Advertising and the Permanent Campaign

Since 2004, Canadians have had four national elections. Except for the 2011 election, each of these has returned a minority government, something that has not happened since the three minority Parliaments in 1962, 1963, and 1965. While we probably will not have another election until 2015, the succession of minority governments has had an obvious impact not only on governing but also on how political parties behave during and between elections.

This chapter will explore two significant consequences of this latest period of minority parliaments. First, we will examine the changes to political parties that now operate in a permanent campaign. In the process, we will attempt to explain why we are in a permanent campaign and how this "new normal" affects the behaviour of both political parties and governments. Second, we will explore the changing nature of political party advertising. Political parties, as a consequence of the permanent campaign, have relied to greater extent on advertising both during and between elections. This has resulted in increasing attention by the media on how parties advertise and in a concern about the alleged increase in negative political advertising. While much has been made of how corrosive this has been to the practice of politics, I will argue, following the work of John Geer, that negative ads deserve a second look. Far from the narrative that appears in the media, they can improve the quality of our political conversation.

MINORITY GOVERNMENTS AND THE PERMANENT CAMPAIGN

While minority governments are not a new phenomenon, the rise of the Bloc Québécois as a strong regional party has made them a more likely occurrence than in the past. In *Two Cheers for Minority Government*, Peter Russell discusses their relative frequency in Westminister systems, noting that Canada has had thirteen minority governments. The UK has had eighteen, five since 1900.[1] The next four years will see a stable majority Parliament, but the behaviour of all parties has been conditioned by this latest period of minority governments.

The success of minority governments is dependent on the prime minister's ability to forge informal coalitions with other parties. Lester B. Pearson's significant legislative accomplishments in the creation of the Canada Pension Plan, a national medicare program, and a new flag, to name three, are proof of their potential. The situation most congenial for them, according to Russell, is a one-party minority government with "an informal but steady alliance of the governing party with an opposition party."[2] The NDP's support of Trudeau's minority in 1972 and the Progressives' support of Mackenzie King's minority government are examples of this. In such an arrangement—or in a more formal codified arrangement, such as the accord between Ontario Liberal leader David Peterson, who became premier, and NDP leader Bob Rae in 1985—the government must work with opposition parties to maintain the confidence of the legislature. In the last three versions of minorities (from 2004 to 2011), the Harper government operated under neither of these arrangements. The result was an unstable Parliament that had little confidence about the timing of an election, and this instability led to all parties being on a permanent campaign footing. "The constant election fever that infects them is the most frequently cited problem," says Russell about minority Parliaments generally.[3] During this period, parliamentary instability shaped the behaviour of parties and changed the way they communicated in the periods both leading up to and during an election campaign.

In such an era of hyperpartisanship, the media play an important role in correcting misinformation but often fall short of that goal. They were largely silent when, in 2008, Stephen Harper incorrectly said, "Mr. Dion does not have the right to be prime minister without an election." With the ambiguity of the legal status of a coalition government, an issue that was raised again in the 2011 election, it is no surprise, then, that a poll commissioned by the Dominion Institute found that 51 percent of Canadians incorrectly believed that voters directly elected the prime minister.[4] Media coverage is seen as a contest between leaders rather than as a discussion of policy differences, a problem compounded by the existence of brokerage parties. In the 2008 election, for example, media coverage of party leaders and the strategic horse race frame dominated the content of stories in the English media.[5]

Competing with a 24-hour news cycle, the existence of cable TV, and now the Internet and the blogosphere, the media are confined to reporting what is episodic and ephemeral rather than thematic and enduring. The fluidity of media topics in the 2011 election speaks to this.[6] The explosion of information that is discrete, targeted, and unrelenting has been described by David Taras as "fragmentation bombs."[7] This dominant style of reporting places a premium on dissecting the minutiae of events and personalities. The drama associated with the Conservatives' claim of the possibility of a "reckless coalition" fit existing media narratives well: it had a clear story line (on the opposition side, righteously taking back power or, from the government's perspective, preventing the opposition from stealing power) and strong characters (David and Goliath as the opposition and government). Combined with the visuals of "spontaneous" coalition rallies across the country, this drama provided a perfect example of what Daniel Boorstin calls a "pseudo-event." In the 2011 election, an example of the emphasis on events rather than substance can be found in the coverage related to a young woman who was prohibited entry to a Conservative rally because she had a photo of herself and Michael Ignatieff on her Facebook page.

In 2011, the permanent campaign was aided by insecurity about the timing of an election but was also related to the coverage of adjuncts of election campaigns and the process of covering them. Here, symbolic stories that report a party's leasing of a campaign airplane, the details of cross-Canada tours of cabinet ministers, and, of course, the content of new election-priming ad campaigns all become fodder for the media. In the last election, much was made about the fact that the media were allotted only five questions at any

Conservative Party event or that the prime minister rarely deviated from his prepared script or controlled environment.

There may be another reason why the media focus on the process of politics rather than its substance. This has to do with the effectiveness and duration of Parliament. First, the average number of sitting days per year has steadily declined from 163 in the 1969–73 parliamentary session to 105 in the 2004–8 session, a 35 percent drop over that period.[8] Second, and perhaps as a consequence of this, the ability of governments, both majority and minority, to pass their legislative agenda has fallen precipitously over the last fifty years. The minority government of Pearson in 1963 had a 90 percent success rate of government bills receiving royal assent. That fell to 78 percent for the majority Trudeau government from 1980 to 1984 and 69 percent for the Chrétien governments from 1993 to 2004. The performance of the recent minority governments shows a similar trend. Whereas the Martin minority in 2004 was successful 60 percent of the time, Harper, from 2006 to 2008, was only able to pass 8 percent of his government's bills, a number that rose to 48 percent in 2009.[9]

These data relate to another reason for the permanent campaign: Parliament is less frequently the place where national issues are resolved and discussed. Until the most recent election, our electoral system, designed to deliver majority governments that are stable and able to pass comprehensive agendas, failed to produce the very values it was designed to support. Instead, it created "a succession of regimes so fragile that the campaign for the next election begins with the first Speech from the Throne."[10]

The redefined role of political parties might also suggest why they are on a permanent campaign footing. John Meisel, in his 1991 classic work on the decline of parties, correctly predicted the increasing significance of advertising agencies, public relations advisors, and other spin doctors in what he called "the grand strategy of parties."[11] Since his writing, the influence on parties of PR agencies, pollsters, and advertisers has become all-encompassing. Meisel describes its latest version as the "Harperization of our Minds," in which the Conservative Party has become the tool of PR and advertising agencies.[12] Party members serve as a backdrop for PR firms in communicating their arguments about how best to sell the party. The purpose of the party organization is now to be a network for the dissemination of ideas that have been focus-group tested and marketed, and appropriately branded.

The blurring of party and government interests through the media management strategies of PR firms is a widespread phenomenon that transcends party ideology. In Alberta, the influence of PR on government was institutionalized through the establishment of the Public Affairs Bureau, a quasi-independent office that reported directly to the premier's office. Created under Premier Peter Lougheed in 1972 for coordinating communications, it was transformed by Premier Ralph Klein into a public relations and news management agency.[13] In Saskatchewan, Premier Brad Wall hired a Toronto advertising firm in early 2010 to create negative ads against the NDP leader, well in advance of the 2011 election.[14] Kirsten Kozolanka writes about the importance of PR firms in selling the new right-wing policies of the Mike Harris government in Ontario.[15] In the UK, the influence of spin doctors in Tony Blair's government became so controversial that it led to the Phillis Inquiry, which examined the practices of government communications.[16]

The political marketing of parties affects what the media do. Esser, Reineman, and Fan found that British newspapers dedicate two to three times more coverage to spin-doctoring activities of parties than do their counterparts in Germany, where PR is less pervasive.[17] The relationships among parties, the media, and marketing firms are symbiotic. The media report on the PR activities of parties and, in doing so, further perpetuate the process-dominated frame of the media.

The role of social media such as Facebook, Twitter, and YouTube, and the use of the Internet by political parties have been cited as another reason for our permanent campaign. While Tamara Small discusses this in greater detail elsewhere in this volume, the Facebook group "Canadians Against Proroguing Parliament" (CAPP) in late 2009 and early 2010 is a strong example of the use of social media. CAPP, which attracted a quarter of a million members in days, shows the capacity of social media sites like Facebook nominally to engage citizens who might not normally participate in political parties.[18]

Alternative party websites can supplement the political marketing of parties. These websites—such as the Not a Leader website (notaleader.ca), which poked fun at Stéphane Dion in 2008, or, in the 2011 election, ShitHarperDid.ca—are useful for parties in two ways. First, they represent a push form of communication whose content is distributed by others. If done successfully, they have the capacity to go "viral" through forwarding via email and posting on websites. Unlike traditional advertising, political parties are not involved in their dissemination but merely provide the platform to facilitate it. The second, and arguably more valuable, purpose of social media and alternative websites is the media coverage that results from these viral websites or videos.

The amount of media coverage devoted to the appropriateness of the "pooping puffin" on the Not a Leader site suggests that the real purpose was to use provocative images to drive viewers to the site. It also demonstrates the potential of viral media to backfire. The media response to the website varied from calling it "mischief making" to more serious allegations of lapsed judgment.[19] A year later, in 2009, it was the Liberals' turn to apologize. An online contest on the party's website asked supporters to post edited pictures of Stephen Harper being "Anywhere but Copenhagen" to draw attention to his planned absence at an international climate change summit. The offending photo that crossed the line was that of Harper on Lee Harvey Oswald's body as he is killed by Jack Ruby. The Liberal Party seemed to be endorsing—at least visually—the assassination of the prime minister. Like the pooping puffin, the negative attention that this garnered far overshadowed the policy point that the website was trying to make.[20] Every election seems to be marked by a new social media. If 2008 was the YouTube election, 2011 was the Twitter Revolution. Yaroslav Baran suggests that the most important effect of social media in this election was that Twitter was novel, sped up the dissemination of communications, and provided "oxygen for a developing story" by allowing journalists to quickly test ideas for a story.[21] If not Twitter, the legacy of this election may be the mobilization of vote mobs on university campuses and the media coverage that a small group of students can generate.

The permanent campaign has also been abetted by changes, both legislative and behavioural, in party fundraising rules. The legislative changes came about first in 2003 through Bill C-24, which amended the *Canada Elections Act*, and later through changes in 2006. The 2003 amendments placed limits on individual donations and a ban on corporate and union contributions. While this changed the rules of the game substantively, fundraising as an important activity of parties has also changed the nature of the game. As Tom Flanagan notes elsewhere in this volume, the Conservatives have been the most successful fundraisers since the 2004 election. This has had two consequences. First, the infusion of cash has been spent between elections, when there are no regulations, rather than during elections, when there is a spending limit. The most visible manifestation of the non-election spending is the increase in political advertisements. The second consequence of this fundraising success is that the Conservatives are the party least dependent on state subsidies for their revenue. State support for parties came from three sources: a $2-a-vote subsidy, tax rebates to individuals on political contributions, and a subsidy of 50 percent on a party's national election campaign. The ability of Conservatives to fundraise successfully means that public support constitutes a smaller share of their total revenue. This gave the Conservative government the impetus to phase out, over three years, the per-vote subsidy for all political parties beginning in 2012.

The disparity in fundraising between political parties is striking. In 2009 and 2010, the Conservatives raised $17 million each year, compared to the Liberals, who raised $7 million in 2010, and the NDP, with $3.9 million in 2009.[22] In 2008, the Conservatives were the first party to raise more than $20 million, a significant number since this is the limit imposed per party on election expenses. Successful fundraising is, in part, related to the resources allocated to fundraising. Fundraising becomes a means (to fundraise further) as well an end in itself. Here, too, the Conservatives far outstrip other parties. In 2008, they spent $7 to $8 million on fundraising, compared to $2 million for the Liberals and $1.8 million for the NDP. These new rules embodied in the changes to limits on political contributions as well as the changes in practice of political parties have had significant repercussions on how parties behave between elections.

PARTY ADVERTISING IN A MEDIA-SATURATED ENVIRONMENT

One of the most visible effects of changed rules related to election financing is the ubiquity of party advertising. It is important to recall that advertising occurs both during elections and now, more significantly, between elections. In both instances, very few limits are placed on what or how a political party can communicate. In Canada, party advertising during elections is modestly regulated compared to other countries, but the prohibitions are few. Parties cannot broadcast on election day and all party advertising must be endorsed by political parties.[23]

Other countries impose greater limits on party advertising during elections. The United Kingdom prohibits election advertising, favouring party election broadcasts, which are longer than our political spots and are allocated according to electoral strength, giving minor parties access to public airwaves. In Germany, the principle that underlies broadcasting ads is "equal opportunity for all parties" and parties are sold airtime at a rate lower than commercial advertising. Moreover, if a TV station accepts ads from one party, it must accept them from all. In Finland and Israel, the content of political advertising is restricted. While comparative party ads are allowed in Finland, negative ads directed at the leader are not. In Israel, military images of any kind are banned from election advertising. Had such a rule been adopted here, the controversial 2004 Liberal ad that showed a tank and gun pointed at the camera would have been prohibited. This incendiary ad used a military drumbeat as a sound track and—with a series of quick visual cuts of tanks, troops, an aircraft carrier, and smog-congested cities—implied that Stephen Harper's motives were not to be trusted. Critics felt that the claims made in the ad through images and the voice-over were without basis.

The justification for not placing excessive constraints on party advertising during elections is based on a number of principles. The first is to ensure a "free marketplace of ideas." Allowing political parties to engage one another and, by extension, the voter and the media, is deemed to have a salubrious effect on democracy. Other than televised debates and, increasingly, party websites, in our system, election ads provide the only opportunity for political parties to have unmediated access to the voter. Ads tell us the priorities of competing parties and the differences in their policy platforms. In short, they are, in Stanley Cunningham's words, a "form of argument." He describes ads as "narrative structures" that tap into larger mythic stories about national values or aspirational leadership.[24] Ads can provide information shortcuts to simplify and distill policies and platforms, taking advantage of the low level of political knowledge among voters.[25] These condensed symbols perform the legitimate democratic goals of obtaining, storing, and evaluating information, according to Samuel Popkin.[26] In other words, political advertising can allow a voter to remember and quickly retrieve an issue or policy position from a candidate or political party.

Increased knowledge is certainly one product of political ads, but our responses to these ads is another legitimate product. Advertising allows a political party to transfer positive or negative feelings toward itself or another party. While this can be understood as preying on the hopes and fears of voters, Ted Brader finds a link between the degree of political sophistication of a voter and the effect that ads might have on them. His research shows that our ability to be swayed by political advertising is related to how much political knowledge we have; as Brader puts it, "Knowing and caring seem to go hand in hand after all."[27] Regulating the content of political ads, therefore, may have some impact on the ability of these ads to transmit knowledge but also to provide memorable shorthand cues.

Advertising by political parties during elections might be an example of path dependency: it is used because communications firms that run elections have always used advertising as a vehicle of persuasion. But does it work? On this question, the research is decidedly mixed: the best answer is that advertising is effective sometimes on some issues by some parties. Subsequent research has both revised and reinforced these findings.

Research on political advertising has used various measurements as a proxy to test advertising effectiveness. Nicholas O'Shaughnessy found that viewers recalled 80 percent of political ads versus only 20 percent of commercial ads.[28] Others, like Tony Schwartz, argue that recall is an improper barometer for political ads and that political affect is more important.[29] The problem with measuring affect is that except in very controlled experimental settings, it is difficult to separate the impact of the ad from the media coverage of the ad from discussions with a friend about the ad. Kathleen Hall Jamieson's work on political advertising argues that the grammar of a political spot—the verbal and visual way an argument is crafted in an ad—is an important way to judge its success.[30] Still others have sought to understand political advertising by categorizing ads as either issue oriented or image based.[31] Collectively, this research points to very different conclusions about the impact of political advertising on voters' attitudes and behaviour.

Notwithstanding this lack of consensus about its effectiveness, political parties in Canada embrace advertising. During elections, it consumes a significant share of a party's expenses. Table 7.1 shows the total advertising expenditures as a share of the total expenses in the last three federal elections for which data are available. Two interesting trends are evident. The first is that even accounting for inflation, total advertising expenses of the three national political parties have increased over the last four elections. The other noteworthy trend in these elections is that in general, advertising has assumed a greater share of all parties' election expenses. This suggests that advertising has become more important to the communication strategy of parties during elections.

Table 7.1   Political party election advertising expenses, 2004–11

	Total advertising expenses (in thousands)	Percent of total election expenses
2011 federal election (41st general election)		
Conservative	10.6	54
Liberal	11.9	61
NDP	10.9	54
2008 federal election (40th general election)		
Conservative	10.5	54
Liberal	8.0	55
NDP	8.3	50
2006 federal election (39th general election)		
Conservative	9.1	50
Liberal	9.4	54
NDP	5.8	43
2004 federal election (38th general election)		
Conservative	7.2	42
Liberal	10.3	62
NDP	5.3	44

SOURCE: Elections Canada, Financial Reports of Political Parties, "Registered Political Parties' Returns in Respect of General Election Expenses," 2004, 2006, 2008, and 2011, http://www.elections.ca/content.aspx?section=fin&document=index&dir=pol/dep&lang=e.

The fundraising success of the Conservative Party has translated into increased advertising expenditures between elections as well as during elections. In 2008, the Conservatives spent $11 million on non-election advertising, in addition to the significant amount spent on election advertising. In the last four non-election years for which data are available, there is a significant disparity among political parties on non-election advertising. Table 7.2 shows that in 2005, the Conservatives outspent the Liberals in advertising by two to one. In the same year, the NDP outspent the Liberals in advertising, perhaps because the media attention to the Gomery inquiry was a liability to Liberal fundraising abilities. The Gomery Commission's first report, in November of that year, may have adversely affected the Liberals' advertising efforts. In 2007, the aggregate amount spent on advertising was down, reflecting the toll on all parties of two elections in the previous three years. But although parties spent less in 2007, the gulf between the Conservative and Liberal advertising budgets had widened significantly. The Tories were now spending five times as much as the Liberals on advertising. In 2009, aggregate amounts on advertising by the Liberals and Conservatives increased but the Conservatives outspent the Liberals by four to one. In 2010, the Conservatives spent twice as much as the Liberals on advertising. While the Conservative amount decreased significantly from the previous year, in 2010, the federal Conservative government spent $136 million on advertising its Economic Stimulus Plan, a central plank in the 2011 election campaign.

It is clear that advertising is an essential element in the arsenal of political parties during elections. The reality of a permanent campaign, brought on in part by a succession of minority governments, suggests that this phenomenon is not confined to the writ period. Since 2004, citizens have witnessed election-style ads with greater frequency in non-election years. In addition to structural reasons, this change might be attributed to the relatively cheaper access to social media as well as leadership factors such as the succession of Liberal party leaders.

The media headlines make it clear that political advertising between elections is newsworthy. If we were to believe the way advertising is discussed in the media, we would see ourselves in a world dominated by increasingly negative advertising.[32] Throughout the media coverage of political advertising are the oft-made claims that party ads are becoming increasingly vitriolic and that this mudslinging is contributing to public disillusionment with politics.

Some academics argue that negative political advertising has a corrosive effect on the practice of politics.[33] In the United States, scholars such as Darrell West claim that negativity has been the most common form of advertising for presidential elections for decades.[34] Ansolabehere and Iyengar are particularly critical of how parties employ ads to demobilize voters, turning citizens off politics and discouraging them from voting.[35] Their research found that in controlled settings, voters were less likely to vote if subjected to negative ads. While much of the literature on negative advertising originates in the United States, Canadian scholars too have worried about the importation of American-style advertising to Canada.[36] It might be time to put some of these assumptions to the test and scrutinize whether parties are using negative advertising as much as the media claim. The balance of this chapter will examine the advertising during the 2008 election, the extent to which political ads in Canada are in fact negative, and if they are, whether this poses a problem.

Table 7.2   Political party advertising in non-election years

	Total advertising expenses (in thousands)
2010	
Conservative	552.6
Liberal	231
NDP	359
2009	
Conservative	4,786
Liberal	1,094
NDP	506
2007	
Conservative	4,194
Liberal	792
NDP	699
2005	
Conservative	6,300
Liberal	2,950
NDP	3,470

SOURCE: Elections Canada, Financial Reports of Political Parties, "Statements of Assets and Liabilities and Statements of Revenues and Expenses," http://www.elections.ca/content.aspx?section=fin&document=index&dir=pol/asset&lang=e.

There are many memorable negative political ads and a few that we wish we could forget. We might recall, for instance, the infamous "Daisy" ad broadcast just once in 1964 by Lyndon Johnson against his opponent, Barry Goldwater. This ad portrayed a young girl picking the petals off a daisy; as she counts down from ten her voice changes to a male voice counting down a rocket launching. The ad ends with a nuclear explosion and a voice-over intoning "Vote for President Johnson on November 3rd. The stakes are too high for you to stay home." Perhaps we think of the Conservatives' 1993 ad "Is this a prime minister?" which showed a still image of Jean Chrétien's face highlighting his facial paralysis. The ad seemed to be questioning his fitness to be prime minister. More recently, we have seen the Liberals' ad titled "Harper and the Conservatives" or the Conservatives' "Just Visiting" ad of 2009, which challenged the Liberal leader's commitment to Canada. These ads—while sharing the qualities of being evocative and quite aggressive—are not similar to one another. Some are based on physical traits or a candidate's history ("Is this a prime minister?" and "Just Visiting") whereas others are implicitly negative by association only ("Daisy"). The suite of Liberal ads that included "Harper and the Conservatives" focused on policy issues rather than on personal characteristics of leaders.

Some negative ads are clearly more acceptable than others. Ads that draw attention to policy differences, even though they may make use of stark images to make that point, should be part of the thrust and parry of political argumentation. Ads that contrast one party's position with another, such as the 1988 Liberal ads, which raised fears of free trade by literally erasing our borders, should also be fair game. In the 2011 election, the Green Party's "Change the Channel on Attack Ads" sought to use the proliferation of attack ads to highlight the difference between them and other parties. These negative ads, which focus on issues rather than personal traits, constitute by far the majority of negative ads, according to the research of John Geer, whose expansive definition of negativity is "any criticism leveled by one candidate against another."[37] Because he is interested in presidential ads, Geer's analysis is limited to presidential candidates during elections. We will use his definition of negativity and add parties as our object of study.

The diverse style of negative ads raises the question of how we should judge the legitimacy of negative political advertising. On normative democratic grounds, most would agree that advertising should be *encouraged* if it helps fill in the information void of most voters. We might think of informational ads as attempts to fill this void, but in politics, negative ads are usually information rich. Geer provides us with several useful criteria to access negative advertising.[38] He believes that negative ads are worthy if they help voters to know certain personal characteristics of leaders. Competence, experience, trust, and integrity, for example, are important proxies for leadership and contribute to needed voter information. Even so, negative ads are more likely to be based on policy differences than personality. In his study of the tone of presidential ads from 1960 to 2000, Geer found that negative ads were four times as likely to be based on issues than on personal traits.[39]

Ads are legitimate if they provide evidence to support their claims, and negative ads are more likely than positive ads to include evidence. All thirty-second spots are a condensed argument. Like all arguments, they comprise a claim (what is the ad saying?), the evidence (what data supports the claim?), and the warrant (what are the assumptions that support the two?). In the last election, Conservative ads made the claim that Michael Ignatieff would lead a "reckless coalition." Broadcast throughout the NHL playoffs in 2011, when the audience was large, they were negative and repetitive and failed to provide any solid evidence. All the same, the ad may have been effective because, like the campaign it mirrored, its strength was based on sheer repetition. It also provides a good counterargument to the claim that all negative ads have value.

Often because negative ads are so polarizing, the mass media and voters are more likely to scrutinize them for evidence than they do positive ads. Indeed, positive biopic ads, which extol humble beginnings or honesty, are rarely examined for evidence as closely as negative ads, which tend to contain more information. The result, as Bob Squier says, is that "most lies in politics are told in positive ads."[40] If more evidence can be found in negative ads than in positive ads, it follows that voters are better served by an information-rich negative campaign than by a positive campaign that does little to engage issues or ideas.

A third criterion used to assess negative ads is whether they focus on issues on which leaders or parties disagree. If there is a divergence in policy, advertising can be a legitimate vehicle to create a bright line. The normative grounds for such a justification is that if elections are about a contest of ideas, and if advertising exposes different ideas, then negative ads serve that democratic goal of informing the electorate and giving voters rational bases on which to make their choice at the ballot box. Some of the most famous negative ads, however, have implied differences where none existed, exploiting the assumption that voters have about the purpose of these ads. The Conservatives' "Soft on Crime Doesn't Work" ad in the 2008 federal election is an example of an ad that makes an implicit claim about a distinction that does not exist: the ad implies but does not state that the Liberals are soft on crime.

The final criterion for evaluating negative ads is whether their focus is relevant to governing. Ads that draw attention to superfluous issues such as gender or physical appearance (as did the 1993 "facial paralysis" ad) would clearly be out of bounds. This criterion would also judge the Conservatives' "Cosmopolitan" ad (June 2009), which criticized Michael Ignatieff for being a "citizen of the world" and "owning a luxury condominium in Toronto," as failing to meet the criterion of relevance. But the large number of negative ads broadcast by parties in 1988 around the free trade issue would be considered legitimate.

To summarize, negative advertisements are acceptable if they are about issues, if they provide evidence, if they delineate differences in candidates' positions, and if their focus is relevant to governing. On this basis, how do the three parties' ads score in the 2008 election ads? We examined a total of thirty-six English-language ads, eleven each for the NDP and the Liberals and fourteen for the Conservatives, using a simple binary division between negative (as Geer defines it, above) and not negative. By this measure, eight (73%) of the NDP election ads were negative, seven (64%) of the Liberal ads were negative, and six (43%) of the Conservatives ads were negative. To a degree, then, the perception of the 2008 election as being dominated by negative ads was correct. The Conservatives had the lowest number because of the "sofa series" ads, which featured Stephen Harper sitting on a sofa discussing his values. These feel-good ads were designed to reframe Harper as a family man (in "Family Is Everything"), as compassionate (in "A Nation of Immigrants"), and as patriotic (in "Lest We Forget"). The NDP scored higher on the negativity rating because all four of their "chalk talk" ads used contrast to disparage other parties. Taking a page from the Liberal playbook, one of the NDP ads, "A New Kind of Strong," had a soundtrack very similar to that of the Liberals' infamous 2006 negative ads that featured austere text accompanied by a militaristic sounding drum. The Liberal 2008 ads either focused on the Green Shift and Dion's support for the environment or used policy differences to attack Stephen Harper. Though the majority of the collective ads by the three parties were negative, they largely meet the criteria of acceptable negative ads.

What is quite striking about all parties' ads in terms of their arguments is that the negative ads are more likely than the non-negative ads to include evidence. Every one of the negative Liberal ads had evidence to support its claims. This usually took the form of newspaper quotes, text from speeches, or data from government or NGO reports. Only half of the fourteen Conservative ads had some evidence and the NDP ads were largely exhortative. Only one of the eleven English-language NDP ads had any evidence: the balance made claims about the economy, prosperity, or the environment without any evidence.[41] In the past, an argument might have been made that as the party that spent the least on election advertising, the NDP needed to make more assertive and bolder claims in its ads just to get the attention of voters. As table 7.1 shows, however, in the 2008 election, the NDP outspent the Liberals on advertising, making them an equal player on that front. The higher negativity of their ads, as well as their relative lack of evidence, may instead reflect the strategy of a party that needed to criticize the government as well as distance itself from the Liberals. This element was found in all their ads.

Negative ads are also justifiable if they further a discussion about a policy. In terms of engagement with issues, all three parties' ads in the 2008 election scored well. The Liberals scored highest on this test because all their negative ads were issue focused, although some, like the ad "New Low," used policy to make claims about the leadership ability of Stephen Harper. On the surface, this ad was about an outbreak of listeriosis-tainted meat, but its real point was to draw attention to Harper's support of his minister who made off-colour jokes about opposition members acquiring the disease. Because of the centrality of the Green Shift in the Liberal platform and because of the complexity of this central plank, five of the eleven English-language Liberal ads examined were about the environment, with the remaining being about economics. The Conservatives ran six negative ads, all of which were policy focused. Only one of their positive ads ("Lest We Forget") was about an issue. The rest consisted of vague statements about Harper's values, such as "I see people who are excited about the possibility of new opportunities" ("A Nation of Immigrants") or "There's no more exciting place for me, as a Canadian, than to go North" ("True North Strong and Free"). These feel-good ads were treated in the media more with gentle bemusement than as the vapid, informationless sound bites they were.

The harshest criticism of the Conservative's negative advertising was reserved for their "Gamble" series, which used a scratch-and-play lottery ticket labelled "Dion's Scratch 'n Lose." This series of three ads ran through a number of proposals by the Liberals with the tagline "You lose." These information-dense ads raised issues about the Liberals' position on the GST, a child care benefit, and a carbon tax. Though they failed the test of providing evidence to support their claims, they were about policy rather than personality.

With the exception of two of the eleven NDP ads, all were about a specific policy and all but one of their negative ads were issue-specific. More than the other parties, in the 2008 election, the NDP ads followed a template that saw Jack Layton narrate the party's position on different issues. Because their ads were largely exhortative, most of them lacked evidence, but they served the purpose of providing information to voters about various planks in their platform such as the economy, environment, leadership, or health care.

The final test for negative advertising is whether they speak about issues relevant to the voter. If they do, they can be said to be providing information to help determine voter choice. Negative ads are often derided for being about the superfluous, but what we find is that, with few exceptions, the negative ads of all three national parties in the 2008 election were relevant to the voter in that they discussed either policy issues or questions of leadership. One of the few notable exceptions was the Liberals' "New Low" ad, which attempted to link a health issue (listeriosis) to leadership. The connection was tenuous and, arguably, the issue was not a salient one in the campaign.

In the Conservatives' advertising campaign, only 43 percent of the ads passed the relevance test. The remaining 57 percent consisted of the "sofa series" of ads, which were positive ads but did not focus on relevant issues. Only one of the eleven NDP ads, a negative one, failed the relevance test: "A New Kind of Strong" responded to the claim that the Conservatives had "strong leadership" (a claim never made in any Conservative ads) by equating strong leadership with a number of economic, environmental, and health failures. The punchline was Jack Layton saying, "The new strong is about fighting for what's right for you." While leadership is certainly a relevant issue in an election campaign, this ad set up a straw man to pull it down.

The 2011 election saw mudslinging ads from all three national parties, suggesting that negative political ads are unlikely to decrease any time soon, for a number of reasons. First, these ads are much more memorable than positive ads, in part because they contain information that aids in understanding politics but also because they have emotional impact. Ted Brader's research demonstrates the importance of emotions in political ads. Positive ads that elicit the emotion of enthusiasm are likely to reinforce status quo beliefs, whereas negative ads that play on fear are more likely to alter the bases of political judgment by causing the viewer to seek out information that either corroborates or repudiates the message of the ad.[42] Because of their visual cues (e.g., tanks) or soundtrack (e.g., drumbeat), or even their form of presentation (e.g., filmed in black and white or animated), negative ads draw our attention to the party's message and resonate with us. Second, negative ads are an attempt by political parties to cut through the thicket of information overload. Communication scholars note that entropic messages—ones that have a high amount of novel information and are unexpected—are more likely to be remembered than redundant messages that reinforce existing knowledge and are routine in their delivery. Negative ads exemplify entropic communication. Related to this is the third reason why negative advertising is likely to continue. The media coverage of negative advertising provides a strong incentive for political parties to use advertising to gain earned or free media.

Canadian political parties are in a permanent campaign brought about by a number of factors that are structural (electoral system, party financing), evolutionary (parties' fundraising abilities, their increasing reliance on public relations firms, and their use of the Internet, including social media), and circumstantial (the destabilizing effect of having four Liberal leaders in five years). As a result, political parties use advertising with greater intensity than they have in the past.

Negative election advertising may have a place in democratic practice. In this chapter, I examined some of the ads in the 2008 federal election to make a case that while all parties use negative ads, it may be time to analyze them with a view to helping voters evaluate them and make decisions at the ballot box. In the past, negative ads have been condemned in and of themselves; they have been seen as a poor form of communication that cheapens our democratic currency. A closer examination, though, suggests that they might have a legitimate role in providing information during an election campaign.

NOTES

1   Peter Russell, *Two Cheers for Minority Government: The Evolution of Canadian Parliamentary Democracy* (Toronto: Emond Montgomery, 2008), 85.

2   Peter Russell, "Learning to Live with Minority Parliaments," in *Parliamentary Democracy in Crisis*, ed. Peter Russell and Lorne Sossin (Toronto: University of Toronto Press, 2009), 35.

3   Russell, *Two Cheers for Minority Government*, 133.

4   Ipsos Reid, "In Wake of Constitutional Crisis, New Survey Demonstrates That Canadians

Lack Basic Understanding of Our Parliamentary System," news release, December 15, 2008, http://www.dominion.ca/DominionInstituteDecember15Factum.pdf.

5 Blake Andrew, Lori Young, and Stuart Soroka, "Back to the Future: Press Coverage of the 2008 Canadian Election Campaign Strikes Both Familiar and Unfamiliar Notes," *Policy Options* 29 (November 2008): 79–84.

6 Media Observatory, "2011 Canadian Federal Newspaper Analysis," McGill Institute for the Study of Canada, McGill University, Media Report, 1 May 2011, http://www.mcgill.ca/misc/research/media-observatory/election2011/.

7 David Taras, *Power and Betrayal in the Canadian Media* (Peterborough: Broadview Press, 2001), 93.

8 C.E.S. Franks, "Parliament and Public Policy: What's to Be Done?" presentation at the Public Policy Forum, "Inside Ottawa: Back to School," Ottawa, Canada, September 9, 2009. (The PowerPoint slides are available at http://www.ppforum.com/events/inside-ottawa-back-school.)

9 Ibid.

10 John Ibbitson, "Six Years, Four Elections: This Political Dysfunction Could Break Us," *Globe and Mail*, September 14, 2009.

11 John Meisel, "The Decline of Party in Canada," in *Party Politics in Canada*, 6th ed., ed. Hugh G. Thorburn (Scarborough: Prentice Hall, 1991), 195.

12 John Meisel, "'Harperizing' Our Minds," *Toronto Star*, April 19, 2011.

13 Simon Kiss, "Selling Government: The Evolution of Government Public Relations in Alberta from 1971–2006" (PhD diss., Queen's University, 2008), chap. 3.

14 Brian Topp, "Bomb the Bridge," *Globe and Mail*, January 21, 2010.

15 Kristen Kozolanka, *Politics of Persuasion: The Politics of the New Right in Ontario* (Montreal: Black Rose, 2007).

16 See for a discussion of Blair's reliance on spin doctors. Nicholas Jones, *Soundbites and Spin Doctors: How Politicians Manipulate the Media—and Vice Versa* (London: Indigo, 2001).

17 Frank Esser, Carsten Reineman, and David Fan, "Spin Doctoring in British and German Electoral Campaigns: How the Press Is Being Confronted with a New Quality of Political PR," *European Journal of Communication* 15 (June 2000): 209–39.

18 Michael Valpy, "Facebook Forums Shouldn't Sway Government, Pollsters Told," *Globe and Mail*, February 18, 2010.

19 Jane Taber, "Pooping Puffin Pulled from Tory Ad," *Globe and Mail*, September 9, 2008.

20 Jane Taber, "Altered Photo on Liberal Website Draws Mea Culpa," *Globe and Mail*, December 16, 2010.

21 Yaroslav Baran, "Social Media in Campaign 2011: A Noncanonical Take on the Twitter Effect," *Policy Options* 32 (June–July 2011): 82–85.

22 Return Details—Summary of Contributions and Transfers, "Financial Reports: Registered Parties Financial Returns," Elections Canada, www.elections.ca.

23 *Canada Elections Act*, Sections 323 and 320.

24 Stanley Cunningham, "The Theory and Use of Political Advertising," in *Television*

Advertising in Canadian Elections: The Attack Mode 1993, ed. Walter I. Romanow et al. (Waterloo: Wilfrid Laurier University Press, 1999), 19.

25 Phillip Converse, "The Nature of Belief Systems in Mass Publics," in *Ideology and Discontent, ed. David E. Apter* (New York: Free Press, 1964); Robert C. Luskin, "Measuring Political Sophistication," *American Journal of Political Science* 31 (November 1987): 856–99.

26 Samuel L. Popkin, *The Reasoning Voter: Communication and Persuasion in Presidential Campaigns* (Chicago: University of Chicago Press, 1991), 44.

27 Ted Brader, *Campaigning for the Hearts and Minds: How Emotional Appeals in Political Ads Work* (Chicago: University of Chicago Press, 2006), 103.

28 Nicholas O'Shaughnessy, *The Phenomenon of Political Marketing* (New York: St. Martin's Press, 1990), 28.

29 See Tony Schwartz, *The Responsive Chord* (New York: Anchor Books, 1973).

30 Kathleen Hall Jamieson, *Dirty Politics: Deception, Distraction and Democracy* (New York: Oxford, 1992), 30.

31 Anne Johnston and Lynda Lee Kaid, "Image Ads and Issue Ads in U.S. Presidential Advertising: Using Videostyle to Explore Stylistic Differences in Televised Political Ads from 1952 to 2000," *Journal of Communication* 52 (June 2000): 281–300.

32 See, for example, Jeffrey Simpson's articles, "Stephen Harper's Legacy: Politics Is War," *Globe and Mail*, June 6, 2009; "Attack Ads Work—And It's Pointless to Resist," *Globe and Mail*, September 9, 2008; "Attack Ads: Kaboom or Bust," *Globe and Mail*, September 5, 2008; and "Harper Has 'Something to Hide,'" *Globe and Mail*, January 10, 2010.

33 See, for example, Thomas Patterson, *The Vanishing Voter* (New York: Knopf, 2002).

34 Darrell West, *Air Wars: Television Advertising in Election Campaigns, 1952–2008* (Washington, D C: CQ Press, 2009).

35 See Stephen Ansolabehere and Shanto Iyengar, *Going Negative: How Political Advertisements Shrink and Polarize the Electorate* (New York: Free Press, 1995).

36 See Jonathan Rose, "The Liberals Reap What They Sow: Why Their Negative Ads Failed," *Policy Options* 27 (March 2006): 80–84; and Paul Nesbitt-Larking and Jonathan Rose, "Political Advertising in Canada," in *Lights, Camera, Action: Media Politics and Political Advertising, ed. David Schultz* (New York: Peter Lang, 2004).

37 John Geer, *In Defense of Negativity: Attack Ads in Presidential Campaigns* (Chicago: University of Chicago Press, 2006), 23.

38 Ibid., 46–47.

39 Ibid., 68.

40 Quoted in ibid., 5.

41 For the one ad that included evidence, see "Chalk Talk—The Economy," YouTube, http://www.youtube.com/watch?v=J2gC-fvhRrY.

42 Brader, *Campaigning for the Hearts and Minds*, 129–31.

Tamara A. Small

E-ttack Politics: Negativity, the Internet, and Canadian Political Parties

One of the biggest digital technology stories from the 2008 American election was Barack Obama's use of social media sites. More than two million people "friended" Obama on Facebook. His Twitter page was one of the highest ranked pages for much of the election year. And the campaign also raised more than half a billion dollars online. Prominent political commentator and blogger Arianna Huffington believes that "were it not for the internet, Barack Obama would not be president."[1] One big digital technology story in the 2008 Canadian election was the "pooping puffin," a graphic of a puffin pooping on the shoulder of the Liberal Party leader Stéphane Dion that was added to the Conservative Party's Not a Leader website during the first week of the campaign. The "pooping puffin" caused considerable embarrassment for the normally gaffe-free Conservatives. The faux pas received significant media attention; according to Globe and Mail writer Jane Taber, it "distracted federal political leaders ... from their policy pronouncements and forced Stephen Harper to make a rare apology to his main rival."[2] Like the 1993 Chrétien face ads, the "pooping puffin" demonstrates what happens when negativity crosses the line.

The juxtaposition of the digital technology stories in these two elections is informative. Democracy and the Internet seem to be inextricably linked—resulting in terms like *e-democracy, e-engagement,* and *netroots.* If Obama's significant online grassroots mobilization is considered evidence of the potentiality of e-democracy in the United States, then what does the "pooping puffin" tell us about Canadian digital politics? In this chapter, I argue that it tells us a lot. Academic research has consistently shown that regardless of the platform—whether it is websites, blogs or social networking sites—and regardless of venue, whether legislative or electoral politics, Canadian parties have not embraced e-democracy. The "pooping puffin" is emblematic of a trend in how Canadian parties actually use digital technology: the rise of attack, or perhaps e-ttack, websites. Indeed, two attack websites, Ignatieff Me! and Cheque Republic, were launched in 2009.

In this chapter, I explore online negativity in Canadian politics. To date, there is little academic literature on this topic, especially in the Canadian context. Therefore, I attempt to shed light on how Canadian parties use the Internet to go negative. Before examining how Canadian parties engage in virtual mudslinging, I begin with a discussion of how Canadian parties have thus far used the Internet. This is followed by an exploration of the concept of negative advertising, both offline and online. Online negativity in Canada is the subject of the subsequent sections, in which I detail the use of attack sites in Canada, with special attention to Ignatieff Me! and Cheque Republic, and then present an analysis of how Canadian parties use the Internet for negativity, identifying five characteristics that define Canadian attack sites. The final section situates attack sites within the Canadian party literature by exploring the concept of the permanent campaign.

HOW CANADIAN PARTIES USE THE INTERNET

Canadian political parties, candidates, and politicians have been online for more than a decade. Without a doubt, the strategic value of digital technologies has increased during that time. The websites of Canada's parties have become technologically sophisticated and integrated with their overall election strategies.[3] Scholarly understanding of Canadian parties' use of Internet politics was greatly enhanced after the 2004 federal election, when several studies by scholars and organizations were published. Two main conclusions can be drawn from these studies: first, party sites are used to perform traditional campaign activities, and second, Canadian parties have not embraced e-democracy.

The Internet is an efficient and cost-effective tool for parties to communicate, fundraise, and organize traditional campaign activities. Party sites serve as a depository for campaign information for both voters and journalists, and also allow people to quickly join the party, volunteer, or donate. Campaign emails focus on the same traditional campaign activities: information dissemination and calls for volunteers and donations. As I have argued elsewhere, even with the rise of Web 2.0, in the most recent election Facebook, Twitter, and YouTube merely provided the parties with other online venues in which to post the same press releases, photos, and online videos.[4] Far from being transformative to party politics, scholars conclude that the Internet is merely "supplementary" to offline campaign activities.[5]

In one of the earliest published works on digital politics in Canada, Darin Barney writes that Canadian "parties have been very reluctant to pursue with vigour and creativity the potentials that ICTs [information and communication technologies] present for the mediation of more routine, deliberative, participatory exercises."[6] Through interactive features such as email, discussion boards, blogs, instant messaging, and social networking, the Internet provides direct and instantaneous communication with others. In the world of politics, this means that whereas in the traditional media, public officials speak and citizens listen (or read), the Internet holds the potential for both public officials and citizens to speak and listen. Despite increasing use of interactive features such as blogs and meetups in the 2004 American election, Kenneth Kernaghan found interactivity to be uncommon in the Canadian election that year.[7] On the basis of interviews, my colleagues and I concluded that Canadian parties avoided interactive features because they "feared that online discussions could knock them off message by raising controversial issues or tarnish their image bringing attention to the 'crazies' that might invade or be planted in party chat rooms."[8] Social networking sites did force some parties to open up in the 2008 election. With the exception of the Conservative Party, supporters were able to comment on the Facebook sites and YouTube channels of the other parties. Despite Barack Obama's effective use of social networking sites like Facebook, in Canadian elections "the engagement between the parties and supporters remained the same. Supporters could make comments on videos or other campaign issues, other users may respond, but the campaigns were still silent."[9] Darin Barney's statement remains true today.

Some suggest that the Internet has the capacity to revolutionize and reinvigorate democratic politics by enhancing public participation and efficacy. For instance, Joe Trippi, the former Howard Dean campaign manager and self-proclaimed cyberoptimist, believes that the Internet is "the best tool we have ever created" to help achieve full participation in democracy.[10] Sarah Bentivegna believes that this is because the Internet "is seen to possess what may broadly be termed 'democratic' potentials untraceable in the traditional media."[11] Canadian parties' use of the Internet appears to defy early expectations about e-democracy.[12] This is not surprising, however, given that Canadian parties are elite-driven organizations: there are very few opportunities for citizens to participate in the internal affairs of political parties.[13] This lack of democracy offline extends into cyberspace. It will become evident that Canadian attack sites fit into this broader use of the Internet by Canadian political parties. Advertising, both positive and negative, has long been a part of Canadian party politics, and it has now moved online. Online negative advertising is another example of using the technology for traditional activities.

NEGATIVE ADVERTISING: DEFINITION AND DEBATES

Negativity has long been a feature of Canadian politics, as is illustrated by the infamous "Mr. Sage" ads from the 1935 federal election This series of dramatized ads featured Mr. Sage chatting with his friend Bill or his wife, making "allegations of fraud, intimidation, lies, blackmail" by the Mackenzie King Liberals.[14] It was later revealed that the Conservative party had sponsored the ads.

There is no universally accepted definition of negative advertising. In the words of David Mark, "Negative campaigning, like beauty, is in the eye of the beholder."[15] That is, what one person might see as mudslinging and attack, another might see as legitimate and informative criticism. Lynda Kaid offers a clear definition: "Most would agree that they basically are opponent-focused, rather than candidate-focused. That is, negative ads concentrate on what is wrong with the opponent, either personally or in terms of issue or policy stances."[16] Negativity can be contrasted with positive advertising, which emphasizes a candidate's own strengths and merits. Buell and Sigelman identify some strategies used in negative advertisements: "Fear arousal is one method, and it is used to paint a grim future if the other side wins. Other methods are ridicule and humor at the opponent's expense, guilt by association or pejorative labelling, apposition (unfavorable comparison with the sponsoring candidate) and accusing the opposition of lying or being inconsistent."[17]

There is much debate about the effects of negative advertising. On one hand, in both the popular and academic literature, negative advertisements are seen as the "electronic equivalent of the plague."[18] That is, negativity is seen to have a deleterious affect on democracy. The demobilization hypothesis, for instance, suggests that exposure to negative advertising suppresses voting. Experimental studies by Ansolabehere and Iyengar support this thesis.[19] Critics also suggest that negative advertising is manipulative because it appeals to emotion rather than rationality. Negativity may affect not only voters but also the ad creators. According to Stanley Cunningham, going negative has a number of "unintended consequences." First, the ad can "boomerang": that is, it "produces more negative feelings against the sponsor than against the target." Next, rather than generating negative feelings toward the target, an ad may inspire positive ones. Cunningham calls this "victim syndrome." Finally, in the case of "double impairment," negativity may generate feelings toward both the target and the sponsor of the advertisement.[20]

However, as noted by Buell and Sigelman, "for all of the aspiration cast on negative campaigning and despite the many ailments of the body politic attributed to it, many a scholar has acknowledged its valuable contribution to free elections."[21] For instance, in his book *In Defense of Negativity*, John Geer argues that "the practice of democracy *requires* negativity."[22] Negativity promotes opposition and accountability, both of which are necessary in a robust democracy. Geer argues that the mass media, rather than being watchdogs, tend to focus their coverage of campaigns on the horse race.[23] As such, candidates must be critical of one another; otherwise, campaign discourse would be superficial at best. Others suggest that negative ads actually increase the quality of information: Darrell West, for example, points out that negative ads are more likely to have policy-oriented content than positive ads because "campaigners need a real reason to attack."[24] Geer concurs, arguing, "For a negative appeal to be effective, the sponsor of that appeal must marshal more evidence, on average, than positive appeals."[25]

In the literature, political advertising, negative or positive, is often considered synonymous with television advertisements, but more recent definitions of political advertising are broader, reflecting the growing importance of the Internet in politics. Holtz-Bacha and Kaid define political advertising as "any controlled message communicated through any channel designed to promote the political interest of individuals, parties, groups, governments, or other organizations."[26] Online political advertising came to prominence in the 2004 American presidential election. Based on that campaign, Kaid identifies five types of online political advertising:

1. Websites
2. Blog ads
3. Ads from other channels
4. Web ads developed for fundraising
5. Original ads[27]

Consistent with cyberoptimistic views, conventional wisdom initially suggested that online appeals are positive in nature. For instance, in his study of websites in the 1996 American election, Robert Klotz found that "the most notable characteristic of web campaigning that supports positive normative assessments of the medium is the low degree of negative campaigning."[28] While this may have been true of the "embryonic era" of online politics, Klotz later changed his assessment, noting that online negativity has become accepted practice in recent campaigns.[29] The 2000 American election featured many hard-hitting online attacks, says Darrell West.[30] He points to the alternative sites GoreWillSayAnything.com, developed by the Republican National Committee, and the Democratic National Committee's IKnowWhatYouDidinTexas.com. Andrew Chadwick suggests that by the 2002 mid-term election, online negativity had become an "entrenched feature" of Internet politics in the United States.[31]

In the 2004 American election, notes David Mark, "many of the nastiest commercials moved away from television to the Internet."[32] For instance, the George W. Bush campaign ad "Unprincipled," which linked Democratic nominee John Kerry to special interest donations, was web-exclusive: that is, it never aired on television. The ad was sent to six million Bush supporters by email. "Unprincipled" also received significant media coverage. Two aspects of this are noteworthy. First, at about a minute in length, "Unprincipled" was significantly longer than most political ads. Second, this ad, like others that followed, did not have the standard "stand by your ad" provision required by American electoral law. Though the *Bipartisan Campaign Reform Act* (2002) requires political advertisements on television and radio to include some sort of statement like "I'm George Bush, and I approve this message," this requirement does not apply to online advertising. According to Mark, this allows online ads to be "more hard-hitting than those featured on television."[33]

The 2008 American election cycle also featured online negativity. Two anonymous emails claimed that Barack Obama was Muslim. One was titled "Can a good Muslim become a good American?" Both emails were widely circulated during the campaign.[43] These emails show that online negativity is no longer the purview of official parties and candidates. Indeed, I have argued elsewhere that "one of the most intriguing aspects of original online political advertising is the level of amateurism. Not only are political parties and candidates creating online content, but so too are independent groups and individuals."[35] Clearly, negative advertising has diversified in the Internet age.

CANADIAN ATTACK SITES: PAST AND PRESENT

Two attack websites, Ignatieff Me! and Cheque Republic, were launched in Canada in 2009. These sites are the most recent in a long line of attack sites: negativity has been a feature of online Canadian party politics for many years. One thing that should be noted, though, is that attack sites have thus far been the purview of only two parties, the Conservatives and Liberals. The NDP, the Bloc Québécois, and the Green Party have not developed such sites.

StephenHarperSaid.ca, developed by the Liberal Party, was the first federal attack site. Prior to the 2004 election, five Liberal TV ads aired targeting the newly selected Harper. With the viewers' curiosity piqued, the ads end by encouraging viewers to log on to StephenHarperSaid.ca, which provided complete quotations and further context. Within days, the Conservative Party responded by launching TeamMartinSaid.ca, which focused on quotations of Paul Martin and members of his caucus. The infamous Not a Leader website appeared in tandem with a series of TV ads aired on Super Bowl Sunday, 2008. These Conservative ads and website were aimed entirely at Liberal leader

Stéphane Dion. Using the image of the now famous "Dion shrug" and the tagline "Stéphane Dion: Not a leader, not worth the risk," the purpose was to frame Dion as an ineffective leader. As Ira Basen points out, "Their coffers brimming with cash, their opponents broke and divided and already weakened by the corruption frame imposed on them by the sponsorship scandal, the Conservatives saw a small window of opportunity to fill the vacuum and hang an unflattering frame around Dion's neck."[36]

The Not a Leader website included features such a create-your-own-Dion ad; an excuse generator, which allowed users to send emails to friends providing Dionesque excuses of why you did not do something; and a blog written by Kyoto, Dion's dog. The site (which no longer exists) was pared down after the "pooping puffin" incident during the election. Again in 2008, the Conservatives launched another multimedia attack on Dion titled "The Dion Tax Trick." The radio ads and the website WillYouBeTricked.ca targeted Dion's carbon tax policy. The Liberals attacked back with the site Scandalpedia during the 2008 election. Using a Wikipedia-like format, the site chronicled the scandals of the governing Conservatives, including the "Chuck Cadman Affair" and the "In-and-Out Scam." According to the press release, "unlike the Conservatives who have launched websites and attack ads that contain character assassinations and outright fabrications, Scandalpedia is fact-based and is fully sourced."[37]

Given the success of Not a Leader, the attack site Ignatieff Me! can be considered another attempt by the Conservatives to frame a Liberal leader. Like StephenHarperSaid.ca, Not a Leader, and WillYouBeTricked.ca, the Ignatieff Me! site was part of a broader multimedia attack plan launched in March 2009. The "Just Visiting" TV ads and Ignatieff Me! website portrayed Michael Ignatieff as an elitist who cares little for Canada and returned only because he wanted to be prime minister. Indeed, the tagline of the website, which was designed to look like a magazine cover, was "It's not about you. It's just about him." The website had five major sections:

- Watch Me!—Featured the four "Just Visiting" television ads, all of which could be shared by email.
- Read Me!—Featured four "magazine" stories: "Just Visiting (The Michael Ignatieff Story)," "Canada & Me!," "Economy and Me!," and "Flip Flops and Me!" Throughout the stories, there

were hyperlinks that opened a pop-up window providing greater context (video or text) and a citation.

- Make Me! Your Cover—Users could make their own Me! magazine cover, choosing between seven different headlines such as "I am horribly arrogant and sure of myself" or "If I do not win, I imagine I will ask Harvard to let me back." The resulting cover could be sent to a friend by email, posted on Facebook, or uploaded to the user's desktop.
- Share Me!—Users could send Ignatieff Me! to a friend by email or add an Ignatieff Me! app to their Facebook site.
- Subscribe to Me!—Users could subscribe "to receive all the latest news about Michael Ignatieff."
- News All About Me!—Five articles about Ignatieff and policy.

The Liberal party launched the attack site Cheque Republic in October 2009 directed at the so-called cheques-gate scandal. The origin of the scandal lies in Conservative MP Gerald Keddy presenting a $300,000 cheque from the Infrastructure Canada fund to a local riding project. Prominently featured on Keddy's oversized novelty cheque was the Conservative Party logo, which contravenes rules of the Federal Identity Program. The prime minister's office responded that the mistake was Keddy's and that this was not an action sanctioned by the government.[38] However, stories of numerous other MPs and numerous novelty cheques began to emerge. In some cases, the fake cheque had the MP's signature while others sported the MP's photograph. The Liberals filed sixty individual complaints to the ethics commissioner, including complaints against twelve cabinet ministers and the prime minister.

According to the Liberals, the website's purpose was to use "humour to draw people's attention to a serious problem."[39] Depicting the leader of the Cheque Republic, the site's logo featured a framed photo of the prime minister wearing a crown. The main visuals on the home page were one hundred thumbnails of photos featuring Conservative MPs presenting Conservative-logo novelty cheques for Government of Canada–related projects. The site had four main sections:

- Get the facts—Provided a chronology of the cheques-gate scandal. In addition to the text written by the Liberals, this page included a link to a Liberal report titled *The Status of Infrastructure Stimulus Spending in Canada* and links to media stories (print and video) on the topic.

- What they're saying—Highlighted public condemnation by some Conservative supporters and MPs and by the mass media (YouTube videos and quotations) of the misuse of tax dollars.
- Cut your own cheque—Users could "Be a Tory MP for a day" by sending a Conservative novelty cheque to their friends by email.
- Blog—Features Liberal press releases in a blog-like format.

Every page of the site offered the option to share the page on various social networking sites or by email. Users could also join the Liberals' Facebook page or donate to the party.

ANALYZING CANADIAN ATTACK SITES

The previous examination of the ways in which parties have used the Internet to go negative suggests five characteristics that define attack sites in Canada: (1) the use of an alternative website to the official party site, (2) extensive evidence to support the attack, (3) the ability of attack sites to be reactive to current and changing events, (4) the cost-effectiveness of attack sites and (5) viral smear—that is, allowing supporters to engage in and spread the mudslinging.

Alternative Sites

The first thing that should be evident about online negativity in Canada is the use of the alternative website. From StephenHarperSaid.ca to Cheque Republic, the main vehicle for negativity is not the official home page but a secondary website. This is similar to the negative sites used in the United States in 2004. In general, the official party websites of Canadian parties are self-regarding, providing biographic information about the party leader, press releases, speeches, multimedia content, policy statements, donation forms, and information about the party organization.[40] The official site is positive in its orientation, emphasizing the attributes and policies of the party.

Thus, attack politics takes place elsewhere on the Web. Unlike American online advertising, these Canadian negative sites do carry a "stand by your ad" authorization statement, in extremely small font at the bottom of the page. This said, there is very little mention of the party sponsor on these pages. In fact, the only mention of the Conservative Party on Ignatieff Me! is the authorization statement. The use of the alternative site allows parties to use their official websites to tout positive messages and to distance their brand from the mudslinging.

More broadly, these attack sites fit into a "virtual omnipresence" of Canadian political parties.[41] In addition to official party sites and attack sites, Canadian parties operate social networking, social bookmarking, social news, news aggregators, and image-sharing sites.[42] There have even been some non-attack alternative sites like the Liberal's This Is Dion and the NDP's Orange Room. The presence of Canadian parties in cyberspace is vast.

Evidence

According to Stephen Brooks, "television advertising by Canadian political parties relies mainly on spot ads whose duration is typically 15–30 seconds.... It is, of course, simply not possible to explore the real complexities of issues in 30 seconds or less, and parties do not try."[43] Certainly this cannot be said of online negativity. Rather, sites such as Ignatieff Me! and Cheque Republic are rich with information and detailed evidence that support the main premise.

Using opponents' words against them is a common strategy in negative television advertisement.[44] This strategy also figures very prominently on Ignatieff Me! and Cheque Republic. For instance, the video on the very first page of Ignatieff Me! shows Ignatieff saying, "You have to choose what kind of America you want, right? You have to decide. It's your country, just as much as it is mine." The video is used as evidence that Ignatieff thinks of himself as an American, that he is merely a political interloper who is "just visiting." Many of the hyperlinks in the "Read Me!" stories are quotations made by Ignatieff himself. Cheque Republic also uses the strategies of presenting plenty of evidence and using the Conservatives' words against them. As noted, the home page features one hundred thumbnail photographs of Conservative MPs presenting large novelty cheques. Additionally, the site links to a Flickr gallery of more than two hundred photos of Conservative MPs holding novelty cheques. Quotes from three Conservative MPs condemning the actions are also presented as evidence. The strategy of using opponents' words and actions against them is long-standing in online attack politics. Indeed, it was the very premise of the first online attack sites, StephenHarperSaid.ca and TeamMartinSaid.ca.

Another common type of evidence is an appeal to authority, or what Richard Davis calls "reinforcement." In examining American blogs, Davis notes that bloggers reinforce their points by "employing sources that bolster [the] bloggers' positions and undermine those of the opposition."[45] On blogs, this occurs through linking to other blogs, websites, or media outlets. This idea of reinforcement appears on Canadian attack websites as a source of evidence: the comments of journalists, media outlets, and other commentators in the form of excerpts, videos, or links are commonplace. The "What They're Saying" section of Cheque Republic, for instance, provides numerous quotations and links to journalists and political commentators, such as Andrew Coyne and Chantal Hébert, who condemn the cheque scandal. Ignatieff Me! uses the same strategy: the "Read Me!" stories contain not only incriminating statements made by Ignatieff but also reinforcing statements. For instance, a quotation from University of Toronto professor Stephen Clarkson, "He told people 15 years ago that he thought about coming back to become prime minister," is provided as evidence that Ignatieff just wanted to be prime minister for his own sake.

Both the Ignatieff Me! and Cheque Republic attack sites are based on extensive evidence, showing that considerable research went into their development. By using the target's own words and actions, and outside sources, the sponsoring party can emphasize that "we are not making this up, this is not just our opinion, this is merely the facts." They can argue that this is not simply partisan politics but legitimate information that people should know.

Reactivity

According to Lynda Kaid, online advertising has several advantages: "First, of course, Web ads are much quicker to produce and distribute than their television counterparts. A second and related advantage is the speed of response and rebuttal made possible by direct access to the Web for immediate distribution."[46] Canadian attack websites have clearly taken advantage of these benefits. Many attack sites were set up very quickly in order to react to very particular situations. Cheque Republic, for instance, was developed in reaction to the emerging cheques-gate scandal. TeamMartinSaid.ca was established in response to another attack website. There is little to suggest that the site was part of a long-term advertising strategy of the Conservatives. Rather, it served as a counter to the Liberal's attack site. As the Conservatives noted in the statement introducing the site: "We can play 'tit-for-tat' all campaign if Paul Martin really wants."[47] It is not just negative sites that can be used in this capacity (though they usually are). During the 2008 election, the Liberals launched their This Is Dion site in an attempt to undo the damage of Not a Leader and to reframe Dion by showing another side of the Liberal leader.[48] The ease of production and low cost makes it easier for parties to react to political events through sites such as these than through high-quality advertising.

In a related way, online ads are not static like TV and radio ads are. New information can constantly be added to the site. For instance, the Liberals reminded visitors to check back often because they would be "posting new material on ChequeRepublic.ca daily—because every day we learn something new about life in Stephen Harper's Cheque Republic!" Photos of Conservative MPs, blog entries, and links to reinforcing stories were added regularly during the height of the scandal. Attack strategies may also be amended, as in the case of the "pooping puffin." This certainly would be more difficult and expensive for TV and radio ads.

Cost-Effectiveness

Advertising is usually the most expensive part of election campaigns: parties spend roughly half of their campaign budget on advertising. With respect to cost, the Internet differs from other channels of political communication; "online advertising" can be a cost-effective means to get out a message.[49] The Internet is cost-effective in terms of both technical hardware and production and transmission. In contrast to television or radio, where what one pays for advertising is often related to the potential reach, "the costs associated with the Web do not increase with the number of people reached."[50] Moreover, Canadian election law does not consider the Internet to be a form of advertising. Therefore, online advertising is not counted as an election expense. Section 319 of the *Canada Election Act* exempts "the transmission by an individual, on a non-commercial basis on what is commonly known as the Internet, of his or her personal political views." This means that Canadian federal election law only applies to paid Internet communcation.[51] A banner ad on a media website or on Facebook that is purchased by an individual or a party is considered advertising and is therefore subject to spending limits. Websites (both official and attack) are exempt from federal election law, as are blogs, social networking sites, and YouTube videos. The Internet as a tool for political advertising, both positive and negative, is therefore very economical for Canadian parties.

It should be recognized, however, that attack websites are not necessarily inexpensive. As we have seen, many sites have been part of a larger multimedia attack strategy. The sites StephenHarperSaid.ca, Not a Leader, and WillYouBeTricked.ca were all released in conjunction with television or radio commercials. When the Not a Leader ads were launched in 2007, the Conservative website announced that the ads aired on "network television and specialty channels including a prized spot during the Canadian broadcast of the Superbowl [sic]."[52] Clearly, this attack campaign was not cheap, although the Liberal party may not be what cyberoptimists had in mind when they suggested that the Internet would aid the resource poor by levelling the playing field for political competition. Compared to the Conservatives, the Liberals do have significant financial challenges as a result of the changes to Canada's party financing regime in 2004: as noted by Flanagan and Jansen, "The reduction of the party to a minority situation in 2004, and then to the opposition benches in 2005 hurt their fundraising capacity.... The major reason why the Liberals have not been able to adapt to the new reality is that they were reliant on corporate fundraising prior to 2004."[53] Whereas the Conservatives have launched three consecutive multimedia attacks, the Liberals have been limited to Web-exclusive attacks. Viewed in light of the Liberal financial woes, Scandalpedia and Cheque Republic did appear to have allowed the Liberals to play on a level field with the Conservatives—a field of mudslinging.

Viral Smear

Another feature of online negativity in Canada is viral smear, which was prominent for both Ignatieff Me! and Cheque Republic. Each site encouraged visitors to share the smear with friends by email and social networking sites such as Facebook and Twitter. In addition to Make Me! Your Cover, the Facebook app allowed users to post Ignatieff Me! magazine covers and TV ads to their Facebook profile. This had the effect of exposing the Conservatives' message to all of the people on users' "friends" lists. The "Share" link on Cheque Republic allowed users to quickly email the page to a friend or post the page on social networking or social bookmarking sites. In addition to exposing new people to the messages of a site, viral marketing also allows for citizen involvement in politics.

The use of viral marketing techniques such as "send to a friend" can be very useful for campaigners for two reasons. First, if users are encouraged to send the item to a friend, someone who may not be as familiar or invested with the campaign, then the original receiver becomes a channel through which candidates may reach untapped citizens. The recipient of a forwarded candidate communication will most likely open the email message and read it because it was sent from someone that person knows: that is, it is not initially interpreted as spam. Thus, email messages may overcome selective exposure, similar to the numerous findings about televised political ads.[54]

Second, in discussions about the democratic potential of technology, the Internet usually comes out on top when compared to television. However, in terms of reach, the Internet has some serious limitations. The Internet is a pull communication in that audiences to websites are self-selected. That is, the audiences of broadcast media are passive; the Internet requires active participation of the user. Users are therefore likely to look only at the information that interests them on a website. In the case of the attack sites discussed in this chapter, a person would have to be interested in politics and be aware of the existence of the site in the first place. Furthermore, the Canadian audience for the Internet is small, at least in terms of political use. Research by the Canadian Internet Project shows that in 2007 only 21 percent of Internet users reported visiting the website of a Canadian political party or individual politician.[55] A CBC/Environics pre-election survey provides similar data, with only 28 percent of Canadians using Internet sources frequently for political information.[56] Therefore, providing opportunities for people to share the smear is crucial because it can make up for what a website lacks in reach.[57]

ONLINE NEGATIVE ADVERTISING AND THE PERMANENT CAMPAIGN

In this volume, Tom Flanagan argues that Canadian politics has evolved into a permanent campaign. The notion of the permanent campaign—a term coined by Sidney Blumenthal—comes from American politics. According to this thesis, there is little difference between the writ and non-writ period. Campaign techniques that once defined elections—such as polling, advertising media management, and fundraising—are now increasingly a feature of everyday politics. Flanagan and Jansen point to two factors in the development of the permanent campaign in Canada: (1) frequent minority government requires that parties "remain campaign ready," and (2) the Conservatives have increased their pre-writ spending in order "to make legal use of resources now available to them."[58] Prior to the 2008 election, the Conservatives made extensive use of non-writ television and radio advertising. More recently, the Liberals and the NDP have also released ads in the non-writ period. For instance, in 2010, the Liberals launched ads targeting Harper's decision to prorogue Parliament until after the Winter Olympics.

The Internet also contributes to the permanent campaign. Political websites, social networking sites, blogs, and email create a permanent presence 24/7. In the United States, the permanent campaign extends in both directions—"beginning earlier and lasting longer."[59] Hopefuls use the Web to "test the waters" for possible presidential bids.[60] Even when candidates lose, many maintain their websites. For instance, the website of Democratic senator and presidential nominee John Kerry (www.johnkerry.com), begun as his senate re-election site in 2002, morphed into his presidential site in 2004. The site still exists in 2011. According to Foot and Schneider, "The infrastructure [of the Internet] enables the organization to engage in the same practices that its electoral incarnations had established, and to build on the databases cataloguing transactional relationships previously established with voters, supporters, contributors, journalists and other political actors."[61] The rise of attack websites in Canada can be viewed in light of the permanent campaign. With the exception of Scandalpedia, every negative site since 2004 has been launched outside of the election period. The Internet now plays a role in both the writ and non-writ periods.[62] As noted earlier, Canada's parties can be found all over cyberspace; this virtual omnipresence allows parties to connect with citizens outside of election periods. The growing use of attack websites by Canadian parties further supports Flanagan's contention that the permanent campaign is now characteristic of Canadian politics.

CONCLUSIONS

The editors of this volume ask, How do Canadians communicate? This chapter has examined how Canadian political parties communicate on the Internet. Earlier, I suggested that two main conclusions could be drawn from how Canadian parties use the Internet during elections. First, parties use the Internet to perform traditional campaign activities, and second, they have not embraced e-democracy. Much of the literature on Canadian parties and the Internet focuses on the writ period. This chapter differs by providing one of the few assessments of parties' use of online technology during the non-writ period. Nevertheless, the trend of attack sites is consistent with the two conclusions noted above.

David Taras points out that "advertising has always been a part of Canadian politics."[63] In *The Newsmakers*, he demonstrates that parties have used the press (both partisan and commercial), posters, pamphlets, radio, and television to sell their messages to the Canadian electorate. Given the importance of the Internet to Canadian society and to politics, it should not be surprising that this "traditional" communication strategy of Canadian parties has moved online. What is, perhaps, surprising is the negative tone of online political advertising. As noted, with very little exception, negativity has defined online political advertising by Canadian parties. Like American politics, there is evidence that the Internet might become the venue for the dirtiest of attacks.

Andrew Chadwick defines e-democracy as "efforts to broaden political participation by enabling citizens to connect with one another and with their representatives via new information and communication technologies."[64] At best, a liberal interpretation of viral smear could be considered e-democracy. Some features of attack sites do encourage citizens to connect with other citizens. Moreover, if we take David Mark's defense of negativity seriously, then viral smear could have some democratic value. This said, attack websites, like official party sites, are not deliberative or participatory spaces. Rather, like official party sites, they are unidirectional. It is difficult, therefore, to reconcile Canadian attack sites with Chadwick's definition of e-democracy.

NOTES

1   Betsy Schiffman, "The Reason for the Obama Victory: It's the Internet, Stupid,"
     Wired, November 7, 2008, http://www.wired.com/epicenter/2008/11/the-obama-
     victo/#ixzzoeZtHulL5.

2   Jane Taber, "Pooping Puffin Pulled from Tory Ad," *Globe and Mail*, September 9, 2008.

3   Tamara A. Small, "Still Waiting for an Internet Prime Minister," in *Elections*, ed. Heather MacIvor (Toronto: Emond Montgomery, 2010), 190.

4   Ibid.

5   Kenneth Kernaghan, "Moving Beyond Politics as Usual? Online Campaigning," in *Digital State at the Leading Edge*, ed. Sandford Borins et al. (Toronto: University of Toronto Press, 2007), 215.

6   Darin Barney, *Communication Technology* (Vancouver: University of British Columbia Press, 2005), 140.

7   Kernaghan, "Moving Beyond Politics as Usual?" 215.

8   Tamara A. Small, David Taras, and Dave Danchuk, "Party Web Sites and Online Campaigning During the 2004 and 2006 Canadian Federal Elections," in *Making a Difference: A Comparative View of the Role of the Internet in Election Politics*, ed. Richard Davis et al. (Lexington: Lexington Press, 2008), 126.

9   Small, "Still Waiting," 190.

10 Joe Trippi, *The Revolution Will Not Be Televised: Democracy, the Internet, and the Overthrow of Everything* (New York: Regan Books, 2004), 226.

11 Sara Bentivegna, "Politics and the New Media," in *The Handbook of New Media*, ed. Leah A. Lievrouw and Sonia M. Livingstone (London: Sage, 2002), 54.

12 See Darin Barney, "The Internet and Political Communications in Canadian Party Politics: The View from 2004," in *Canadian Parties in Transition*, ed. Alain G. Gagnon and A. Brian Tanguay (Peterborough: Broadview Press, 2007); and Small, "Still Waiting."

13 See William Cross, *Political Parties* (Vancouver: University of British Columbia Press, 2004).

14 Carolyn Ryan, "The True North, Strong and Negative," *Canada Votes 2006: Analysis and Commentary, CBC News*, 2006, http://www.cbc.ca/canadavotes2006/analysiscommentary/negativeads.html.

15 David Mark, *Going Dirty: The Art of Negative Campaigning* (Lanham: Rowman and Littlefield, 2006), 2.

16 L.L. Kaid, "Ethics in Political Advertising," in *Political Communication Ethics*, ed. R. E. Denton, Jr. (Westport: Praeger, 2000), 157.

17 Emmett Buell and Lee Sigelman, *Attack Politics* (Lawrence: University of Kansas Press, 2008), 12.

18 Darrell West, *Air Wars: Television Advertising in Election Campaigns, 1952–2008* (Washington, DC: CQ Press, 2009), 70.

19 Stephen Ansolabehere and Shanto Iyengar, *Going Negative: How Political Advertisements Shrink and Polarize the Electorate* (New York: Free Press, 1995).

20 Stanley B. Cunningham, "The Theory and Use of Political Advertising," in *Television Advertising in Canadian Elections: The Attack Mode, 1993*, ed. Walter I. Romanow et al. (Waterloo: Wilfrid Laurier University Press, 1999), 24.

21 Buell and Sigelman, *Attack Politics*, 7.

22 John Geer, *In Defense of Negativity: Attack Ads in Presidential Campaigns* (Chicago: University of Chicago Press, 2006), 6.

23 "Horse race coverage" refers to a focus by the media on how parties and/or candidates are faring in the polls.

24 West, *Air Wars*, 71.

25 Geer, *In Defense of Negativity*, 6.

26 Christina Holtz-Bacha and L. L. Kaid, "Political Advertising in International Comparison," in *The Sage Handbook of Political Advertising*, ed. Christina Holtz-Bacha and L. L. Kaid (California: Sage, 2006), 4.

27 L. L. Kaid, "Political Web Wars: The Use of the Internet for Political Advertising," in *The Internet Election: Perspectives on the Web in Campaign 2004*, ed. Andrew Paul Williams and John C. Tedesco (Lanham: Rowman and Littlefield, 2006).

28 Robert Klotz, "Positive Spin: Senate Campaigning on the Web," *Political Science and Politics* 30 (September 1997): 482–86.

29 Robert Klotz, *The Politics of Internet Communication* (Lanham: Rowman and Littlefield, 2004).

30 West, *Air Wars*, 62.

31 Andrew Chadwick, *Internet Politics: States, Citizens, and New Communication Technologies* (London: Oxford University Press, 2006), 84.

32 Mark, *Going Dirty*, 161.

33 Ibid., 220.

34 Ben Smith and Jonathan Martin, "Untraceable E-mails Spread Obama Rumor," *Politico*, October 13, 2007, http://www.politico.com/news/stories/1007/6314.html.

35 Tamara A. Small, "Regulating Canadian Elections in the Digital Age: Approaches and Concerns," *Election Law Journal: Rules, Politics, and Policy* 8 (September 2009): 189–205.

36 Ira Basen, "Commentary. A Schlemiel Is the Elephant in the Room: The Framing of Stéphane Dion," *Canadian Journal of Communication* 34 (2009): 299.

37 "Campaign Gets Nasty in Cyberspace," Canwest News Service, September 9, 2008, http://www.canada.com/saskatoonstarphoenix/story.html?id=3a9376b9-617b-4107-8a58-e14ccaf255fa&p=2.

38 Rosemary Barton, "Big Cheque, Big Logo," *CBC News*, October 14, 2009, http://www.cbc.ca/news/canada/politicalbytes/2009/10/big-cheque-big-logo.html.

39 "You Have Entered the Cheque Republic," Liberal Blog, October, 23, 2009, http://www.liberal.ca/en/blog/16764_you-have-entered-the-cheque-republic.

40 Barney, *Communication Technology*, 136–37.

41 Paul McFedries, "All A-Twitter," *IEEE Spectrum*, October 2007, http://spectrum.ieee.org/computing/software/all-atwitter.

42 Small, "Still Waiting," 180.

43 Stephen Brook, "Televison Advertising by Political Parties: Can Democracy Survive It?" in *Canadian Parties in Transition*, ed. Alain G. Gagnon and A. Brian Tanguay (Peterborough: Broadview Press, 2007), 362.

44 Mark, *Going Dirty*, 5.

45 Richard Davis, *Typing Politics: The Role of Blogs in American Politics* (New York: Oxford University Press, 2009), 77.

46 Kaid, "Political Web Wars," 69.

47 "Pre-election Campaigns Debut on TV and Online," *Election 2004, CTV News*, May 19, 2004, http://www.ctv.ca/CTVNews/TopStories/20040519/liberal_ads_040518/.

48 Basen, "Commentary," 302.

49 Michael Cornfield, *Politics Moves Online: Campaigning and the Internet* (New York: Century Foundation Press, 2003), 414.

50 Carol Ann McKeown and Kenneth D. Plowman, "Reaching Publics on the Web During the 1996 Presidential Election," *Journal of Public Relations Research* 11 (1999): 325.

51 Small, "Regulating Canadian Elections," 196.

52 "Stéphane Dion Is Not a Leader," Conservative Party website, January 9, 2007, http://www.conservative.ca/EN/1091/67584.

53 Tom Flanagan and Harold J. Jansen, "Election Campaigns Under Canada's Party Finance Laws," in *The Canadian Federal Election of 2008*, ed. Jon H. Pammett and Christopher Dornan (Toronto: Dundurn Press, 2009), 198.

54 Andrew Paul Williams and Kaye D. Trammell, "Candidate Campaign E-Mail Messages in the Presidential Election 2004," *American Behavioral Scientist* 49 (December 2005): 560–74.

55 Charles Zamaria and Fred Fletcher, *Canada Online! The Internet, Media and Emerging Technologies: Uses, Attitudes, Trends and International Comparisons 2007* (Toronto: Canadian Internet Project, 2008), 226.

56 "Pre-election Poll: Full Results," *CBC News*, September 7, 2008, http://www.cbc.ca/canada/story/2008/09/07/f-full-poll-results.html.

57 Tom Spring, "Political Smears Thrive Online: Presidential Campaign Camps Push Video, Other Ads into Your In-box," *PC World*, March 23, 2004, http://www.pcworld.com/article/115291/political_smears_thrive_online.html.

58 Flanagan and Jansen, "Election Campaigns," 207.

59 Kristen Foot and Steven M. Schneider, *Web Campaigning* (Cambridge: MIT Press, 2006), 202.

60 David Dulio and Terri Towner, "The Permanent Campaign in the United States," in *Routledge Handbook of Political Management*, ed. Dennis W. Johnson (New York: Routledge, 2008), 88.

61 Foot and Schneider, *Web Campaigning*, 204.

62 See Small, "Still Waiting."

63 David Taras, *The Newsmakers: The Media's Influence on Canadian Politics* (Scarborough: Nelson Canada, 1990), 198.

64 Chadwick, *Internet Politics*, 84.

Alvin Finkel

Myths Communicated by Two Alberta Dynasties

During its first 105 years as a province, Alberta has had only three changes of government. Its last two regimes, Social Credit from 1935 to 1971 and Progressive Conservative from 1971 to the present, have been extraordinarily long-lived for elected governments. The province's oil wealth aided both dynasties, allowing them to spread money around and buy voters' support, but in each case, communication of a particular image has also been crucial. In this chapter, I examine the means that the two dynasties used to project a certain image, and then I explore the extent to which these images accurately portrayed the performance of the government. I suggest that the images were largely spin and that both regimes proved able to use communications strategy to project false images of their performance. The spin worked best when a dynasty's leader appeared to embody the image that the regime sought to put forward, and the dynasties only faced collapse when the party proved unable to find a leader whom the image-makers could use.

Political dynasties in Alberta have also benefited from the limited presence of an opposition, unlike other provinces, where two or three parties have vied for office, with an established opposition party with ample legislative representation over many years replacing a governing party when it could persuade voters that it was time for a change. In Alberta, the first two changes of government in 1921 and 1935 brought to office parties that had not even existed at the time of the election that preceded their victory. The Progressive Conservatives of Peter Lougheed had formed the Official Opposition in the 1967 election that preceded their victory, but it was the Liberals that occupied most of the small number of opposition seats during most of the Social Credit period, with the Tories failing to win any seats in 1963. Effectively, voters began turning to a "Lougheed party" in 1967 and put that party over the top when a change in leadership in the Social Credit Party weakened what had become the "Manning party." Without strong opposition parties, Albertans have tended to view the governing party and its leader as the embodiment of the province. Image-makers had to take heed of popular desires as they spun their narrative of a government's works, but they had the advantage over their counterparts in other provinces of dealing with significant numbers of voters who did not view the opposition as a way of dealing with their dissatisfaction with a given government.[1]

SOCIAL CREDIT

Social Credit's image throughout its period in office was infused with the religious affiliations of its first two premiers, "Bible Bill" Aberhart and Ernest Manning, who, between them, governed for all but the last three years of the Social Credit era. The religious mantle of the government was important because the government's elected officials, including the Social Credit premiers, at their outset had only modest claims to expertise relevant to government. Aberhart was a school principal and mathematics teacher, but he was also the founder of the fundamentalist Calgary Prophetic Bible School Institute. He had never served in any elected or appointed position in government before becoming premier. Manning was a farm boy and the first graduate from Aberhart's institute. He also had no experience outside of that restricted religious world before being elected at age twenty-seven as an MLA in the Social Credit sweep in 1935 and immediately being appointed to cabinet.[2]

In many respects, the key, if unofficial, communication between the Social Credit premiers and the people of Alberta was the "Back to the Bible Hour" broadcast on radio that Aberhart began before becoming premier and that continued throughout his premiership. The immense popularity of Aberhart's radio ministry had been the fuel that ignited the Social Credit movement of the 1930s, and it reflected the importance of religion in the self-identification of Albertans in the early years of the province. With 300,000 listeners, two-thirds of them in Alberta, Aberhart reached a large audience both before and after becoming premier.[3] When he died in 1943, Manning took over as both premier and host of the Bible Hour, continuing the broadcasts even after he retired as premier in 1968. The fire-and-brimstone quality of those broadcasts cast an aura of righteousness over the government, and the portrayal of the government as religious and honest through these non-formal means replaced a formal communications policy.[4] As Simon Kiss argues, the Social Credit government lacked an overarching communications policy. No government agency linked messages from the various departments of government to put a brand on government messaging. Communications staff in most departments were political appointees, but they relied mainly on the government's Publicity Bureau for advertising. The Publicity Bureau, initially established in 1906 to promote the province to potential settlers, did little more than contract out these requests for promotional materials to two advertising firms of questionable competence but with ties to the government.[5]

The informal policy worked well enough during the Aberhart and Manning periods. The party leaders personified the party while their cabinet ministers and backbenchers seemed little more than cheerleaders for the leader. It is clear from his papers during his time as premier that Aberhart was a rambunctious, authoritarian individual who devised policy on the fly and who quickly lost his grip on efforts to implement the largely fanciful Social Credit policies that had won him election in 1935.[6] But the combination of his religious views, fanaticism, and anti-establishment rhetoric allowed him to survive a concerted challenge by the establishment parties to push him out of office in the 1940 provincial election.[7] Manning, when he became premier in 1943, significantly toned down the anti-bank, anti-business rhetoric of his predecessor. He followed conservative economic and social policies while retaining enough of the early Social Credit message to appear as something more than a shill for big oil companies, which he increasingly became. His "Back to the Bible" persona gave the government the aura of honesty and prudence in its management of public monies.[8] As Manning biographer Brian Brennan writes: "Before 1955, the Social Credit government had a reputation for honesty and integrity that went virtually unchallenged. Its public persona as a party of devoted Christians kept it free from allegations of dishonesty and corruption. The personality and image of its leader defined the persona of the party, and most Albertans viewed Ernest Manning as a man of sincerity, rectitude and moral correctness."[9] But the glow seemed to fade in the months preceding the election of 1955, an election called only three years after the previous election so that Premier Manning could gain a public vote of confidence before allegations of government incompetence and dishonesty became too overwhelming to refute.

Opposition MLAs and the media made a variety of allegations of Social Credit improprieties in tendering government contracts, in government procurement policies, and in MLAs transacting business with the government, including receiving loans from the Alberta Treasury Branch. The ATB was a quasi-bank with branches throughout the province established by the Aberhart government when the courts and the federal government rebuffed his efforts to control the lending policies of the chartered banks in the province. The *Alberta Assembly Act* forbade MLAs from transacting business with the government, and Manning introduced legislation to exempt dealings with the ATB from that provision after revelations that Social Credit MLAs routinely received loans from the Treasury Branch. When the Liberals challenged the retroactive character of this exemption and, along with it, the legality of laws passed in Alberta since MLAs began receiving Treasury Branch loans, Manning argued that the voters would have to make the ruling as to whether the laws passed by the Social Credit administrations since 1940 were valid. Though Manning won the election by focusing on his own integrity and downplaying the accusations against his underlings, Social Credit dropped from fifty-two of the legislature's sixty-one seats in 1952 to only thirty-seven seats in 1955.[10]

After the election, Manning set up a Royal Commission with a restricted mandate to report on some of the specific opposition allegations made before and during the election. This would spare the government a more general inquiry about how contracts were awarded and how the government interacted with the Treasury Branch. Manning's reputation for rectitude was such that the commission trusted him to provide it with the requisite government documents necessary for its work. But even with the limited information provided to them, the commissioners expressed concern about the casual character of the government's procurement and contracting policies. Possibilities for ministers to benefit personally or politically from the awarding of contracts were endless. The commission saw no evidence, however, that the government had behaved corruptly or irresponsibly.[11] Premier Manning, agreeing to implement the commission's recommendations to establish arm's-length agencies for contracting and procuring, claimed that the government had been vindicated.[12]

But Premier Manning had a secret. He had withheld documents that would have led the commissioners to different conclusions. What the commissioners would have learned, as Bob Hesketh demonstrates in an impressive and largely unknown master's thesis for the University of Alberta, was that the Manning government was urging the managers of the Treasury Branch to make loans to certain business people with little collateral.[13] Other government departments—such as Public Works, which handled all the highway contracts—were then urged to award contracts to Treasury Branch business clients. When the commission examined highway contracts, they were given only partial information about fifteen contracts for which Public Works had negotiated with companies rather than seeking competitive bids and no information at all about fourteen other contracts, nine of which involved O'Sullivan Construction or Mannix-O'Sullivan, two large recipients of underperforming loans from the Treaury Branches. Social Credit's veneer of prudent management of government funds was fraudulent. Religious spin spared the government from being forced to make revelations that might have removed Social Credit from power a decade or more before they were finally defeated. Hesketh concludes: "Yet, under Manning's leadership, the Alberta Social Credit government created a fiction of the Treasury Branch operating as an orthodox banking institution; the Main Highways Branch rigged contracts to benefit the Treasury Branch and its customers; and the government lied to the public and to a Royal Commission to cover up its guilt."[14]

In the late 1960s, just after Manning had retired as premier, another commission report suggested questionable behaviour, though no clearly illegal actions, by two government ministers. Premier Harry Strom, Manning's colourless successor, could not weather the storm in the manner that the long-time Social Credit premier had done. Strom, an old farmer, typified a Social Credit membership that had become unrepresentative of the province as a whole: old, rural, and religious in an Alberta that was increasingly young, urban, and secular. The

Strom government had only weak strategies, both substantive and communicative, to harness changing demographics in its own favour.[15]

THE CONSERVATIVES: LOUGHEED AND GETTY

The Progressive Conservative (PC) Party of Alberta, led by Peter Lougheed, worked to take advantage of urban, educated, secular Albertans' alienation from Social Credit. Winning a beachhead of seven seats in the 1967 provincial election, the PCs followed the earlier Social Credit tradition of making their leader the party message. As the 1971 election approached, the PC communication directors worked to shape a John Kennedyesque version of their leader. Party candidates, especially in urban areas, were mainly university-educated professionals and business people, and the Conservatives projected an image of expertise and hipness that contrasted with the tarnished Social Credit brand of rural religiosity.[16] Telegenic and comfortable before microphones, Lougheed had his party spend more than 85 percent of its advertising budget in 1971 on television spots. Social Credit, by contrast, used that medium for only 25 percent of their ads.[17]

Once in office, Lougheed worked to create a communications policy that matched his party's urbane image. He gutted the Publicity Bureau and created the Public Affairs Bureau (PAB) in its stead. This centralized agency with about two hundred positions would hire trained communications professionals and lend expertise to all departments. According to Simon Kiss, it was run along civil service lines and was not politicized in the Lougheed period.[18] It was always in the hands of a junior minister and the cabinet made no direct effort to control its work. Roger Epp has argued, however, that it was a centralized operation under the control of the politicians and modelled on public relations departments in the corporate world. It was meant to provide a particular spin about the government to the media. Rich Vivone has also claimed more recently that the PAB was set up by Lougheed "to centralize and control communications and to put a protective barrier between politicians and the media."[19]

Lougheed's fixation with secrecy, with not letting the media define the issues, and his swift retaliation against Tory MLA Tom Sindlinger for expressing views contrary to the Conservative position on several issues, sent a clear message to PAB employees that their employer would brook no conflict with the premier's perspectives.[20] Perhaps, though, as Kiss suggests, the overall favourable environment within which Lougheed worked—no serious opposition party, a soaring economy, a largely supportive media—meant that he did not see the need to take the drastic, formal steps to bend the PAB to his absolute direction that Ralph Klein would take in the 1990s.

Nonetheless, Lougheed took care to cultivate a particular media image, making himself available to the media only at tightly controlled news conferences. Essential to that image was the notion that Lougheed was not simply the leader of a political party but the leader of all Albertans as the province fought alleged federal government efforts to prevent Albertans from controlling their provincial resources. This "Captain Alberta" approach was invoked during both the 1975 and 1979 provincial elections, to good partisan effect. In 1980 and 1981, the premier was unchallenged when he used government rather than party funds to pay for special addresses on television regarding the province's position in its dealings with the federal government regarding the proposed National Energy Policy.[21]

The premier was prickly and sued CBC in 1976 over a dramatization of the provincial and federal government's dealings with energy companies in negotiating the Syncrude tar sands project. The network agreed to pay a $250,000 out-of-court settlement and make a public apology.[22] Mostly, however, the media aided the government in projecting an image of being at once fiscally conservative and innovative regarding economic policy. While Social Credit presented itself as unwilling to risk public expenditures on efforts to lure private investors, the Lougheed PCs were bolder on the economic front. Lougheed argued that the province's dependency on oil revenues was not sustainable over the long run because Alberta's supplies of conventional oil were dwindling. Immediate economic diversification was necessary, and his government would attempt to promote the development of new economic sectors and the expansion of existing ones. In addition, the government would save petroleum royalty revenues for future generations in the Alberta Heritage Savings Trust Fund (AHSTF), which was promised in the 1975 provincial election and established the following year. Thirty percent of resource revenues were henceforth to be placed in the fund annually and to be invested prudently. There was an urgency in the government's message that convinced even its left-wing critics that it intended to diversify the provincial economy and that it had the support of a burgeoning urban middle class in

Calgary and Edmonton to use government policies to promote an industrial policy for the province.[23] The major enemy of such a province-building exercise, in Lougheed's view, was the federal government, which allegedly wanted to make use of Alberta's oil and gas to provide cheap feedstocks for central Canadian industries and to maximize federal government revenues from Alberta's resources.

While energy prices continued to climb throughout the 1970s and early 1980s, the Lougheed government had little to fear from either forces to its right or its left. The former complained about the rapid growth in the province's expenditures while the latter complained that the distribution of wealth in the province was more skewed than ever and that government policies did little to counterbalance market-created inequities. Only the recession that began with the collapse in the international price of oil in early 1982 raised questions about whether the Tories were good economic managers. Though Premier Lougheed had left office before such questioning began in earnest and his successor, Don Getty, would bear the brunt of criticisms, some of the questionable decisions for which Getty would have to take the blame had been made during the Lougheed period.

Getty became premier in 1985 and had a public image of someone who was more interested in playing golf than in governing. His loss of a significant chunk of the Tory vote in 1986 and his failure to regain it in 1989, which can be partly attributed to dissatisfaction with the province's sluggish economic performance, are also sometimes attributed to Getty's inability to maintain the Tory brand of expertise, innovation, and at least moderate fiscal conservatism.[24]

Lougheed had initially responded to the recession in 1982 with spending programs, particularly mortgage subsidies, which were meant to ensure his reelection. Afterwards, however, he focused on spending cuts, which included a get-tough policy on single unemployed people. After three weeks in an urban homeless shelter, individuals were expected to look after themselves. The policy—according to Tamara Kozlowska, associate director of the Unemployed Action Centres set up by the Alberta Federation of Labour—was to persuade the single unemployed to leave the province.[25] By contrast, both the Lougheed and Getty governments treated families in poverty with relative compassion.[26]

The governments of these two premiers also made marginal cuts in programs that affected the middle class, such as health and education. They attempted to maintain their image of good fiscal managers by reducing the revenue flow into the AHSTF by half as a means of increasing current revenues. This proved enough to maintain surpluses until 1985, when the government's net assets were reported to be $12.6 billion.[27] But in 1986, the bottom fell out of oil prices and the government began a series of budgets with annual deficits. While the first Getty budget in 1985–86 recorded a $761 million deficit, that figure increased to $3.1 billion by 1992–93. It was only after the fact that it became clear that the Lougheed government had successfully communicated a comfortable mistruth to Albertans: that it had collected enough revenues through taxation and set aside sufficient funds to deal with rainy days and a post-energy future. In fact, the cupboard was almost bare and the province's low-tax strategy, in which low corporate and personal income taxes and no sales tax figured prominently, left few alternatives other than debt or substandard social programs.

By 1992, the failure of a variety of private companies to which the government had committed significant public revenues or on which it had failed to impose sufficient regulation had wrecked the image of the Getty Conservative government as a good manager of public finances. The first domino to fall was the Principal Group, a large investment fund in which thousands of Alberta investors had placed their trust. After Principal's collapse in 1987, a judicial inquiry concluded that weak laws and weak enforcement had contributed to the investors' predicament. The cost to the government of the inquiry and compensation to investors was about $100 million.[28] The problems had begun under Lougheed's watch, but the Getty government suffered the political consequences. Another Lougheed-era financial decision, the financing of a canola-processing company, cost taxpayers about $68 million before it was sold in 1994. But, according to Mark Lisac, "the biggest of the Conservatives' business failures was probably the pouring of billions of dollars into land and housing development during the boom years," which boosted the overheated land market of the Lougheed years, a pro-cyclical set of investments that contradicted Keynesian theory and belied the government's image of fiscal prudence.[29]

Getty continued Tory financial recklessness with a combination of privatizations of government firms (particularly Alberta Government Telephones) and socialization of risk for private ventures. Loan guarantees under Lougheed had amounted to $9.7 billion, and Getty added another $2.5 billion to the pot.[30]

This money was risked on firms that were supposed to either diversify the Alberta economy or preserve existing jobs. The biggest loss was $566 million, which the government had to write off for its investment in Nova Tel, a wireless manufacturer, but it was only the tip of the iceberg, with losses recorded for investments in a smelter, a meatpacking plant, pulp mills, a steel plant, a computer design firm, a laser-cutting machine manufacturer, and a port operation in British Columbia.[31] The smelter alone cost taxpayers over $100 million.[32] Losses in Nova Tel, though, were a particularly bitter pill for Alberta taxpayers to swallow because Nova Tel had been hived off from AGT when the government privatized its telephone company in 1990 and 1991 to help balance its recession-battered books; during 1990 and 1991, the province earned about $1.7 billion (minus costs of sale) for AGT shares.[33] The announcement in 1992 of the Nova Tel writeoff meant that at least one-third of that profit would be spent on the government's earlier mismanagement of AGT.

With so much of the government's program going wrong, Don Getty was badly in need of a communications policy that would help him get across a positive message to the media. Several of his ministers urged a reorganization of the Public Affairs Bureau to make it more of a political propaganda agency, but Getty opposed such a change.[34] Instead, he set up a cabinet committee chaired by Peter Elzinga, minister of Economic Development, to coordinate communications campaigns and work on a long-term strategy for government messages. But it was composed mainly of low-ranking ministers and developed little clout with the cabinet.[35]

The government's amateurish communications were evident in 1991 when it began a campaign, produced by the Department of Economic Development and Trade, to advertise that the administration had finally balanced the budget after six years of deficits. The budget was not balanced, though, and the opposition had a field day attacking the government both for lying and for using public funds for a clearly partisan campaign.[36] By the time Getty announced his resignation as premier in 1992, the mighty Conservatives of Alberta had fallen well behind the provincial Liberals in public opinion polls.

COMMUNICATIONS IN THE KLEIN ERA

Ralph Klein, who succeeded Getty as Progressive Conservative leader and premier, faced a difficult task. He had been part of the Getty cabinet since

1989 and had therefore been part of the decision-making group that the public believed had inflicted severe damage to the public finances of the province. He faced a strong opponent in Liberal leader Laurence Decore, a former mayor of Edmonton, who was calling for "brutal cuts" in government spending to balance the budget, while attracting enough small-l liberal candidates to alleviate fears about how unfair the cuts would actually be. Klein fought fire with fire, dissociating himself from the previous government, of which he had been a key minister, to call for "massive cuts." Trading on his popularity as the former mayor of Calgary and several years of attending every rural Conservative constituency meeting that he could, Klein successfully convinced 44 percent of Albertans, enough to give him a majority of seats, to keep the Alberta Tories in power, but with Decore's Liberals having received 40 percent of the vote, Klein could not take power for granted.

Klein therefore developed a communications strategy that he hoped would ensure that the cabinet and caucus spoke with only one voice and with a united message. Along with his chief of staff, Rod Love, he further tightened control over the Public Affairs Bureau, eventually having it report directly to the premier, a centralization of communication that matched an overall centralization of government authority under Klein.[37] The bureau was to provide strategic advice to the premier and cabinet and to ensure that the government had a consistent, positive image within the media and with the public. All government public relations messages were scrutinized to make certain that they followed the party line.

But Klein wanted more than consistent messages from communications staff. It was also important that his ministers say only things that were pre-approved and in line with the government's overall message of frugality. Through the PAB and Love, ministers received "talking points" on most issues and were told never to diverge from these points when they spoke to the media. "Talking Points devalued political discourse," notes Rich Vivone, a one-time executive assistant to a Conservative minister and later the publisher of *Insight into Government*, a perceptive journal regarding the government's manipulative media strategy throughout the Klein years.[38]

Klein, a long-time TV anchor before he entered politics, manipulated the media by allowing only reporters who provided favourable reports on government activities to receive leaks—thus allowing their coverage to be disguised as investigative journalism—or indeed, to be given any interviews at all.

Pliant reporters received complete "stories" assembled by the PAB and needed to do little digging, the price for the story often being an agreement not to include opposition reaction to the government's perspective.[39] Annual television addresses in which the premier summed up the government's strategies and successes, without any reporters or members of the public present to ask any questions, served as an emblem of the overall approach to communication. Simon Kiss, who has provided the most extensive examination to date of the government communications strategy, sums it up as "manipulative and aggressive news management tactics, politicizing and centralizing the public relations staff and integrating the entire range of public relations techniques into regular politically contentious advertising campaigns."[40]

One word summarized the government's agenda: cutbacks. Within a few years of coming to office, the government had reduced government spending by 28 percent in real per capita terms. The message that it communicated was that it had no choice: spending was wildly out of control, and deficits and debt would strangle the provincial economy unless the government took tough action. Through more controls over its own spending and more contracting out to the private sector, the government could still assure basic social protections to citizens, but at reduced cost. While cuts in health and education spending spread grief throughout the population, social services and housing cuts were far deeper and targeted mainly the poor. The government received national attention when it gave about four thousand social service recipients one-way tickets to British Columbia.[41] The PC's communications strategy stressed the need to minimize the information given to the public about the impacts of the cuts and to maximize the alleged ultimate benefits to all Albertans, and especially the poor, of reducing the "nanny state" and giving individuals and families more responsibility for their own well-being.

Obviously, such a message was hampered when public employees revealed hardships that cutbacks were creating for their clientele and/or for the workers. So the government informed its employees that they would be disciplined if they made public comments about impacts of government cutbacks. Minister of Family and Social Services Mike Cardinal was quoted in the media with explicit warnings to social workers to stay silent. When Guy Smith, a provincial social worker and well-known activist in the Alberta Union of Public Employees, defied this ban, he was suspended from his position for three weeks in 1996 and was warned that a repeat could cost him his employment.[42]

Klein even attempted to interfere when he was criticized by university professors. He asked the president of the University of Alberta to eliminate the Parkland Institute, a left-leaning research body that scrutinized Klein's ideology and policies. He tried to stop the University of Alberta Press from publishing *Shredding the Public Interest*, a book by Kevin Taft that demolished the government's fiscal arguments. For good measure, he publicly labelled Taft, whom he had not met, as a "communist." Taft was, in fact, a non-partisan business consultant with a PhD in business. He later became leader of the provincial Liberal party.[43]

The universities did continue to defend academic freedom but, like most public bodies, they were paranoid of the government's willingness to punish its critics. This caused all four public universities to obfuscate and almost perversely defend Klein when, through strange circumstances, he posted an essay that he had written for Athabasca University on his website, only to have critics note that 27 percent of the essay was taken word for word from Internet sites that he had failed to credit.[44] Athabasca University, rather than follow normal academic channels to deal with a situation that could have resulted in a normal student receiving a grade of zero and a plagiarism note on his or her student file, gave the issue over to a media relations company.[45] An academic issue became instead a communications/damage-control issue. The presidents of the other three universities succumbed to a request from Learning Minister Lyle Oberg and "wrote public letters defending the Premier's 'commitment to learning.'"[46] Only Athabasca president Dominique Abrioux declined to send such a letter. These letters were sent even before Athabasca had contentiously cleared the premier of the plagiarism charge, making dubious use of the word "willful" as if the premier of a province and a long-time journalist could be seen as too ingenuous to know that failing to cite Internet sources was plagiarism.[47]

Of course, policies of manipulating the media and intimidating government employees, while reprehensible, do not, in and of themselves, demonstrate that a government is communicating false information. So how accurately did the Klein government convey the state of the province's finances? Much of the literature to date suggests that the Klein cuts—with their promise of creating a leaner, meaner government—were based on faulty economics and false promises. Kevin Taft demonstrated in *Shredding the Public Interest*, published in 1997 after the cutbacks had largely ended, that

Premier Klein had exaggerated increases in Alberta's expenditures in the years preceding the government's cuts. Expenditures had actually been tightly controlled during the Getty years, and deficits and debts were mainly the result of revenues having temporarily declined during the period of low prices for oil; they would be quickly restored when oil prices rose again. Klein had also ignored the province's considerable tax room, the envy of every other province, in favour of a business narrative that suggested that an "Alberta advantage" of low across-the-board taxes was necessary for attracting investment. With regard to medical care spending, for example, Alberta spent 7.9 percent of its GDP on health care before the cuts began, while the country as a whole spent 9.7 percent. Per capita spending on health care had peaked in 1987; Taft writes, "I have never seen reliable data to support Ralph Klein's claims that in the years before he became premier, health care spending in Alberta had 'tripled,' or that costs were 'soaring,' 'skyrocketing,' or 'out of control.'"[48]

Taft's conclusions are echoed by economist Greg Flanagan, who suggests that program spending during the Getty period was relatively stable. The main reason for provincial deficits and debt was the money risked and then lost on new industries. Since oil and gas revenues were temporarily low when Klein assumed office but it was inevitable that they would pick up again, "the deficit would soon have disappeared regardless of what the government did on the expenditure side of the ledger."[49] As for tax room, in 1993, before the Klein cuts started, Alberta spent the lowest proportion of provincial GDP on government expenditure: 22 percent, compared to a mean for all the provinces of 27 percent. By 2003, the Alberta figure had dropped to 13 percent against a provincial mean of 22 percent. Flanagan notes that "the role of government as stabilizer was abandoned, as regulator was considerably reduced, and as provider of public goods was diminished."[50] The poor, he suggests, were hit hardest by the government's cutbacks, a claim that various articles in two books by the Parkland Institute documented closely.[51] The wealthy were favoured by the Klein tax policies. Flat taxes alone cost the provincial treasury $5.5 billion in potential income from higher-income Albertans in 2006.[52]

The government's message that spending was out of control in 1993 and that therefore weapons of mass destruction were the antidote for the provincial budget was, on the whole, false, or at least an artifact of ideology rather than an accurate portrayal of either the state of provincial finances or the capacity of the Alberta government to spend. But it might nonetheless be argued that the government was reflecting the views of Albertans generally that reining in spending rather than maintaining social programs should be the government's first priority. Klein's re-election with large majorities in 1997, 2001, and 2004 does demonstrate that his party remained the most popular party in the province. Klein could also argue that he had consulted widely in the period after provincial deficits gave way to surpluses on how the province should spend. Certainly, his government carried out a series of consultations and polls leading to the Alberta Growth Summit in September 1997. The consultations and polls indicated that what people wanted most was to rebuild the programs that had been slimmed down during the first Klein mandate. The Alberta Growth Summit was more conservative, but that was because the government chose the participants, provided all the background documents, and steered the overall summit in the conservative direction that it felt most appropriate. In any case, the government did not bind itself to following the advice that came from its various consultations, treating them all as part of an exercise in communicating the openness of what was, in fact, a very closed government.[53]

Indeed, the jury is out as to how conservative Albertans truly are. On the one hand, as sociologist Harry Hiller has argued, the province's conservative reputation has attracted migrants from other provinces who see it as a low-tax province without the heavy hand of the state on citizens' behaviour or their pocketbooks.[54] Yet, as political scientist Doreen Barrie maintains, there is a large liberal element in the province as evidenced in surveys on a variety of social and economic issues. She believes that conservatives in the province succeed both provincially and federally because they have proven able to create and maintain a mythology of an evil federal government determined to rob them of their birthright.[55] While that may explain why the Progressive Conservative Party has done so well in Alberta, it does not help to explain why the Klein Conservatives, whose battles with Ottawa were tame compared to those of the Lougheed Conservatives, managed to sell a far more conservative agenda than their Conservative predecessors. Klein's consistent message provides much of the explanation: he did not usually sell cuts as an absolute good to create more freedom for individuals because that would not have gone over well with Albertans, who wanted to have their cake and eat it too: they wanted both low taxes and exceptional public services. Instead, he sold cuts as necessary because the province was going broke, and his ability to control communications within the province meant that only a minority of Albertans got a glimpse of the arguments of those who claimed that Klein was exaggerating the province's financial problems, if not fabricating the evidence for impending financial disaster out of whole cloth.

Klein and his advisors also had their ears to the ground as to how far they could go before the public turned against them. After a November 1995 strike by unionized Calgary hospital laundry workers, who faced job losses, almost triggered a province-wide strike of all health care workers, the government, aware that the laundry workers were being embraced as heroes by much of the population, not only made concessions to the laundry workers but significantly scaled back further health care cuts it was planning. Klein was quite public about his turnaround, noting in good populist fashion: "I've said before if we reach a roadblock and we have to make a detour, we will do that.... We're getting the feeling people are impacted by the overall health care restructuring."[56] From the 1997 election onwards, as the government began to spend money on health care and other services again, it always insisted that funds were available for such spending because the earlier cuts had allowed the government to gradually get the province out of debt.

Klein's ability to use his communications strategy to convey the government's priorities went beyond the success of the campaign to make cutbacks look necessary. In the early 2000s, the Alberta government, which was vigorously opposing the Kyoto agreement on behalf of the energy companies that were the Conservatives' chief financial backers, was dismayed to find that national polls suggested that two-thirds of Albertans, along with a similar majority of Canadians as a whole, wanted Canada to ratify this agreement that required Canada to make substantial cuts in its greenhouse gas emissions. Much as it did with the National Energy Program, the governing party, assuming that its position allowed it to use government revenues to promote the views of the governing party, filled every home with slick pamphlets and television, radio, and newspaper advertisements that used scare tactics to condemn Kyoto. The campaign suggested that the Alberta government had a plan to preserve the integrity of Alberta's environment at the same time that it allowed unrestricted growth in the energy industry, including the Alberta tar sands. This campaign succeeded since polls demonstrated a substantial decline in Kyoto support in Alberta over a short time.[57]

But how honest was the message that this communications campaign conveyed? As with the financial message, it would seem that the government was disguising the potential harmful impacts of its plans. It appears to have had no plan other than to let the tar sands companies carry on as they saw fit. While $200 billion had been invested in the tar sands by 2008, including pipelines and upgraders, making it the world's largest energy project and largest construction site, journalist Andrew Nikiforuk wrote in 2009, "No comprehensive assessment of the megaproject's environmental, economic, or social impact has been done."[58] He added, "Easy wealth has turned Alberta into a petrotyranny, while Canada has adopted all the trappings of an imperious oil kingdom, with a profound bitumen bias."[59] Though he would never use such tough language to describe the policies followed by Ralph Klein, Peter Lougheed became one of the province's toughest critics of the government's unwillingness to regulate the pace of tar sands development and its failure to require that the companies involved be required to build upgraders in Alberta rather than simply export raw bitumen.[60]

ED STELMACH'S CONSERVATIVES

When Ralph Klein resigned as premier in late 2006, his replacement, Ed Stelmach, was virtually unknown to most Albertans. But he was able to win another mandate for the Tories easily in 2008, despite some grumbling from energy companies about his plans to modestly increase royalties on resources. At the time, Big Oil saw the alternative to the Tories, the provincial Liberals, as less friendly to their interests than the Conservatives. In the period following the election, they would hedge their bets on the Tories by generously funding the Wild Rose Alliance, previously viewed as a fringe right-wing party mainly interested in defending rural interests and social conservatism. The goal of the energy industry seemed to be both to have an alternative government friendly to their industry ready to govern should the Tories falter and to use support for that alternative governing party as a lever to pressure the Tories to renege on their royalty increases.[61]

Ed Stelmach, though his own impulses seemed initially less authoritarian than Ralph Klein's, seemed gradually to follow almost instinctively both substantive and communication policies that had worked in the Klein era. Communications remained centralized, and critics of the government were silenced.[62] Members of the legislature who said anything critical in public were removed from caucus.[63] Stelmach, however, lacked the charisma to get away with such bullying. Perhaps Albertans were finally simply getting sick of the Tories. Perhaps the nasty recession that struck in late 2008 and ended what had seemed an unending energy boom made people anxious to look for new leaders. Stelmach's key problem, though, was that he was not a showman like Ralph Klein. Like Harry Strom and Don Getty, he did not project much of anything to Albertans. He lacked Klein's populist impulse that could make a premier who was arguably in the pockets of oil companies seem to be an everyman, whose concern at all times was, as he said endlessly, to think about the views and needs of "Henry and Martha." Stelmach resigned in 2011, and the party chose Alison Redford, formerly the provincial minister of justice, as the new party leader and premier in September of that year.

CONCLUSIONS

Parties that present themselves as the personification of all Albertans rather than mere policy-driven political organizations have struck a chord with voters throughout most of the province's history. They have been able to create long-lasting political dynasties when they have found charismatic leaders who embodied aspirations of significant sections of the population at a given time. Communication strategies reflected efforts to create a unity of purpose between the governing party and the people. Christian beliefs in the period before significant urbanization united most Albertans. Social Credit relied on an image of righteousness and tight controls of the public purse that appeared to hide the fact that for much of its period in power, the party was venal and secretive about at least some of its economic policies. The imposing personalities of Aberhart and Manning caused their Christian-minded supporters to have few doubts about the integrity of the regime. It was only when the rather boring Harry Strom took power at a point when younger Albertans and newcomers to the province failed to identify with a religious-based Social Credit regime that the dynasty, unable to create a more modern image, began to crumble rapidly.

Peter Lougheed, who kept whatever religious beliefs he had to himself, developed a more sophisticated communications strategy that gave him the aura of JFK and "the man from Prudential" of advertising fame rolled into one. He and his cabinets presented themselves as prudent but visionary economic managers, taking advantage of the very real concerns that Albertans had developed about whether the province could survive over the long haul as a one-trick pony. While his government did indeed have ambitious plans to diversify the Alberta economy, it largely failed in this objective. The spectacular failure of the Principal Group in the early Getty years raised questions about just how deserved the Lougheed government's "prudent economic manager" image really was. His successor, Don Getty, proved unable to develop a communications strategy that would give his government the same image of competence that the Lougheed government exuded. If the Lougheed and Getty governments could nevertheless at least be given credit for having some vision of the public good, however flawed, the Klein government seemed obsessed with cutbacks and reducing the overall role of government in Alberta. It developed a centralized, intelligent policy for conveying its neo-liberal policies as in the interests of balanced economic development for Alberta. But all that materialized was uncontrolled tar sands development, which will likely define the province's economic and political directions for the forseeable future. Klein's populist anti-government spin proved almost as effective as Lougheed's patrician approach in limiting the advance of a partisan opposition in Alberta. While Lougheed caught the wave of concern about apparently depleting energy resources in the 1970s to create a somewhat state-centred version of Conservatism for the province, Klein took advantage of the disillusionment with the failure of the Lougheed-Getty vision to refashion the provincial Progressive Conservative Party as the party of minimal government and minimal taxation. Each man had both the personality and a supportive communications strategy to use the same party as the tribune for their rather different approaches to the role of government.

NOTES

1   C. B. Macpherson, in *Democracy in Alberta: Social Credit and the Party System* (Toronto: University of Toronto Press, 1953), was the first to accuse Albertans of subscribing to plebiscitarian ideas rather than accepting the party system. While the first-past-the-post system wildly exaggerates the extent to which Albertans as a whole fail to consider opposition parties as the answer to governments that seem to be failing their citizens, it also creates legislatures in which such parties have little representation. That leads to demoralization. So, for example, when the CCF won one of every four votes in 1944

but only two seats in the legislature, it began to fall apart; by the time the 1948 election occurred, it had a membership only one-third as large as its 1944 membership. Alvin Finkel, *The Social Credit Phenomenon in Alberta* (Toronto: University of Toronto Press, 1989), 125–26.

2   For background on Aberhart, see David R. Elliott and Iris Miller, *Bible Bill: A Biography of William Aberhart* (Edmonton: Reidmore, 1987). On Manning, see Brian Brennan, *The Good Steward: The Ernest C. Manning Story* (Calgary: Fifth House, 2008).

3   Finkel, *The Social Credit Phenomenon*, 29. On religion in Alberta more generally, see W. E. Mann, *Sect, Cult and Church in Alberta* (Toronto: University of Toronto Press, 1955).

4   Elliott and Miller, *Bible Bill*, 307–14; Finkel, *The Social Credit Phenomenon*, 137; John A. Irving, "Psychological Aspects of the Social Credit Movement in Alberta. Part III. An Interpretation of the Movement," *Canadian Journal of Psychology* 1 (1947): 127–40; Bob Hesketh, *Major Douglas and Alberta Social Credit* (Toronto: University of Toronto Press, 1997), 237–38.

5   Simon Kiss, "Selling Government: The Evolution of Government Public Relations in Alberta" (PhD diss., Queen's University, 2008), 68.

6   Finkel, *The Social Credit Phenomenon*, 57, 59, 61–62.

7   A perceptive analysis of the 1940 election is found in Edward Bell, *Social Classes and Social Credit* (Montreal and Kingston: McGill-Queen's University Press), chap. 8.

8   Finkel, *The Social Credit Phenomenon*, chaps. 3 and 4; Elliot and Miller, Bible Bill, chaps. 15–18.

9   Brennan, *The Good Steward*, 120.

10   Finkel, *The Social Credit Phenomenon*, 128–30; Brennan, The Good Steward, 120–24.

11   Finkel, *The Social Credit Phenomenon*, 130–32.

12   Ibid.

13   Robert Hesketh, "The Company A, Company B Charges: The Manning Government, the Treasury Branches and Highway Contracts" (master's thesis, University of Alberta, 1989). The extent to which this thesis is unknown is clear in Brian Brennan's biography of Manning, which makes no reference to Hesketh's thesis and provides mainly Manning's side of the story of the 1955 charges, election, and commission.

14   Ibid., 371–72.

15   Finkel, *The Social Credit Phenomenon*, 168–69, chap. 7.

16   Meir Serfaty, "The Conservative Party of Alberta Under Lougheed, 1965–71: Building an Image and an Organization," *Prairie Forum* 6 (Spring 1981): 57–74; Howard Palmer and Tamara Palmer, "The 1971 Election and the Fall of Social Credit in Alberta," *Prairie Forum* 1 (November 1976): 123–34; Edward Bell, "The Rise of the Lougheed Conservatives and the Demise of Social Credit in Alberta: A Reconsideration," *Canadian Journal of Political Science* 26 (September 1993): 455–75.

17   Roger Epp, "The Lougheed Government and the Media: News Management in the Alberta Political Environment," *Canadian Journal of Communications* 10 (Spring 1984): 41.

18   Kiss, "Selling Government," 3, 69.

19   Rich Vivone, *Ralph Could Have Been a Superstar: Tales of the Klein Era* (Kingston: Patricia Publishing, 2009), 69.

20 Epp, "The Lougheed Government," 42.

21 Kiss, "Selling Government," 57, 81–82.

22 Paul Eichorn, "For the Record: Watching Canadian Reality," *Take One*, June 22, 1998, http://www.highbeam.com/doc/1G1-30555250.html.

23 John Richards and Larry Pratt, *Prairie Capitalism: Power and Influence in the New West* (Toronto: McClelland and Stewart, 1979), chap. 7.

24 Elections Alberta, "General Election Results: Candidate Summary of Results," May 8, 1986, and June 15, 1993, http://www.elections.ab.ca/public%20website/746.htm#1986.

25 Tamara Kozlowska, interview with Alvin Finkel, Edmonton, December 1, 2009.

26 Peter Faid, "Poverty Reduction Policies and Programs in Alberta: Extending the Alberta Advantage" (Ottawa: Canadian Council on Social Development, 2009), 6–7.

27 Ronald D. Kneebone, "From Famine to Feast: The Evolution of Budgeting Rules in Alberta," *Canadian Tax Journal* 54 (November 2006): 665.

28 Marc Lisac, *The Klein Revolution* (Edmonton: NeWest, 1995), 31. See also David Leyton-Brown, ed., *Canadian Annual Review of Politics and Public Affairs, 1990* (Toronto: University of Toronto Press, 1991), 225.

29 Lisac, *The Klein Revolution*, 30, 32.

30 Kiss, "Selling Government," 90–91.

31 Lisac, *The Klein Revolution*, 33–35.

32 Leyton-Brown, *Canadian Annual Review*, 247.

33 Anthony E. Boardman, Claude Laurin, and Aidan R. Vining, "Privatization in North America," in *International Handbook on Privatization*, ed. David Parker and David S. Saal (Cheltenham, UK: Edward Elgar, 2003), 137.

34 Kiss, "Selling Government," 106–7.

35 Ibid., 113.

36 Ibid., 124–26.

37 Centralization of government under Klein is examined in Keith Brownsey, "Ralph Klein and the Hollowing of Alberta," in *The Return of the Trojan Horse: Alberta and the New World (Dis)Order*, ed. Trevor Harrison (Montreal: Black Rose, 2005), 23–36.

38 Vivone, *Ralph Could Have Been a Superstar*, 6.

39 Shannon Sampert, "King Ralph, the Ministry of Truth, and the Media in Alberta," in *The Return of the Trojan Horse: Alberta and the New World (Dis)Order*, ed. Trevor Harrison (Montreal: Black Rose, 2005), 40, 44; Vivone, *Ralph Could Have Been a Superstar*, 53–54.

40 Kiss, "Selling Government," ii.

41 Claude Denis, "'Government Can Do Whatever It Wants': Moral Regulation in Ralph Klein's Alberta," *Canadian Review of Sociology and Anthropology* 32 (August 1995): 365–83.

42 Natasha Mekhail, "Free Radicals: Edmontonians Who've Mobilized, Motivated and Raised a Little Hell," *See Magazine*, May 1, 2003; Vivone, *Ralph Could Have Been a Superstar*, 110–11.

43 William Marsden, *Stupid to the Last Drop: How Alberta Is Bringing Environmental Armageddon to Canada* (and Doesn't Seem to Care) (Toronto: Alfred A. Knopf, 2007), 128; Vivone, *Ralph Could Have Been a Superstar*, 107; Shannon Phillips, "Parkland Institute Turns Ten," *Vue Weekly*, October 11, 2006.

44 This calculation was made by my colleague Jeff Taylor after he read Klein's essay. Taylor noted that Klein, despite his conservatism, was lifting materials at random from the web, including materials that were clearly Marxist in their orientation that he quoted uncritically along with more conservative materials, all mishmashed together without any indication that the student saw the differences among these various materials.

45 As a professor at the university, I joined a conspiracy of silence in which we refused media requests for comment. No one in management directed us to remain silent. There was a general understanding that any comments to the media or any effort to punish this student for failing to cite his sources could result in arbitrary reductions to the Athabasca University government grant.

46 Vivone, *Ralph Could Have Been a Superstar*, 112.

47 Athabasca University's plagiarism policy at the time defined *plagiarism* as follows: "The willful act of presenting another person's work as one's own without the proper academic acknowledgment and recognition." *Athabasca University Calendar 2007–08*, 258.

48 Kevin Taft, *Shredding the Public Interest: Ralph Klein and Twenty-five Years of One-Party Government* (Edmonton: University of Alberta Press, 1999), 95.

49 Greg Flanagan, "Not Just About Money: Provincial Budgets and Political Ideology," in *The Return of the Trojan Horse: Alberta and the New World (Dis)Order*, ed. Trevor Harrison (Montreal: Black Rose, 2005), 118.

50 Ibid., 122.

51 Gordon Laxer and Trevor Harrison eds., *Trojan Horse: Alberta and the Future of Canada* (Montreal: Black Rose, 1995); Trevor Harrison, ed., *The Return of the Trojan Horse: Alberta and the New World (Dis)Order* (Montreal: Black Rose, 2005).

52 Parkland Institute, "Giving Away the Golden Egg: Alberta's Tax Giveaway and the Need for Reforms," December 16, 2009, http://parklandinstitute.ca/research/summary/giving_away_the_golden_egg/parklandinstitute.ca/downloads/.../givingawaythegoldenegg-factsheet.pdf.

53 Jerrold L. Kachur, "Orchestrating Delusions: Ideology and Consent in Alberta," in *Contested Classrooms: Education, Globalization, and Democracy in Alberta*, ed. Trevor Harrison and Jerrold Lyne Kachur (Edmonton: University of Alberta Press, 1999), 59–74.

54 Harry H. Hiller, *Second Promised Land: Migration to Alberta and the Transformation of Canadian Society* (Montreal and Kingston: McGill-Queen's University Press, 2009).

55 Doreen Barrie, *The Other Alberta: Decoding a Political Enigma* (Regina: Canadian Plains Research Centre, 2006).

56 Lois Harder, *State of Struggle: Feminism and Politics in Alberta* (Edmonton: University of Alberta Press, 2003), 134–37.

57 "Alberta Launches Campaign Against Kyoto," *CBC News*, September 18, 2002, http://www.cbc.ca/news/canada/story/2002/09/18/alberta_kyoto020918.html; "Kyoto Protocol, Daily Rolling Poll," October 20–November 4, 2002, http://www.gov.ab.ca/home/documents/kyotopollnov2002.pdf.

58 Andrew Nikiforuk, *Tar Sands: Dirty Oil and the Future of a Continent* (Vancouver: Greystone Books, 2008), 2. As Nikiforuk notes, before the 1980s, bitumen sands were

commonly referred to by all as tar sands. The term conveys the extent to which bitumen is a viscous entity, which requires that large amounts of fresh water be mixed with it before it becomes a usable petroleum product. Critics of tar sands development emphasized the large-scale use of fresh water and the huge carbon dioxide emissions that characterized the extraction of bitumen. In an effort to minimize the differences in environmental degradation associated with the tar sands in comparison to conventional oil, during the 1980s the energy industry rebranded the tar sands as "oil sands." By 2000, most of the conventional media forbade the use of the term "tar sands." Nikiforuk's views are echoed in a number of works on the tar sands, including Marsden, *Stupid to the Last Drop*, and Don Woynillowicz, Chris Severson-Baker, and Marlo Reynolds, *Oil Sands Fever: The Environmental Implications of Canada's Oil Sands Rush* (Drayton Valley: Pembina Institute, 2005). The government's own take on the oil sands is found at Alberta Energy, "Oil Sands Frequently Asked Questions," http://www.energy.gov.ab.ca/OilSands/792.asp.

59 Nikiforuk, *Tar Sands*, 166.

60 "Peter Lougheed Speaks Out: An Interview with Alberta's Iconic Ex-Premier," *Oil Week*, January 30, 2008.

61 *Insight into Government* reported on the large donations that oil companies were making to the Wild Rose Alliance in 2009.

62 For example, when four top public health officials quit in June 2008, the government did not allow them to speak publicly about their reasons for resigning and claimed that they left for other jobs because they wanted more money than the government was willing to pay. But infectious disease expert Dr. Stan Houston of the University of Alberta revealed publicly that one of the health officials who was leaving claimed that she was getting little government support for combating a syphilis epidemic in the province. The acting chief medical officer of the Department of Health, Dr. Gerry Predy, responded by filing a complaint against Houston with the College of Physicians and Surgeons for his public comments. The College, according to Houston, simply asked him to elaborate on his comments, and no discipline was applied. But the lengthy process, during which Houston was unsurprisingly advised by his lawyer not to comment on the matter to the media, allowed the original issue to slip by before Houston was in the clear. Brian Mason, MLA, Highlands-Norwood, *Alberta Hansard*, November 5, 2008, 1778–79.

63 Guy Boutilier, a cabinet minister under Klein, criticized the government for doing an about-face on its promise to build a long-term care facility in his constituency of Fort McMurray-Wood Buffalo. Premier Stelmach ousted him from the PC caucus for this action, claiming that MLAs who had criticisms of the government should make those criticisms behind closed doors in caucus meetings, not in public.

Robert Bergen

Throwing the Baby Out with the Bathwater: Canadian Forces News Media Relations and Operational Security

On March 24, 1999, Canadian CF-18 fighter jets from CFB Bagotville, Québec, dropped their first of 568 bombs on military targets in Kosovo and Serbia, Almost exactly twelve years later, Canadian CF-18s from Bagotville once again took to the skies over the northern coast of Libya as part of a US-led coalition to enforce a UN Security Council–endorsed no-fly zone over the troubled North African country. Two days after that, shortly after 1:00 p.m. on March 23, Major-General Tom Lawson, Canada's Assistant Chief of Air Staff, confirmed at a media briefing at National Defence headquarters in Ottawa that four Canadian CF-18s had dropped their first bombs on an ammunition depot near Misurata in north Libya. Canada's jets were once again officially at war in a distant land. Major-General Lawson's briefing to the media was quite detailed, and he produced stunning cockpit video of the air strikes. "What you see here on the screen behind me," he said, "is what is seen by the pilot in his aircraft. The flashing crosshairs indicate where he has placed his laser indication. In a second, you'll see the impact of his laser-guided bomb on the riveted bunkers carrying Libyan armed forces ammunition. Shortly after this, you'll see a secondary explosion to the right side of your screen, indicating that there were weapons held there."[1] For the first time, Canada was involved in two simultaneous conflicts involving its army in Afghanistan and its navy and air force off the shores and over the skies of Libya. Quite predictably, when federal politicians rose to their feet in the House of Commons to speak about the Libyan mission, they made comparisons to the air force's role in the 1991 Persian Gulf War and over Serbia and Kosovo.

Canadians know little of the jets' missions during the Gulf War and even less about the 1999 Kosovo air war: this lack of knowledge resulted from a host of factors that saw the Canadian Forces effectively undermine the democratic role of the Canadian media and stifle coverage of Canada's first protracted war efforts since the Korean War. The key restrictive element cited in 1999 and again in 2011 is "operational security." At the time of this writing, the mission over Libya has ended, and it therefore offers an opportunity to make comparisons about the state of the Canadian media coverage of conflicts and the military's management of the media over time. A brief review of the history will highlight how that management has evolved and how it is being implemented now.

THE 1991 PERSIAN GULF WAR

In the months before the war, the Canadian Forces viewed the impending conflict as an opportunity to build popular support for the military. Internal military documents, obtained using the *Access to Information Act*, show that the military anticipated "maximum disclosure of information consistent with maintaining the operational security of Canada's forces and those of other allied nations participating in the Gulf operations."[2] In its "After Action Report" on its public affairs planning, the Canadian military stated that it knew the media would play an influential role in that communications strategy because they would be the key conveyors of information about, and interpreters of, the war's events to the Canadian public.[3]

The plan specified:

a. Within the scope of operational security, media will be accorded every possible assistance in the preparation and filing of their reports;

b. Censorship will not be invoked by DND or by CANFORCOMME. The imposition of censorship can only be derived from censorship policy of the Canadian government.

Therefore it is paramount that a good working relationship with the news media be established to ensure they understand the necessity to voluntarily comply with in-theatre security screening guidelines. Accordingly, media covering the roles, operations and activities of the Canadian Forces Middle East should be prepared to submit their copy for security screening only;

c. There will be no suggestion that media expunge critical commentary from their reports unless there is an impact on security of operations;

d. Before they are provided access to in-theatre operations, all media are to be provided unclassified briefings about Canadian Forces operations and activities in the Persian Gulf, security considerations and requirements, and what is expected of them while they are visiting CANFORME units;

e. Media embarked in HMC ships may use ships' communications resources, when appropriate and available. The Canadian Forces will provide protective clothing and equipment to media representatives when they are embarked in HMC ships;

f. All interviews with news media representatives will be "on the record";

g. Journalists will be requested to dateline their articles and reports generically, such as "… with the Canadian Forces in Bahrain/Qatar/Persian Gulf." No specific locations will be used when filing stories;

h. Media representatives will be assisted by on-site public affairs officers;

i. Diplomatic clearances, visa and inoculations will be the responsibility of the media members; and,

j. Media who are not prepared to work within these guidelines will not be provided access to CANFORME operations, activities and units.[4]

Journalists had to accept those guidelines in order to be accredited. Despite the military's claim that it wanted to be as transparent as possible, the media howled over the restrictions placed on them, referring to them as "censorship guidelines." For example, the *Globe and Mail* reported on January 19, 1991, that military censors aboard Canadian ships reviewed journalists' stories to determine whether they jeopardized operational security using guidelines that mirrored US Defence Department guidelines on the prohibition of information that would reveal military operations' details, size, location, or movement.[5]

In the Canadian Forces' lessons-learned analysis of its media management, the authors of the report wrestled with the two conflicting imperatives of their practices: openness and candour versus operational security. The report recommended: "We should standardize with our allies who have had more operational experience than we have and adopt their more liberal release of info policies."[6]

THE 1999 KOSOVO AIR WAR

Some eight years after the writing of the Persian Gulf "After Action Report," the Canadian Forces, during the 1999 Kosovo air war, completely ignored its own recommendation to adopt more liberal release of operational information. University of Leeds scholar Philip M. Taylor noted in 1995 that, despite rapid advances in communications technologies, there remained two ways militaries can effectively censor the media during conflict. First, access to troops can be denied altogether, and second, military leaders can control messages about the conflicts by inserting themselves into the news-gathering process.[7] Air wars, in particular, lend themselves to such censorship quite easily because it is impossible for journalists to accompany pilots on their combat missions. As a result, crews can only be interviewed before or after their missions, and journalists' reports can be supplemented by cockpit footage of bombings.[8] Taylor argued that such images could not convey the "sounds, sight, smell, touch and taste of the nasty, brutal business of people killing people" that would frighten, appall, and repel most people.

During the Kosovo air war, the Canadian Forces applied both censorship techniques. Members of the media who travelled to Aviano, Italy, to report on Canadian air force participation in NATO's 78-day bombing campaign were confined to the US sectors of the Aviano air base. Completely denied access to Canadian crews, the media had to rely on the goodwill of Colonel Dwight

Davies, which was in short supply.[9] Davies, who commanded Canada's Task Force Aviano, had no time for members of the media who he thought belittled the efforts of his air crews by questioning their proficiency at hitting targets.[10] He also believed, wrongly, that the Canadian pilots identified in news reports during the 1991 Gulf War had body bags thrown on their families' lawns by protestors opposed to the war. As a result, he would not allow the few pilots who eventually did speak to reporters to identify themselves or discuss details of their missions.

The Canadian Forces in Ottawa staged daily briefings on the war, but those briefings contained very little specific information about operations and no accounts of mission successes or failures. During one of them, in the most high-profile interview of the campaign, journalists talked in a conference call to one unidentified Canadian CF-18 pilot in Aviano about his feelings about flying into combat for the first time, but raised little else.[11] Effectively, all life was stripped out of the journalists' few print or TV reports from Aviano. In Ottawa, the Department of National Defence invoked "operational security" time and again, sometimes ludicrously, as a reason for not releasing information. The June 1, 1999, briefing is one example. That day, a journalist tried to get a sense of what the Canadians were doing in the bombing campaign by asking about the number of bombs dropped. Chief of Joint Operations Brigadier-General David Jurkowski stonewalled on the grounds of security. Asked for the cost of the weapons dropped to date, Jurkowski replied: "That could lead one to think about the number of weapons and by way of policy and security, we don't talk about the number of weapons employed."[12] The journalist pressed, wanting to know why the number of bombs was a security issue and arguing that Canadians had a right to know the cash value of munitions dropped. Jurkowski responded: "I don't have those numbers for you right now and for security reasons, I'm not going to address it any further."[13]

The journalist then dropped that line of questioning but picked it up the next day with Deputy Chief of Defence Staff Lieutenant-General Ray Henault. Henault went on the offensive in response: "We have been, I think, fairly open. In fact, very open throughout this whole process now at seventy-one days of giving you briefings daily so I think our process has been very open and transparent, probably in a way unprecedented in the past."[14] Henault then contradicted Jurkowski's decision that, for policy and security reasons, the bombs' costs would not be revealed by saying that Operation Echo had cost

$20 million to date and about 45 percent of that was on bombs.[15] The journalists did not question the apparent inconsistency—why that precise information was withheld for security reasons one day and was not a security threat the next.

In the end, a content analysis of the entire daily print and TV coverage of the 78-day war revealed that nearly 60 percent of the coverage had two sentences or less about the CF-18s' involvement. Slightly more than 75 percent had six sentences or less. Not much can be learned about the activities of air crew in a war in six sentences or less.[16]

As a result, the Canadian public knows nothing about Canada's involvement in the Kosovo air war. They don't know that within days of beginning the bombing campaign, the air force ran out of bombs and had to buy more from the Americans with government-issued credit cards. They don't know that the Canadian CF-18s' highly touted four-power magnification NITE Hawk B targeting pods were old school and paled in comparison to modern GPS equipment. They don't know that the pilots fought most of their missions at night without night-vision goggles and had to develop special flying formations to avoid crashing into each other. Canadians don't know that the CF-18s had old radios and had them jammed by the Serbs with Celine Dion's music. Canadians don't know that the ground crews suffered terribly working in the heat and rain in improper clothing. Most of all, they don't know about the effects of Canadian actions on the outcome of the war or even what kind of war it was. In short, Canadians deserve much better information about the courage of their military in the face of adversity.

AFGHANISTAN

Canadians have been deploying to Afghanistan since February 2002, and the Canadian Forces has studied media coverage and learned lessons about it—even if at times the lessons are ignored. Members of the Canadian Forces write about it in a scholarly fashion in refereed journals to diffuse the accumulated body of wisdom throughout the Forces' command chain in order to better manage it. They work from a 123-page *Public Affairs Handbook* first published January 15, 1974, amended in September 1985, and amended again in March 1999 specifically to describe how to control all manner of messages and images that could affect how the Forces appear publicly, including in the media.[17] There is no equivalent document in Canadian newsrooms or journalism schools. The most comprehensive guide that journalists have for dealing with the Canadian Forces comprises five pages in *The Canadian Press Stylebook*. It sets out the proper way to refer to the Forces, where headquarters are, the proper way to use titles and ranks before a name, and how to refer to retired officers; it specifies that courts martial are open to the media and contains a section on ceremonies and miscellaneous details, including the fact that Canadians do not go to boot camp, but they take basic training.[18]

The military's studied approach to the media was on display in an article in the Fall/Winter 2004 issue of *Canadian Army Journal* by Major Jay Janzen, who examined the relationship between the media and the military during Rotation Zero (ROTO 0) of Operation Athena in the summer of 2003, when Canadian journalists were embedded with the Third Battalion of the Royal Canadian Regiment (3 RCR) based in Kabul, Afghanistan. That relationship came from a ground rules agreement, borrowed from the American experience in Iraq to manage the journalists hosted by the 3 RCR.[19] The Canadian military quickly learned that there were big differences between the American concept of embedding in Iraq and the Canadians' Afghanistan experience. In the Iraq war, for example, individual journalists were assigned to specific units for the duration—eating, sleeping, and travelling with the same unit for weeks or even months, and receiving briefings from platoon or company commanders with scant public affairs experience.[20] As a result, they had little contact with public affairs officers or senior commanders, and the military lost its ability to influence the journalists from a strategic perspective.[21]

The Canadian journalists, meanwhile, were based at Camp Julien in separate living quarters from the troops. There were eight of them from five different media organizations, and they were in regular contact with public affairs and senior officers, who learned, as an effective media relations tactic, that by informally engaging the journalists, they could often influence what they covered. Major Janzen explained:

> On many occasions, senior officers would join members of the media for meals or a cup of coffee. These impromptu gatherings suggested to journalists that they were not regarded as an inconvenience or something to be avoided. Further, it gave both parties an opportunity to hold informal discussions that would often lead to positive story ideas being passed to journalists. Many

company commanders also sought out journalists when their troops were about to embark on interesting or important missions. Reporters appreciated being given information on upcoming activities rather than having to discover it on their own. By pushing information to the media, the battalion was also able to exercise some influence over what journalists decided to cover. When an opportunity to cover a mission or event was proactively presented to a reporter, it almost always received coverage.[22]

Major Janzen wrote that the military would prefer to have journalists remain in theatre for extended periods because interactions with them tended to be more cordial than with those who remained for only short periods or who chose not to be embedded. Those non-embedded journalists, called "uni-laterals," who did not sign the embedding agreement sometimes just came and went, or lived off-camp. It was much more beneficial for the military to have embedded journalists with the Canadian troops rather than journalists reporting as unilaterals.[23]

The single biggest problem Major Janzen documented was disputes over access to information that the Forces refused to provide for reasons of operational security. Major Janzen notes that media members were routinely briefed on impending operations and provided with sensitive material to help them understand and report to Canadians about the overall Canadian mission in Kabul, but they weren't allowed to file reports until authorized to do so by unit commanders.

Embedded journalists signed a ground rules agreement far more restrictive than the ground rules agreement for the 1991 Persian Gulf War, which the media at the time claimed was censorship. While the later agreement didn't require media covering the roles, operations, and activities of the Canadian Forces in Afghanistan to submit their copy for security screening, as did the 1991 agreement, it detailed nineteen categories of information that could not be released unless specifically approved by the Task Force Commander and only ten categories that could. For reasons that appeared eminently reasonable, the information that could not be reported included such categories as "specific information on troop strength, equipment or critical supplies (e.g. artillery, radars, trucks water, etc.)" and "information on future operations, current operations, postponed or cancelled operations."[24] Among those that could be reported were the "arrival of military units in the area when officially announced," "non-sensitive, unclassified information regarding air and ground operations, past and present," and, laughably, "weather and climate conditions."[25] These detailed restrictions were imposed even though not one responsible journalist—or news organization, for that matter—would report on future operations.

Many journalists became impatient when, for example, during rocket attacks against Camp Julien, they could only leave their assigned protected areas seeking imagery, sounds, and impressions of the event under the escort of a public affairs officer. The problem with that approach, Major Janzen noted, was that Canadians reading or watching the news at home "can be left with impression the Canadian Forces are involved in a soft peacekeeping mission, when in fact troops are being deployed on some dangerous and sensitive missions."[26] The challenge, he wrote, was to strike a balance so the media could report on aspects of the missions while maintaining elevated levels of operational security.

The point is that Canadian journalists do not approach the Canadian Forces in the studied fashion that the military approaches them. There are no peer-reviewed journals to which they contributed reflections on their successes or failures as an industry in their coverage of the 1991 Persian Gulf War or the 1999 Kosovo air war.

Sharon Hobson, the Canadian correspondent for *Jane's* and a research fellow of the Canadian Defence and Foreign Affairs Institute, authored a paper for CDFAI that took an in-depth look at *operations security* (a term used interchangeably with operational security) as applied in Afghanistan. She examined the coverage of Afghan detainees and Canadian Special Forces operations and determined that one could learn very little from media reports about Afghan detainees and nothing at all about the Special Forces who have been in Afghanistan continuously since 2001. She argues: "The use of OPSEC [operations security] to deny information to the public is often understandable and justifiable when the CF deploys on a combat mission. But if it is to be acceptable, it must be applied with surgical precision, to specific events, materiel, or personnel. To apply the broad brush of OPSEC to deny information as a matter of convenience, without explanation or with false explanations, undermines the military's credibility not only on the operation in question but in all areas."[27]

An example of what Hobson meant was the February 2008 media briefing provided by Brigadier-General Peter Atkinson, director of General Operations with the Strategic Joint Staff, in which he talked about operations security. It shows exactly how far operational security has evolved since it was first institutionalized in the 1991 ground rules agreement. He acknowledged the media's requirement for information but pointed out the problems associated with providing it:

> Simply put, OPSEC is keeping the good guys' secrets from the bad guys. We firmly believe that Canadians have the right to know about our operations in Afghanistan. We also understand the importance of independent reporting and analysis of the government of Canada in this complex environment. Your appetite for information serves positive and lawful objectives of our Canadian democracy. OPSEC allows the safeguarding of some information that has an operational impact on our mission while permitting Canadians to know as much as possible about their soldiers and members of the whole government team....
>
> Simply, the smallest piece of information may be invaluable in the hands of personnel employed in the counter-intelligence world, given the fact that they have access to a much broader spectrum of information. In the hands of a journalist, unrelated pieces of information can be turned into an excellent story.
>
> The same is true for sensitive information, which may not in and of themselves be sensitive but formed together they create a comprehensive picture of significant use to our adversaries....
>
> To close, here is an excerpt from an Al-Qaeda training manual with respect to their use of information sources. They identify that an organization must gather as much information as possible about the enemy, in other words about us. Information in their words has two sources:
>
> Public sources. Using this public source openly and without resorting to illegal means it is possible to gather at least 80% of the information about the enemy.
>
> Now secret sources. It is possible through these secret and dangerous methods to obtain 20% of the information that is considered secret.

So we need to make their collection efforts as difficult as possible, by denying them 80% of the solution. This will make it difficult for groups like Al-Qaeda to plan their operations.[28]

Using a baby-and-the-bath-water analogy, if the baby is 20 percent of information that is considered secret and the water is 80 percent of the information that is available publicly, Brigadier-General Atkinson proposes a 100 percent solution that would throw the baby out with the bath water. In his application of operational security, the Canadian media would have absolutely no understanding of or knowledge about what the Canadian Forces do on the ground.

LIBYA

Much like during the Kosovo air war, daily press conferences on the Libya conflict began at National Defence headquarters on March 21, 2011, the first day of Canadian operations. The previous week, the air force had been tasked with contributing to the UN Security Council–backed no-fly zone over Libya. In-theatre operations comprises two task forces. Task Force Charlottetown consists of about 250 personnel aboard the frigate *HMCS Charlottetown*, contributing to a multinational flotilla of sixteen ships escorting and providing air defence for more vulnerable vessels. Task Force Libecco consists of some 265 personnel, the seven CF-18 Hornet jet fighters, two CC-150 Polaris in-flight refuellers, and two CP-140 Aurora maritime patrol aircraft. The planes fly from Italy's Trapani-Birgi Airbase in Sicily, while the task force headquarters is in Poggio Renatico, about thirty kilometres northeast of Bologna.[29]

Canadian CF-18 operations began on March 21, and later that day, politician after politician rose in the House of Commons hours after the press briefing to speak to a motion supporting the mission presented by Defence Minister Peter MacKay. None of them referred to the Canadian military action as an act of war. The key words in the motion were the following: "The government shall work with our allies, partners and the United Nations to promote and support all aspects of UNSC Resolution 1973, which includes the taking of all necessary measures to protect civilians and civilian populated areas under threat of attack in Libya and to enforce the no-fly zone, including the use of the Canadian Forces and military assets in accordance with UNSC Resolution 1973."[30] In the same way in which the politicians had dodged the question of whether Canada was at war during the 1999 Kosovo air war, no Canadian political leader used the word "war" in 2011. In Kosovo, Canadian pilots dropped 568 bombs, some 500,000 pounds of high explosive, but it was not a war. "All necessary measures including the use of military assets," it seems, has become the euphemism for war.

Two prominent Canadian journalists, Rosie DiManno of the *Toronto Star* and Eric Reguly of the *Globe and Mail*, travelled to the Trapani-Birgi Airbase in Sicily to talk to Canadian fighter pilots. They were each only allowed to interview Lieutenant-Colonel Syvlain Ménard, commander of the 425th Tactical Fighter Squadron. Reguly arrived first. He reported on the importance the pilots place on hitting their targets with pinpoint accuracy, but also avoiding civilian casualties—even if that meant returning home without dropping bombs. He noted that the pilots are often provided with their target information while they are en route to the no-fly zone. He also reported that only one of the twelve pilots based in Sicily had flown in combat missions over Serbia and Kosovo. Sadly, Reguly was not allowed to talk to any of them. There was no explanation why.[31]

Five days later, DiManno published a story also quoting Colonel Ménard on the importance of the pilots not dropping their bombs if they think they can't do so without killing civilians. That made the mission particularly difficult when Colonel Gadhafi's troops routinely placed their weapons near civilians, effectively making them human shields. She also went into some detail about the amount of flying required—that a mission can begin around 8:40 a.m. and return to the tarmac at 1:32 p.m, and that the pilots are routinely provided with their target information en route to the no-fly zone. Colonel Ménard was also the only pilot she interviewed.

Why was Colonel Ménard the only one who talked to Reguly and DiManno? Were there operational security concerns, and if so, what were they? Were they the same as those of the Canadian commander in Aviano more than a decade earlier—that families in Canada would be threatened if pilots were identified in the news media? Those questions were put to Major Leah Byrne in Poggio Renatico. She replied:

The concern is that not everyone is in favour of this air campaign and what we are doing. Until a thorough threat analysis could be completed it was determined that only the detachment commander would speak to the media. Due to their positions they have an added level of responsibility and with this comes any additional risk that might (or might not) be associated with having their name in public. As you can appreciate this campaign started with very little notice, and so in due time we will be able to determine if a more liberal approach is warranted. We know there is a demand from the media to talk to pilots and so we have adopted this approach until it can be further reviewed.[32]

No one in Ottawa mentioned the need to conduct a threat assessment in the interest of operational security. The argument that not everyone is in favour of the war and there is a need for a threat assessment, however, has the potential to be even more draconian than the previously advanced "mosaic" argument that even small amounts of information could reveal much about the larger picture. It is unlikely that those who are opposed to the bombing will have an epiphany and suddenly support it. That means a thorough threat analysis could last until the last bomb is dropped and the last airplane returned to Canada. The result is that the restrictions placed on journalists could last that long or even longer, and, just as in the Kosovo air war, very few Canadians will have a current understanding of what their airmen and women are doing in battle.

It is also ironic that the Canadian commander of the NATO bombing campaign, Lieutenant-General Charles Bouchard, told the media at Allied Joint Forces Command in Naples, "It's not about me, it's about the whole gang here that NATO was able to so quickly put it together."[33] In an interview, the general was candid about his role directing the war and the pressures he faced to minimize civilian casualties, but he was disingenuous in stating that it is not about him and a handful of others who have been named in relation to the war. In fact, the coverage is about him rather than his troops since through the constraints placed on the media, their coverage has made him and his commanders the faces of the war, not the hundreds of Canadians actually fighting and supporting it.

It is just as Philip Taylor highlighted: access to troops can be denied altogether and military leaders can control messages about the conflicts by inserting themselves into the news-gathering process. An example appeared in the *Globe and Mail* after reporter Paul Koring flew on a Canadian Hercules mid-air refuelling mission. He quoted a pilot's joke that bomb-laden Italian Tornados arrive early for fuel but said he could not name the pilot; he did not, however, include why he was prevented from doing that. The Canadian Forces–supplied picture showed the backs of two pilots' heads. Surprisingly, Koring did identify a Captain Andre Kratochvil, who commanded the ground crew keeping the Hercules flying, although the captain didn't say more than one sentence about what they were doing: "You name it, we fly it, trash hauling [airlifting of supplies], refuelling, northern resupply, medevac."[34] That story of flying skill under less than ideal conditions was interesting but is just the tip of the iceberg of what could be reported about the bombing campaign without some of the needless restrictions imposed by the Canadian Forces.

CONCLUSIONS

Much has changed since two *Calgary Herald* journalists took portable computers and one of the first digital cameras to cover the Canadian Forces in Croatia and Bosnia in the war-torn former Yugoslavia in 1994 and transmitted stories and digital pictures to Canada via satellites from a war zone. Email was then in its infancy.

Journalists, some of whom work for multi-billion news organizations, now have cell phones, Blackberrys and iPhones, voicemail, email, text messaging, YouTube, Facebook, Twitter, satellite phones, and portable satellite dishes that can keep them in instant touch with their newsrooms and people all around the world. The media's modern technology can also connect soldiers, sailors, and airmen and women with Canadians at home to tell their stories in ways that were unthinkable even in Croatia and Bosnia in 1994. The live coverage of the invasion of Iraq and the war in Afghanistan are prime examples. Canadians are more connected, but are they more and better informed about the Canadian Forces in conflict in the new millennium? Sadly, the answer is no. The operational security restrictions developed in 1991 to manage the Canadian news media during the first Gulf War have been refined and codified to the point where, according to some members of the Canadian military, enemies can gather valuable battlefield advantages by building intelligence pictures in a mosaic-like fashion, similar to how a journalist begins with one nugget of information and uses it to build a coherent story. That possibility, they argue, necessitates the denial of all information, even if 80 percent of it is available publicly.

As that spectre unfolds, others talk about the need for threat assessments, which do the same thing: deny journalists the information that they want and that Canadians need until the threat picture is understood in its entirety. If one operational security concern is no longer valid, a new one rises like a phoenix to replace it. The central issue is that the principle of operational security—or not jeopardizing a mission or troops—is so broad that there is no one single definition or standard for its application. That is apparent from the last category of information that can't be released under the Canadian embedding agreement for Afghanistan. Added to an alphabetical catalogue of specific information that can't be released is "any other information" that the commander of Joint Task Force Afghanistan orders restricted for operational reasons. That gives absolute power to the field commander to censor what Canadians can or can't learn about Afghanistan. Who or what is the driving force behind withholding information about equipment, training, mission preparedness, or other information that would allow an assessment of what is or is not being accomplished? Is it the chief of defence staff, who may want to avoid questions that might embarrass the Defence minister? Is it the Defence minister himself, or the Privy Council Office? I can find no smoking gun that points anywhere but to the military public affairs officials who wrote operational security into their public affairs plans. After that, the gun points to individual spokespeople in Ottawa and field commanders, who have wide latitude to decide what the news media can and cannot know and report.

Censorship has been officially invoked by the Canadian government only during the First and Second World Wars. Now, with "operational security," there is no need for official censorship. This didn't start with the war in Libya; it started in the 1991 Persian Gulf War and followed through to the role of Canadian troops in the battle of the Medak Pocket in Croatia in 1993, to the 1999 Kosovo air war, to Afghanistan, and to Libya. The implications for Canadian democracy are profound. Canadians will not be able to make timely and informed judgements about the military's performance and actions, and the government's ability to oversee the military's conduct of war. That is not how democracies are supposed to work and not how militaries are supposed to behave. It does, though, give credence to the old adage that militaries defend democracy, but they don't always practice it.

That is one half of the concern. The other is that there are less than a dozen journalists in Canada who specialize in covering the Canadian Forces. Only a handful—like Graeme Smith, Matthew Fisher, Murray Brewster, Louie Palu, Francis Silvaggio, Bill Graveland, and Adam Day—have returned to Afghanistan six times or more. They have the opportunity to see the evolution of Canadian operations in the Kandahar region, unlike the vast majority of Canadian journalists who embed with the Forces there for six weeks and never return or cover the military again. Only this select few have the opportunity to see for themselves how the mission has changed and to assess its successes or failures. It is to that handful's great credit that they have been able to accomplish much of that and, as a result, deserve their rightful place in Canadian journalism history. No one can or should compel a journalist to risk his or her life to go to places like Afghanistan to cover wars. The tragic death of the *Calgary Herald*'s health care reporter, Michelle Lang, in Afghanistan on December 30, 2009, underscores the risks involved. The ones who do go, go voluntarily, but there aren't enough of them to do the job as well as the Canadian news media ought to during troubled times.

The Canadian combat mission in Afghanistan ended in the summer of 2011, and later that fall, *The Savage War*, a book on the combat mission in Afghanistan and the Ottawa backroom politics written by the Canadian Press's defence correspondent, Murray Brewster, was published. What comes screaming off its pages is the unstated message that it is virtually impossible for even the most dedicated readers and viewers to entirely understand a complex mission like Afghanistan by reading daily snippets about it in newspapers or watching TV. The war only becomes somewhat comprehensible when someone like Brewster compiles as much of his knowledge about it as possible in one place. Having said that, until books like Brewster's are written, the media is the only way possible for most Canadians to learn about wars in distant lands. It should be noted that Brewster's book focuses mostly on infantry operations and uses the word *tanks* only twice. The fact of the matter is that the Lord Strathcona's Horse (Royal Canadians) had rotated a squadron of tanks into Afghanistan continuously since the fall of 2006 with virtually no media coverage. Brewster also delves into his journalistic relationships with the Forces and politicians. Obviously, it is easier to cover an army or a navy than it is to cover a tank squadron because a tank has no room for passengers.

Similarly, journalists can't travel with pilots to see what they do. They can only watch on the ground as warplanes thunder into the skies and listen to the stories that emerge after the fact, if someone will talk.

Following the death of Libya's dictator Colonel Moammar Gadhafi on October 20, 2011, the Canadian government announced that its CF-18s would be returned to Canada by late October or early November. At the bombing campaign's conclusion, only Canadian Lieutenant-General Charles Bouchard, who commanded the NATO operations, spoke to the media, and even then, he only talked about the importance of avoiding civilian casualties. Sadly, it will probably be historians, not journalists, who will have to tell Canadians the whole stories of the Afghanistan and Libyan campaigns. That, in turn, and despite the best efforts of a courageous handful, speaks volumes about the gulf that still separates the Canadian military and the Canadian media in the fulfillment of their social and democratic responsibilities.

NOTES

1   Department of National Defence Canada, news conference transcript, March 23, 2011. Obtained from Media Q Inc, for a fee.
2   Director General of Public Affairs, "After Action Report: Operation Friction," Department of National Defence Canada, July 24, 1991. Obtained under *Access to Information Act*: request A-2003-00394.
3   Ibid.
4   Ibid. CANFORCOMME stands for Canadian Forces Commander, Middle East, and CANFORME for Canadian Forces Middle East.
5   R. W. Bergen, "Balkan Rats and Balkan Bats" (PhD diss., University of Calgary, 2005), 78.
6   Director General of Public Affairs, "After Action Report: Gulf War Public Affairs," Department of National Defence Canada, April 23, 1991. Obtained under *Access to Information Act*: request A-2003-00394.
7   Philip M. Taylor, "War and the Media" (keynote address at a conference on military-media relations, Royal Military Academy at Sandhurst, Surrey, UK, 1995), http://ics.leeds.ac.uk/papers/vp01.cfm?outfit=pmt&folder=34&paper=39.
8   Taylor, "War and the Media."
9   Bergen, "Balkan Rats and Balkan Bats," 342.
10 Ibid., 285.
11 Ibid., 343.
12 Deputy Chief of the Defence Staff Canada, news conference transcript of briefing, June 1, 1999. Obtained from the National Defence Public Affairs Office (Calgary).

13 Ibid.

14 Deputy Chief of the Defence Staff Canada, news conference transcript of briefing, June 2, 1999. Obtained from the National Defence Public Affairs Office (Calgary).

15 Ibid.

16 For a full examination of Canadian Forces management of the Canadian news media coverage of the Kosovo air war and its results, see Bergen, "Balkan Rats and Balkan Bats," 258–394.

17 Department of National Defence Canada, *Public Affairs Handbook* (Ottawa: Director General Public Affairs, 1999).

18 *The Canadian Press Stylebook*, 14th ed. (Toronto: Canadian Press, 2006), 253–55.

19 Major J. Janzen, "OP Athena ROTO 0-Embedded Media," *Canadian Army Journal* 7, nos. 3–4 (2004): 43–51.

20 Ibid., 43–44.

21 Ibid., 44.

22 Ibid., 45.

23 Ibid., 47–48.

24 Assistant Deputy Minister (Public Affairs), J5PA Instruction 0301, Department of National Defence Canada, November 12, 2003.

25 Ibid.

26 Ibid.

27 Sharon Hobson, "Operations Security and the Public's Need to Know" (Calgary: Canadian Defence and Foreign Affairs Institute, 2011), 15.

28 Brigadier-General P. Atkinson, ADM(PA), "Government Officials Hold Technical Briefing to Provide an Update on Canada's Activities in Afghanistan," news conference transcript, February 14, 2008. Obtained from National Defence Public Affairs Office (Prairies and NWT); Robert Bergen, *Censorship: The Canadian News Media and Afghanistan; A Historical Comparison with Case Studies* (Calgary: University of Calgary Press, 2009).

29 "Operation MOBILE," National Defence and the Canadian Forces, last modified November 4, 2011, http://www.cefcom.forces.gc.ca/pa-ap/ops/mobile/index-eng.asp.

30 House of Commons of Canada, *Debates*, vol. 145, no. 145 (March 21, 2011), 9071

31 Eric Reguly, "Inside the Cockpit of a CF-18: Avoid Civilians and Don't Get Shot," *Globe and Mail*, April 4, 2011.

32 Major Leah Byrne, email message to author, May 19, 2011.

33 Paul Koring, "'It's a Knife-Fight in a Phone Booth': Canadian Directing the War in Libya Speaks," *Globe and Mail*, June 13, 2011.

34 Paul Koring, "The Delicate Ballet of Mid-Air Refuelling," *Globe and Mail*, June 15, 2011.

PART II   **CITIZENS AND POLITICS IN EVERYDAY LIFE**

David Marshall

Exceptional Canadians: Biography in the Public Sphere

Biography humanizes history. It makes what are often complex, impersonal, and abstract matters tangible for those who seek some understanding of the society in which they live. Biography, therefore, is a good prism through which to explore popular attitudes of a nation's history. People look to biographies to examine and re-examine the past. And in the case of Canada, a nation that is perpetually unsure of its identity, biography often plays a role in the quest to define or understand the Canadian identity. Because so much is invested in biographical writing, the measure of a biography's quality or importance is not merely a matter of assessing the biographer's ability to recreate a person's life as it was lived. Often the biography is assessed according to what it tells Canadians about who they are, where they have been, and why they have come to a certain point in history.

A few years ago, the Canadian Broadcasting Corporation (CBC) under-took a national search to discover the greatest Canadian. Through a series of TV programs, CBC engaged Canadians in a debate about the contributions and significance of a wide range of well-known Canadian citizens. The lives of those being considered were presented to viewers by familiar public figures, such as television journalists Rex Murphy and George Stroumboulopoulos, actor and filmmaker Paul Gross, and author Charlotte Gray.[1] Viewers voted for the person they thought was most worthy of the title. This exercise in populist hero-making led to a storm of controversy, demonstrating both the virtues and perils of using biography as a means to understand the national historical experience. The eventual winner of the contest was Saskatchewan CCF Premier Tommy Douglas, the conscience of social reform and an exponent of the social gospel and democratic socialism in post–World War II Canada. Douglas's pioneering role in introducing a system of universal public health insurance over the protests of the medical doctors in Saskatchewan was the major reason for his emergence in the public mind as the greatest Canadian. Critics of CBC's process were not surprised by this outcome, for it revealed much about contemporary social concerns. At the time, Canada's national public health care system was in crisis and under serious scrutiny; some thought that it was no longer fiscally sustainable and therefore should be reformed, if not entirely dismantled. Douglas had become a weapon in the debates over the sustainability and wisdom of Canada's health care system.

The most controversial aspect of CBC's quest to identify the greatest Canadian, however, was the network's mini-series about Douglas titled *Prairie Giant: The Tommy Douglas Story*. This docudrama indulged in some of the worst failings of biography, including the tendency to attribute far too much to the subject of any biography and thus heroize the subject while demonizing anyone who stands in the way or is an adversary. In *Prairie Giant*, Douglas's political opponent, Saskatchewan Liberal leader Jimmy Gardiner, is presented as a hard-drinking thug.[2] Such a characterization grossly misrepresents Gardiner's personal attributes and moral code. He was a Presbyterian, one of the signatories of the United Church of Canada, an advocate and supporter of Prohibition, and a teetotaler himself.[3] At the same time, the less noble qualities of Douglas's life, such as his advocacy of eugenics in the 1930s, were overlooked.[4]

A challenge to CBC's "greatest Canadian" quest was undertaken by another popular forum for Canadian history, *The Beaver: Canada's History Magazine*. Instead of seeking the greatest Canadian, the editors asked readers and a panel of Canadian historians to identify "the worst Canadian." Not surprisingly, some of those selected as CBC's "greatest Canadians" were also chosen as "the most contemptible" by the readers of *The Beaver*. Canada's recent prime ministers—Mulroney, Chrétien, and Harper—were all selected for the magazine's rogues gallery. But Pierre Trudeau, who was on CBC's top ten list, was catapulted to the place of lowest esteem and selected as the most "contemptible Canadian" by the magazine's readers. His darkened profile graced the cover of the magazine. This gallery of prime ministers was joined by the predictable mass murderers and other controversial characters, such as the discredited entrepreneur Conrad Black and abortion crusader Henry Morgentaler.

One of *The Beaver*'s expert panelists also selected a figure from CBC's top ten list. Native advocate and Cree historian Winona Wheeler selected John A. Macdonald for his callous treatment of Native and Métis people. Her condemnation of Macdonald and his policies was devastating. Identifying him as the "oppressive" prime minister, she wrote:

> Under Macdonald's government breaches of treaty obligations, starvation, negligence and manipulation fanned Indian and Métis fears, culminating in the 1885 Indian Treaty Grievance Movement and Métis Resistance. The resulting Canadian military campaigns ended in the largest mass hanging of Indians in Canada, the execution of Métis leader Louis Riel, and the imprisonment of many more Métis and Indian people. The Métis were dispersed, and Indian people were subjected to oppressive policies under the Indian Act.... Thousands of Indian and Métis people were left destitute and leaderless, but Macdonald got his Canadian Pacific Railway.[5]

Of course, this is a gross oversimplification of the complicated situation that Macdonald and his government had to deal with in the late nineteenth-century Canadian west. But it nicely demonstrates the crucial role biography can play in the task of challenging comfortable national or social myths and in generating debate.[6] Wheeler's view of Macdonald contrasts sharply with the view of Macdonald as the leading father of Confederation and nation-builder that was immortalized in Donald Creighton's magisterial two-volume biography published in the 1950s. In a fascinating twist of fate, the arch-villain in Creighton's biography was Métis leader Louis Riel, who challenged Macdonald's vision of a transcontinental nation in both the Red River Resistance of 1870 and the North-West Rebellion of 1885. As Canadian society was becoming more self-consciously aware of its identity and character and thus more open to minority rights, ethnicity, and the country's Native heritage, Riel the villain was transformed into the new heroic figure of Canadian history. He was portrayed as a spokesman for Métis and Native rights, for the protection of the French language and Catholic religion, and for the aspirations of the west.[7] He was the defender of minority rights of all descriptions in Canadian society. The villain became a hero and the hero was being vilified. Biography plays a role in the shaping, maintaining, and revising of a nation's self-image. Biographies of nation-builders are at the very centre of a nation's self-image.

These exercises in popular history and biography reveal the shortcomings of using biography as a way to understand Canada. By focusing on the individual, the broader responsibility for injustices—or, conversely, the sacrifices made by other Canadians—can be overlooked. Indeed, one of the panelists for *The Beaver* refused to name a particular individual. Instead, John Herd Thompson of Duke University selected "common Canadians" for their support and duplicity in the residential schools that systematically undermined Native culture, health, and family life. But despite scholarly dismissal of biography, it endures and remains one of the more popular and accessible ways for citizens to explore their nation's history and society. Biography is essential to any liberal democratic society. As Nigel Hamilton asserts in his recent historical overview of biography, "the pursuit of biography, controversial in its challenge to received ideas of privacy and reputation since ancient times, is integral to the Western concept of individuality and the ideals of democracy."[8] Biography plays a central role in democratic societies, for it is a forum for public debate about a broad range of issues. Biography makes debates concrete because people can more readily identify with individuals and personalities than with abstract concepts such as tolerance or identity. As the searches for the greatest or most despicable Canadian indicate, biography has the ability to reach into popular culture through book sales, magazines, and TV shows. It is not merely part of academic discourse. In Canada, biography has always been at the very centre of the illusive Canadian search for identity. The nature of biographical writing as well as its subject matter has always reflected broader political realities, social concerns, and cultural trends.

As early as the Confederation era, Canadians began to deliberate on what kind of a nation they were creating. Between 1862 and 1903, nine different biographical dictionaries, three of them multivolume, were produced in Canada.[9] The first of these was H. J. Morgan's *Sketches of Celebrated Canadians* (1862) with 424 entries. A picture of Canada's development from colony to nation emerged from the entries. An individual's contributions to political and military events such as the War of 1812, the constitutional development of Upper and Lower Canada, and the more recent political debates were the criteria for selection. The sketches were primarily of generals and colonial politicians. The more modest three-volume *Portraits of British Americans* (1865–68), edited by J. F. Taylor, was dedicated to those politicians who had played a prominent role in the confederation debates. Through these biographical sketches, Taylor produced an early history of Confederation. The broader purpose in these enterprises was to inform readers about exemplary individuals who were builders of the Canadian nation. Each entry was accompanied by photographic portraits. Cochrane assumed that the photographs illustrated the "intimate connection between the features and expression of the face and the qualities and habit of mind."[10] The accomplishments of the subjects were tied directly to character traits. The biographies were designed to serve as lessons in achieving middle-class Victorian respectability.

Biographical writing in Victorian Canada reached a pinnacle with the publication of the twenty-volume Makers of Canada series, published in the early twentieth century. Each volume of approximately 250 pages was based on archival records and other primary sources, such as newspapers, but they were designed for the popular market.[11] Early volumes were dedicated to the major figures in the history of New France and especially those men considered responsible for its major institutions, such as Bishop Laval and Governor General Frontenac. For the era of imperial rivalry from the conquest of New France to the end of the War of 1812, military figures such as Wolfe, Montcalm, and Sir Isaac Brock were featured. Most of the biographies of nineteenth-century figures focused on the politicians from the British North American colonies who were integral to constitutional developments, especially responsible government and confederation. Other volumes were dedicated to the explorers and governors who helped to open the west. The tone of the biographies was celebratory, and few, if any, notes of criticism were sounded. What was considered important was the subject's public life and contribution to Canadian political and social development. The emphasis was on nation-building. For example, the authors of the biography of Egerton Ryerson, the architect of Ontario's public school system and advocate of the separation of church and state, explained that they "made no attempt, except in the first brief chapter, to trace the record, either of his personal or public life, or the development of his character, or the lessons which might be gathered from the example of his life. We have rather considered his work as one of the makers of Canada, and necessarily with that, something of the great movements of the days in which he lived."[12]

The exception to the "great man" conventions that prevailed in the Makers of Canada series was the manuscript written by the career civil servant and iconoclastic thinker William Dawson LeSueur, who was also an editor of the series.[13] With respect to the Upper Canadian reformer William Lyon Mackenzie, who led the 1837 rebellion, LeSueur suggests that he was a flawed human being whose overly passionate disposition impeded his ability to make a positive contribution to Canadian national development. He noted that Mackenzie adopted "methods more adapted to promote strife and discord than constitutional progress."[14] LeSueur was not only questioning the character of the hero of the rebellions of 1837; he was also questioning his contribution to Canadian history. He laid down the gauntlet against the myth of Mackenzie and the "great man" thesis with the observation that "had William Lyon Mackenzie never come to Canada, the old system of government would none the less, through the action of general courses, infallibly have given place to government of a more democratic type."[15] Such a statement contradicted the widely held belief that without Mackenzie and the Rebellion of 1837 in Upper Canada, responsible government would not have been achieved. According to LeSueur, social and political conditions were the key to understanding the achievement of responsible government, not the contribution of any one individual. By extension, LeSuer's challenge to the "great man" thesis indicated that not many of the characters who had received special attention in the Makers of Canada series were indispensable to Canadian political and institutional development.

Little wonder, then, that George Morang, the publisher of the series, charged LeSueur with "destroy[ing] the usefulness of the rest of the series."[16] In a long letter to LeSueur, he outlined the parameters of Canadian public opinion with respect to what could be written about their leaders and historical figures: "I have always understood that there is an unwritten canon in the writing of biography, which demands from the biographer a certain amount of sympathy with the subject of the narrative. This I am afraid is entirely wanting in your estimate of Mackenzie and his struggle with the admittedly evil system of government which prevailed."[17] LeSueur's biography would not be tolerated because "scant justice is done to Mackenzie's virtues—to his highest and noblest qualities of head and heart." LeSueur's response indicates how far removed he was from the conventions of contemporary biography that Morang was determined to defend. In a letter to John L. Lewis, the author of the volume on the Reform politician George Brown in Morang's Makers of Canada series, LeSueur wrote that he was opposed to writing anything that merely confirmed "popular opinion," especially when the evidence pointed in another direction. The task of the biographer, he believed, was "to make the image vivid, to make the man live." The biographer of Mackenzie, LeSueur contended, had to show "to what terrible excesses of scurrility he did not hesitate to give way ... how little he cared about misleading the ignorant as to the conditions of public affairs; how his hatred of opponents completely dominated his interest in practical measures of reform; and then show how, in spite of all this, there was a sound core of humanity in the man; that he had a soul above mere party politics; that, unscrupulous as he was to means, he had, in the largest sense, good ends in view."[18]

LeSueur insisted that his biography was in fact a balanced account and that those who overlooked the underside or less-than-noble features of Mackenzie's personality were indulging in myth-making.[19] Canadians were able to tolerate criticism of its politicians in the cut and thrust of political debate but not in the canons of historical or biographical writing. William Lyon Mackenzie was regarded in the annals of nation-building historiography as one of the founders of responsible government and of the reform tradition in Canada; therefore, his character had to be above reproach in the literature. LeSueur's sophisticated approach to biographical writing was far ahead of the times.[20] Morang did not publish the manuscript in the Makers of Canada series; indeed, the manuscript was not published until 1979.[21]

LeSueur's manuscript remained mired in obscurity, and there were no challenges to the heroic tradition in Canadian biographical writing throughout the first half of the twentieth century. Donald Creighton's two-volume biography of Sir John A. Macdonald, *The Young Chieftain* (1952) and *The Old Politician* (1955), stood out as the pinnacle of Victorian biography. In many ways, it read like a Victorian novel, with its florid prose and keen novelist's sense of time, place, and character with regard to a particular moment or circumstance. Creighton continued the traditions of biographical writing that had begun with the Makers of Canada series. He combined the virtues of Makers of Canada dramatic narratives with the authoritative reliance on documentary evidence that characterized the "life and times" approach that emerged in the interwar years.[22] In contrast to the volumes in the Makers of Canada series, however, in the political narrative of Creighton's biography Macdonald's personal life was fully integrated with his public life. Creighton presented Macdonald's private life as evidence to explain the qualities and force of his character that were behind his contributions on the national political stage. In this regard, the conventions of Victorian biography were not challenged. Few notes of criticism or harsh lights were allowed into the portrait or exploration of personal life. If there were any uncomfortable facts, they were glossed over.[23] But while other authors who used the life and times approach tried to disappear and allow the subject's own voice to prevail through letters and other documents, Creighton's voice intruded throughout his life of Macdonald to the point where readers had trouble discerning Macdonald from Creighton.[24]

The task of understanding Creighton, therefore, is almost as necessary for reaching an understanding of Canada, and certainly of the mid-twentieth century, as it is for understanding Macdonald.[25] To this end, Creighton's biographer, Donald Wright, argues that the caricature of Creighton as temperamental, intolerant, francophobic, and basically unlikeable needs to be revised with a "proper biography" because he was "too important a figure in the intellectual, cultural, and political history of this country to ignore."[26] Wright indicates that the caricature of Creighton is only part of the story, as is every caricature. Creighton was a remarkably complicated man and someone who struggled, like many Canadians did, with disappointment and concerns about the future of the nation. When Canada, under the direction of the Liberal Party, was redefined, with little reference to its British heritage, as a bilingual and multicultural nation, Creighton got angry and lashed out against what he considered to be a betrayal of what Macdonald had created at Confederation. But this anger was rooted in grief. "'He grieved so for Canada,' his wife wrote after his death."[27] Creighton was a voice for the looming concern about the future of Canada that lurked underneath the brimming confidence of the 1950s. Canada was changing: it was becoming more strongly oriented within North America, Québec and the west were beginning to assert themselves, Métis and Native peoples were undergoing a cultural and demographic renewal, and Canada was becoming far more multicultural.

On the one hand, Creighton's biography of Macdonald was a nostalgic book, for it looked back to the certainties of an English-speaking Canada that was quietly being transformed into something quite different.[28] On the other hand, the popularity and critical acclaim that the book enjoyed rested in the fact that Creighton's vision of Macdonald was consistent with the confident Canadian national feeling of the 1950s. Canada had emerged from World War II with a renewed sense of purpose and optimism. The country's contribution to the war and its postwar diplomacy and prosperity fostered a real sense of national achievement and destiny. One issue that troubled Canadians was that of the Americanization of the Canadian economy and culture.[29] Creighton's portrait of Macdonald ameliorated their concerns about Canada's sovereignty and identity: Macdonald emerged as a politician who had the vision to create a new Dominion that averted the perils of the American constitution by insisting on a strong central government and that resisted American commercial and expansionist designs through its national policies. In Donald Creighton's hands, Macdonald became the grand orchestrator of a transcontinental Canada. It was his vision, his skill, his ability that ensured the success of the young Dominion.

The appeal of Creighton's Macdonald, however, went beyond the particular dilemma facing Canadians about their national identity. Creighton was an eloquent exponent of the biography as a way to understand the human condition: "I think an historian's chief interest is in character and circumstance. His concern is to discover the hopes, fears, anticipations and intentions of the individuals and nations he is talking about. His task is to reproduce as best he can the circumstances, problems and situations faced by another person in another time. He seeks insight and understanding that cannot be gained through the application of sociological rules and general explanations."[30] In the 1950s, people were anxious to see historical change as the product of individual actions and choices. This recognition of the role of the individual in history was important to the generation who lived under the shadow of World War II and the Holocaust, and who experienced the threat of the Cold War. At a time when the perils of ideologies such as Nazism, fascism, or communism were dangerously apparent, history that emphasized the role of the individual was part of the arsenal of liberal democracies in their battle against these forces of tyranny that robbed people of their freedom of choice. "History is not made by inanimate forces and human automations," Creighton explained;

"it is made by living men and women, impelled by an endless variety of ideas and emotions, which can best be understood by that insight into character, that imaginative understanding of people, which is one of the attributes of literary art."[31]

This biographical approach to Canadian history was institutionalized in the 1950s with the creation of the *Dictionary of Canadian Biography*, an ambitious collaborative scholarly enterprise. The *Dictionary* was the brainchild of James Nicolson, a philanthropist who believed that Canada would benefit from a comprehensive biographical dictionary of "noteworthy inhabitants of the Dominion of Canada."[32] In keeping with Nicolson's objectives, the editors requested that contributors "leave the reader with a definite impression of the personality and achievements of the subject in relation to the period in which he lived and the events in which he participated."[33] Nicolson's wish was to create a biographical dictionary that would help readers understand that Canada's past harkened back to its Victorian predecessors as much as it looked forward to modern scholarship; he insisted on a complete and impartial realistic portrait that indicated "strengths weaknesses, success and failure" in assessing the subject's life and contribution to Canada. This seemed to be a "golden age" of biography in Canada, with the launching of the *Dictionary of Canadian Biography* in 1959 and the publication of numerous critically acclaimed political biographies—aside from Creighton's, most notably J.M.S. Careless's two-volume biography of George Brown of the *Globe* and Kenneth McNaught's eloquent biography of J. S. Woodsworth, the founder of the CCF.[34]

But just as the *Dictionary of Canadian Biography* was getting off the ground in the early 1960s, the certainties surrounding biographical writing in Canada came crashing down. Profound change that shook Canadian society to its foundations occurred in many areas, including the arts and letters. A general mood that questioned almost every aspect of Canadian society, including its political traditions and the certitudes of Victorian morality and respectability, prevailed.[35] Things that would once have been considered scandalous or even sacrilegious were tolerated and seriously considered by an increasing number of Canadians in the 1960s. A good barometer of the new cultural values, which propelled further change, was the more liberal understanding of what constituted obscenity in Canadian society. Controversy was launched by the presence on Canadian newsstands of a new edition of *Lady Chatterley's Lover*, a novel that had been considered obscene since its publication in 1928.

In Montreal, the morality squad raided newsstands and seized copies of the novel. A local judge found *Lady Chatterley's Lover* to be obscene, ruled that the police action was lawful, and ordered the confiscation of the remaining copies of the offensive book. This ruling was unanimously upheld by the Québec Court of Appeal and ultimately the case was heard before the Supreme Court of Canada in 1962. In a narrow decision, the Supreme Court overturned the ruling of the lower courts and defined new grounds for obscenity. It was not sufficient, the justices argued, to quote certain passages containing foul language or descriptions of sexual activity and declare the work obscene. To prove that undue exploitation of sex is a dominant characteristic of any work, they reasoned, the whole book in its entirety and not certain isolated passages must be considered. Moreover, they declared that to discern whether the dominant characteristic of a book was obscene, the intention or purpose of the author must also be considered. Artistic and literary merit had to be taken into account.[36] Judicial decisions alone cannot change literary traditions, but in this case, the decision signalled a more open and tolerant attitude that was emerging in Canadian society about what could be discussed, written, and printed.

Soon after the Supreme Court decision, an early indication of the changing atmosphere was the publication of Peter C. Newman's *Renegade in Power*. What was significant about Newman's book was that he laid the responsibility for the indecision, confusion, and chaos of the Diefenbaker administration squarely at the feet of Diefenbaker; more specifically, he attributed it to Diefenbaker's personality. It was a flaw not in his managerial style but rather in his character that was responsible for the paranoid style of politics that characterized his government.[37] It was becoming clear that no longer would a veil of secrecy protect concerns about propriety and respectability. Biography was ultimately transformed in this process of cultural reorientation.

One of the most dramatic examples of this new spirit came from the pen of a distinguished historian, C. P. Stacey (born in 1906), whose own life was rooted in the Victorian respectability of the early twentieth century. Stacey was familiar with the Mackenzie King Papers; they included King's diary, which he kept almost religiously on a daily basis from the time he was a student at the University of Toronto in the early 1890s to the end of his life in 1950. Much to Stacey's delight, this intensely private diary was remarkably candid and detailed about personal matters, particularly family life and King's mother, his many women friends, and, perhaps most sensational of all, his involvement with the world of spiritualism. Stacey understood that little was known about Mackenzie King's life outside of politics, and he decided to write a book about his fascinating private life. As Stacey explained in his own memoirs, "At an earlier day this simply would have been 'not done.' Twenty years before, I should not have dreamed of doing it myself. But times, and public taste, had changed."[38] He also understood that "no conspiracy of silence was going to last long and in any case it seemed to me that conspiracies of silence were out of date."[39]

Stacey hoped to shed light on the conundrum of Mackenzie King's character. In public life and politics, he was rational, skilful, shrewd verging on ruthless, and highly successful. In his private life, he allowed the superstitious to influence him; he was frequently very emotional to the point of becoming irrational; and in terms of his relationships with women, especially in relation to marriage, he had failed. Stacey's exposé was published under the provocative title *A Very Double Life: The Private World of Mackenzie King*, a reference to one of the more revealing and introspective excerpts in the diary. After yet another episode in which the young Mackenzie King had to fight off the temptations of the flesh, he had written:

> There is no doubt I lead a very double life. I strive to do right and continually do wrong. Yet I do not do the right I do to make it a cloak for evil. The evil that I do is done unwillingly, it comes of the frailty of my nature, I am sorry for it.... I fear I am much like Peter, I deny my Lord when the maid smiles at me, but with God's help I will overcome even this temptation.[40]

This reference to the temptations of evil fighting against King's desire to follow the Lord and lead an upstanding Christian life captures the theme of the book perfectly. It is not a flattering portrait of King. He is portrayed as a tortured soul, at best, if not a habitual hypocrite in his personal life. Throughout the book, Stacey presents King as a man who pursued women, sometimes obsessively; befriended other men's wives; and communicated with deceased "dear ones" and political celebrities through seances. *A Very Double Life* smashed the convention that a public figure's personal life was "private" and that only the public record mattered. Somehow, the book made King more attractive but also somewhat comic and even pathetic.

Although Stacey had a serious intent for his exposé of King's "very double life," the book became the subject of media frenzy. The *Toronto Star* had received the right to publish excerpts of the book in advance of its publication. With its eye on mass readership, the *Star* printed the most sensational sections.[41] The documentary references and Stacey's careful explanations of background and historical context were not published, so the book appeared to be little more than an exercise in cheap gossipmongering. In Stacey's own words, the excerpts were "crude."[42] While many Canadians enthused over the fact that in boring Canada, where nothing of interest happened, there could be scandal and sex involving its usually dull politicians, others were outraged. In his memoirs, Stacey comments that many Canadians were still of the mind that "the conspiracy of silence should have continued."[43] More substantial criticism suggested that Stacey's prurient obsession with the women in Mackenzie King's life had misled him and that he had overlooked many of the more telling aspects of his personal life. So much was missing with respect to King's private life that the reviewer for the *Canadian Historical Review* remarked that the book was little more than an "excursion on the margins of the biographical lake."[44] Stacey was charged with being superficial in his exclusive focus on the women in King's life, his beloved Irish terriers, and his flirtation with seances and spiritualism. Whatever the verdict on Stacey's book, it clearly signalled the end of the Victorian insistence on propriety and respectability. Moreover, it was abundantly apparent that restricting biographical detail to the public record, as was done in the official multivolume biography of Mackenzie King, was inadequate for understanding public figures.[45]

Questions relating to the most private matters and intimate activities, such as marriage and sexuality, were no longer exclusively in the private sphere; they were part of public discourse in post-1960s Canada. Canadians were vigorously debating legislation relating to divorce, human reproduction, and sexual orientation. In announcing amendments to the Criminal Code that included the Divorce Reform Bill and measures decriminalizing abortion and homosexual acts between consenting adults, the minister of Justice, Pierre Elliot Trudeau, famously quipped that "there was no place for the state in the bedrooms of the nation." Perhaps so, but this more liberal attitude toward marriage, family life, and sexuality meant that what had been fiercely private became public. Indeed, the *Divorce Act* of 1968, sponsored by Trudeau as Justice minister, was one of the many pieces of social legislation indicating that the grasp of the old Victorian belief systems had finally been broken.[46] The social dimension of the human experience was also critical to understanding what it meant to be Canadian.[47] The personal was now political, and biographies that fully integrated personal life with public life only reflected this trend.

It was therefore ironic in the extreme that Trudeau was subjected to a terribly public and painful divorce in the late 1970s. Trudeau's marriage became the subject of a sensational memoir by his ex-wife, who commented extensively on their marriage and the reasons for the marital breakdown.[48] Margaret Trudeau's *Beyond Reason* was one of the first memoirs to discuss the most private matters of marital sexuality and divorce openly. In his recent biography of Trudeau, John English interweaves Trudeau's public and private life so effectively that new revelations and insights about his life emerge. For example, English demonstrates that Trudeau's electoral defeat in 1979 at the hands of the hapless Joe Clark was in no small part the result of his declining passion for politics and public life. He was tired, bitter, depressed, and overwhelmed by his collapsed marriage. Although plenty was known about Trudeau before English's biography, as journalist Paul Wells points out, his private and public life "had tended to be kept separate" in the many previous biographies. "But," Wells protests, "nobody lives like that.... Every life is a whole, and English treats Trudeau's prime ministerial career as a whole to an extent none of his predecessors did."[49] In English's biography, the integration of public and private allows readers to understand Trudeau the man as well as his political career with more sensitivity and to see that his personal life, in some ways deeply tragic, had a profound impact on his political career and his stewardship of the nation. Exploration of the most private matters cannot be neglected, for it can shed light on some of the most public matters. Any insistence that biography should primarily be about public life cannot be sustained.

There are, however, important matters of propriety that must be taken into account. What is perhaps the final frontier of privacy relates to the most secretive of activities: extramarital affairs. Here again, the barriers have come down very slowly and painfully. On no other subject is the biographer so constrained by the feelings of the living and the memory of the dead. With respect to Prime Minister Pearson, his biographer, John English, was circumspect but suggestive about his "affair" with Mary Greey, writing that "Mike found her thoroughly admirable and magnetic, and she was a scintillating companion in the absence of his family during those 'siren years.'"[50] Confronted with more concrete evidence, English was blunter in the second volume when discussing philosopher George Grant's anti-Liberal 1963 polemic, *Lament for a Nation*. Here, English suggests that some of the bitter tone of Grant's attack on the Liberal Party of Canada may have been rooted in the fact that "he believed that in London during the Blitz, Mary Greey had fallen in love with Mike and he with her," and Grant was distressed by how Pearson had treated his family friend: Grant's sister, Alison, had been Mary Greey's flatmate in London. But, in a footnote, English clarifies things by muddying the waters. He notes that he interviewed people who were in a position to know about the relationship. The most important were Alison Grant and her future husband, George Ignatieff, who was a colleague and friend of Pearson. According to English, Alison indicated that "the extraordinary circumstance of the Blitz transformed" Mary and Mike's "acquaintanceship into friendship." She did not elaborate upon the nature of the friendship. She and George Ignatieff agreed that Mike became a much more private person after he returned to Canada, and, from then onwards, his life played out primarily in the public forum.[51]

Not surprisingly, William Christian, the biographer of George Grant, is much less circumspect about the affair, claiming without hesitation that Pearson and Greey were romantically involved.[52] Of course, absolute certainty on this very private matter is impossible. As P. B. Waite reminds us in his sensitive discussion of "invading privacy," the biographer

> need not, should not, be prurient, raking up scandal for titillation of contemporary taste: but neither ought he to blink it away. Should one not openly and candidly accept such evidence, judging it as part of a man's life? I think so. The alternative seems unacceptable. Deliberate suppression of the essential is deliberate distortion. But there is a world of fighting in what constitutes essential.[53]

It is no small matter, in the case of Pearson, to understand that the leader who prodded and pushed Canadians to consider a new Canada that was not tied to old colonial traditions—through the Commission on Bilingualism and Biculturalism, the recognition of multiculturalism, the building of the welfare state, and the adoption of a new flag—also struggled in his personal life with the new post-Victorian social and moral realities of the late twentieth century. It also opens up the possibility of reaching some understanding that the source for new morality was rooted in the disruption of family life imposed on individuals by the demands and pressures of World War II. In this regard, the biographies of Pearson and Trudeau are much more than lives of national leaders; they are also lives of two individuals who dealt with the myriad of pressures, disruptions, and opportunities that many other Canadians, in some form or another, also faced in that era.

Despite the growing fascination with the private details of people's lives, it was often public life that still caused the greatest stir and interest. For example, the details of Trudeau's life that elicited the most commentary were those relating to his position on French-Canadian nationalism and separatism, not his prolonged bachelorhood or his many relationships with beautiful women. It came as a shock for many readers that Trudeau's youth, in the late 1930s, was characterized by obedience to his Jesuit teachers and ardent commitment to traditional French-Canadian nationalism, which included espousal of the anti-Semitism of the times and harbouring romantic dreams of leading French-Canadian youth in a military coup to establish an independent Québec.[54] What is significant about this phase of his life is that when Trudeau organized his extensive personal archive, he did not destroy or bury this incendiary and incriminating material that clearly compromised his image as a "citizen of the world" who rejected nationalisms based on race, religion, or language. Perhaps Trudeau understood that this aspect of his life explained both the necessity of and his passion for entrenching the Charter of Rights and Freedoms in the Canadian Constitution. His youthful prejudices were poignant evidence of why he became so opposed to race-based definitions of nationalism and the "two nations" concept of Canada. It is easy enough to suggest reasons why Trudeau thought the Charter was necessary. Indeed, he suggested many of the reasons himself when he referred to the treatment of minorities in Québec under Duplessis and the internment of the Japanese during World War II. Trudeau understood that in a democratic multicultural nation such as Canada, fundamental freedoms could only be protected in law in a binding constitution. These considerations were rooted in the social and political history of the nation. But the best way to appreciate Trudeau's passion about these matters and his willingness to play high-stakes politics in order to achieve his goal and entrench the Charter of Rights and Freedoms is through his own past or his biography.[55] One can go only so far in understanding the history of the nation through studying the grand sweep of political, social, intellectual, economic, or cultural history. There is a dimension of a country's past that can only be appreciated and understood through the biography or the lives of its citizens.

One hundred years after the publication of the Makers of Canada series, a multivolume series of biographies of "extraordinary Canadians" was completed in 2011 under the editorship of John Ralston Saul. Much as in the Makers of Canada series, the purpose of this work is to explore the Canadian identity through biography. In introducing the series, Saul writes: "How do civilizations imagine themselves? One way is for each of us to look at ourselves through our society's most remarkable figures." Saul hastens to add, however, that the series is not an exercise in "hero worship or political iconography" but rather an attempt to understand those people from Canada's past who seem to remain relevant for Canadians long after their deaths.[56] "Their ideas, their triumphs and failures," writes Saul, "all of these somehow constitute a mirror of our society. We look at these people, all dead, and discover what we have been, but also what we can be. A mirror is an instrument for measuring ourselves."[57] The editors of the Makers of Canada series would recognize the sentiment underlying Saul's rationale. What would be shocking to the editors of the older series are the lives Saul selected. These Canadians were, to use Saul's phrase, "people of the word." In a clearly postmodernist explanation for his selection criteria, Saul argues that while civilizations or nations are built around many themes and actions, they also require a shared public language or a broadly understood narrative or discourse: "Words, words, words—it is around these that civilizations create and imagine themselves."[58]

It is instructive to compare the names in the Makers of Canada series with those in the Extraordinary Canadians series to consider the changes over the past century in Canadian biography and the Canadian identity. The editors of the earlier series would have been shocked that so few politicians, only four, were included in the later work. They would have been astounded by the number of literary figures and artists—Stephen Leacock, Lucy Maud Montgomery, Marshall McLuhan, and Mordecai Richler, Emily Carr, and Glenn Gould. Most shocking, indeed scandalous, for early twentieth-century Anglo-Protestant Canadians would be the presence of a volume dedicated to the Cree chief, Big Bear, and another to Louis Riel and his military lieutenant, Gabriel Dumont, who in 1910 were considered little more than traitors, and violent, bloodthirsty ones at that. Also surprising would be the three women in the series: Lucy Maud Montgomery, Emily Carr, and Nellie McClung. The latter also represents the activist or reformist orientation, as does Norman Bethune, the activist medical missionary who worked alongside Mao during the 1949 revolution. Finally, from the world of sport, a volume on Maurice "Rocket" Richard has recently been added. Extraordinary Canadians is not dominated by politicians or military leaders. Indeed, there is not one military figure in the series except for the insurgent Métis, Gabriel Dumont. Canada's World War I hero Arthur Currie is not included.

One of the most widely commented-upon volumes in the series is the biography of René Lévesque by Daniel Poliquin, a Franco-Ontarian and a federalist. He portrays Lévesque's appeal as a politician both inside and outside of Québec's borders with insight and sensitivity, for he understands the affection Canadians had for this vulnerable, all too human but fiercely democratic man. On the controversial question of separatism, however, Poliquin is devastating in his condemnation of Lévesque and the politics of separatism. With reference to the FLQ crisis and the killing of Pierre Laporte, Poliquin suggests that Lévesque was most concerned about the possibility that the FLQ's radical militancy might destroy the sovereignist movement. He charged Lévesque with "intellectual dishonesty" and worse. "Overall, Lévesque's take on the October Crisis was a political gambit of the vilest sort. He was not seeking the truth; he was trying to regain the political terrain he had lost. The polls were not good."[59] Lévesque shifted the blame for the crisis away from its terrorist perpetrators and onto Trudeau, the federal government, and the RCMP. This conspiracy theory, fostered by Lévesque, led to the perversion in politically correct Québec nationalist circles "to say that Laporte 'died,' which is a curious way to describe Paul Rose's strangling of the minister with the chain of his scapular medal. But using the word *died* instead of the word *murdered* keeps Laporte's abductors absolved." For Poliquin, this absolution of the terrorist acts of October 1970 "was a callous perversion of the truth, and a technique Lévesque resorted to again in very different circumstances."[60] Of course, Poliquin is referring to the vague and, in his view, misleading wording of the 1980 referendum question. Poliquin's assessment of Lévesque's character is equally frank. He mentions that Lévesque had affairs, was a less than devoted father, and handled money poorly. He was a likeable but seriously flawed individual. Poliquin suggests that Lévesque's immaturity was in part responsible for the failure of his political vision and certainly the failure of his tactics in his disputes with federalists such as Trudeau. The private and public are merged into a seamless web in this controversial biography.

Saul's selection of "extraordinary Canadians" can be criticized for reflecting the old Canada of Natives, Québécois, and members of the English-Canadian elite. The only volume on an immigrant or ethnic Canadian, representing the nation's multicultural character, is the one on Mordecai Richler. Where one does see multicultural Canada is in the series' authors, who were selected for their proven ability to communicate with Canadians. They include Adrienne Clarkson, born in Hong Kong; Nino Ricci, from a Canadian family of Italian immigrants; M. G. Vassanji, born in Kenya; and Vincent Lam, from a Chinese community in Vietnam. Rudy Wiebe, who wrote the volume on Big Bear, is a deeply committed Mennonite, and Joseph Boyden, author of the dual biography of Riel and Dumont, is Métis.

The central importance of Canada's multicultural character is reflected in two very recent biographies. Richard Gwyn's second volume of his biography of John A. Macdonald, published in 2011, confirms that, although the veneration for Creighton's earlier account of Macdonald's life has by no means disappeared, it has at least reached the point where the clear limitations of Creighton's achievement are recognized.[61] Gwyn does not debunk what Creighton achieved. As H. V. Nelles points out in the *Literary Review of Canada*, Gwyn

> might have cavalierly rejected the Young Politician and the Old Chieftain, turning them on their heads, finding a yet unknown counter-Macdonald to unveil. In rejecting Creighton, for example, he might have taken a Strachey-esque tack ... exposing the abundant vanity and readily displayed hypocrisy of his subject. The siren song of a psychobiography of a man of inexplicable ailments, tragic marriages, lost children, mad relatives, monstrous binges, and mysterious power over other men might have been tempting, especially with an eye to sales.[52]

Instead Gwyn's purpose is to provide a new generation of Canadians with a means to rediscover Macdonald.[53] He portrays Macdonald differently than

Creighton did, seeing in him a man "as complex and contradictory as his own country."[54] Gwyn approvingly cites Goldwin Smith's 1884 observation that Macdonald's lifelong mission was "to hold together a set of elements, national, religious, sectional and personal, as motley as the component patches of any 'crazy quilt.'"[65] Macdonald understood diversity and the necessity of some degree of tolerance as central to the Canadian character. Gwyn points to Macdonald's Scottish background as a main reason why he could appreciate the diversity of Canada. But more than this, Gwyn suggests, he understood that Canada was a nation in the making without a definite identity. He knew, perhaps like no other politician of his generation, that "for Canada to survive on its own, it had to demonstrate that it possessed the will and nerve it took for a nation to survive. Confederation was the essential means to that end."[66] In a statement that makes clear the importance of biography above all other studies in understanding the Canadian identity, Gwyn asserts that to understand Macdonald is to discover "where we came from and ... why we are the way we are now, no matter all the transformational changes since—demographic, economic, technological, lifestyle." Macdonald is somehow a transcendent figure.

No historian has made a more forthright, powerful defense of biography than American historian David Hackett Fischer. In his recent biography of Samuel de Champlain, whom Canadians consider the Father of New France, he informs readers that he began his inquiry with a set of open questions about Champlain: "Who was this man? Where did he come from? What did he do? What difference did he make? Why should we care?"[67] These questions appear simple and straightforward, and indeed, they are. Moreover, they are questions that are basic to any biography. But they also led Fischer to a probing investigation and bold conclusions about the nature of Canadian society during its formative colonial period. He reveals Champlain as a man of the French Enlightenment. When Champlain arrived in the New World, he did not try to conquer, abuse, or drive the Natives out.[68] Here, Fischer does not indulge in the much-maligned "great man" thesis but instead demonstrates that Champlain was a product of his times: "He came to maturity in a time of cruel and bitter conflict: forty years of religious strife, nine civil wars in France, and millions of deaths. As a soldier he had witnessed atrocities beyond description. After that experience, this war-weary soldier dreamed of a new world where people lived at peace with others unlike themselves."[69] He was genuinely appalled at the cruelty, violence, and enslavement that Europeans had inflicted upon Native peoples. His dream was to create a new society where Native North Americans and newcomer Europeans could co-operate and thrive. Champlain strove to maintain close relations with First Nations people, often living among them, while establishing three francophone colonies and cultures—Québécois, Acadian, and Métis. A cornerstone of the Canadian character, Fischer observes, remains its French-speaking heritage. In revealing Champlain's humanism and especially his respect for the values and traditions of other cultures, Fischer identifies one of the essential qualities that characterizes Canadian history and society: respect for minorities. The fact that Canadians increasingly view multiculturalism and tolerance as being at the core of the Canadian national character indicates that they have embraced "Champlain's dream."

In both Gwyn's and Fischer's recent biographies, respect for diversity is presented as a defining aspect of the lives of their subjects and, by extension, as a central component of the Canadian experience. Both biographers are reflecting contemporary Canadian attitudes as much as they may be shaping and deepening these attitudes. They have added a new dimension to the prevailing view of Canada as a multicultural nation. Although biographical writing has undergone significant change throughout Canadian history, its central role in assisting Canadians to ponder, debate, and revise their views of the Canadian experience and identity has not changed. Contemporary Canadians are more skeptical about human nature and certainly about the ability of any biography to be the final word on anyone's life or character. But this greater skepticism aside, biography still holds a unique ability to provide a window through which readers can explore what it is to experience life in Canada.[70]

NOTES

1   The top ten were Tommy Douglas, Terry Fox, Pierre Elliot Trudeau, Dr. Frederick Banting, David Suzuki, Lester B. Pearson, Don Cherry, Sir John A. Macdonald, Alexander Graham Bell, and Wayne Gretzky. See "The Greatest Canadians," CBC Digital Archives, November 2004, http://archives.cbc.ca/society/celebrations/topics/1455/.

2   For this controversy surrounding the historical accuracy of *Prairie Giant*, see "The Revisionist History of 'Prairie Giant: The Tommy Douglas Story,'" http://members.shaw.ca/prairiegiant/public_html/index.html. See also Bill Waiser, "Story About the Father of Medicare Needed More Time on the Waiting List," *National Post*, March 9, 2006;

Christopher Moore, "Another Prairie Giant: Who Was Jimmy Gardiner Anyway?" *The Beaver*, October–November 2006.

3 See Norman Ward and David Smith, *Jimmy Gardiner: Relentless Liberal* (Toronto: University of Toronto Press, 1990).

4 This aspect of Douglas's career is dealt with in Angus McLaren, *Our Own Master Race: Eugenics in Canada, 1885–1945* (Toronto: McClelland and Stewart, 1990), 7–9, 166–67. Early biographies of Douglas include Thomas H. McLeod and Ian McLeod, *Tommy Douglas: The Road to Jerusalem* (Markham, ON: Fitzhenry and Whiteside, 1987).

5 Winona Weaver, "The Worst Canadian Contest: Sir John A. MacDonald," *The Beaver*, August–September 2007, 35.

6 Joining Macdonald in the rogues gallery of contemptible Canadians selected by the panel of historians was the Nazi firebrand from 1930s' Québec, Adrian Arcand, anti-Catholic and anti-French journalist Edward Farrer, and racist Indian commissioners Duncan Campbell Scott and Joseph Trutch, among others. All these men represent a powerful and disturbing challenge to the prevailing mythology of a peaceable, tolerant Canadian society.

7 On the transformation of the image and historical understanding of Riel, see the seminal work by Doug Owram, "The Myth of Louis Riel," *Canadian Historical Review* 63 (September 1982): 315–36; and Jennifer Reid, *Louis Riel and the Creation of Modern Canada: Mythic Discourse and the Postcolonial State* (Albuquerque: University of New Mexico Press, 2008).

8 Nigel Hamilton, *Biography: A Brief History* (Cambridge: Harvard University Press, 2007), 2.

9 These biographical dictionaries receive a critical analysis in Robert Lanning, *The National Album: Collective Biography and the Formation of the Canadian Middle Class* (Ottawa: Carleton University Press, 1996).

10 This principle was applied even more vigorously in H. J. Morgan, *Types of Canadian Women* (Toronto: William Briggs, 1903), where the often full-length photographs were designed to demonstrate that physical attractiveness, grace, and tasteful dress were signs of social standing and indications that the subject possesses qualities necessary for her contribution to family life and the community.

11 Donald Wright, *The Professionalization of History in English Canada* (Toronto: University of Toronto Press, 2005), 21–22, 43.

12 Nathanael Burwash and Alfred Henry Raynor, Egerton Ryerson (Toronto: Morang, 1909), preface (n.p.).

13 For LeSueur's contributions to late Victorian intellectual life, see A. B. McKillop, *A Disciplined Intelligence: Cultural Inquiry and Canadian Thought in the Victorian Era* (Toronto and Kingston: McGill-Queen's University Press, 1979).

14 William Dawson LeSueur, *William Lyon Mackenzie: A Reinterpretation* (Toronto: Macmillan, 1979), 48.

15 Ibid., 1.

16 "Feared Book Would Destroy the Series—Publisher's View of LeSueur's Work ... According to Lawyer," Toronto *Globe*, November 15, 1912, quoted in A. B. McKillop, *A Critical Spirit: The Thought of William Dawson LeSueur* (Toronto: McClelland and Stewart, 1977), 257.

17   George Morang to W. D. LeSueur, May 6, 1908, quoted in McKillop, *A Critical Spirit*, 273–75.

18   W. Dawson LeSueur to John L. Lewis, December 26, 1911, quoted in McKillop, *A Critical Spirit*, 281–82.

19   See McKillop, *A Critical Spirit*, 275–80. McKillop cites W. Dawson LeSueur to George N. Morang, May 11, 1908.

20   LeSueur was anticipating the challenges to Victorian biographical writing so brilliantly developed by Lytton Strachey in *Eminent Victorians* (New York: G. P. Putnam's Sons, 1918), a book of four biographical portraits that caused a scandal. Strachey humanized his subjects by "shattering the pretensions of Victorian morality" that surrounded them. They came alive because he exposed their pretensions, ambition, and hypocrisy.

21   William Dawson LeSueur, *William Lyon Mackenzie: A Reinterpretation* (Ottawa: Carleton University Library, 1979). The fullest account of the fate of LeSueur's manuscript is "Introduction: The Critic as Historian," in McKillop, *A Critical Spirit*, 247–67.

22   See O. D. Skelton, *Life and Letters of Sir Wilfrid Laurier*, vol. 1, *1841–1896* (Oxford: Oxford University Press, 1921); O. D. Skelton, *Life and Letters of Sir Wilfrid Laurier*, vol. 2, *1896–1919* (Toronto: Oxford University Press, 1921); C. B. Sissons, *Egerton Ryerson: His Life and Letters*, 2 vols. (Toronto: Clarke, Irwin, 1937, 1947).

23   See Ged Martin, "Macdonald and His Biographers," *British Journal of Canadian Studies* 16 (2001): 300–319. For a sensitive treatment of Macdonald's deeply troubled personal life, see Ged Martin, "John A. Macdonald and the Bottle," *Journal of Canadian Studies* 40 (Fall 2006): 162–85.

24   P. B. Waite, "Donald Creighton and His Macdonald," introduction to Donald Creighton, *The Young Politician, The Old Chieftain*, Reprints in Canadian History (Toronto: University of Toronto Press, 1998), xx; Frances Halpenny, "Expectations of Biography," in *Boswell's Children: The Art of the Biographer*, ed. R. B. Fleming (Toronto: Dundurn Press, 1992).

25   For a historiographical assessment of Creighton, see Carl Berger, *The Writing of Canadian History: Aspects of English Canadian Historical Writing Since 1900* (Toronto: Oxford University Press, 1976).

26   Donald Wright, "Reflections on Donald Creighton and the Appeal of Biography," *Journal of Historical Biography* 1 (Spring 2007): 18. On the francophobic aspect of Creighton's thought and personality, see Donald A. Wright, "Donald Creighton and the French Fact, 1920s–1970s," *Journal of the Canadian Historical Association* 6 (1995): 243–72.

27   Wright, "Reflections on Donald Creighton," 19–20.

28   There is a growing literature on the transformation in English-speaking Canada that was of such huge concern to Creighton, including Jose Igartua, *The Other Quiet Revolution: National Identities in English Canada, 1845–71* (Vancouver: University of British Columbia Press, 2006), and C. P. Champion, *The Strange Demise of British Canada: The Liberals and Canadian Nationalism* (Montreal and Kingston: McGill-Queen's University Press, 2010). For Creighton's lament, see Donald Creighton, *Canada 1939–1957: A Forked Road* (Toronto: McClelland and Stewart, 1976), and Donald Creighton, *Canada's First Century*

(New York: St. Martin's Press, 1970).

29 See J. L. Granatstein, *How Britain's Economic, Political and Military Weakness Thrust Canada into the Arms of the United States: A Melodrama in Three Acts* (Toronto: University of Toronto Press, 1989), and Ryan Edwardson, *Canadian Content: Culture and the Quest for Nationhood* (Toronto: University of Toronto Press, 2008).

30 Quoted in John S. Moir, ed., *Character and Circumstance: Essays in Honour of Donald Grant Creighton* (Toronto: MacMillan, 1970), x.

31 Quoted in Wright, "Reflections on Donald Creighton," 24.

32 Nicolson, Last Will and Testament, quoted in George W. Brown, introduction to the *Dictionary of Canadian Biography*, vol. 1, *1000–1700* (Toronto: University of Toronto Press, 1966), xi. Brown, the *Dictionary*'s first general editor, provides a brief biographical sketch of Nicolson on pp. vii–xii.

33 Directives to contributors, *Dictionary of Canadian Biography*, vol. 1, xvii.

34 J.M.S. Careless, *Brown of the Globe*, vol. 1, *The Voice of Upper Canada, 1818–1859* (Toronto: Macmillan, 1959); J.M.S. Careless, *Brown of the Globe*, vol. 2, *Statesman of Confederation, 1860–1880* (Toronto: Macmillan, 1963); Ken McNaught, *A Prophet in Politics: A Biography of J. S. Woodsworth* (Toronto: University of Toronto Press, 1959).

35 On the 1960s in Canada, see Doug Owram, *Born at the Right Time: A History of the Baby Boom Generation* (Toronto: University of Toronto Press, 1996), and Bryan Palmer, *Canada's 1960s: The Ironies of a Rebellious Era* (Toronto: University of Toronto Press, 2009).

36 Brodie, Dansky, Rubin v. The Queen, [1962] S.C.R. 681, at 702–5..

37 Peter C. Newman, *Renegade in Power: The Diefenbaker Years* (Toronto: McClelland and Stewart, 1963).

38 C. P. Stacey, *A Date with History: Memoirs of a Canadian Historian* (Ottawa: Deneau, 1982), 262–63.

39 Ibid., 263.

40 C. P. Stacey, *A Very Double Life: The Private World of Mackenzie King* (Halifax: Formac, 1976), 50.

41 *Toronto Star*, March 6–11, 1976.

42 Stacey, *A Date with History*, 264.

43 Ibid.

44 James A. Gibson, "A Very Double Life," *Canadian Historical Review* 58 (June 1977): 236–38.

45 See R. MacGregor Dawson, *William Lyon Mackenzie King: A Political Biography, 1874–1923* (Toronto: University of Toronto Press, 1958); H. Blair Neatby, *William Lyon Mackenzie King: The Lonely Heights, 1924–1932* (Toronto: University of Toronto Press, 1970); and H. Blair Neatby, *William Lyon Mackenzie King: Prism of Unity, 1933–1939* (Toronto: University of Toronto Press, 1976).

46 On the defense of the sanctity of marriage at all costs, see James G. Snell, "'The White Life for Two': The Defense of Marriage and Sexual Morality in Canada, 1890–1914," *Histoire Sociale/Social History* 16 (May 1983): 111–28; James G. Snell, *In the Shadow of the Law: Divorce in Canada, 1900–1939* (Toronto: University of Toronto Press, 1991).

47 This point is developed in a more general way with regard to Canadian historiography in A. B. McKillop, "Who Killed Canadian History: A View from the Trenches," *Canadian Historical Review* 80 (June 1999): 272, 297.

48 Margaret Trudeau, *Beyond Reason* (New York: Grosset and Dunlap, 1979).

49 Paul Wells, "We're Still Watching: Will Our Obsession with Trudeau Ever End?" *Literary Review of Canada* (November 2009), 9.

50 John English, *Shadow of Heaven: The Life of Lester Pearson*, vol. 1, *1897–1948* (Toronto: Knopf, 1989), 232.

51 John English, *The Worldly Years: The Life of Lester Pearson*, vol. 2, *1949–1972* (Toronto: Knopf, 1992), 255.

52 William Christian, *George Grant: A Biography* (Toronto: University of Toronto Press, 1993), 71, 78–81, 119–20.

53 P. B. Waite, "Invading Privacies: Biography as History," *Dalhousie Review* 69 (Winter 1989–90): 484.

54 See Max and Monique Nemni, *Young Trudeau: Son of Quebec, Father of Canada, 1919–1944*, trans. *William Johnson* (Toronto: Douglas Gibson, 2006); John Hellman, "Skeleton in Jackboots? An Intellectual Historian Makes Sense of Trudeau's 'Shocking' Papers," *Literary Review of Canada* (September 2006): 20–21

55 See William Johnson, "Just Watch Me? How Could You Not?" *Globe and Mail*, October 31, 2009.

56 John Ralston Saul, introduction to Margaret MacMillan, *Stephen Leacock* (Toronto: Penguin, 2009), vii.

57 Ibid., viii.

58 Ibid., ix.

59 Daniel Poliquin, *René Lévesque* (Toronto: Penguin, 2009), 126.

60 Ibid., 127.

61 See Richard Gwyn, *John A—The Man Who Made Us: The Life and Times of John A. Macdonald*, vol. 1, *1815–1867* (Toronto: Random House, 2007), and *Nation Maker—Sir John A. Macdonald: His Life, Our Times*, vol. 2, *1867–1891* (Toronto: Random House, 2011).

62 H. V. Nelles, "The First Northern Magus," *Literary Review of Canada* (November 2007): 6.

63 See Gwyn, *John A*, 6.

64 Ibid., 3.

65 Goldwin Smith, quoted in Gwyn, *John A*, 2.

66 Gwyn, *John A*, 5.

67 David Hackett Fischer, *Champlain's Dream: The Visionary Adventurer Who Made a New World in Canada* (New York: Random House, 2008), 11.

68 Fischer, *Champlain's Dream*, 528.

69 Ibid., 529.

70 See, for example, Michael Bliss, *Right Honourable Men: The Descent of Canadian Politics from Macdonald to Mulroney* (Toronto: HarperCollins, 1994), x.

Roger Epp

Off-Road Democracy: The Politics of Land, Water, and Community in Alberta

Democratization is not about being "left alone." ... To become a democrat is to change one's self, to learn how to act collectively, as a *demos*. It requires that the individual go "public" and thereby help to constitute a "public" and an "open" politics, in principle accessible for all to take part in it.[1]
—Sheldon Wolin

If we persist long enough, preach and protest long enough, we may be able to support this fragile, ancient bio-diverse landscape. Somewhere democracy may still breathe.[2]
—Francis Gardner, southern Alberta rancher, Pekisko Group member

I

The question of how Albertans communicate politically—and whether, in fact, they do—deserves a serious answer, not a flippant one, though it may need to be exploratory and circuitous in nature. The temptation to be flippant is obvious enough. By appearance and reputation, Alberta is easily the most apolitical, perhaps anti-political, province in the country. It elects dynastic parties for generations at a time—the current one since 1971. Its elections are rarely real contests where the outcome is in doubt, and even when they are, voter turnout is still puzzlingly low. In the past decade, Alberta's political life has been characterized variously as hollowed-out, enigmatic, impoverished, the "false front" of a self-deceived frontier town.[3] Its legislature typically sits for fewer days a year than any other in the country. One former premier (Don Getty) mused that if it met even less often, it would pass fewer laws—presumably a good thing. Another, Ralph Klein, famously dreamed of a government run on "autopilot" and questioned the need for an Official Opposition since all it ever did was oppose.[4] Such comments did not exactly light up the radio talk shows. Indeed, Albertans sometimes seem to accept the contradictory caricatures spun about them: that they are maverick, live-free-or-die libertarians, or at least indifferent to politics unless roused momentarily against a threatened federal raid on either the provincial pantry or their gun cabinets—in which case, they need to speak with one voice—and that dissenters, by definition, are not real Albertans.[5] Alternatively, they are cast as timid inhabitants of what is, in effect, one big resource-based company town where industry calls the shots, government generally does its bidding, and individuals think twice before taking public positions that put their jobs or their community projects in jeopardy.

Caricatures often contain a measure of truth, to be sure, but they are also dangerous foundations for political action and weak substitutes for political understanding. If they do not tell the whole story, neither do they necessarily tell the right one or the most fundamental one. Alberta is a complex, openly heterogeneous, globally connected place. There are, in fact, many "Albertas"—delineated, for example, by geographic region, subculture, and economic sector. The province is no monolith. It is certainly not downtown Calgary writ large. It is home to an impressive number of policy institutes and political-cultural magazines, as well as a flourishing blogosphere populated by both insiders and outsiders, from Conservative MLAs to libertarian-pagan socialists. The letters pages of its newspapers, even in smaller centres, reflect a diversity of views and, at times, enough criticism directed at the provincial government that an unfamiliar reader might wonder how it ever received the votes to get itself elected.

And yet Alberta is somehow different. There is, I want to argue, a frustrated, elusive, almost subterranean quality to its politics. For a province once steeped in a robust conception of skilled citizenship and a populist distrust of representation, what is now striking is how difficult it is for people to have an honest, meaningful, and public conversation about the interlaced policy challenges that confront Alberta. Those challenges include the roller-coaster public finances of a resource-based economy, the right levels of oil and gas rents, societal expectations for a high level of public services but without high taxation, the environmental and social costs of energy development and their uneven distribution across the province, the national and international politics of climate change, and the capacity of government to chart a constructive path through such complex terrain. Where and how do Albertans say what they want—and what they don't want? How do they begin to test ideas, disagree in good faith, and strike tentative balances? Is there, in fact, common ground? Is there enough interest to find out? As will be evident, my focus is on political communication not as the tactical domain of government, political parties, and organized interests, but rather as the characteristic activity of citizens when they engage the state and each other. This is, of course, a more elusive subject. As the political philosopher Charles Taylor observes, the "malaise of modernity" is partly the inability of individuated societies to form an "effective common purpose through democratic action."[6] But this problem has a specific coloration in Alberta. What makes public conversation so difficult and, perhaps, so promising here?

II

Sometime around the start of the latest energy-fuelled boom-and-bust cycle, around the ebbing of Klein's premiership—when his aspiration to a government run on autopilot had been turned against him by impatient critics, even inside his own party—the sense of political opening was impossible to ignore. The most self-assured days of the Alberta Advantage had passed. The sense of a province out of balance had become a subject of coffee-shop analysis, and with it, the anxiety of not frittering away another economic boom. The talk did not emanate only from the usual suspects: the small opposition parties, say, or activist think-tanks like the Parkland Institute, which a prickly Klein once helped boost to prominence by denouncing as a communist the author of its first sponsored book, future Liberal leader Kevin Taft.

Instead, it came from a host of less-expected sources. By mid-decade, for example, the Calgary-based Canada West Foundation had published a series of research studies championing the idea of a provincial sales tax, a political near-heresy, as the key piece in a reform of the province's public finances to increase savings and achieve greater revenue stability. Other mainstream economists followed suit.[7] Rural municipal leaders had begun to be bold enough to say, as a government strategy paper conceded, that the prosperity of the Alberta Advantage was concentrated inside the Edmonton-Calgary corridor even though the resources that produced it were extracted mainly outside it and that reinvestment in public infrastructure was required for rural communities to have a future.[8] Big-city mayors had claimed more resources to build infrastructure in the new engines of the economy. Most notably, former premier Peter Lougheed had chided the government for leaving the province in a "mess" because of its aversion not just to planning, especially the "orderly development" of the oil sands, but also to collecting a fairer share of non-renewable resource rents for the people of Alberta, who were its collective "owners."[9]

Lougheed's intervention, however, was not necessarily the most pointed or provocative at the time. Like the others, it identified the problems as managerial or distributional in nature. In the fall of 2004, Preston Manning went a step further in a column published in several newspapers, including the province's major dailies. Part punditry, part positioning, the column began by recalling the peculiar historical pattern of Alberta politics, in which a new political movement with a "big, new idea" eventually sweeps a tired dynastic party from office. Manning speculated that the "idea that will elect the next provincial government" would not be spending more on public services or building firewalls between Alberta and the rest of Canada—the cause to which Stephen Harper and other Calgary-based policy thinkers had committed themselves by an open letter. Rather, it would be environmental conservation. Manning noted the surprising prominence of environmental issues in public-opinion surveys of Albertans, as well as the proliferation of conservation groups—"many disillusioned with the provincial government's responses to their concerns and organizing increasingly at the grassroots level." Perhaps he had in mind the newspaper photographs of the iconic singer-rancher Ian Tyson and his neighbours riding horseback into the foothills south of Calgary to make a statement against oil-and-gas development in their heritage rangelands.[10] In any case, Manning's column concluded: "If some group, properly led and organized politically, were to figure out how to marry the Alberta commitment to marketplace economics and fiscal responsibility, with a genuine, proactive, approach to the conservation of the province's natural capital, the times and conditions are nearly ripe for such a group to form the next government."[11]

Whatever Manning's motives at the time—he did, after all, consider and decide against a run for the Progressive Conservative leadership in 2006—he has persisted in the idea that a new "blue-green" politics is both necessary and possible in his home province. The concept of "living within our means" is his proposed common ground for fiscal conservatives and conservationists.[12] As recently as February 2010, the Manning Centre organized the "Conference on Alberta's Future," in which the three lead agenda items were the "handling of public money," "balanced" and "responsible" economic growth, and environmental conservation. My interest here is precisely *not* to revisit the journalistic speculation about what impact such an event might have on the ruling coalition that is the Progressive Conservative government, in which, safe to say, Manning has long been a divisive figure and the subject of as much suspicion as admiration. Even less does it lie in the merits of his quixotic attempt to orchestrate a conservative unity of free-market economics, little-guy populism, and deliberative democracy, though he is not the first politician to assume that "the people," rightly informed, would align with him ideologically.

Rather, my interest lies in at least three important instincts represented in Manning's formulation of a blue-green political agenda. One is that environmental issues cannot be disentangled from the core cluster of policy issues in Alberta. Indeed, they are the best-bet "next wave"—the simmering discontent waiting to be captured by a savvy, ear-to-the-ground political movement that can speak its language. A second, by implication, is that the environmental issues facing Albertans are, in good measure, within the realm of policy choices made in Alberta. In other words, they amount to more than the external threat to oil-patch jobs routinely conjured up in the form of carbon-taxing politicians in Ottawa, regulators in Washington, or "climate-change jihadists" in Copenhagen, as the business-page columnists and radio talk-show hosts took to calling them. Consequently, they require more than marketing campaigns to counteract the glare of negative national and international publicity. The third instinct—possibly the most important, if also the most presumptuous—is that there is now no adequate deliberative forum in which a genuine conversation could happen. The legislature alone could not be that forum. Nor could an election campaign. It had to be created new. Regardless of whether the "Conference on Alberta's Future" was sufficiently representative (predictably, it wasn't), regardless of whether its deliberations were too much entangled in the prospects of the upstart Wildrose Alliance (predictably, they were), the point is that the challenge facing the province was not just managerial or distributional. It was also political.

III

A short history lesson from an ill-remembered agrarian past: in late June 1921, Henry Wise Wood took to the stage of Medicine Hat's Empress Theatre to make the evolutionary case for co-operation (the "higher law") over competition, democracy over plutocracy, and popular self-government over the "primitive" party system. The occasion was a federal by-election rally on behalf of the United Farmers of Alberta candidate. Though the Lincolnesque, Missouri-born Wood, the UFA's leader, had been unsuccessful in keeping the movement out of electoral politics, he insisted for his audience that the purpose was to build a counterforce that could transform the political system itself—so that people were no longer powerless, suspended in weakness, but instead developed the capacity for self-government.[13] The UFA movement was steeped in the notion of democracy as capacity. Its modestly titled pamphlet, *How to Organize and Carry on a Local of the United Farmers of Alberta* (1919), was a primer not only on how to run a meeting but also on how to develop the "power of self-expression of every member" through small libraries, formal debates, and meetings for community discussion of "all public questions."[14] The UFA won its federal by-election and, within months, swept into office in Alberta with a majority of legislature seats. While it proved to be a fairly cautious provincial government—caught between fiscal limits, the impulse toward technocratic, "non-partisan" administration, and the demands of a more radical membership—the widest impact of the farmers' movement arguably was experienced at the local level through both the UFA and the Wheat Pool. Agrarian populism in Alberta was motivated by more than grievance at malevolent economic forces and indifferent governments. It has been credited fairly with having "contributed more to Canadian thought about the nature and practice of democracy than did any other regional or class discourse."[15]

Its adherents lived out the idea of self-government in a generation of local institution-building: school boards, creamery co-operatives, credit unions.

It took the shock of the Depression and a political scandal in the premier's office to bring the UFA era to a close. What emerged in its place was another movement, Social Credit, whose woolly economic cure was scarcely understood except as a desperate hope and whose leader, William Aberhart, was very much the central figure in its popularization. He held Albertans spellbound by radio, encouraged them to "put aside politics," and asked merely for a declaration of the general will—in this case, to be delivered from hunger and want—while trusting the "experts" to bring "results." Commentators have described the new populism as "plebiscitarian."[16] While the transition was not so dramatic as one election in 1935, there is no single, unbroken populist tradition in the West—no straight line, as Manning would have it—from Riel to Reform. In the words of historian W. L. Morton: "Social Credit was the end of politics in Alberta and the beginning of popular administration."[17]

From the vantage point of its early democratic history, what Alberta has experienced since is a process of political deskilling.[18] After 1947, the economy shifted toward oil production and refining, bringing with it a new reliance on US-based capital and expertise. The traditional resentment of central Canadian domination shifted targets from the railroads and banks to Ottawa. The provincial government, in turn, had significant new resources with which to provide a relatively high level of services—roads, schools, hospitals, seniors' lodges—without having to fund them through onerous levels of taxation. Alberta was no longer poor. But along with prosperity, I have argued, came a paralyzing patron-client politics, especially in overrepresented rural areas. At the heart of it, essentially, has been an exchange of state largesse, less generous by the mid-1990s, for fairly passive citizen support, mostly at election time. Within two generations, the memory of a more robust politics of community self-defence has been buried deep beneath an increasingly industrial landscape.

IV

Alberta's political communication might seem elusive or subterranean in several senses, though in this essay I address only one of them. I am not concerned here with the question of whether real debate happens, as we are assured, inside the "big tent" of the government caucus; or whether energy executives have routine back-door access to the premier; or whether the furtive undercurrents of elite discontent might someday surface as an electoral coalition that changes the party-political landscape. Nor am I concerned here with whether the government's high-profile, highly politicized Public Affairs Bureau is so effective as to merit the nickname bestowed by its critics and sometimes by its staff: the Ministry of Truth.[19]

Instead, I am concerned with a species of political communication that is subterranean not because it is secretive—if anything, it can be downright noisy—but because it occurs mostly out of range, in the "other" or "outer" Alberta. It is off-road politics, invariably local or regional, often rural. It organizes under banners like the Voice of Community and Land (VOCAL), Citizens for Responsible Development, the Pekisko and Livingstone Landowners groups, the Peace River Environmental Society. Their activity may not always sound and feel like politics even to participants. Its primary focus is not to replace the party in power, though its target commonly is the provincial government or, say, its health authority or its energy regulator. It is seldom enlisted successfully by the opposition parties. The intent is more immediate and practical, set within the parameters of what people experience as a single-party state. It may be to save something—like a hospital, a watershed, a stretch of heritage rangeland, a market-garden belt within a sprawling city or newly minted industrial "heartland"; or it may be to stop something—like sour-gas flaring, a factory farm, a massive coal-mine project, or a high-voltage transmission line; or, in rare cases, it may be to build something—like a co-operative to buy and operate a short-line railroad otherwise destined for abandonment.

This list of examples is suggestive but reflects the fact that, in the past two decades, Alberta has become a place of intense conflict over land and water use, and over competing resource, residential, and recreational development pressures. Iconic landscapes have been crowded by the industrial countryside of pipelines and wellsites, petrochemical plants, forestry cutlines, waste-disposal dumps, intensive livestock operations, gravel pits, and utility corridors.[20] The conflicts they have provoked are, in essence, about alternative futures, local and provincial. Typically, they are eruptive and short-lived; they may generate no more than an inchoate proto-politics. They may cause participants, for example, to ask critical questions—why doesn't "our government" defend us?—but not always to connect the dots, join forces on a larger scale, or arrive at a sophisticated understanding of power, institutions, and decision-making. The outcome may be nothing more than a more resolute fatalism. Nonetheless, such groups are a recurring feature of the landscape—notwithstanding the national media preoccupation with isolated, decidedly apolitical individuals such as Wiebo Ludwig.[21] Some of these groups show signs of effective communication, organization, and political re-skilling.

While land-use conflict is inherent in a resource economy such as Alberta's, the landscape arguably shifted in the late 1980s, when, as oil prices tumbled, the province responded to desperate pressures for job creation by supporting the development of a large-scale, export-oriented pulp industry in the north. The proposed Alberta-Pacific (Alpac) mill on the Athabasca River was a centrepiece of the government's resource diversification strategy.[22] While it enjoyed the support of municipal and business leaders in the region, as well as the construction industry, it also became the focus of intense opposition expressed most notably during the lengthy public hearings that were required as part of the environmental impact assessment. Ultimately, the project was too big and too important politically to be derailed. But, as one critical account later put it, the province had been "dragged" into "the most comprehensive scrutiny of a pulp mill ever conducted in Canada"—mostly by the efforts of local people, "relatively uninformed, unorganized individuals in rural northern communities," who were up against corporate money, the government's clear preference, and "the authority of specialists and experts." They had to assert their own complex knowledge. They also had to "violate the rules of country etiquette to ask tough, public, and sometimes embarrassing questions" of company officials who otherwise were treated like "guests" by mill boosters.[23] In some ways, though, the challenge to the Alpac project was unusual. It benefited from the presence in the region of professors recruited to a new university and from a fairly generous scope of environmental impact assessment for a project that fell under both provincial and federal review. It was not typical of what was to come, though the project itself symbolized a decisive policy shift in favour of resource extraction. Consequently, the rural landscape of the past two decades has been dominated by large-scale industrial development representing at least four Ps: pulp, petroleum, pigs, and power.

In the economic downturn of the mid-1980s, the provincial government had also responded by scaling back oil and gas royalties and, in the next decade, making significant changes to its regulatory regime. The Energy Resources Conservation Board was absorbed into a bigger agency, the Energy and Utilities Board. Its new mandate stressed "discovery, development, and delivery," but not "conservation" of resources; its ability to monitor the industry and enforce regulations was further limited by staffing reductions; and its application process was streamlined to reduce opportunities for public participation in decisions. As one environmental scholar has observed, this last shift reversed a decade in which "rural citizens" had succeeded in broadening the scope of assessment beyond mere technical-geological considerations and had learned to represent their concerns effectively in both public hearings and informal consultative processes on issues such as sour-gas emissions.[24] Not surprisingly, the renewed intensity of conventional oil-and-gas activity across the province in the 1990s was accompanied by pockets of white-hot anger in the countryside. In places—for example, west of Grande Prairie—it produced a constructive citizen-led effort to establish a monitoring regime for airshed quality. More often, that anger was aggregated in venues like the Alberta Surface Rights Federation, whose annual meetings in Camrose drew landowners armed with file folders containing the documents and photographs of their individual quests for redress against the industry for improper land reclamations, wellsite abandonment, corrupted water sources, or the downwind health effects of sour-gas flaring. While the federation produced materials and engaged counsel to give members a clearer sense of their legal rights, it struggled to point their anger in a political direction. Instead, it was caught in the calculations of patron-client politics and the greater provincial "public interest." The federation did not necessarily possess more power than to summon a sacrificial senior EUB staff member to absorb the anger in the room.

When the Klein government, like New Democratic governments in Saskatchewan and Manitoba, embarked on a plan to boost livestock production and processing, anticipating that grain transportation reforms would shift grain-growers from export wheat to feed barley, it did so with a model that provoked sharp divisions in proposed site communities. In Alberta, beef was the flagship industry; the result was the emergence of cattle feedlots as large as 100,000 head in the south. Perhaps because beef is more deeply embedded in the provincial mythology, it was pigs that produced the strongest local reactions, most notably around the unsuccessful efforts of Taiwan Sugar Corporation, which had been recruited by the province, to find sites in sparsely populated eastern Alberta on which to build a 7,200-sow, multi-barn complex. The company first tried in Forty Mile County in the south, where the municipal appeal board revoked a development permit in the face of a local campaign led by two farm women between seeding and harvest. One of them, Lisa Bechtold, recalled later:

> Our municipal politicians … didn't feel the need to find out what the people in the community or the people that were living in the area, if they thought that was OK, and didn't bother to do the research themselves to find out what negative impacts there could be.… We started petitions and we asked the county if they would hold a meeting, trying to present some of the facts for both sides, not just the one public relations side. They felt that was adequate. And so we held our own meeting, and we advertised it in the paper. And we had a soil scientist come out, and a biologist, and held our own public meeting, and we had 150 or more people just at that first meeting.… So we educated them, we put letters to the editor in the paper every week.[25]

Following the decision, Bechtold spoke at international conferences, lobbied in Washington, and helped form a national organization to oppose factory farming: "I never thought I'd know this much about pigs or manure and, or politics for that matter."[26] Taiwan Sugar, meanwhile, eventually abandoned its second site—in Flagstaff County, three hundred kilometres north—after area residents mounted a campaign at the municipal level and then in the courtroom. Midway through the campaign, one of them admitted: "Out here in the rural, we've got to learn to do politics all over again."[27] The province's legislative response, in short, was to transfer authority over confined-feeding livestock developments from the "emotional" domain of local government to a "science-based" provincial regulator with limited provision for community intervenors beyond those "directly affected."[28]

A variation of the same pattern played out in the more publicized recent case of opposition from central Alberta landowners to a 500-kilovolt, north-to-south transmission line. Although the project was initially approved without public notice, a landowners group quickly organized to force a second round of hearings to review the original decision and then seek a Court of Appeal ruling against the EUB on the basis of procedural irregularities. In the meantime, as hearings continued, it was revealed that the EUB had hired private investigators to gather information about protestors who, because the board feared violent disruption, had already been banished to watching regulatory hearings on closed-circuit television.[29] In the political and legal fallout, the EUB chair was replaced and the agency ultimately dissolved, the hearings were cancelled, and the project was postponed pending a new application and new regulator. The leader of the landowners group, Joe Anglin, contested the 2008 election as a Green Party candidate; he received 23 percent of ballots cast in a rural riding in which the turnout was slightly less than half of the eligible electorate. In 2009, the government reintroduced legislation whose most controversial provision, deleted prior to third reading, would have exempted "critical transmission infrastructure" from the requirement that the new Alberta Utilities Commission consider the public interest—in particular, the social and economic impact—of any development applications it hears.[30]

The other major "power" development proposed in the same period was a coal mine and gasification project one hours' drive southeast of Edmonton. The project, led by Sherritt International and the Ontario Teachers Pension Fund, would involve the excavation of more than three hundred square kilometres of land—much of it good farmland—over several decades to generate a synthetic alternative to natural gas for oil sands and other industrial purposes. In the 1970s, residents of this rural district had mobilized against a Calgary Power coal-mine project that Lougheed intervened personally to stop in the late stages of development. Three decades later, the district was older; some of its farm people, especially those who had no children interested in succeeding them or those who had grown tired of the economic stresses, were readier to sell; and a rich seam of coal still lay underground. Municipal and business leaders in the nearest town, Tofield, quickly swung in behind the promise of more than a thousand jobs during the construction period and three to four hundred jobs on an ongoing basis. Edmonton's municipally owned utility, Epcor, entered the partnership to explore how it might provide water and generate onsite power.[31]

While Sherritt was careful from the start to consult openly with residents and commit to environmental best practices and above-market compensation for those who were displaced, organized community opposition eventually coalesced around the multi-generational farm families whose place and livelihood were directly threatened. In this and other cases, some land uses simply do not coexist easily with others. In the district, the new group Voice of Community and Land (VOCAL) emerged alongside the older Round Hill-Dodds Agricultural Protective Association, which had been formed in the 1970s and took a more cautious position this time. VOCAL committed itself to be "a unified voice in opposition to the project"; to raise awareness of its environmental, social, and economic impact; to evaluate risks independently; to help regulatory authorities, "with their appreciation of the public interest," promote conservation and alternative energy sources; and to work with like-minded groups.[32] Since its establishment, VOCAL has met regularly with Sherritt and with the local MLA, former Premier Ed Stelmach. It has exercised care not to split the neighbourhood. It has sponsored practical workshops on energy topics. It has also built relationships with university researchers and students, resulting in a participatory social-impact assessment, a thesis, and a YouTube video ("Julie's Story"). VOCAL's website attests to communication by member newsletters, a billboard, meetings with politicians (government and opposition), national TV and radio coverage, a folk-music festival, Rotary Club speeches, and the active use of social media in circulating the message even into the heart of Ontario.[33] Bill Sears, chair of VOCAL, has described the group's method as talking to as many people as possible so that they are in a better position to determine the province's future: "Because industry will develop—that's their job. Government's job and people's job is to say how we want that development to take place.... What are we leaving for our kids?"[34] The Sherritt project has been in limbo since mid-2008, though VOCAL remains active.

The same combination of rootedness, environmental concern, and diffuse, web-based communication characterizes the Pekisko and Livingstone groups. They represent landowners and grazing-leaseholders—mostly ranchers—in adjacent southern foothills regions, the focus of recent sour-gas and coalbed methane exploration, and a pipeline development application. They describe themselves as "families bound together" and "stewards" of a "special place" (Pekisko), and as dedicated to "community consultation and participation with industry and government in the planning of future development" (Livingstone).[35] Their websites post the details of industry applications, documents filed with regulators, sample legal agreements, fact sheets, press releases, research studies, media coverage, videos, and eclectic links. What's perhaps most interesting is that they represent traditional ranch country—in other words, people culturally averse to collective action, land-use planning, and politics. In 2005, in a letter to the EUB, two government ministers, *and* opposition environment critics, the Livingstone group challenged plans for "high-density" energy development within its region: "Let us remind you that the Public Interest is not legitimately defined as maximum development of the energy sector, stunning profits to corporations, and royalties to the Government of Alberta, with a much-ballyhooed trickle-down 'Alberta Advantage' effect for the rest of us—while landowners and residents bear the extreme costs of this kind of development."[36]

The two groups and municipal governments were among the sponsors of what became the Southern Foothills Study, an independent environmental assessment and future modelling of "business as usual" cumulative effects.[37] The goal is to establish key indicators at the community level, invite the resource industries to talk, and set land-use parameters for what activity occurs where, partly in order to conserve rangeland. Long-time rancher Francis Gardner, a Pekisko leader, has identified a more immediate, positive outcome: "What I guess I [am] most proud of is that the entire area in the foothills has come together to help set some bearings on the compass of land use. We have created a community that corresponds with each other more than it used to, meets more and has more hope for the future. We have in real terms challenged the model, found it lacking and have been able to do something about it.... The facts were simple, do it ourselves or we would lose the opportunity for any meaningful input."[38]

It may have been no coincidence that late in 2008, the provincial government unveiled a long-awaited *Land-Use Framework*. The document acknowledged that Alberta had reached a "tipping point"—marked by "conflict" among users and "stress" on the land. It made commitments both to regional planning based primarily around major watersheds and to a regime of cumulative-effects management.[39] Alberta Environment had already announced a number of model cumulative-effects projects with community stakeholders: one, coincidentally, in a three-county region in east-central Alberta that included the proposed Sherritt mine, another in the southwest. While rural activists approached the subsequent consultations and model projects warily, unsure that their investment of time really would be rewarded with meaningful opportunities to map "desired outcomes," unsure that the policy shift was more than rhetorical, it is hard to imagine that any such shift would have occurred without them.[40]

V

The kinds of activism I have described in this essay are not easily dismissed as mere self-interested, "not in my backyard" behaviour. For one thing, they draw attention to the fact that, however the benefits of resource development may be distributed in Alberta, the messes associated with it have been concentrated in particular places—mostly out of sight, out of mind—in what is now a very urban province. For another, they demand serious learning on the part of those who are mobilized, even if members begin, as VOCAL's Bill Sears told a journalist, as "just ordinary farmers that want to be farming but are forced into this situation to protect their land."[41] The campaigns in the countryside build political capacity—though not always, and not always easily. They may require a crash course in regulatory law and the science of parts-per-million, emergency zones, clay liners, or soil reclamation. They require of leaders the courage to speak publicly for a community, name its values, meet with political leaders without being intimidated, and deal with journalists, scientific experts, and national environmental organizations with their own agendas. They require the ability to sustain organizations with ideologically and socially complex memberships and to deal tactfully with the tensions that result in face-to-face local settings where municipal leaders, Main Street businesses, or neighbours might see an economic opportunity rather than a threat—for there is no such thing as a simple, tight-knit community. This kind of political re-skilling recalls what the nineteenth-century European political thinker Alexis de Tocqueville observed in his classic work, *Democracy in America*: only when private people are drawn out of their homes to join in some association, even for reasons mixed with self-interest, and learn from that experience to speak, listen, and act can they develop a "taste" for the public realm and its "dangerous freedom."[42]

From the perspective of political communication, particularly citizen communication, the kinds of activism described in the preceding section do merit serious attention. They represent real instances of political mobilization in rural Alberta. As training grounds, they are perhaps the closest contemporary equivalents of the Wheat Pool or the United Farm Women's campaigns for hospitals early in the last century. At the same time, though, quasi-judicial regulatory hearings, environmental impact assessment processes, and other such venues have obvious political limits. They are reactive, fear-filled, and adversarial; they pose narrow, technical questions; they routinely discount local knowledge; and, in the words of Daniel Kemmis, they "set science up by expecting it to give us the answers without having done the civic work of first deciding what the questions are."[43] They can be a substitute for civic work. By default, they assume that the public interest lies in large-scale resource development and the jobs it promises. In a large, diverse province—filled with self-selected *arrivistes* recruited by economic opportunity, not the Sierra Club, and living mostly in the cities[44]—they can serve to quarantine environmental concerns geographically so that it is left to small host communities to absorb the intense conflict generated by provincial economic imperatives. Citizens who are mobilized around development decisions rarely get a platform from which to address a larger audience on bigger questions. Even less likely is a two-way conversation. Their talk, moreover, is directed at authorities—often in the strange dialects of science and law—but not at each other, as equals, "negotiating and acting together" and thereby "exercising power *together* as citizens" in relation to communities, places, watersheds.[45] In other words, they struggle for meaningful settings for words and actions; without them, democracy is "managed."[46]

Still, it is a start. The example of VOCAL or the Pekisko group suggests that local self-defence, however subterranean, can generate a sense of common interest, a broader environmental analysis, a democratic sensibility, and, not least, the surprise of citizenship. Those organizations are not defined strictly by the regulatory processes that may lie ahead of them. What they require as a next step, though, is the kind of larger, honest, difficult conversations toward which some Albertans keep groping, and in which rural people on the front lines of land-use choices must be able to speak for themselves and for their communities and livelihoods, their landscapes and watersheds. More than most know, the province's political vitality may depend on it.

ACKNOWLEDGEMENTS

I am grateful to Jordan Vitt for his research assistance on this project and to Lars Hallström, Karsten Mundel, Norma Williams, and the editors of this volume for their suggestions and comments.

NOTES

1   Sheldon Wolin, *Democracy, Inc.: Managed Democracy and the Specter of Inverted Totalitarianism* (Princeton: Princeton University Press, 2008), 289.

2   Francis W. Gardner, "Rangeland Home Maintenance: What It Means to 'Get It'—When You Live on the Grasslands," in *Homes on the Range: Conservation in Working Prairie Landscapes*, ed. Robert G. Warnock et al. (Regina: Canadian Plains Research Centre, 2008), 54.

3   Keith Brownsey, "Ralph Klein and the Hollowing of Alberta," in *The Return of the Trojan Horse: Alberta and the New World (Dis)Order*, ed. Trevor Harrison (Montreal: Black Rose, 2005), 23; Doreen Barrie, *The Other Alberta: Decoding a Political Enigma* (Regina: Canadian Plains Research Centre, 2006); Mark Lisac, *Alberta Politics Uncovered: Taking Back Our Province* (Edmonton: NeWest Press, 2004), 2, 58.

4   Mark Lisac, "Tory Leaders Ponder Their Legacy: Klein Promises to Pay Off Debt but Reluctant to End Medicare Premiums," *Edmonton Journal*, October 30, 2000. The premier repeated the "autopilot" comment on several other occasions, among them his victory speech after the 2001 election.

5   Mark Lisac, a long-time newspaper columnist with a circumspect, non-partisan reputation, and now the publisher of a weekly political newsletter, does a masterful job on all this in his book *Alberta Politics Uncovered*.

6   Charles Taylor, *The Malaise of Modernity* (Toronto: House of Anansi, 1991), 117.

7   See, for example, Kenneth McKenzie, *Replacing the Alberta Personal Income Tax with a Sales Tax: Not Heresy but Good Economic Sense* (Calgary: Canada West Foundation, 2000); L. S. Wilson, ed., *Alberta's Volatile Government Revenues: Policies for the Long Run* (Edmonton: University of Alberta Press/Institute for Public Economics, 2002).

8   Government of Alberta, *A Place to Grow: Alberta's Rural Development Strategy*, February 2005. The strategy followed the report of a task force of government MLAs, *Rural Alberta: Land of Opportunity*. The task force was struck after a Conservative candidate won a by-election in east-central Alberta by a large plurality but with the votes of only one in seven eligible voters.

9   See, for example, "Ex-Premier Reflects on Alberta," *Calgary Herald*, September 3, 2006; and John Gray, "The Second Coming of Peter Lougheed," *Globe and Mail*, August 28, 2008.

10 Wendy Dudley, "Heritage Ranchers Take On Oil Industry," *Western Producer*, October 10, 2002.

11 Preston Manning, "Will Alberta Turn Green When Conservatives Fade to Black?" *Edmonton Journal*, September 27, 2004.

12 Preston Manning, Nicholas Gafuik, and Peter Andreasen, "Development, Conservation Can Be Achieved," *Calgary Herald*, October 26, 2006.

13 In this section, I draw on Wood's short articles and the transcript of the Medicine Hat speech found in the Walter Norman Smith and Amelia Turner Smith finds (M-1157-103;

M-1157-50) in the Glenbow Museum's digital archive. See my book, *We Are All Treaty People: Prairie Essays*, especially chap. 5: "Statues of Liberty: The Political Tradition of the Producer" (Edmonton: University of Alberta Press, 2008).

14 See Epp, *We Are All Treaty People*, chaps. 4 and 5. The UFA pamphlet is available in the University of Alberta's digital archive at http://peel.library.ualberta.ca/bibliography/4540. html.

15 David Laycock, *Populism and Democratic Thought in the Canadian Prairies, 1910 to 1945* (Toronto: University of Toronto Press, 1990), 3.

16 See Epp, *We Are All Treaty People*, 68–69. I owe this characterization in part to Laycock's *Populism and Democratic Thought*.

17 W. L. Morton, "A Century of Plain and Parkland," in *A Region of the Mind*, ed. Richard Allen (Regina: Canadian Plains Research Centre, 1973), 178.

18 I have described this phenomenon at greater length in "The Political De-skilling of Rural Communities," in *Writing Off the Rural West: Globalization, Governments and the Transformation of Rural Communities*, ed. Roger Epp and Dave Whitson (Edmonton: University of Alberta Press/Parkland Institute, 2001), 301–24.

19 The most careful and substantial study of the bureau over the long period of Progressive Conservative government is in Simon J. Kiss, "Selling Government: The Evolution of Government Public Relations in Alberta from 1971–2006" (PhD diss., Queen's University, 2008). Kiss argues persuasively that for all the Lougheed administration's skilful use of television, it was under Klein that control over the bureau was centralized in the premier's office and its activity—increasingly in advertising, opinion polling, and "aggressive news management"—thoroughly politicized. Kiss characterizes the result as "the public relations state" (chap. 5), though he is careful not to attribute the Conservatives' longevity simply to media manipulation or to suggest that the lessons of Alberta are easily implemented by other governments in more competitive political environments. For other critical accounts, see, for example, Shannon Sampert, "King Ralph, the Ministry of Truth, and the Media in Alberta," in *The Return of the Trojan Horse: Alberta and the New World (Dis)Order*, ed. Trevor Harrison (Montreal: Black Rose, 2005), 37–51; and Don Martin, *King Ralph: The Political Life and Success of Ralph Klein*, rev. ed. (Toronto: Key Porter, 2003), chaps. 11 and 15. Martin, a former legislature reporter and columnist, described the bureau as a "streamlined and scripted communications empire," "a tightly disciplined, highly partisan and powerful tool for the Klein government" (134), especially while it made deep budget cuts in the mid-1990s. Curiously, as if to reinforce the case for the bureau's power and ubiquity, its home website was the top result of my Google search for "Alberta" + "Ministry of Truth." See http://publicaffairs.alberta.ca/index.cfm.

20 I have described these land-use pressures in more detail in "Farming Out Our Future," *Alberta Views*, October 2007, 38–41; and "1996—Two Albertas: Rural and Urban Trajectories," in *Alberta Formed, Alberta Transformed*, Provincial Centennial History Project, ed. Michael Payne, Donald Wetherell, and Catherine Cavanaugh (Edmonton: University of Alberta Press; Calgary: University of Calgary Press, 2006), 726–46.

21 Ludwig is patriarch of the multi-generational Trickle Creek Farm in northwestern

Alberta, near the centre of some of the most intense energy activity in the province. After a series of attacks against wellsites and a pipeline, he was charged in 1999 and eventually found guilty on several counts. He spent nineteen months in jail. In January 2010, he was arrested but not charged in relation to a series of explosions in the Tomslake area of northeastern British Columbia. One account of the earlier period is Andrew Nikiforuk, *Saboteurs: Wiebo Ludwig's War Against Big Oil* (Toronto: Macfarlane, Walter and Ross, 2001). See also Byron Christopher, "Maclean's Interview: Weibo Ludwig," January 20, 2010, http://www2.macleans.ca/2010/01/20/macleans-interview-wiebo-ludwig/.

22 A good account of this period is Larry Pratt and Ian Urquhart, *The Last Great Forest: Japanese Multinationals and Alberta's Northern Forests* (Edmonton: NeWest Press, 1994).

23 Mary Richardson, Joan Sherman, and Michael Gismondi, *Winning Back the Words: Confronting Experts in an Environmental Public Hearing* (Toronto: Garamond Press, 1993), 2, 175, 125.

24 See Arn Keeling's "The Rancher and the Regulator: Public Challenges to Sour-Gas Industry Regulation in Alberta, 1970–1994," in *Writing Off the Rural West: Globalization, Governments and the Transformation of Rural Communities*, ed. Roger Epp and Dave Whitson (Edmonton: University of Alberta Press/Parkland Institute, 2001), 279–300.

25 Lisa Bechtold, quoted in "The Canadian Clearances," CBC *Radio One: Ideas*, a two-hour radio documentary produced by Dave Whitson and Roger Epp, first broadcast September 7–8, 2004.

26 Lisa Bechtold, interview by Roger Epp for the CBC radio documentary "The Canadian Clearances."

27 The comment was made to the author in a telephone interview. See also *We Are All Treaty People: Prairie Essays* (Edmonton: University of Alberta Press, 2008), 150–53.

28 *Natural Resources Conservation Board Act*, Revised Statutes of Alberta, Chapter N-3 (Edmonton: Queen's Printer, 2000), http://www.qp.alberta.ca/574.cfm?page=N03. cfm&leg_type=Acts&isbncln=9780779744923.

29 See, for example, Andrew Nikiforuk, "Not in Our Back Yard!" *Canadian Business*, October 22, 2007, 77–83; and "Tories Urged to Fix Spy Scandal," *Calgary Herald*, September 14, 2007.

30 Legislative Assembly of Alberta, Bill 50, *Electric Statutes Amendment Act* (2009). The revised act, however, was part of a suite of legislation that gave the provincial cabinet more direct authority to designate land use and approve major development projects. The legislation and revived AltaLink transmission line project have caused a political firestorm, particularly in the countryside, though the reaction has been framed primarily and narrowly around "property rights" and the spectre of expropriation rather than, say, the quality of democratic decision-making or community-level participation in conceptualizing the public interest. The final amendments are found in the *Alberta Utilities Commission Act* (Art. 17), Statutes of Alberta (Edmonton: Queen's Printer, 2009), http://www.qp.alberta.ca/574.cfm?page=A37P2.cfm&leg_type=Acts&isbnc ln=9780779746651.

31 Sherritt International, *Dodds-Round Hill Coal Gasification Project*, Public Disclosure

Document, January 2007, environment.alberta.ca/documents/Sherritt_Dodds-Roundhill_
PDD.pdf.

32 See the group's website, http://www.vocalalberta.com/about.html.

33 Ibid.

34 Quoted in Scott Harris, "Not in Anyone's Back Yard," *Vue Weekly*, July 31, 2008; "Round
Hill Landowners Want to Repeat History-Changing Victory over Coal Barons," *Edmonton
Journal*, January 18, 2008.

35 See http://www.pekisko.com/pk_about.html and http://www.livingstonelandowners.net/
about-us.

36 Letter from Jillian Lynn Lawson on behalf of the Livingstone Landowners Group, June 15,
2005, http://www.livingstonelandowners.net/archive.

37 *The Changing Landscape of the Southern Alberta Foothills*, Report of the Southern
Foothills Study, Business As Usual Scenario and Public Survey, June 2007. An Executive
Summary of the report can be downloaded at http://www.salts-landtrust.org/sfs/sfs_
reporting.html. See also the community visioning report, released in fall 2011, at http://
www.pekisko.ca/pk_sfi_results.html.

38 Gardner, "Rangeland Home Maintenance," 52–53.

39 Government of Alberta, Sustainable Resource Development, *Land-Use Framework*,
December 2008, 6. The framework's release followed three years of work beginning with
a report commissioned by the province: Roger Gibbins and Barry Worbets, *Managing
Prosperity: Developing a Land-Use Framework for Albertans* (Calgary: Canada West
Foundation, 2005). The Canada West report, striving for balance, noted that there
was "heightened competition for a limited land base," that natural areas had been
"compromised," and also that "investment uncertainty" had become prevalent among
resource industries unsure of their access to land for development. It also recommended a
shift to cumulative-effects management.

40 The outcome in the case of the East Central Alberta Cumulative Effects Project was not
entirely reassuring. After a diverse group of regional stakeholders had made considerable
and imaginative progress in charting a desired future, the project was brought to an
abrupt conclusion—ostensibly to redirect government staff resources to the Land-Use
Framework.

41 Bill Sears, quoted in Harris, "Not in Anyone's Back Yard."

42 Alexis de Tocqueville, *Democracy in America*, vol. 2, trans. Henry Reeve, rev. Phillips
Bradley (New York: Random House, 1954), 127. Alternatively, Alberta's rural landowner
groups can be understood in terms of what social scientists have called "new social
movements"—that is, organizations that exist for purposes other than that of achieving
state power or building electoral coalitions. George Konrad, the dissident Hungarian
intellectual, defined such activity in the 1980s as "antipolitics," not in the sense in which
that word is sometimes applied to Alberta but as a form of struggle that is built around
informal "networks of friends," that rejects the goal of conquering state institutions or
"deputizing others to do our work for us," and that instead sustains a "debate between
power and creativity" and defends place and work from deterioration: "The success of

this independent ferment cannot be measured by the replacement of one government by another, but by the fact that under the same government society is growing stronger, independent people are multiplying, and the network of conversations uncontrollable from above is becoming denser. Let the government stay on top, we will live our own lives underneath it." George Konrad, *Antipolitics: An Essay*, trans. Richard Allen (New York: Henry Holt, 1984), 176, 198. I am grateful to Lars Hallström for reminding me of Konrad's work from an earlier time and the different world of late-communist Eastern Europe.

43 Daniel Kemmis, "Science's Role in Natural Resource Decisions," *Issues in Science and Technology Online*, Summer 2002, http://search.nap.edu/issues/18.4/p_kemmis.htm.

44 See the extensive study by Harry Hiller, *Second Promised Land: Migration to Alberta and the Transformation of Canadian Society* (Montreal and Kingston: McGill-Queen's University Press, 2009).

45 James Tully makes this distinction in "On Local and Global Citizenship: An Apprenticeship Manual," *Public Philosophy in a New Key* (Cambridge: Cambridge University Press, 2008), 2:290–91.

46 This is Wolin's point in *Democracy, Inc.*, especially chaps. 12 and 13.

Dominique Perron

Two Solitudes, Two Québecs, and the Cinema In-Between

For Pierre Falardeau

Traditionally, Québec cinema has been used in Anglo-Canadian universities as a pedagogic tool for the teaching of Québec culture. Without question, Québec cinematic productions have provided many Anglo-Canadian undergraduate students with a compelling look into Québec's so-called "distinct society" in its main historic forms. Examples include Claude Jutra's *Mon oncle Antoine* (1971), Michel Brault's *Les ordres* (1974), Jean Beaudin's *J. A. Martin photographe* (1977), Gilles Carle's *Maria Chapdelaine* and Claude Fournier's *Bonheur d'occasion* (both 1983), Denys Arcand's *Le déclin de l'empire americain* (1986) and *Jésus de Montréal* (1989), and Jean-Claude Lauzon's *Un zoo la nuit* (1987) and *Léolo* (1993). Such films could be regarded as authentic and linear cultural reflections on the francophone community and on its cultural differences with what Québécois have long perceived as a mythical anglophone bloc called "Canada Anglais."

In such a perspective, in which traditional forms of relatively good-quality cinema were viewed as unequivocal statements about a certain state of Québec society as a whole, the result was also a paradoxical confirmation of English Canada's distinct identity. In fact, the many points of dissimilarity depicted by what I shall call the "classic Québec cinema" offered reassuring ways to measure the cultural disparities between the two solitudes. There was, of course, the use of the French language, both in its standard form and as a *joual* dialect, but the lines of separation were also drawn by the subject matter of these films: the influence of Catholicism on gender relations and on family and social structure, the economic and political subordination of French Canada, the translation of canonical Québec literary works onto the screen, and the alleged post-referendum breakdown in Québec cultural output after 1980. The cinematic expressions of such topics were not especially shocking to English Canada. Viewers of these films were, in a way, expecting such themes and could reflect on them as a paradoxical part of Canada itself, whatever pointed criticisms of Canada the films implied through their portrayal of French-Canadian conditions.

Francophone Québécois instructors teaching Québec culture courses in the early nineties faced a decade of Québec-Canada relations in motion. The decade began with the failure of the Meech Lake Accord in 1990, followed five years later by the second referendum on Québec sovereignty. These events were close enough in time that instructors could use them to remind their students about the role of René Lévesque and the first referendum of 1980, and, before that, the October Crisis of 1970. I was one of those instructors, and the memory was fresh enough to allow me to convey to students the emotions attached to those events and their fundamental importance and significance for both solitudes. In more than one way, history and culture were alive, and they marked the defining and familiar lines of the historic Canada-Québec confrontation, in which everyone knew their roles and positions.

My own experience as professor of Québec culture and literature at the University of Calgary somehow induced me to conclude that the year 2000 presented a new fault line in the perceptions and role of Québec cinema for each solitude. As I reflect on teaching a course on Québec cinema as recently as the fall of 2009, I realize that those opposed and comforting positions of culture in Québec and Canada, responding to each other with perpetual reminders of past rights and wrongs, did not and could not be translated in the same manner any longer. Multiple factors need to be examined in a more detailed way to assess precisely a remarkable change not only in the way Québec communicates its culture through its cinematic productions but also in the way a new wave of Québec movies can be received by a new set of Canadian viewers.

One of these factors is a well-known phenomenon experienced by all university professors: the growing generation gap between teachers and pupils. Although this gap may have minimal significance in the case of the pure or applied sciences, it does have an impact when it comes to explaining historic events or conveying memory and emotions about such events as the military occupation of 1970 or the close call of 1995, depending on your degree of involvement at the time.

In 1970, most of the parents of the students of 2009 were toddlers who probably had no direct or indirect memories of this event. These same parents were barely teens during the first referendum of 1980, and, knowing what teens make of politics, they probably do not remember even having seen René Lévesque on television. In the same vein, the students of 2009 were still babies during the failure of the Meech Lake Accord and were probably watching *Sesame Street* rather than the big public demonstrations in Montréal during the second referendum in 1995. These generational considerations and the resulting "memory gap" regarding recent historical landmarks in Canada-Québec relations produce the uncomfortable but unmistakable sense that one is being viewed by one's students as a "geezer," or as what Québécois call a "mon oncle" (or, in my case, a "ma tante").

Adding to the generation gap, another change in the very composition of the Canadian university population becomes indisputably clear when one is discussing Québec and its stormy relations with Canada: an increasing number of undergraduate students are "neo-Canadians". That is, they were not born in Canada, or their parents were not born in Canada. So all the above-mentioned elements of recent Canada-Québec relations are almost completely alien to them. They may know certain facts, but they are culturally, as well as generationally, disengaged emotionally from these conflicts between the two solitudes, which in their minds could be merged in a bigger entity in which all the components are equally problematic: francophones, anglophones, First Nations, immigrants, West, Centre, East, North.

It is this experience of cultural communication with a new generation of Canadian and neo-Canadian students that I would like to reflect on through a collection of Québec films produced after 2000, using the reaction of the student viewers to evaluate the communication value of this more recent cinema. In other words, what do these newer films say about Québec that is not said in the classic Québec cinema?

For my 2009 class, I selected the following films, whose only common feature is that they were produced after the year 2000: Pierre Falardeau's *15 février 1839* (2001); Charles Binamé's *The Rocket* (2005); Jean-François Pouliot's *La grande séduction* (2003); Benoît Pilon's *Ce qu'il faut pour vivre* (2008); Robert Morin's *Le Nèg'*, (2003); and Éric Canuel's *Bon Cop, Bad Cop* (2006). Although all produced recently, the films have little in common, nor have they been received in the same way. For example, the comparison between *15 février 1839* and *La grande séduction* is not an obvious one. How should one compare a highly artistic film that describes a difficult time in the history of Canada and Québec, one that is characterized by an atmosphere heavily charged with British imperialism, with a charming comedy that illustrates, with almost an Italian flavour, the daily contemporary life of a tiny fishing hamlet? What should students make of the biography of Maurice Richard, with its rather fast-paced and Hollywood-like account of the life of a hockey player, in comparison to the slow and poetic narrative of *Ce qu'il faut pour vivre*? How do you juxtapose a slapstick comedy like *Bon Cop, Bad Cop* and the shocking account of racism in *Le Nèg'*?

These contrasting movies presented students with diverse points of view. I was anxious to understand how they would process and comment on what these movies communicated to them, and whether that message would be similar to that received by Québec audiences. I assumed their reactions would be somewhat varied, given the diverse backgrounds of the students in the class, but I ended up with unexpected surprises.

Let's start with *15 février 1839*, directed by the ultranationalist Pierre Falardeau, who, among his earlier productions, released a film in 1994 about the October Crisis. *Octobre* was not well received in English Canada. The same anglophone reviewers were more open to *15 février 1839* (if not necessarily to the director), largely becasue both Canadian and Québec critics focused on the more artistic dimensions of the movie—the plot, the elegance of the images, the magnificent lighting, and the strength of the interpretation by the actors, notwithstanding the occasional interruption by a few nationalist diatribes delivered by secondary characters.

Even with the lapse of time since the actual events, the story of *15 février 1839* provoked different responses in the two solitudes. The intervening 170 years allowed this paradoxical effect. Québécois perceived the hanging and deportations of the Patriotes through the galvanizing effect of the well-known

"Je me souviens," conveniently forgetting that the revolution of 1837–38 was an all-Canadian insurrection involving both Upper and Lower Canada against the British Crown. Instead, Québécois viewers turned the rebellion into a uniquely French-Canadian event. For their part, if Anglo-Canadians could use the argument that Falardeau turned terrorists into heroes in *Octobre*, the historically accurate depiction of the fate of the Patriotes on *15 février 1839* could lead to a more ambiguous reaction. Did English Canadians really hang the Patriotes? Or deport them? Are Chevalier de Lorimier and Charles Hindelang heroes of English Canada's making? One can see different cathartic potentials at work here: an obscure feeling of historic guilt, a vague acknowledgement of the importance of this episode, or a fatalism in the face of a complicated past that remains unresolved by giving way to a harmonious present.

The students who viewed the movies told me that they were moved. Some even cried at the final scene of the very graphic hanging of the five men on that cold morning in February. Needless to say, Falardeau spared nothing in his efforts to produce the greatest possible pathos in that scene. But, interestingly, none of the students seemed to experience any particular sense of guilt or unease in their momentary identification with the Patriotes. For this generation, who weren't yet born in the 1970s, the emotional baggage that my generation still carries about Canada-Québec history is nonexistent. My generation, anglophone or francophone, would still find this a subject for a history class, but the students saw the same history as what it perhaps should be: an object of interest that did not involve them. As a result, for them *15 février 1839* had a universal appeal: it was about the historic battle between two unequal military and political forces and what happens when the more powerful wins.

In this film, the one who wins and subsequently punishes the one who loses is the villain, but not necessarily because he is British. For the students, it all depends on their perspective. Some of the non-Canadian students even transposed the events into the context of their own history or the history of their parents in another country on another continent. From that perspective, the failure of the Patriotes, as narrated by Falardeau, transcended the narrow frame of nationalism and resentment. It could be appropriated into other historical frameworks and imbued with other cultural references.

The next film I presented, *The Rocket,* had a wider appeal for the students, as this biography of hockey star Maurice Richard takes place within a highly symbolic dimension of Canadian identity: hockey. Indeed, director Charles Binamé, like Pierre Falardeau before him, made sure that the life of "the Rocket," especially from start of his NHL career to the riot of 1955, was framed within the same Québec nationalistic perspective, something that was duly noted by the Anglo-Canadian reviewers. Moreover, in comparison to *15 février 1839*, *The Rocket* had a more upbeat plot, one featuring the familiar theme of the ethnically different underdog who competes in a national sport and manages to overcome all obstacles and achieve stardom for himself and, by extension, his people. This angle, which clearly gave *The Rocket* an American flavour, produced an easy cathartic reaction from the Canadian public. Professional critics may have noted with irritation the film's ideological context, but as I witnessed myself at the release of the DVD version of the movie, the average Canadian viewer—especially those who remember seeing the Rocket on the ice—enjoyed the film for what it is: a good story about Canadian hockey. The affronts to Maurice Richard perpetrated by the anglophone directors, owners, and coaches of the Montréal Canadiens and the NHL are in a way devoid of bad and good connotations, which is the preferred way to frame history in both solitudes. My students said they could compare *The Rocket* to *Remember the Titans*, where the identification with the underdog is in a way decontextualized from political overtones and moves to a universal level, where, in turn, it can be fused with elements from another culture. The students with a European background, and especially the ones with Arabic origins, certainly appreciated the narrative of *The Rocket* since it played into the elevated and emotional world of the national sport, whatever the origins and the linguistic identity of the player. One just has to think of the European soccer teams formed of players of all nationalities, lending themselves to form part of a united national symbol, as is the case for France.

The next film presented in the course is the largest grossing film in Canadian history: *Bon Cop, Bad Cop*. After the historical narratives assigning the bad role to Anglo-Canadians, this satire presents the absurdities of the two solitudes through the relations between Québec and Ontario. The students saw this film as welcome comic relief, as well as a golden opportunity to explore many incongruities: Canada's officially bilingual status, the reluctance of Québec to stay in Canada, and the numerous insults and prejudiced comments the two solitudes daily throw at each other, such as those currently being tossed between Québec and Alberta regarding the oil industry and the tar sands.

Bon Cop, Bad Cop (especially its French version, which required that the viewer truly be bilingual to appreciate the humour fully) operated at different levels for the Canadian students and the neo-Canadian ones. For the Canadian students, *Bon Cop, Bad Cop* lampoons the encyclopedia of all that can go wrong in any exchange between francophones and anglophones in this country. Actually, director Éric Canuel and writer Patrick Huard deserve credit for presenting the relations between Québec and Canada for what they often are: a hilarious set of droll performances that are increasingly remote from the tensions, even tragedies, that characterized our initial history. Moreover, most of the students in Québec universities, as well as those in the rest of Canada, have a completely different experience with bilingualism than past generations did, given that many of today's students were educated in a French- or English-immersion system from elementary or secondary school on. They have a comfortable and ironic familiarity with all the sidesplitting and hyperbolic differences shown in the movie, some of which are pushed to the absurd. The film allowed expressions of prejudice, distrust, rejection, tension, incomprehension, clumsiness, and conflicts of interest and pushed them to nonsensical conclusions with which the students could easily sympathize.

Bon Cop, Bad Cop perceived the effective separation between Québec and Canada as enjoyable, something that can only be the privilege of this younger generation. Remarkably, all the Canadian-born students in the class had seen the movie before our fall 2009 screening. The students born outside Canada, many of whom had lived through the dire consequences of political dissent in their countries of origin, found the movie hilarious—amusing, yet also reassuring. For them, the film showed that it is possible to highlight ludicrous aspects of the relations between the two solitudes without threatening the actual structure of the country as a whole.

The next film was the very moving *Ce qu'il faut pour vivre*, which takes place in the Québec of 1952 and tells the story of an Inuit hunter displaced from Baffin Island, who speands a year in a sanatorium run by Catholic nuns and doctors. The uncomplicated plot, the slow flow of the images and action, the quiet performances of the main actors, and the dialogue in Inuktitut all contrasted strongly with the nervous and high-octane montage of *Bon Cop, Bad Cop*. Perhaps for that reason, *Ce qu'il faut pour vivre* was not perceived as exciting. Nevertheless, the students were intrigued by the very rare presence of First Nations people in any Québec and Anglo-Canadian films, and especially by the rarity of films that depict the Inuit, along with their language. Following a question asked by a francophone student from Belgium, the discussion of *Ce qu'il faut pour vivre* provided a new and unexpected experience for both the Canadian students and the Québécois professor. Both had to explain to our neo-Canadian classmates the nature and history of Québec-Canada relations with respect to the country's Aboriginal communities. Attention was very high among the Canadian students as I explained to Romanian, Jordanian, Russian, Japanese, and Belgian students the actions taken against the various First Nation communities in Canada and Québec from the sixteenth century onward: expropriating their lands, confining them to reserves, infecting them with our diseases, depleting their resources, putting them in residential schools, and so on. At this point, the Canadian students and I embarrassingly felt that *Ce qu'il faut pour vivre* was a Canadian movie as well as a Québec movie, that the message it conveyed went far beyond Québec's cultural borders. In fact, since the in-class test regarding this film focused on a particularly racist scene, the best answers came from students born outside Canada: they could easily identify with the character of Tivi, the Inuit hunter, who is treated as if his culture, his language, and his emotional needs are of absolutely no importance to white people, whether francophone or anglophone. Foreign-born students could relate to this denial of Native identity by the majority.

The next movie, *Le Nèg'*, is far more shocking than a film that quietly chronicles the way in which Inuit culture has been dismissed and denied. It is a graphic movie about pure racial hatred that depicts in detail the torture and murder of a black teenager at the hands of rednecks from the Québec backcountry, as well as the cover-up that follows. In fact, the violence of the movie would make the depiction of an actual lynching in the American South during the 1950s pale by comparison. But the point of this almost unbearable account of an extremely racist act had to be explained to the students, and despite the discomfiture of an entire Québec social class, it was difficult to find a rationalization for the actions in *Le Nèg'*. As I listened closely to the film's dialogue in *joual*, I realized that I had to move to a psychosocial commentary in order to understand, and help the class understand, the extreme acts committed in the movie.

Here, I was describing the conditioning and behaviour of a certain social class, easily recognizable to both Canadians and Québécois. These are people characterized by economic vulnerability, emotional instability, the inability to project oneself into the future and envisage consequences, feelings of resentment and suspicion in the face of differences of any sort since those differences could provide the rationale for a position of superiority, the view of any event solely in terms of its impact on the individual and not on the collectivity, thinking driven by emotion rather than reason, a distorted sense of morality, violence as a ready answer to any situation seen as challenging, and that violence well magnified by the abuse of alcohol. As well, it is clear that racist psychological and physical abuse becomes an obscure but reliable way to get a certain "satisfying" revenge for one's own dissatisfying life. The young black teenager in the movie serves as an ideal scapegoat for the meaningless lives of his torturers. But, at this point, I was describing only a specific class within Québec society rather than the whole society, and the students could all recognize what I was talking about. As with *Ce qu'il faut pour vivre*, *Le Nèg'* has a universal dimension, albeit a darker and more tragic one embodying racism as it is expressed in a particular situation, to which the whole class could relate.

After these films, *La grande séduction* provided welcome relief for everyone. It is a light comedy about a small seashore community that tries to retain a doctor in order to attract some job-providing industry to their unemployment-plagued hamlet. I remember that *La grande séduction* played for a long time in a commercial cinema in Calgary, rivaled only in that respect by *Jésus de Montréal* and *Les invasions barbares*. If we keep in mind that *La grande séduction* won the World Cinema Audience Award at the Sundance Film Festival in 2004, it is clear that the movie has a strong appeal for the general public, like *Ce qu'il faut pour vivre* but unlike *Le Nèg'*, which provides no feel-good optimism about the possibility of overcoming racism.

There are a variety of reasons for the Canadian and international success of *La grande séduction*. It describes in French the specific conditions of fishermen who lost their livelihood as a result of the structural changes occurring in the fishing sector but who try to turn their lives around by convincing a local developer to locate his business in their isolated outpost. The energy, creativity, good humour, and tenderness displayed by the inhabitants of this tiny village, and their ultimate victory in saving it, effectively inspire in the audience an enormous optimism. The story of the film doesn't belong exclusively to Québec society. Canada's West Coast and Atlantic provinces are dotted with small towns that have witnessed the collapse of their industries, and Canada as a whole is marked by one-industry lumber or mining towns, often struggling to survive. The first images of abandoned boats and fishing gear thus speak not only to Québec but also to a good part of rural Canada and the United States. From such a perspective, Québec's culture and society matter less than its creative capacity to translate what could be the object of a social tragedy into a humorous presentation.

So what are all these Québec films made after 2000 saying about Québec society or the ability to define this society? Do they provide us with an obvious way of describing this society as "distinct," do earlier films such as *Le déclin de l'empire américain, Mon oncle Antoine, Léolo, J. A. Martin photographe*, and, above all, *Octobre*? Clearly not, as the more recent films provide us with a representation of another Québec, or another view of Québec, which cannot be explained in terms of a single point of view. Instead, our understanding of these films must take account of components: the sense of history (*15 février 1839*), xenophobia and racism (*Ce qu'il faut pour vivre, Le Nèg'*), the power of myth and the capacity of mythification, the sense of irony related to the concept of two solitudes (*Bon Cop, Bad Cop*), and the deep social fissures caused by declining economic circumstances (*La grande séduction*).

Historian and political scientist Jocelyn Létourneau offers an explanation as to why Québec society can no longer be represented through its film as one-dimensional. He questions the usefulness of viewing Québec as having only one identity and one social level—the traditional view that does not account for what is communicated in post-2000 films, including the Falardeau film. Létourneau speaks of a phenomenon that is not exclusive to the Québécois and should be borne in mind in communication with contemporary Canada. Québec's socio-economic space has split into two distinct identities: metropolitan Montréal and the new ROQ—the Rest of Québec.[1] Létourneau singles out Montréal as an emerging global and world-class city—a francophone reference point in the world, like Paris, but characterized as well by a different identity and culture that he calls "Montreality." It could be defined as polyglot, educated, and independent of ethnic or linguistic origins, a cultural identity that can easily circulate in the international environment of industrial, financial, or cultural capital. This "first Québec," to use Létourneau's expression, does not depend solely on the French language, although it can retain it as an important feature of its self-identity. It is also highly mobile and does not consider the territory of Québec as a limitation on its goals and visions. This is particularly true among the artistic and business community. Belonging to the first Québec creates a distance from another kind of Québec, one that is not blessed with these prerogatives and privileges—the Québec outside of Montréal, the Rest of Québec.

The population of the latter is typified by unilingualism that is not the product of a political will. It is the result of insufficient education, and it is not marked by a mastering of standard French. Both the intellectual capacity and the professional competence of those who live in ROQ lie in the realm of the ordinary and do not allow them access to the same global mobility that those from the first Québec enjoy. In fact, Létourneau goes so far as to divide Québec society between winners and losers, integrating differences confronted in the process of centralization of identity by the different groups who are living at the periphery. They share more or less the same "Québecitude": unemployed school dropouts, workers in the traditionally soft sector of primary industries, older generations uncomfortable with changes of all kinds, people living in the increasingly empty regions outside Québec City and metropolitan Montréal, for whom any idea of globalization or contact with outsiders represents a threat to their fragile integrity.

I would argue that such a social fracture, as described by Létourneau, can be found as well in the more recent wave of Québec films and can help explain the response of Canadians to these movies. For example, *Bon Cop, Bad Cop*—which depicts the bilingual communication between Québec and Canada as a funny and sometimes absurd performance—and its popularity in Québec are undeniably related to a sense of "Montreality" that can be fully appreciated (whatever the lowbrow traits of the film, such as slapstick clownery) by those familiar with the sometimes hilarious effects of bouncing between the two official languages of Canada, as my students and Montréalers often do.

One might argue, however, that Pierre Falardeau's *15 février 1839* cannot be so easily understood by framing it within the "Montreality" effect. But if we compare the highly political *Octobre* (1994) and the more artistic *15 février 1839*, we notice with no difficulty the passage between a raw description of the Felquistes as especially belonging to this second Québec—the Québec with no hope, no real prospect of improving its situation except by literally turning violence onto itself, as it did with the murder of Pierre Laporte—and the more artsy (and also quite accurate) interpretation of the final journey of the Patriotes. In *15 février 1839*, one can feel that the sense of political urgency of *Octobre* has shifted into something more universal, something that does not properly belong to any specific class or even nation. Imperialism can be found in all countries, and the main theme of *15 février 1839*, beyond its specific political context, is really how men agree to die for a cause and find the courage and the dignity to do so. In that sense, the last words of Chevalier de Lorimier on the gallows—"Vive la liberté! Vive l'indépendance!"—fit perfectly into global history. In this way, the film moves the Québec problem into a realm that can no longer be controlled just by the political will of Canada. For that reason, my students (Canadian and neo-Canadian) reacted emotionally to a film in which the conflict in Canada was not localized within the specific relationships between the two solitudes but became part of a global history and could be recognized by any citizen of this world.

The case of *Ce qu'il faut pour vivre* illustrates the same shift of perspective. Here, it is the Inuit hunter who is the target of the structural racism with which French Canada is familiar, although viewers (regardless of their social origins) don't identify with the racists. The doctors at the sanatorium where Tivi is treated, the nuns who run the institution, the working-class men with whom he shares his hospital room, even the bishop who wants to make sure that Tivi is duly Catholic, are all references to the Québec of the great Duplessis darkness in the fifties. But was that darkness exclusive to Québec of the fifties, in Louis St. Laurent's Canada? How many provinces shared the scandal of residential schools? Was the systematic displacement of Inuit people in order to ensure Canada's sovereignty merely a matter of provincial policy?

I am not making these comments to accuse one government more than another but to point out how the story depicted by *Ce qu'il faut pour vivre* relates to nineteenth- and twentieth-century Canadian history as a whole. When one of the roommates of Tivi makes fun of him and his table manners, and then highlights the complicity of everybody in the room when he says, as if it were something scandalous, "Il ne comprend rien, il ne comprend rien là," he is expressing the same discriminatory attitude most of us harboured about First Nations people. How was it possible to speak, and to keep speaking, Inuktitut, Cree, or Innu? That question is not exclusive to Québec, and certainly not to the Rest of Québec. It is certainly shared, not just by global Canada, but by the other Rest of Canada that we can easily imagine: this fringe of multiple vulnerabilities identical to those in Québec who cannot see Otherness as anything but a threat.

The same comment can be applied to the tragic movie *Le Nèg'*, except that the "racisme ordinaire" is here pushed to an extraordinary level that can be explained not only by the nature of an accomplice society but also by a deep rupture between two states of a society. Létourneau reminds us that the first Québec is also made up of polyglot, educated immigrants who greatly enjoy their ability to circulate globally. In the first Québec, especially after the Bouchard-Taylor Commission, any blatant declaration of racism would be a sign that you do not and cannot belong to this circle of winners. That is why the racist violence and the subsequent murder of a young black teenager in the film is accompanied by all the social characteristics that describe the hopeless losers: unemployment, insufficient or nonexistent education, lack of mastery of standard French, dependence on welfare, living at the edges of legality with a deep sense of insecurity. None of these characters can leave their birthplace. They obscurely understand that they would not survive long in an urban area such as Montréal, Toronto, Vancouver, or Calgary. This condition is not exclusive to Québec: it can be found in a careful reading of the local crime news in any small-town newspaper in Canada. *Le Nèg'* is a deeply disturbing movie precisely because it focuses on a specific phenomenon that transcends the linguistic and ethnic borders of the two solitudes. On this point, Québec and Canada can communicate. Each can recognize its own "rest of" in that of the other.

As mentioned earlier, it is the very same dynamic that produces a totally different effect for *La grande séduction*. This quaint comedy presents the positive side of the communities who cannot go global, who cannot move, who cannot offer something beyond what they are: people idealistically united and determined to avoid being swallowed up in a greater market. *La grande séduction* does not expose anything uniquely Québec but instead connects with all the rest of Canada as well—those small hamlets dotting the country and coasts where livelihoods are threatened by every crisis with a global origin: the market, demography, delocalization, the exhaustion of natural resources. In those little villages on the edge of disappearance, a certain kind of Canada— the winner—can invest, generating a lot of nostalgia for a communal country that perhaps never existed but that can provide a space where an easier and traditional definition of identity still seems possible. In the movie, the people of the village of Sainte-Marie-la-Mauderne want to develop a little industry that will help them to avoid the first Québec, the Montréal where they would no longer know who they are. Considering the same imbalances between rural and urban Canada, I would say that Sainte-Marie-la Mauderne is more Canadian that Québécois, inasmuch as we assume that it is the first Québec that gives us, by default, our identity.

In conclusion, I want to propose a reformulation of the problem of identities that haunts the always difficult relation between the two solitudes. But I would also question the very principle of those solitudes, given that, in a global world, they are delineated on the basis of something other than ethnicity or language. Socio-economic determinants, rather that political choices, define new solitudes both within and beyond the historical relationship between Canada and Québec. The lines of each flow from their ancient respective solitudes, and they have common elements, but there is no easy way to join them. One can always become bilingual and talk to the Other, provided that each has the means to learn the Other's language: education, employment opportunities, chances to travel, social exchanges. Today, while a class of Canadians and Québécois takes for granted that they can effectively change places if they so desire, another class has none of the luxury of these options for movement, for change, for the future that mobility can provide. They cannot talk to Canada any longer unless they adopt something similar to the approach used by the first Québec to communicate with the Rest of Canada. In both solitudes, the losers do not communicate. They are rather the object of the communication within each solitude, as lovers form their very own country, so to speak.

NOTE

1   See Jocelyn Létourneau, *Le Québec, les Québécois: Un parcours historique* (Saint-Laurent: Les Éditions Fides, 2004).

Shannon Sampert

Verbal Smackdown: Charles Adler and Canadian Talk Radio

For reasons I have never fully understood, televised wrestling events are enormously popular in Canada and the United States. Fans of wrestling programs appear to like the clearly defined heroes and villains, the extravagant costumes, and the outrageous posturing. It is as if they watch the over-the-top antics in the wrestling ring in suspended disbelief, aware that what they are seeing is a tightly rehearsed act but believing the dramatic storyline anyway. I am struck by the similarities between wrestling and commercial political talk radio in Canada. Talk radio also has clearly defined heroes and villains, pageantry, outrageous posturing, and high drama, and it attracts fans in much the same way that wrestling does. Using wrestling as a metaphor, I examine in this essay the rhetorical devices employed by Charles Adler, billed as Canada's only national private-radio talk-show host.[1]

I will argue that Adler creates, on a number of topics, a pan-Canadian viewpoint that is decidedly right-leaning, neo-conservative, and populist. This is important for many reasons. First, it becomes clear that talk radio in Canada is a medium from which Canadians receive political information. Moreover, the primary audience that listens to programs like *Adler*, Canadians over the age of thirty, is also the audience more likely to vote and participate in the political domain by donating time and, more importantly, money to political parties.[2] Thus, their opinions and viewpoints are important to politicians when determining policy initiatives and party platforms. As well, as demonstrated by the guests who have appeared on Adler's program, the radio host is vetted by journalistic and political elites alike, including columnists, federal opposition party leaders, members of Parliament, and even the prime minister, all of whom have appeared on his program. Finally, there is considerable evidence that the type of journalism practised on *Adler* has a contagion effect in that his views are reinforcing and reinforced by other media outlets, including columnists writing for Canada's major newspapers, political pundits appearing on TV news panels, and—more recently, with the announcement of the new "Fox news of the north"—Quebecor's Sun Television, a station on which Adler now appears.[3] Thus, Adler, along with his perspective, must be viewed as an agenda setter, selecting and framing central issues of the day for other political and journalistic elites.

In North America, professional wrestling has grown from a relatively minor sport to an extremely popular multi-million-dollar industry. According to Michael Atkinson, the mandate of wrestling is to entertain and excite audiences through contrivance and hyperbole.[4] This echoes the mandate of commercial talk radio, which is to entertain and excite. As an insider working in talk radio explains, the purpose of commercial talk radio is to keep listeners thinking and interested, and it is clear that Charles Adler's talk radio program meets those criteria.[5]

There are other similarities to wrestling. Canada's talk radio market, the metaphorical ring in which all the action takes place, is home to a cast of colourful characters who participate in this highly specialized medium. Moreover, Adler, as the headline act, works the ring with intricate and colourful arguments that punctuate his perspective on Canadian politics and public policy. While he is often the main event, he at times assumes the role of the referee, attempting to control his unruly radio guests. Adler also sometimes works as part of a tag team, building and expanding on his broadcast partner's positions with creative and intricate verbal costuming, another similarity to wrestling. But it is the verbal smackdown, the ultimate take out, at which Adler is particularly skilled. He throws to the mat any perceived enemy of "Adler Nation's" citizens (as he calls his listeners), leaving these opponents bloodied and beaten.

I begin by providing an overview of the "ring," Canada's talk radio market, and then move into the rhetorical devices Adler uses in his radio broadcasts. I analyze some of the discussions that have occurred on Adler's programs, relying on podcasts found on the Charles Adler website (www.charlesadler.com) between October 2009 and February 2010.[6] Podcasts such as these illustrate radio stations' increasing recognition that the Web "holds promising opportunities as an outlet for programming content."[7] Placing program content on the Web solidifies "a station's brand image and its programming in the minds of site visitors, resulting in increased audience retention."[8] These podcasts were chosen because they were, and still are, characteristic of Adler programs.

THE RING: CANADA'S RADIO MARKET

Like wrestling, the action of Canada's talk radio environment takes place inside a ring within the Canadian media market. Political talk radio is among the "new media," a format that includes the Internet, talk television, television news magazines, and electronic town hall meetings.[9] The talk radio/information format is a popular one for AM stations coping with the desertion of music listeners in favour of FM radio, which, because of technological advances, now features superior sound quality.[10] In 2009, in Canada, news/talk radio programs broadcast on privately owned stations captured 11.5 percent of the tuning shares of English-language radio, while Canada's public information radio station, CBC Radio One, captured 9.4 percent.[11] Talk or information radio stations are winners, regularly breaking the top three in the Bureau of Broadcast Measurement books.[12]

Like its newspaper competitors, radio in Canada sustained losses in 2009. For the first time since 1993, private commercial broadcasters saw their generated revenues drop by 5.2 percent.[13] Corus Entertainment, which is responsible for the Adler program, is one of the top three radio operators, accounting for 17 percent of the revenues in the English-language market and operating fifty radio stations across the country.[14] Adler, heard in thirteen cities across the country, is billed as Canada's only national talk-show host. As such, he offers a specifically pan-Canadian voice on political affairs in Canada. Because Adler runs in multiple venues, he has to present issues of interest to a national audience; his focus, therefore, is on the national agenda rather than the local political story. One insider suggested that Adler chooses stories that interest all Canadians.[15]

The number of hours that Canadians spend listening to the radio has been declining as well. In 2008, the average number of hours each week that people spent tuned to radio was 17.7, down 1.4 hours since 2005, and people between the ages of 12 and 24 listened to radio even less. Those aged 35 and older listened to radio more often, with listening times increasing with age.[16] This is perhaps not surprising. As the Canadian Media Research Consortium points out, "Canadians over 50 tend to be habitual consumers of news while those under 30 are more likely to check in with online news sources and to pick up a newspaper for a particular story or because they are in a particular location."[17]

Detailed demographic information about Canada's talk radio audience is unavailable; however, Statistics Canada does provide some comparative information. Given that young people—in particular, teenagers—are less likely to listen to radio, it is not surprising that the talk radio audience tends to consist of older consumers, with the percentage share of listeners increasing with age. Statistics also indicate that talk radio is more popular with men than women, at least up to the age of 65.[18] In addition, one can infer that, because listening to talk radio requires a greater degree of attention than does listening to music stations, those who are alone in their homes or who spend much of their day in a vehicle are more likely to be relatively heavy users of talk radio. Indeed, conversations with producers of talk radio programs reveal that listeners are either tuning in from their vehicles or are working at home. Additional research is available about the American market. In 2008, Pew's annual report on journalism indicated that 63 percent of "the 'talk/personality' audience was male." The report also noted that "more than 36% of the talk audience is between 25 and 44 years old, compared with 22% in the news/talk/ information grouping."[19]

Despite the declining listening rates in Canada, radio remains an important source of information for Canadians, particularly for those living in rural locations. According to the Canadian Media Research Consortium, in 2008, 61 percent of Canadians spent at least some time listening to the radio, almost tied with the number of Canadians who said they had read a newspaper offline (62%).[20] Moreover, newspapers and radio stations were virtually tied when respondents were asked how important various media were as sources of information.[21] In an Ekos survey conducted during the 2008 federal election,

44 percent of Canadians polled said that they had relied "somewhat" on radio to inform themselves about the election. This compares to 49 percent who relied on traditional print media and 48 percent who relied on TV news.[22] Radio is clearly still one of the top sources for news for many Canadians.

In the United States, extensive research on the impact and effect of political talk-show programs reveals that talk radio and, more specifically, political talk radio has both an agenda setting and framing function when it comes to politics and political opinion. However, its effect on the voting public has been contested. It is still not clear if listening to talk radio makes a person more politically active or if a person who is politically active is more likely to listen to talk radio. Clearly, though, politicians ignore its presence at their peril. Bill Clinton's bid for the White House in 1992 aggressively enlisted new social media like political talk radio to engage voters.[23] Given the audience shares and the political discussions on Canadian talk radio, political parties would be foolish if they did not regularly monitor these programs, both locally and nationally, to determine the "hot topics."[24]

There is some evidence that those who have a specific political leaning deliberately search out media outlets that share their perspectives. Natalie Jomini Stroud's analysis of selective exposure of those seeking information yielded interesting results. As she asserts, "not everyone who seeks out political information from the media wants to find outlets with a congenial political perspective." However, in the United States, a substantial percentage of the population seek out media that share their political predispositions. Jomini Stroud suggests that "political beliefs play an important role in determining where people turn for political information." Furthermore, she issues a warning about the impact of this selective exposure on the non-commercial role of the press. As a "commercial enterprise, the media are subject to market pressures. If political partisanship is a viable segmentation strategy, news outlets may increasingly target their news towards consumers with specific political leanings."[25]

Canada's talk radio market is a paltry one compared to the United States, which has over two hundred talk radio stations.[26] Not surprisingly, given the large audience, US talk-show hosts are given celebrity status. *Talkers*, a magazine dedicated to the talk-show market, annually lists its Heavy Hundred: the top one hundred radio talk-show hosts in the country.[27] Rush Limbaugh, Sean Hannity, and Glenn Beck consistently make the top three, with each boasting millions of weekly listeners. In 2008, Rush Limbaugh signed an eight-year, $400 million syndication deal; at that time, his show attracted nearly twenty million regular listeners every week on six hundred stations.[28] According to an online business website, Glenn Beck has more than eight million weekly listeners on 350 radio stations across the United States; he has a five-year $50 million contract for his syndicated program.[29] Clearly, there is no equivalent market in Canada for these levels of salary or celebrity status.

Canada has had its stars, albeit more modest ones than in the United States. However, information about commercial talk radio hosts, both past and present, is hard to come by, mainly because their presence on the air is both ephemeral and parochial. The market for talk radio remains limited, and there are no syndication deals similar to those enjoyed by Rush Limbaugh or Glenn Beck. Moreover, when Canadian talk-show hosts leave the market—either by their choice or the stations'—publicity is limited. Therefore, the following overview of the market cannot be construed as a complete list of radio talk shows in Canada but should instead be viewed an illustration of the range of hosts who have appeared over the years. One thing that they all seem to have in common is an interest in holding those in authority accountable. All of them have been described as avid commentators on news events in their community, and all gained reputations for asking thoughtful, if not tough, questions of politicians and others in positions of authority. Their styles, however, are vastly different.

One of Canada's longest running radio talk-show hosts is Winnipeg's Peter Warren, who worked for Adler's station, CJOB, for twenty-eight years. Now living in Victoria and working independently on voice-over projects, Warren's colourful career includes work as a columnist, investigative journalist, author, and talk-show host. In 1997, he won the Western Broadcasters Broadcaster of the Year Award for his work on his program *Action Line*. As his website points out, "He has interviewed ten Canadian prime ministers head-to-head and had four escaped convicts give themselves up on-the-air. Former Canadian Prime Minister Pierre Trudeau once said that an interview with Warren 'was worse than Question Period.'"[30]

Vancouver's Rafe Mair held court over the airwaves at CKNW for almost twenty years. Before he was turfed by the Corus station in 2003, Mair earned an estimated $300,000 a year and "delivered Canada's largest local talk show audience—some 239,000 listeners." As Ken Macqueen writes in *Maclean's*,

Mair listeners were of the "wrong demographic" for advertisers and for that he was let go, but during his career, politicians, bureaucrats, media moguls, and environmentally unfriendly corporations were subject to a "Rafing," a public tongue lashing by Mair and his audience.[31] Jack Webster, who broadcast out of Vancouver, was another well-known and highly popular radio talk-show personality. Webster, with his memorable Glaswegian brogue, was a pioneer of this format when he began his talk radio career for CJOR in 1953. In 1979, he took his show to television, to BCTV, where he remained until his retirement in 1987. Webster died in 1999 but leaves as his legacy the Jack Webster Foundation, which promotes and recognizes the accomplishments of BC journalists with an annual Websters Awards Dinner.[32] In Alberta, Ron Collister, working out of CJCA in Edmonton, was an extremely popular host who was slightly less fiery than Mair or Webster, but still a media icon in the Alberta capital. Collister, a former CBC journalist in Ottawa, left CJCA in the early 1990s, when the station changed ownership, and found a home on CHED, also a Corus station, where he continued to operate his style of reasonable debate. In 1995, Collister retired from CHED after forty years as a journalist and eighteen years on the air. During his final broadcast, former Prime Minister Jean Chrétien and Canadian writing icon Pierre Berton called to pay tribute. Collister died in 1997.[33] Collister, Mair, and Webster were critical of those in positions of authority, and while they could be aggressive when needed, their style of talk was more muted than some of their more recently minted counterparts.

For example, at CHQR in Calgary, Dave Rutherford is known for his bombastic style. He has been working for CHQR for more than twenty years, and his program runs in Edmonton as well on CHQR's sister station, CHED, which is part of the Corus Entertainment network. Rutherford is fiery, strongly opinionated, and clearly neo-conservative. There was little doubt of his support for Conservatives, particularly former Alberta Premier Ralph Klein. His on-air style mirrors the popular American-style talk radio, and he has built on his notoriety in Alberta to assume the role of political pundit on television and in newspapers. Toronto's huge radio market has also seen many colourful and popular radio talk-show hosts. Ed Needham made a name for himself in this medium. Described as a no-nonsense, take-no-prisoners type of host, Needham worked out of CFRB, Toronto's oldest radio station, in the 1980s and 1990s. In 1992, a complaint was filed with the Canadian Broadcast Standards

Council after Needham commented that "if you allow yourself to be sexually harassed, so you can keep your job, you deserve it" and that women, when harassed, should "quit … or take action … and quit your whining." He also said, "If you wear a skirt with your bum sticking out and somebody makes a crack and you get upset, now who's setting who up?" In the CBSC decision, Needham was found to have violated the code of ethics in relation to sex-role stereotyping.[34] Called the "King of Rant Radio," the 260-pound Needham was larger than life both physically and figuratively. A self-described "right-wing guy" and "a real conservative," he was known for his direct attacks on feminists, calling the Ontario Women's Directorate "fascistic fascist fascist feminists."[35] At the height of his career, he was pulling down $100,000 a year working on-air in the evenings for the most highly rated radio station in Toronto in the mid-1990s.[36]

In Ottawa, Lowell Green, who has been dubbed the "King of Talk Radio," hosts a late-morning talk radio program on CFRA radio (owned by CTV). Green began broadcasting in 1966, and while he attempted politics and ran unsuccessfully as an Ontario Liberal candidate in a 1984 by-election, he returned to CFRA in 1993.[37] According to his website, Green's show has been "the top rated throughout Eastern Ontario and Western Quebec and one of the top rated talk shows in North America."[38] Green's book May Day! May Day! calls for a halt to multiculturalism and a substantial reduction in the number of immigrants allowed into Canada, which suggests that despite his liberal affiliations, he too shares a right-wing viewpoint on the air.[39]

The prototype of the Canadian talk-show host appears, then, to be a white male who is critical of authority and, certainly in more recent years, right-leaning ideologically. Those who have captured audiences and imaginations are seemingly unafraid to state their viewpoints in a controversial and flamboyant way. For them, being condemned as a tough interview would seem to be the highest accolade, since controversy is their ultimate goal.

THE MAIN EVENT: CHARLES ADLER

Broadcasting for Corus out of CJOB in Winnipeg and heard across the country, Charles Adler prides himself on being the "boss of talk," and he is clearly the headliner in Canadian commercial talk radio. His radio program, *Adler on Line*, is heard in Vancouver, Kamloops, Kelowna, Regina, Saskatoon, Edmonton, Calgary, Winnipeg, London, Hamilton, Wingham, Toronto, and Cornwall. The three-hour show is broadcast live in the afternoon, but not all stations carry the entire three hours. For example, CKNW does not pick the program up live but instead broadcasts the show later in the day, from 7:00 to 9:00 p.m. Vancouver time. Adler works alone or in conjunction with other guests in pontificating on the topic of the day, and those topics vary. His website directs users to podcasts of show segments on topics ranging from social and gender roles, including chivalry and dating after thirty-five, to business stories like the launch of the iPad, Toyota's recall woes, and unemployment, to political stories about Prime Minister Stephen Harper, Liberal leader Michael Ignatieff, and the late NDP leader Jack Layton.

Behind the scenes, Adler has a content producer who works out of Montreal and a technical producer based in Winnipeg at CJOB. He and his content producer, Stephanie Tsirgiotis, work as a team, sharing story ideas. Tsirgiotis, the "Queen of Groove," books the guests. According to a radio insider, the purpose of programs like *Adler on Line* is to explore topics "that every Canadian will have an opinion on. Something they can talk about at the dinner table."[40]

Adler attempts to create an environment in which listeners are encouraged to participate. That he often sets himself as a contrarian in a world of politically correct media is demonstrated by his denigration of Peter Mansbridge and the CBC, which he suggests are supporters of the Liberal Party. According to Adler, the mainstream media, as typified by the CBC, are too politically correct. In one segment dealing with the issue of reverse racism, Adler asks his listeners if they think Peter Mansbridge would ever want to tackle this topic. By criticizing the CBC, Adler positions himself as the only media host who is really getting to the truth by going beyond the "politically correct" and saying what real Canadians are thinking. It is in this way that his program follows the lead of political talk radio programs in the United States, where his show is viewed as a rebellion against the demands of new civility and special interest groups.[41] By taking on themes of political discourse and liberalism, talk radio hosts have the opportunity to attack "specific policies and oppos[e] leaders while using their position as a way to advance their own ideologies."[42]

Adler often relies on a tag-team approach to advance his arguments. By pairing himself with like-minded guests, his ideas and opinions are supported and built upon by others who agree with him. In this way, he performs what Peter Moss and Christine Higgins call an "enabling function," in which the radio host "facilitates the making of meaning, by his guest, by means of the question he asks, but he does not actually *contribute* content to the text."[43] Adler controls and shapes the discourse completely and relies on other members of the media—in particular, columnists from English Canada's newspapers who share his ideological perspective, including the *Globe and Mail's* Matt Cook and the *National Post's* Matt Gurney. David "The Menzoid" Menzies, a *Toronto Sun* columnist, has appeared on the show and suggested, among other things, that women who are menstruating should be required to wear a coloured ribbon so that men would take that as a signal to leave them alone. The ensuing discussion illustrates the modus operandi of the "tag team." First, Adler took a step backwards and suggested that Menzies had gone too far. He then called on women to support or criticize the Menzoid's argument. Adler specifically asked female callers to respond, suggesting that they are the only ones with the experience to do so. One caller, Jennifer, did just that. She said that the Menzoid was not too far off the mark because wearing the bracelet could signal to a woman's husband that it was time "to leave me the heck alone." Jennifer went even further, arguing that men should be required to wear a brown bracelet to let women know when they are "full of crap." Adler laughed and told the audience, "She just set us up."[44] In this exchange, Adler acted as the ring's referee, ensuring that each party—the Menzoid and the female callers—"played fair." Much of this segment was filled with laughter, making it clear that Adler, his listeners, and Menzies were joking with each other and signalling to the listener that it was not to be taken seriously and was merely "a casual entertaining chat."[45] However, inherent in this casual discussion is a narrative of women as dangerous, mercurial, and unpredictable at certain times of the month. The joke is clear—true understanding between the sexes is impossible.

In a particularly interesting two-part segment called "Angry White Males," Adler again relied on a tag-team combination, working in tandem with an anonymous listener who, through his email, sparked Adler's interest in the topic. The main theme of the segment was that young men are not doing well in university, so for some of these men, a better choice may be enrolling in the trades. Adler began the broadcast with an email from a trades worker in the Greater Toronto Area who complained that he is sick and tired of trades people being portrayed as buffoons, opining that union halls in the GTA are often dominated by specific ethnic groups who only hire from within their culture and ethnicity. It is within this context that Adler defaulted to populist scripts such as the notion that white men are unjustly disadvantaged by Canada's multicultural ethic. As he pointed out in the broadcast, "The Human Rights Commission, when it comes to these sorts of things, is about always finding the white guys guilty of discriminating against minorities and never the other way around." Adler then segued, without discussion, stating: "Lots of young guys are carrying a lot of anger around for a lot of reasons," and from there, without an explanatory transition, he launched into a discussion about the explosion of guns and knives at parties attended by university-aged men. By speaking about multicultural hires, the Human Rights Commission, and male violence, in that order, Adler intimated that violence is a justifiable outcome of the "race wars" in Canada. He expressed sympathy with white men, particularly young white men, who may resort to violence, given that they have been denied a fair opportunity to participate in the job and academic market because of Canada's multicultural practices.

In this segment, Adler relied on stereotypes to help his listeners make a number of argumentative jumps that presumably the listener is well equipped to make. The first is that honest working men are too often unfairly viewed as second-class citizens. The subtext is that white men are being unfairly treated and minorities are the ones holding them back. By extension, violence is the only natural outcome. Outrage at the treatment that good, working-class, white men are experiencing at the hands of special minority groups is similar to the outrage that Murray Levin documented in his study of talk radio in the late 1970s and early 1980s in the United States. Levin concluded that talk radio provided a discourse "preoccupied with emasculation" in which the natural world order was inverted. In other words, white men no longer were considered to have power. Instead, minorities and women had taken over.[46]

Using a tag-team approach, Adler builds on the ideas proffered by his audience and columnists. As a result, he entertains by playing off of the action inside the ring, building on the excitement and entertainment values, and then delivering his assessment with his rhetorical verbal posturing.

Wrestling Costumes and Verbal Posturing

Wrestlers' extravagant costumes allow them to display their musculature, and in that same vein, Adler uses his verbal posturing as a way to demonstrate his own discursive musculature. Despite his position as a member of Canada's media elite, he takes on the persona of the Everyman and he does it with great style. His ability to speak for, as he puts it, the "guy who buys his coffee from Tim Hortons" allows for an exploration of anti-establishment and anti-authoritarian views in opposition to the views of those he deems "Latte Lovers."[47] Many of his past shows indicate that he is in the "Tim Horton guy's" corner, speaking for the regular folk. For example, he began a segment titled "Ignatieff": "In a cold, cold, red meat Canadian winter, the opposition granola is not selling." In other words, Canada's opposition political parties are not reflecting the harsh realities that real Canadians are facing.

Even when discussions are not on political topics, Adler challenges Canadian political elites. For example, he began his segment titled "Dating, Who Pays?" with this: "Ladies and gentlemen, you deserve a break today.... You deserve a break from unelected, unaccountable bodies like the Senate getting in the way of legislation that everybody wants, having to do with revolving door sentencing and all the rest, the crime and the crime." This seems unrelated to dating, but it provides Adler with the opportunity to take a jab at those who are not the Everyman, the Liberal-appointed senators who at the time were dominating the upper chamber. By saying that his listeners deserve a break, Adler framed the actions of the Senate as antithetical to the values and interests of ordinary Canadians. Such discursive fulminations are an example of the elite-challenging aspect of talk radio.[48] Furthermore, Adler's message dissociates the Liberal elites from the people and, by extension, from common sense.[49]

Adler hooks listeners by labelling his callers "Citizens of Adler Nation." By doing this, he immediately creates a group dynamic and implicitly asserts that there is a homogeneity among his callers on politics and public policy. Within that dynamic, Adler is the "boss"—or more specifically, the "boss of talk." For example, in a segment called "No Hyphen Canada," which took aim at Canada's multicultural policies, Adler managed to align himself against the policy of multiculturalism without actively marginalizing minorities: "It's not about the minorities," he said. "It's about different people who want to run for government—right? Politicians pandering to some members of minority groups and I really think that's what keeps this hyphenated thing going. I—I don't perceive that there are millions and millions of individuals who are members of the so-called minority groups who are *demanding* hyphens."

Adler did not aim to alienate his potential minority listeners. Instead, he condemned multiculturalism as a cynical attempt to grab votes. Most of his listeners are aware of the host's own history of arriving in Canada as an immigrant child from Hungary. He relies upon this experience of escaping from Communist rule in his home country. The "epistemological populism" borne out by an assertion that "individual opinions based upon first-hand experience are much more reliable as a form of knowledge than those generated by theories and academic studies" allows him to assert himself as trustworthy, legitimate, and the possessor of the truth.[50]

Clearly, Adler does not demand a hyphen and he refuses to be pandered to. It is this personal experience that he returned to in a segment titled "Communism." Adler summed up his view of his responsibility as a host: "Do the folks understand where I'm coming from? And then the more important question do I understand where they're coming from? So look. I just can't be the companion I want to be for you unless you get a chance to know who I am and sometimes that means taking a piece of my own life story and putting it right up there on the dashboard for you." The alleged primacy of the experiential is evident here, and it supports Paul Saurette and Shane Gunster's observation that Adler "effortlessly shifts back and forth between personal experiences (either one's own or others) and broader social and political questions."[51]

In that vein, Adler provides a moving piece on the issue of snobbery to underscore his Everyman status. "Snobs" began with Adler reading of a number of emails from people who were responding to an earlier email from a salesman who was derided by a colleague because he talked to the woman janitor. In his summation of the lengthy segment, Adler thanked one of his email listeners, another janitor in Vancouver, with this: "You make a lot of lives easier. Much easier. And you've made my life much easier because you've reminded me of a person who did the kind of thing you're doing for many people over the years. Made their lives a lot more comfortable. It wasn't always easy work but she made things easier for the people she worked for. Her bosses, her customers. Her name was Rose and it's extremely personal [voice breaking]." That Rose is Adler's mother is revealed in the second section of this piece. By this declaration, Adler secured himself as one of the people, a man whose parents worked hard and did not expect much from the state but managed to make a home and a life in Canada—lessons he has clearly not forgotten.

Heroes and Villains: The Smackdown

The modern world of wrestling is a "morality play" that features "mighty heroes and monstrous villains."[52] In many ways, Adler adjudicates issues of morality, setting up easily identified heroes and despicable villains. Adler, like his wrestling counterparts, delivers the ultimate smackdown, a verbal undressing of those he deems to be unworthy. His articulation of clear winners and losers, heroes and villains, is evident in his unabashed support of Prime Minister Harper and his very clear opposition to former Liberal leader Michael Ignatieff.

In one segment, titled simply "Stephen Harper," Adler provided the prime minister with an opportunity to discuss the initiatives of the Canadian government in responding to the devastating earthquake in Haiti in 2010 as part of a special broadcast to raise money for the Red Cross effort in Haiti. This segment opened with dramatic music and a series of short clips from government officials, including the prime minister, discussing responses to the disaster. Adler then had the prime minister on live. He was given full access to Harper, a prime minister well known for his control of the media.[53] Harper was interviewed for over ten minutes about how the government was responding to the needs of Haitians following the earthquake.

Adler's tone with the prime minister was markedly different from the tone he has used with other guests. He was obviously deferential, calling him, rather formally, "Mr. Prime Minister." Harper, by comparison, called Adler "Charles," repeating his name several times. Since Adler is normally so flippant in dealing with those in authority, his deference suggests that the prime minister is the one person for whom he has respect. Conversely, the prime minister's use of Adler's first name leaves the listener with the impression not only that Harper is familiar with Adler and his work, but also that he recognizes Adler as a peer.

Much of the interview came across like a promotion for Canadian nationalism and pride. Adler's first comment to the prime minister was about the generosity of the Canadian people in donating money to the Haitian relief efforts. He also played up the role of the Canadian Armed Forces:

ADLER: Prime Minister, we're also hearing from some terrific number of our military and of course they're all terrific, but we're hearing from some of them who have done a couple of tours of duty already in Afghanistan. They just cannot get enough of public service and now some of these young men and women who have done so much time and so much important work in Afghanistan now want to contribute by going to Haiti.

HARPER: Well, you can never say enough about the people in the Canadian Forces. First of all, I can't say enough about all the government officials involved in this from RCMP to development workers to the diplomats who are actually coordinating the effort, but as you know, particularly the Canadian Forces.

This exchange allowed the audience the opportunity to act as "eavesdroppers overhearing a cosy chat."[54] Also significant is the ideological function of the conversation, which suggests the importance of a strong military, the selflessness of the Canadian soldiers, and the efficiencies of government workers made possible by the Conservatives under Harper's capable command.

In another segment, "Harper the Piano Man," Adler portrayed Harper as "a control guy" not known to be trendy. But as he pointed out, Harper's by now famous surprise appearance at a National Arts Centre gala in Ottawa in October 2009—a gathering that, according to Adler, was filled with Liberal supporters—allowed the prime minister to make the transformation from a "stiff" to a doting husband who was bravely performing live with the famous cellist, Yo-Yo Ma. This praise for Harper provided Adler with an opportunity to critique Ignatieff, who he claimed could never be cool enough to pull off such a manoeuvre. The language he used to describe Harper's actions is the language of a fan: he gushed that "Steve's" performance was impressive.

It is interesting that in this segment, Adler humanized Harper by focusing on the prime minister's personal life. He suggested that Harper's decision to play piano at the National Art Centre was nothing more than a husband doing a favour for his wife—the type of thing that many husbands do. In the Haiti interview, Adler provided Harper with the opportunity to talk about how the earthquake had affected his wife and family, thereby providing listeners with an inside glimpse into a man who has been portrayed as stiff, difficult to read, and uncomfortable showing affection to his family. Harper therefore revealed the man he claims to be—an ordinary Canadian, a loving husband who is doing the right thing by his family and by his country.

Adler's deferential treatment of Harper stood in stark contrast to his treatment of NDP leader Jack Layton, who was also given a rare (according to Adler) opportunity to speak on the program. Adler, in introducing Layton as his guest, began by saying that people have asked him if he had anything nice to say about his friend Jack Layton. He replied that the day Layton did something with which he agreed, he would invite him on the program, and the NDP's decision to oppose the Harmonized Sales Tax, an attempt to rethink sales tax legislation in Canada, was apparently what prompted the invitation. While Adler called Stephen Harper "Mr. Prime Minister," he called Layton "Jack" throughout the segment. He was also much more relaxed and informal in his interview, laughing with Layton and at times gently chiding him.

I could not find one segment in which Ignatieff was offered the same courtesy as Layton or Harper. Instead, Adler relied on news clips of the opposition leader or he interpreted Ignatieff's political moves in a negative light. Moreover, he referred to Ignatieff by a number of somewhat insulting monikers, including "Iffy Iggy," "the big-brained visiting professor," "frat boy," and "arrogant."[55] There is no indication of respect, no deference, and no collegiality in these labels. Adler characterized the Liberal leader as a political outsider, a foreigner who wants to infiltrate the Adler Nation. He is therefore not a "true" Canadian but a visiting professor from the United States, and it is clearly intimated that once his political term is completed, Ignatieff will return to the States, echoing the Conservative ad campaign "Just Visiting."

In a long piece titled "Why Is Ignatieff Shooting?" broadcast when Canada was potentially on the verge of yet another federal election because of an anticipated non-confidence motion, Adler read an open letter he had written to the opposition leader. He called Ignatieff an "unreliable character" and suggested that he was falling short of Canadians' expectations:

> Ordinary Canadians are expecting that the dude who's been touted as their big brain with the big heart with the big, big database of phone numbers and email addresses that includes members of Barack Obama's inner circle—these poor salts are expecting a vision, a show, an attitude, a vibe, a feeling of change in the

northern air. A change in the economic spring after a very long and dark and dank economic winter. Who can blame them? Michael, you talked incessantly about the PM giving you a report card on what his government is doing about infrastructure, the deficit, EI, isotopes, it goes on and on. But what have you been doing?

The juxtaposition of the ordinary against the elitist, the working man against the political inner circle in the United States was deliberate and effective, and emphasized Ignatieff's outsider status. Adler summed up Ignatieff's effectiveness by giving him a letter grade of C-, suggesting that he was a lightweight and calling into question his establishment attachments and Harvard training.

The final blow to the mat occurred in the last minutes of the segment. Adler opined: "Those members of the general public—remember, the ones who don't read the reviews of your books and don't pretend to read the book—can read you pretty well at this point, Michael. You're the guy who will jump on or jump off any little red wagon that's moving." The red wagon, of course, is the Liberal party: Adler was intimating that Ignatieff's tenure as leader is temporary and opportunistic. He continued by saying that if Ignatieff wanted to commit political suicide, he should not get his "pathetic DNA on the prime minister's Harry Rosen suit." This comparison was an interesting one. Harper was clearly being depicted as a member of the elite because he dresses in expensive suits. But Adler went further by suggesting that Ignatieff was a morally weakened leader who was not up to the job.

CONCLUSIONS

While several studies originating in the United States discuss the power of talk radio, few studies have examined exactly how talk radio operates, particularly in Canada. As Saurette and Gunster argue, talk radio is limited in that it does not promote real debate but instead naturalizes "certain political and policy conclusions" while dismissing others as "worthy of ridicule."[56] Adler's approach is to provide the context of interpretation on the topic of the day. Indeed, his heavy-handed treatment of Ignatieff and his somewhat uneven interview with Layton reveal where his political allegiances lie. While he may claim that he is on the forefront of breaking news, for the most part he is merely a news commentator: like other members of the new social media, he relies on the mainstream media for information. In this respect, Adler and talk radio in Canada can only be viewed as reactive rather than as cutting edge or innovative.

Moreover, Adler's clearly articulated views on who is the hero and who is the villain support a normative populist view that suggests how things should be. There is little room for those who do not share that view, including feminists and "special interest" groups. As Saurette and Gunster suggest, there is no space for alternative viewpoints. Adler's program is very much a show in which "nobody ever changes their mind or demonstrates any willingness to recognize, accommodate or learn from those with differing perspectives." Indeed, Adler is great on talk, and not so great on "listening and thinking."[57]

Adler uses talk radio as his wrestling ring and his Canadian audience as his devoted fans, listening as he and his tag team slam to the mat anyone with whom they do not agree. It is not clear whether these fans buy into his message, but it is clear that the match has been carefully crafted to keep them entertained and to narrow the parameters of political discourse in this country. In an era of declining revenues, traditional media, including radio, are facing serious challanges in maintaining and building audiences. Presumably, then, Adler and his "smackdowns" will be with us for as long as they are profitable for the radio station, leaving limited room for alternative voices in Canadian private talk radio.

NOTES

1   Adler is not truly national, as he does not broadcast in the Atlantic provinces; however, he is still the only private radio talk-show host who is heard in multiple markets.
2   Paul Howe, "The Electoral Participation of Young Canadians," Working Paper Series on Electoral Participation and Outreach Practices, Elections Canada, 2007, www.elections.ca/res/rec/part/paper/youth/youth_e.pdf.
3   "Charles Adler Signs On with Quebecor TV News Operation, Promises Tough Talk," Canadian Press, September 15, 2010.
4   See Michael Atkins, "Fifty Million Viewers Can't Be Wrong: Professional Wrestling, Sports-Entertainment, and Mimesis," *Sociology of Sport Journal* 19 (Summer 2002): 47–66.
5   Radio insider, email interview with Shannon Sampert, February 16, 2009. The interviewee, whose remarks are also cited in nn. 15 and 40, prefers to remain anonymous.
6   Adler's website has since been updated, and the podcasts have been taken down. They are also no longer available on iTunes. The segments I downloaded were titled "Adler 2,"

"Angry White Males," "Communism," "Dating, Who Pays?" Friday Rant, October 30,"
"Harper the Piano Man," "Ignatieff," "Snobs," "Stephen Harper," and "Why Is Ignatieff
Shooting?"

7   Robert F. Potter, "Give the People What They Want: A Content Analysis of FM Radio
Station Home Pages," *Journal of Broadcasting and Electronic Media* 46 (December 2002):
369, http://www.theaudioprof.com/Research/Pubs/potter.jobem02.pdf.

8   Ibid., 371.

9   Stephen Earl Bennett, "Americans' Exposure to Political Talk Radio and Their Knowledge
of Public Affairs," *Journal of Broadcasting and Electronic Media* 46 (March 2002): 73.

10 See Shannon Sampert, "Jock Radio/Talk Radio/Shock Radio," in *Mediating Canadian
Politics*, ed. Shannon Sampert and Linda Trimble (Toronto: Pearson, 2010), 33.

11 CRTC (Canadian Radio-Television and Telecommunications Commission),
Communications Monitoring Report, July 2010, http://www.crtc.gc.ca/eng/publications/
reports/policymonitoring/2010/cmr2010.pdf.

12 Sampert, "Jock Radio/Talk Radio/Shock Radio."

13 Government of Canada, "Radio Broadcasting Industry, 2009" (Ottawa: Statistics Canada,
2010), 5, http://www.statcan.gc.ca/pub/56-208-x/56-208-x2010000-eng.pdf.

14 CRTC, *Communications Monitoring Report*, 2009 (Ottawa: Government of Canada,
August 2009), 87; "Corus Radio," Corus Entertainment, http://www.corusent.com/home/
Radio/tabid/1663/Default.aspx.

15 Radio insider, email interview with Shannon Sampert, February 23, 2010.

16 CRTC, *Communications Monitoring Report*, 2009, 32.

17 Canadian Media Research Consortium, *The State of the Media in Canada: A Work in
Progress* [2009], 9, http://www.cmrcccrm.ca/documents/SOM_Canada_0702.pdf.

18 See Statistics Canada, "Radio Listening: Data Tables," 2007, tables 3 and 4, http://www.
statcan.gc.ca/pub/87f0007x/87f0007x2007001-eng.pdf.

19 Pew Project for Excellence in Journalism, *The State of the News Media, 2008: An Annual
Report on American Journalism*, "Talk Radio," http://stateofthemedia.org/2008/radio-
intro/talk-radio/.

20 Canadian Media Research Consortium, *The State of the Media in Canada*, 10.

21 See the "Importance of Information Sources" table in the Canadian Media Research
Consortium's 2008 report "The Credibility Gap," http://www.cmrcccrm.ca/en/projects/
TheCredibilityGapCanadiansandTheirNewsMedia.htm.

22 "Post-Debate Post-Script," Ekos Politics, October 7, 2008, http://www.ekospolitics.com/
index.php/2008/10/post-debate-post-script.

23 See Diana Owens, "Talk Radio and Evaluations of President Clinton," *Political
Communication* 14, no. 3 (1997): 333–53.

24 Indeed, when I worked in the 1990s with the opposition party in Alberta, we regularly
monitored talk radio stations for hot-button topics and attempted to offer our leader as a
potential guest to offer an alternative perspective.

25 Natalie Jomini Stroud, *Niche News: The Politics of News Choice* (Oxford and New York:
Oxford University Press, 2011), 361.

26 Bob Michaels, "R and R Talk Radio Seminar 2003: Top Arbitron Performers in News Talk," Arbitron, 6, 2003, http://www.arbitron.com/downloads/RR_TRS_2003.pdf.

27 "2010 Talkers 250 Featuring the Heavy Hundred," *Talkers*, February 2010.

28 "Right Wing Radio Host Rush Limbaugh Signs 400 Million Dollar Deal," Monsters and Critics, July 2, 2008, http://www.monstersandcritics.com/news/usa/news/article_1414676.php/Right_wing_radio_host_Rush_Limbaugh_signs_400_million_dollar_deal%27.

29 Dan Colarusso, "Glenn Beck's Cash Machine: Radio," *Business Insider: The Wire*, April 27, 2009, http://www.businessinsider.com/the-empire-of-glenn-beck-radio.

30 Peter Warren, "Warren—The Broadcaster," accessed 12 August 2010, http://peterwarren.ca/peterwarrenpages/broadcaster.htm.

31 Ken MacQueen, "In Like a Lion, Out Like a Lion," *Maclean's*, June 23, 2003, 29.

32 "A History of the Jack Webster Foundation," The Jack Webster Foundation, 2011, http://www.jackwebster.com/foundation/index.php?page=information#history.

33 "Veteran Journalist Dies at 69," Canadian Press, June 6, 1997.

34 Canadian Broadcast Standards Council, Ontario Regional Council, "CFRB-AM re the Ed Needham Show (Harassment)," CBSC Decisions, accessed 12 July 2010, http://www.cbsc.ca/english/decisions/1993/930526b.php.

35 Michele Landsberg, "That Old 'Mrs. Lewis' Insult Bid is Tiresome," *Toronto Star*, February 9, 1993.

36 Warren Girard, "The King of Rant Radio," *Toronto Star*, March 14, 1993.

37 "Lowell Green," *Wikipedia*, last modified November 13, 2011, http://en.wikipedia.org/wiki/Lowell_Green.

38 "About Lowell Green," Heresproof.ca, accessed 12 August 2010, http://www.lowellgreen.com/About__Biography_.html.

39 Heresproof.ca, accessed 12 August 2010, http://www.lowellgreen.com/Writings.html.

40 Radio insider, email interview with Shannon Sampert, February 23, 2010.

41 See Susan J. Douglas, "Letting the Boys Be Boys: Talk Radio, Male Hysteria, and Political Discourse in the 1980s," in *Radio Reader: Essays in the Cultural History of Radio*, ed. Michele Hilmes and Jason Loviglio (New York: Routledge, 2002), 485–503.

42 C. Richard Hofstetter and Christopher L. Gianos, "Political Talk Radio: Actions Speak Louder Than Words," *Journal of Broadcasting and Electronic Media* 41, no. 4 (1997): 501.

43 Peter Moss and Christine Higgins, "Radio Voices," *Media Culture Society* 6 (October 1984): 361.

44 This exchange took place in a segment titled "Adler 2."

45 Moss and Higgins, "Radio Voices," 367.

46 Murray Levin, quoted in Douglas, "Letting the Boys Be Boys," 491.

47 These remarks are from the "Ignatieff" segment.

48 See Barry Hollander, "Fuel to the Fire: Talk Radio and the Gamson Hypothesis," *Political Communication* 14 (July–September 1997): 355–69.

49 Paul Saurette and Shane Gunster, "Ears Wide Shut: Epistemological Populism, Argutainment and Canadian Conservative Talk Radio," *Canadian Journal of Political Science* 44 (March 2011): 199.

50 Ibid.

51 Ibid., 201.

52 John W. Campbell, "Professional Wrestling: Why the Bad Guy Wins," *Journal of American Culture* 19 (Summer 1996): 128.

53 On Harper and the media, see Jennifer Paterson, "PMO vs. the Gallery: Final Round?" *Ryerson Review of Journalism*, January 15, 2007, http://rrj.ca/m4054/.

54 Moss and Higgins, "Radio Voices," 362.

55 The quotations are from "Friday Rant, October 30."

56 Saurette and Gunster, "Ears Wide Shut," 211.

57 Ibid., 214.

Troy Patenaude

Contemporary Canadian Aboriginal Art: Storyworking in the Public Sphere

In 1974, Canada's first Aboriginal art curator, Tom Hill, impatient with the lack of artistic reaction in Canada to Aboriginal political issues, prophesied that "in the future, art will probably manifest the political struggle more, especially as Indians become more vocal in their demands to be treated fairly."[1] Throughout the 1970s and 1980s, many contemporary Canadian Aboriginal artists found new ways of expressing "the political moment."[2] Visual artists such as Carl Beam and Robert Houle (both Anishinaabe), Edward Poitras (a Métis), and Joane Cardinal-Schubert (a Kainai) built on the earlier political interests of Alex Janvier, a member of the Dene Suline First Nation, and began producing works that were not merely a means of cultural expression but instruments for making non-Aboriginal audiences aware of the real issues facing Aboriginal peoples.[3]

From the 1990s onward, Aboriginal artists broadened their expressions even further to incorporate complex ways of understanding social and political issues facing all Canadians, but now from and including an Aboriginal perspective.[4] Works such as *Honour and Balance* (2005) by Métis artist Michael Robinson, *Ayum-ee-aawach Oomam-mowan: Speaking to Their Mother* (1991) by Anishinaabe artist Rebecca Belmore, and Kʼómoks artist Andy Everson's *Watchmen* (2008) interweave traditional ways of knowing and identity formation with artistic expressions of broader Canadian social and political issues, including cultural diversity, social-ecological holism, and intercultural sharing. Such works confront the Euro-Canadian grounds upon which mainstream society largely operates. To these artists, Canada is quite clearly a place shaped by many hands.

Aboriginal creative works and projects such as these have given Aboriginal people an important voice within Canada.[5] Rediscovering, within a very old Indigenous way of living, this interconnection between an individual, art, the geophysical land, and an intercultural society lies at the heart of the political consciousness of Aboriginal visual art in Canada today. Contemporary Canadian Aboriginal art not only visualizes aspects of this consciousness *for* others but also communicates it, or performs it, *with* others. It does not import ideas from political science but generates subtle political resistance through the practice of Indigenous storytelling in a visual medium.

STORYWORK: THE POWER OF STORIES AS TEACHERS

Aboriginal art has always been a significant part of what we now call Canada. Today, it is key to how Canadians—including non-Aboriginal Canadians— represent themselves.[6] Non-Aboriginal people in Canada account for the majority of purchases of Aboriginal art, but these purchasers are not buying the art merely because it was created by an Aboriginal artist. There is more emotion involved, more thought, more physical influence, and more spiritual connection, even if there may not be a culturally informed understanding.[7] Aboriginal voices are clearly becoming more influential, respected, and popular in mainstream Canada—so much so that, as John Ralston Saul suggests, some Canadians are "starting to imagine ourselves in another manner."[8]

Contemporary Canadian Aboriginal art varies from region to region, artist to artist, and it deploys new kinds of subject matter and new systems of style within the mainstream art world. It is part of a cultural continuum that emerges and adapts, now including the city, the reserve, technology, modernity, the market, imported Western aesthetic techniques, industry, and new forms of government. Yet across this continuum, Aboriginal art is rooted in the ecosystems, cultures, aesthetics, spirituality, and experiences of this land.[9] Aboriginal artists often express this broadening sense of interrelationship in their art. For this reason, contemporary Canadian Aboriginal art does not necessarily seek to depict a specific traditional teaching or way of knowing consciously or directly, and exhibits considerably different formal and functional characteristics within communities than does traditional Aboriginal art. Together, those characteristics have helped create a distinct and new (although very old) visual model in Canada wherein Aboriginal voices, teachings, and perspectives appear to deepen non-Aboriginal Canadians' awareness. Politically, contemporary Canadian Aboriginal art expresses a distinctly Aboriginal blueprint for building mutually respectful and reciprocal partnerships analogous to what Ralston Saul has termed "a philosophy of minorities."[10]

The colonial system in Canada reinforced an assimilative educational model based on affirming "the political and social status quo."[11] Contemporary Canadian Aboriginal art, however, engages people in a reciprocal process that enacts the enormous social-ecological benefits to Canadian societies of Aboriginal ways of knowing (through language, story, spirituality, and the land), experiential learning, and Aboriginal independence and self-determination. This list is greatly simplified, but it approximates the political consciousness of contemporary Canadian Aboriginal art.

This consciousness does not come through an artist's intention, ideological standpoint, or formal skill alone, nor through a viewer's receptivity alone, but through the practice of art, which synergistically includes artist, artwork, viewer, and context of the viewing encounter(s). The aesthetic reference through which this process can best be understood is what Jo-ann Archibald calls "storywork." It can be briefly defined as a methodology, rooted in Indigenous ways of knowing and oral traditions, that effectively educates the spirit, heart, mind, and body through the power of story and storytelling.[12] Canadian Aboriginal artists engage the principles of storywork in a fashion that is not just about delivering a message but about unfolding story meanings in relation to personal lives.

Storywork is a process of Indigenous education that interweaves the teachings of elders, cultural stories, and personal experiences within a story. The storyteller can guide the process but does not control it. Storywork sings when it engages the heart, the mind, the body, and the spirit together. This is the essence of learning. When stories are taken seriously, they become critical teachers in and for our lives, not only as containers of valuable messages but also as active expressions of social-political insight that contribute to the ways in which humans participate in their everyday lives and the world.

Storywork is ultimately the vehicle through which the political consciousness of contemporary Canadian Aboriginal art is communicated. Stories only
become alive and have value if shared. Storywork involves many kinds of
sharing, including elder with learner, storyteller with listener, context with
story, and listener with story. Jo-Ann Archibald, with the help of, among
others, various Stó:lō and Coast Salish elders, identifies seven principles that
elucidate storywork: respect, responsibility, reciprocity, reverence, holism,
interrelatedness, and synergy. These principles are storywork markers, each
"like a long flat piece of cedar bark used for weaving a basket."[13] They are also
the elements of a political consciousness inherent in contemporary Canadian
Aboriginal art.

STORYWORK AND CONTEMPORARY CANADIAN ABORIGINAL ART

Storywork provides a reference through which to understand not only story
and storytelling but also contemporary Canadian Aboriginal art, its political
consciousness, and its effects on the public sphere. It applies to contemporary Canadian Aboriginal art for three main reasons: (1) many contemporary Aboriginal visual artists and commentators have referred to artwork as
a form of education or sharing; (2) they also refer to artwork as a story or as
a reciprocal process of communication and meaning making through a kind
of language, like storytelling; and (3) Canadian Aboriginal art, like stories and
storytelling, is to be taken seriously as an important teacher in our lives.

One of the most important commentators on Indigenous education,
Gregory Cajete (a Tewa) points out that "art becomes a primary source of
teaching since it integrates and documents an internal process of learning."[14]
This describes an aspect of contemporary Canadian Aboriginal art that helps
motivate a storywork process. Anishinaabe artist Norval Morrisseau, one of
the most respected and influential artists in Canada, provides an example of
this. Morrisseau (1931–2007) was raised by his Anishinaabemowin-speaking
grandfather in northern Ontario and, through a life flecked with health and
alcohol-related issues, became the first to paint traditional Anishinaabe stories; this was a controversial action that inspired generations of Aboriginal
artists and made him the founder of what would later be called the Woodland
School of painting.[15]

From the beginning, Morrisseau's art was intertwined with a learning process, and he eventually flowered into a crucial teacher—storyworker—in the lives of many Canadians. When he was young, his grandfather taught him about the Anishinaabe way of life as a spiritual quest, drawing on knowledge of the scrolls and on stories, oral history, and ceremonies. Morrisseau began painting what he had been taught on almost anything he could find: birch bark, cardboard, canvas. His grandfather encouraged this, despite the discontent of many other elders about Morrisseau's representations of oral and sacred knowledge. His learning included lessons about the intricacies of paint as a medium; ancient Anishinaabe art, such as the regional petroglyphs; European and Mayan art, such as stained-glass windows and stone friezes with people in profile; the natural world around him, such as the rugged forests, lakelands, and intense colours of northern Ontario; and the social-political issues arising within Anishinaabe communities, where younger generations were no longer learning the important stories and knowledge of their culture like he had. These all converged in his art.

Morrisseau's desire to teach what he had learned (as a now-recognized storyteller by companions) began merging with the very form and subject matter of his work, as can be seen in his *Observations of the Astral World* (see figure 1). Here, his traditional Anishinaabe cultural and social-ecological teachings combine with ideas from the new age religion, Eckankar, which he joined in the 1970s. "Eck" is the Divine Spirit believed to connect all living things to each other and to God, a concept easily grounded by an Anishinaabe context, where interrelatedness between human communities, the local animals, local plants and trees, and the spirit world is central.[16] Eck, in the painting, is given its power through Morrisseau's association of it with the school of fish bridging the human and astral planes: a traditional Anishinaabe awareness, where fish remind society of its dual responsibilities of teaching and learning. On one hand, teaching involves the necessary training to support one's physical needs, and on the other, it must enlarge one's spiritual awareness of oneself and one's sacred place in existence.[17] The references balancing out both planes in the painting are the life-giving trees of the natural world. The formal qualities of the painting—the framing and connecting of all physical and spiritual activities by stark trees and waterborne fish emerging from the enlightening depths through a hole in the all-encompassing blue, watery background— are linked to a prior and interdependent relationship with northern Ontario.

Morrisseau's homeland is powerfully experienced through its two key features
of large mixed-forested woodlands and glacially incised basins and veins of
water, both complementing the rugged bedrock of the Precambrian shield.
It is this original context that shapes the subsequent ideas of Eckankar in the
painting, and not the other way around. In other words, the imported Eckist
ideas are tested first against their ability to adapt and fit in with the primary
relationship to the land and context of Morrisseau's own life. Significantly, it
is not the Eckist ideology that is given primacy over the land or the license
to adapt the land in its own image; rather, the painting overturns a colonial
mentality, rooting everything once again in a partnership with the "natural
context." This element of holism, which continually grounds internal learning

processes for many Aboriginal artists in the geophysical lands of Canada, gives many formal aspects of contemporary Aboriginal art incredible educational, and hence, storywork power in Canada.

An internal learning process also fuels Morrisseau's storywork by helping to substantiate a reverence for the stories and teachings he was stimulated to share, a profound sense of responsibility to his culture and world as instilled by his grandfather, and an important reciprocity that spread through the lives of many viewers. These included the relations established with younger generations of Anishinaabe, who were inspired to reconnect with their culture in the wake of the tragedies ignited by the residential school era, as well as those built through important non-Aboriginal visitors to his community, such as artist and writer Selwyn Dewdney and Toronto art dealer Jack Pollock.

Following his first successful exhibition with Pollock in 1962, Morrisseau's work contributed to such educational experiences as the renewal of Anishinaabe heritage and communities, the first solo exhibition featuring a First Nations artist at the National Gallery of Canada in 2006, and countless personal life-experience stories within the lives of Canadians, such as the impact of his *Androgyny* (1983) on former Governor General Michaëlle Jean, who chose it to hang in the ballroom of Rideau Hall in 2008.[18]

This educational role for contemporary Canadian Aboriginal art gives it an enduring storywork energy that has also prompted many Aboriginal artists and commentators to emphasize the important "sharing of knowledge" inherent in the art process.[19] In so doing, contemporary Canadian Aboriginal artists are sustaining an age-old tradition of communicating with other generations, species, entities, and cultures through forms of art, or story, from the ground up.[20] What people and artists communicated and shared throughout this tradition was crucial knowledge about "the worlds they lived in, the Land they walked on, the Beings they shared the Land with," and how they came to "'walk' in the many worlds they inhabited both physically and spiritually."[21] This communicative practice equally motivates storywork in Canadian Aboriginal art today.

As important knowledge is gained through an artist's own internal learning process, traditional Aboriginal aesthetics teach that it must be shared if it is to stay alive in and contribute to the world. This is a matter of respect and responsibility, where personal gain, skill, or perfection are less important than the quality of the communication itself.[22] With such an emphasis on quality in the communication process, it becomes imperative that artists stay aware of the various nuances characterizing their interrelatedness with everything in the world around them, with the "core" of their stories, and with the language they use to convey them. Contemporary Canadian Aboriginal artists continue to share some of the most telling, striking, and powerful stories about that rich social-ecological diversity, and about shades of social, ecological, historical, and political life in Canada.[23]

Coast Salish artist Lawrence Paul Yuxweluptun (b. 1957) studied at Vancouver's Emily Carr College of Art and Design (1978–83) and is well-known for his large-scale, colourfully vivid, and expressive paintings that engage contemporary Aboriginal social-political issues, often with a biting humour.[24] His art has occasionally been reproved for its use of and similarity to Western aesthetic traditions, but he has responded confidently that "to deal with the contemporary problems that interest me I have to have a contemporary language."[25] This highlights his awareness of the need for quality communication through his art in order to uphold his responsibilities as an artist to his community and the world in which he lives. Métis film artist and producer Loretta Todd's impassioned words allude to the intimacy and power Yuxweluptun achieved in the quality "translation" and communication of his story told through *I Have a Vision That Some Day All Indigenous People Will Have Freedom and Self-Government* (see figure 2):

> In that first painting I was startled. I marvelled at the scale, the humour, the use of colour in relationship to traditional use of colour. These were all proud but not arrogant innovations. This was boldness without vanity, expansion without destruction; this was risk with responsibility ... even as he took chances with images millennia old, he sought to respect the integrity of the design form to honour the meaning behind the aesthetics while making images none had seen before.... This was a path that was utterly new, yet old as the hills. We learn in many ways and from many teachers. From his first canvases Lawrence Paul Yuxweluptun was a teacher.[26]

The calling Yuxweluptun felt to alter the way he shared his knowledge also demonstrates an awareness of knowing what stories to tell, as well as their abilities to engage a viewer in a way that the stories can grab hold—spiritually, emotionally, intellectually, and physically. A clear sign of his ability to do so is evident when we consider how the title of Yuxweluptun's work alone, *I Have a Vision That Some Day All Indigenous People Will Have Freedom and Self-Government*, reflects aspects of Todd's simultaneously unfolding life and work as an impassioned filmmaker frequently concerned with the struggles of Aboriginal peoples in Canada.

Aboriginal artists do at times feel apprehensive about the part of the communicative process where meaning becomes interdependent with a viewer's attentiveness and level of participation. Giving the story and viewer space and time to unfold is necessary to keep the spirit and power of the story alive. Joane Cardinal-Schubert stated:

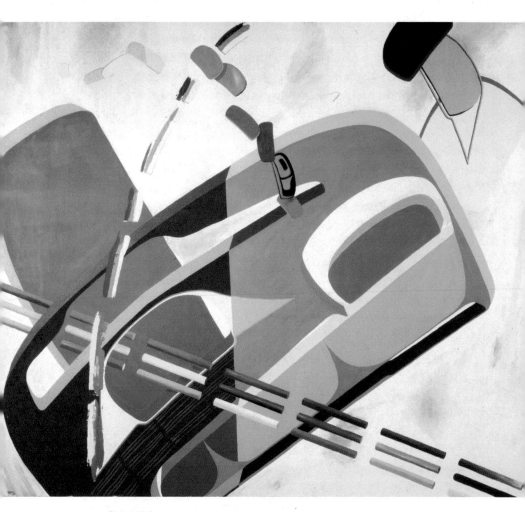

Figure 15.2
Lawrence Paul Yuxweluptun, *I Have a Vision That Some Day All Indigenous People Will Have Freedom and Self-Government*, 1989. Acrylic on canvas. 174 x 211 cm (68.5 x 83 in.). Ethnologisches Museum, Staatliche Museen zu Berlin.

When I'm in the process of making something, that's when it's all going on for me; the discovery, the exploration, the challenge. Then when you take it out of that realm … there is a kind of separation for me because when the viewer looks at it I don't have any control over how they do that. I try and create things that are going to be a mirror for people, so that when they do look at it there is something within it where their own knowledge and memory can take off, so everyone can relate to it on some level.... Part of my strategy is to create things that have a metaphorical jump—allow someone to understand Native issues in terms that they can relate to in their own culture.... What I usually try to do is make something terribly beautiful so that if people don't get it on an intellectual or emotional layer, then they'll get it on the personal [physical] layer of it's nice to look at. Then when they really figure out what it's really about, it gives them a double whammy.[27]

Cardinal-Schubert's awareness of her stories' interrelatedness with the viewer is echoed in the work of Métis artist Heather Shillinglaw, a relative of Alex Janvier. Shillinglaw (b. 1971), who graduated from the Alberta College of Art and Design in 1996, now produces mixed-media paintings of native Alberta plants and wildflowers that call attention to social-ecological relationships, thus honouring the knowledge carried by her great-grandmother, a Cree medicine woman. Shillinglaw's artwork, when viewed from a distance, depicts a flower, plant, or herb almost with the scrutiny of a botanical study. On closer look, a viewer quickly notices that her subject matter comprises a collage of diverse materials that might include layers or accents of leather, buttons, newspaper clippings, watch parts, musical scores, beads, patchwork, and much more. On one hand, these layers obscure or filter a clear perception of the partly painted subject. On the other hand, they also enhance the subject by enriching its relationship to the viewer. Shillinglaw's work relies on the coming together of diverse ways of knowing and experiencing—Aboriginal and non-Aboriginal—in order to "see" the natural world in its fullness.

Similar to what we see in the work of Morrisseau, Shillinglaw's collage elements, while including various human ways of experiencing an aspect of nature, are adapted and come together primarily from a responsibility to the holistic relationship with the natural world. The layering of the prickly currant shrub in *Bear's Delight* (2010)—with its three-dimensional, long, thin, golden-brown beads, hand-stitched on a patch of leather to evoke the shrub's tiny spines, complemented with two-dimensional, painted currant berries and background—interrupts a viewer's Western aesthetic or scientific training, as well as the socially ingrained way of seeing paintings. In this way, Shillinglaw's work potentially initiates various storywork threads in the interrelated lives of viewers.

The titles of Shillinglaw's botanical works also help to stimulate story-work. Her titles—*A Headache, I'm So Itchy, Little Savage, Which Direction Do I Grow?*—are often deliberately tantalizing, providing just enough information to pique an interest in her subject matter without actually providing any explanations. The effect is to tease the viewer, thus helping to create a story-work synergy among the artist, the artwork, and the audience. *Little Savage*, for example (see figure 15.3), depicts beautiful camas plants in flower, but the variety of camas is highly poisonous and can easily be confused with the tasty wild onion and other edible types of camas that form part of the diet of local Aboriginal peoples. The title, *Little Savage*, refers to a very real social-ecological relationship, inviting viewers to learn about the plant but also suggesting that they may need to do so, as is indeed the case: this is a matter of life and death. Shillinglaw's approach to titles is in keeping with the way that natural elements are named in Aboriginal languages: rather than serving simply to identify, names often emphasize the relationship between the thing named and human beings.[28] Shillinglaw's titles and formal combinations together tell the story of the intimate and intrinsic social-ecological relationship that humans have with the natural landscape when they are respectfully and responsibly "listening" or paying attention. Her distinct ways of communicating this relationship help to initiate storywork, from the ground up.

Intercultural layerings and metaphorical associations also create many situations of great irony and humour. Works of contemporary Aboriginal art can provoke laughter—a response that, like crying and expressing anger, engages a person in a story emotionally, intellectually, spiritually, and physically.[29] Encounters with contemporary Canadian Aboriginal art, especially with works that deal more overtly with highly charged social and political issues, can also produce tears. Joane Cardinal-Schubert's installation *The Lesson* addresses the effects of residential schools on Aboriginal communities. First created in 1989 in Montreal, *The Lesson* was subsequently installed at the Toronto International Powwow in 1999 as well as widely exhibited elsewhere. *The Lesson* depicts a claustrophobic classroom, with chairs tied together, seats with screws through them, and chalkboards with some of the past and present injustices that took place in such classrooms scrawled across them. One of the chalkboards, the "Memory Wall," invites Aboriginal people to come up and write their names and thoughts on the board. It is estimated that more than 2,500 people—Aboriginal and non-Aboriginal—viewed the installation, many of whom were observed to leave crying.[30] An artwork might also be experienced one way initially, but it evolves as viewers themselves do, taking on new meanings as a viewer's understanding and sensitivity grow. In this way, contemporary Canadian Aboriginal art constitutes a powerful communication process.

In a place encompassing as many edges of social-ecological diversity as Canada does, contemporary Aboriginal art has its work cut out for it. Along each of these edges are opportunities for learning more about oneself in the world and about other ways to experience the world. It is the well-honed ability to communicate and the long-standing expertise in communicating important knowledge across cultural and ecological edges in Canadian contexts that makes contemporary Aboriginal art especially important to social and political consciousness. In the endeavour to enliven that consciousness, the storywork process generated through contemporary Canadian Aboriginal art, is a proven methodology for working with these edges in Canada. It demonstrates that the edges are less like rigid and hierarchical borders in everyday life and more like permeable membranes across which equally important "stories," or ways of knowing one's place and role in the world can "intergrade producing a richness of knowledge and practices that enhances the resilience of local societies."[31] This is the heart of the political consciousness of contemporary Canadian Aboriginal art, and Indigenous storywork gives it legs.

SOCIAL-ECOLOGICAL RESILIENCE: THE WORK OF CONTEMPORARY
CANADIAN ABORIGINAL ART

In a still strongly colonial society like Canada, one contributing system tends to overwhelm or dominate others, and benefits generally tend to flow top-down in one direction through rigid borders between different cultures.[32] The storywork process in contemporary Aboriginal visual art actively engages viewers in the experience of living in a Canada in which this structure has been overturned. The principles of holism, interrelatedness, reciprocity, respect, responsibility, reverence, and synergy, functioning together in a contemporary Canadian Aboriginal art encounter, engage Canadians in the experience of a sharing or partnership based on consent, mutual respect, and mutual adaptation, unlike experiences that may emerge in the political, institutional, and hierarchical structures of mainstream society.

Figure 15.3
Heather Shillinglaw, *Little Savage*, 2009.
Mixed media on canvas. 38 x 89 cm (15 x 35 in.). Private collection of the artist, Edmonton.

This rich form of sharing harks back not only to the original Indigenous knowledges concerning living in this place but also to modern lessons about "the real spirit of intent in treaty making," reconciliation, and sustainable development.[33] It is a sharing that involves more than just an intellectual somersault or a linear relationship between artist, artwork, and viewer. Active

participants in this contemporary Aboriginal art process reciprocally perform together what John Ralston Saul has called "a philosophy of minorities," even if only temporarily or subconsciously.[34] Here, an equal sharing between different people, cultures, and communities can enhance the collective knowledges and practices contributing to living in society. In short, contemporary Canadian Aboriginal art communicates and engages Canadians in a political relationship that is, as Michael Murphy argues, based on "equality ... an equal right to exercise choices and make decisions that for too long have been the exclusive privilege of non-Aboriginal peoples through their control of the modern state."[35] This political relationship involves two key and overlapping dimensions, one social and one ecological. Indigenous politics, traditional knowledges, and aesthetics dovetail in the storywork of contemporary Aboriginal art through its expression of stories that do not claim to give answers from a privileged position. Rather, they rely equally on the contributions—with spirit, heart, body, and mind—of others for meaning-making within everyday life. The eventual outcome is a more social-ecologically resilient society for all those living together in this same place.

Not every person in Canada who encounters contemporary Aboriginal art engages with it in the way that has been described. Storywork "is hard work," and if not done successfully, could reduce stories to communication without a purpose other than entertainment.[36] Even if the story is told in the right (read "most responsible") way, the listener might not be prepared to engage with it fully—spiritually, emotionally, intellectually, and physically.[37] Significantly, however, many Canadians are "grabbed" by an Aboriginal art story, and it does work in various ways on and through their lives.

In an effort to learn more about this equally important dimension of Aboriginal storywork through visual art, I interviewed several Albertans who have engaged with contemporary Canadian Aboriginal art. Lily, a nurse and stay-at-home mother, spoke of her encounters with Heather Shillinglaw's mixed-media collages, which first grabbed her attention by being totally unexpected—"because how can you expect that? Look at what she does! How can you even possibly in your little imagination even expect something like that? Because if you look at art and you look at Aboriginal art, it's not what she does." She was struck by what seemed to her the "life" and "joy" in Shillinglaw's botanical paintings. Her relationship with this art eventually deepened to include an appreciation for the artist's use of collage, "the way she creates these images, and the way they jump out at you." Shillinglaw's art attracted Lily in part because, as a hobby gardener, she loves plants and is especially interested in species native to Alberta, where she has lived all her life. Lily mentioned the connection she felt between her experiences gardening and her childhood memories of walking around local ravines and her experience of Shillinglaw's art, which seemed to her "familiar ... but not familiar." Even while hanging on her wall inside her home, the art in some way amplified, or brought to life, her walks and outdoor life, as well as the flow of the seasons. As she recalled one encounter with Shillinglaw's art: "It was wintertime, and it's dark, and we're covered in snow, and then you have these beautiful, beautiful things that remind you of a season that's coming or a season that's passed."[38]

Lily's observations echo the stages of learning as they develop into storywork. Together, she and Shillinglaw moved from a predominantly one-way conversation (in which the artwork was doing most of the unexpected talking), to a two-way conversation (through a dialogue about the uses of collage, texture, and media), to chat (as Shillinglaw's artwork hanging in her house became more familiar with each viewing), to storytelling.[39] The last was expressed through Lily's reciprocal sharing with me, now also a participant in her storywork process with Shillinglaw's art, as Lily is now in mine. Lily shared stories about doing art workshops with Shillinglaw in order to learn how to make art herself; about childhood memories that Shillinglaw's art brought back, like being with the wild roses in the ravine behind her house; about her curious connection, as a nurse, with Shillinglaw's art as an honouring of the medicinal knowledge carried by Shillinglaw's great-grandmother; about the "joy" that Shillinglaw's art invokes in her life, which she related to her love for her two daughters; and about her own passion for native plants in Alberta. Shillinglaw's art has indeed become a part of Lily's own life-experience story through all these connections, unfolding equally on a physical, emotional, or spiritual level as on an intellectual one.

Even though there may be no overt intellectual message pertaining to politics in Canada immediately passed on through Shillinglaw's story, she and Lily perform a partnership that embodies a radical political consciousness where intercultural relationships are mutually respectful and accommodating. Here, they are rooted in the natural geophysical context stabilizing their everyday lives, and each person is guided and supported in everyday life—not necessarily only with gentleness—rather than being imposed upon from an abstract or "artificial context."[40] The storywork of contemporary Canadian Aboriginal art quite literally arises from the ground up, neutralizing the force of Canada's top-down political and social structures.

A rising number of similar storywork relationships in Canada's Prairie provinces have altered the philosophy and politics underpinning prairie arts and institutions, such as the Banff Centre, Calgary's Glenbow Museum, and the statues of Louis Riel in Regina and Winnipeg. Each has been reorganized over past decades to acknowledge a regional Aboriginal presence that has become increasingly and integrally linked to their social-political success.[41] Canadian prairie art has undergone significant change in this regard. Canadian studies commentator George Melnyk observes a change in the way non-Aboriginal painters have painted the prairie west throughout the twentieth century. He points out that the region's current aesthetic shifts are being developed "in the sweat lodge," pointing to a possible "post-continentalist phase [of post-modernist prairie populist art] in which the settler audience naturalizes itself by incorporating the Indigenous worldview into regional identity rather than relying on the agrarian myth." Melnyk calls this shift "the métisization of art."[42] Regional identity has been significantly negotiated as well by Aboriginal aesthetic contributions to society from the ground up. The métisization of art is not simply a trend that non-Aboriginal Canadians alone have ushered into the Prairie provinces. Rather, it has been equally forged out of the Aboriginal–non-Aboriginal relationships engaged by the storywork of contemporary Aboriginal art and its foundational knowledge systems. These relationships, based on mutual respect and interrelatedness, have helped give the settler audience the knowledge and practice to re-vision the agrarian myth—like colonial and top-down political structures generally. It is just as important and critical to acknowledge the very aware elders, or artists, who have invited or welcomed non-Aboriginal peoples into the sweat lodge, or artwork, as it is to acknowledge those people who have subsequently applied or reciprocated their experiences in the lodge, or with the art, in their everyday lives. The synergy developing between non-Aboriginal and Aboriginal Canadians—in part, through the growth of opportunities to experience contemporary Aboriginal art—is increasing the social resilience of Canadian society. The storywork of contemporary Canadian Aboriginal art has stimulated a political consciousness by initiating a working partnership between Aboriginal and non-Aboriginal individuals and communities. Such a partnership entails the sharing of knowledge and practice through local consensus and mutual adaptation from the ground up, rather than through mainstream political, social, and institutional hierarchies.

One of the most famous examples of a contemporary Canadian Aboriginal artwork that has generated much social-political reverence, power, and authority is *The Spirit of Haida Gwaii* (see figure 4) by Haida artist Bill Reid. Reid (1920–1998) was a carver and goldsmith who, inspired by the art of his great-great-uncle Charles Edenshaw (1839–1920), combined Haida traditions with European jewelry techniques to make his own art, which subsequently influenced a growing awareness of Aboriginal art traditions, a wave of emerging Northwest Coast Aboriginal artists, and a surge of intercultural sharing in Canada.[43]

The Spirit of Haida Gwaii, installed in the courtyard of the Canadian Embassy in Washington, DC, tells the story of thirteen travellers—animal and human from Haida Gwaii—journeying together in a traditional Haida canoe. The accompanying text introduces layers of the sculpture's metaphorical depth as it came to Reid in a stream of consciousness dictated to his wife, Martine. Right from the beginning, Reid made no provision for an "answer," or meaning, contained in the work alone: "Here we are at last, a long way from Haida Gwaii, not too sure where we are or where we're going, still squabbling or vying for position within the boat, but somehow managing to appear to be heading in some direction."[44] He introduces the thirteen travellers, each embodying aspects of their relationship to the land of Haida Gwaii, as well as to each other and the Haida people. In the end, Reid returns to the use of the inclusive pronouns *we* and *us* when concluding with still more uncertainty: "Is the tall figure who may or may not be the Spirit of Haida Gwaii leading us, for we are all in the same boat, to a sheltered beach beyond the rim of the world as he seems to be, or is he lost in a dream of his own dreamings?"[45]

It is telling that Reid includes all Canadian viewers—us, we—in this multi-species boat from Haida Gwaii. The storywork relationship, including the viewers and their contexts, guides the viewer into a profound relationship with Haida Gwaii: its people, land, and ecosystems. The sharing and partnership forged here is not always easy—some of the characters in the boat interact through an embrace (Bear Mother and her children), others in a quarrel (the Wolf and the Eagle)—but it is a partnership shaped by a distinct Aboriginal way of knowing about equality, mutual respect, and mutual accommodation between humans and the more-than-human world in a Canadian context.

This is the kind of relationship that many sustainable development and business commentators in Canada have increasingly been seeking. David Lertzman and Harrie Vredenburg, from the Haskayne School of Business at the University of Calgary, argue that "global sustainable development will not be achieved in a cultural vacuum. In the global context, sustainable development is by its nature and of necessity a cross-cultural endeavor. With their long-standing use and

Figure 15.4
Bill Reid, *The Spirit of Haida Gwaii* ("The Black Canoe"), 1991. Cast bronze with black patina.
6 x 4 x 3.5 m (20 x 13 x 11.5 ft.), 4,900 kg (10,800 lb.). Collection of Foreign Affairs and International Trade Canada. Courtesy of the Canadian Embassy, Washington, DC. Gift of Nabisco Brands Limited, Toronto, 1991. Photograph by Glen Bullard.

knowledge of ecosystems, Indigenous peoples play an especially important role in the cross-cultural dialogue on sustainable development."[46]

Around Haida Gwaii and along BC's West Coast are found many examples of failed government policy and unethical industrial practices for resource extraction.[47] It is not difficult to find examples of this in other provinces as well. Mark, an Aboriginal art collector and retired oil industry executive in Calgary, told me that, while employed in the oil industry, he became very aware of environmental issues and that he felt "somewhat conflicted" as a result. As he acknowledged, people in his position work within an established structure driven by growth and profit, and many of the policies and practices that corporations put in place encourage employees to feel a sense of entitlement—to feel that, in carrying out their work, they are simply "being responsible." Mark's experience suggests that while conscience and hindsight may lead one to question the ethical grounds of one's activities, the corporate structure tends to demand that one repress these thoughts and dampens any inclination an employee might have to challenge that structure as a respected and engaged citizen. The storywork inherent in contemporary Canadian Aboriginal art dissolves just such a hierarchical imbalance within a viewer's own experience.

In the storywork that Mark shared with me, Aboriginal and landscape art—both of which he collects and both of which find a place in his home—mesh with his own experience, making him aware of his surroundings in a more reciprocal and holistic way. Referring to the Canadian Aboriginal and landscape art in his living room, he remarked, "You know it's so peaceful, it's so uncontaminated, there's no buildings, there's no people … it's serene." He saw this purity as contrasting with the modern environment: "You go walking around town and you see garbage all over the place, and run-down buildings, and … yeah, it affects me … subconsciously." Gradually, he said, "you become more and more aware that people, houses, buildings, roads are taking over the world and leaving fewer and fewer pristine places."[48] When Mark walks the streets of Calgary, the sense of ecological harmony he finds in his contemporary art collection is thrown into relief by the seemingly rampant disrespect surrounding him. The stories expressed in his art collection take on a life of their own: they become teachers, conveying subconscious lessons.

Contemporary Canadian Aboriginal art carries significant political and ecological weight. It communicates by engaging viewers in a distinct intercultural partnership, based in Aboriginal storytelling traditions, that embodies a solution to the socially and ecologically unsustainable practices promoted by mainstream industrial and political structures. This solution is related to principles like holism, reciprocity, and interrelatedness. The embodiment of this political consciousness in the storywork experiences of contemporary Canadian Aboriginal art engages viewers in an expression of themselves as interrelated with the land and the other beings that share it. This sustains the life and importance of aesthetics, particularly Aboriginal aesthetics, for contemporary Canada.

As we have seen, a sharing of knowledge through the arts has always been integral to the resilience of Canada. Today, the process is being adapted by artists to confront the colonial attitudes and behaviours that have contributed to many of the social-ecological imbalances currently experienced in Canadian societies. Contemporary Canadian Aboriginal art continues to engage societies in the age-old process of learning from each other, interacting with mutual respect and adaptation, and maintaining balanced relationships with the surrounding world.

The Spirit of Haida Gwaii was one of Reid's crowning works in a long career, life, and learning process largely concerned with this theme of reciprocity and balance. The importance of theme can be traced through Reid's lifelong work on an essay he called "Haida Means Human Being." In 1979, while confined to a Vancouver hospital, Reid began this essay, which he revised several times throughout his life: it explored the question "What is a human being?" For Reid, becoming human beings was a creative act where "we first had to invent ourselves." This self-invention is more effectively sustained in communities such as early Aboriginal communities, where "access to [artistic/creative] skills was denied to no one." Reid argues that over the course of Canadian history, some people became less human by turning their attention away from supporting this kind of creativity and toward the taking away or destruction of this basic creative ability in others around them. In the end, he envisions a time when Canadians will be "neither displaced aborigines nor immigrant settlers" but will realize how becoming human is wholly dependent on how we creatively invent ourselves in relation to our homeland and the world around us. This is a theme that fuels his courageous, vulnerable, and powerful conclusion: "In the Haida language, Haida means human being.... I wish for each of us, native or newcomer—or, as so many of us are now, both—that however we say it, we can recognize ourselves someday as Haida."[49]

Aboriginal art expresses a unique soul-connection between humans and the more-than-human world immediately around them. In *The Spirit of Haida Gwaii*, not only is everyone equal or "in the same boat," but the "boat goes on, forever anchored in the same *place*" (my emphasis).[50] The storywork of this sculpture ultimately expresses a political statement that reverses the process that destroyed the creative ability for humans to invent themselves in relation to here. It subtly works to rebuild the necessary relationships for a balanced life in Canada. It reinstates Aboriginal knowledges and practices as crucial contributions to the sustenance of life in this place and also engages non-Aboriginal Canadians as equal contributors in this working partnership.

Contemporary Canadian Aboriginal art succeeds at doing this when it is purchased by non-Aboriginal collectors. Over time, the motives behind the collecting of Aboriginal art have changed. There is frequently much more emotion, thought, even spiritual connection in such transactions than in the past. Whatever their initial reasons, collectors have the advantageous position of being able to "hear" the story again and again as they view their works day after day. Each time they do, the story unfolds, from the ground up, in a different context and presents different layers of meaning within their lives and in the Canadian public sphere.[51] The political consciousness inherent in a storywork encounter with contemporary Canadian Aboriginal art can be at work even for people who do not become purchasers.

In another interview, Leo, the son of Italian immigrants who was, like Lily, greatly moved by the work of Heather Shillinglaw, began discussing his experiences with her art in the context of his own background and upbringing. He told me that when he and his siblings were growing up in industrial Ontario, they felt little connection either with their Italian heritage or with the land. Cultural and ecological considerations took a back seat to just living and working. Leo later moved to Alberta and encountered Shillinglaw's art at the same time he discovered the prairie landscape. Her art "confronted him," he said, with something he was not used to in his day-to-day life—an acknowledged connection with the land. It also helped him make sense of his new surroundings and inspired him to think more about his own relationship to the land. He went on to say that Shillinglaw's art and its stories keep appearing for

him in unexpected ways as he grows with and learns about Alberta as "home."
He is inspired "to connect all the time with the creative process" in his own
work. Shillinglaw's art has also helped him to grow more aware and prouder
of his own Italian heritage.[52]

In a similar way, when Reid envisions a time when all people "in the same
boat ... forever anchored in the same place," Canada, can call themselves
"Haida," a paradox immediately arises. When human beings are engaged in a
respectful and accommodating partnership, the self is not destroyed, appropriated, replaced by someone else's way of doing or understanding things, as is
frequently an overwhelming fear in many relationships with "others." Rather,
the self becomes clearer, as an integral contributing member to the diversity
of the world around.[53] The storywork inherent in contemporary Canadian
Aboriginal art engages viewers in an experience where all participants, whatever their background, are rooted in the "natural context." This dissolves the
validity of the "artificial context" of Canadian politics and clears space for
an equal partnership to be expressed and affirmed. Leo's story demonstrates
that his deepening relationship with the land in Alberta through Shillinglaw's
art also helped him deepen his relationship to Italy. "Italian," like "Haida," is
ultimately an expression of "human beingness" and, when in equal partnership with Aboriginal knowledges in Canada, it too can enrich local society,
making life here more whole and resilient.

THE SPIRAL CONTINUES TO UNFOLD

The expression of this distinctly Aboriginal political consciousness through
storywork in contemporary Canadian Aboriginal art is contributing to the
slow awakening of more social-ecologically resilient societies in Canada. In
a recent public opinion survey, 77 percent of respondents agreed that there
is "a great deal" for Canadians "to learn from Aboriginal heritage, culture,
and the unique relationship between Aboriginal Peoples and the land."[54] The
increasing popularity of contemporary Canadian Aboriginal art also demonstrates that the relationships formed and knowledges shared resonate with
Canadians.[55] Indigenous storywork engages Canadians in stories that enact
a wild, accommodating, and respectful partnership in this culturally and
ecologically diverse place, through an aesthetic methodology that has been
doing this same work here for millennia. As an Indigenous aesthetic and way

of knowing, storywork establishes the independence of Aboriginal cultures, art, and knowledge systems on their own terms. This awareness is unavailable through current mainstream, colonial, social-political practices and structures alone, which are generally organized hierarchically top-down from an abstract or "artificial context." The subtle social-ecological partnerships between Aboriginal and non-Aboriginal Canadians within their own stories and contexts form a significant and unfolding political dynamic. Within its more "natural context," contemporary Canadian Aboriginal art helps to enrich, respectfully and reciprocally, Canadians' lives with a deeper experience of living together in this place.

ACKNOWLEDGEMENT

I want to express my sincere and deep gratitude to Frits Pannekoek. Without his dedicated patience, help, time, and encouragement, this essay would not have been possible.

NOTES

1   Tom Hill, quoted in James Hickman, "The Quiet Birth of the New Indian Art," *Imperial Oil Review* 59, no. 2 (1975): 20. Winner of a Governor General's Award in Visual and Media Arts, Hill, a Konadaha Seneca, has played a key role in the development of Aboriginal Arts in Canada, which has included two terms on the board of directors of the Canada Council for the Arts. See also Gerald McMaster, "Contributions to Canadian Art by Aboriginal Contemporary Artists," in *Hidden in Plain Sight: Contributions of Aboriginal Peoples to Canadian Identity and Culture*, ed. David R. Newhouse, Cora J. Voyageur, and Dan Beavon (Toronto: University of Toronto Press, 2005), 1:150.

2   McMaster, "Contributions to Canadian Art," 151.

3   Ibid.

4   Cree artist and curator Gerald McMaster states that these artists primarily help "their audiences understand how to move into the larger world *with an Aboriginal sensibility.*" Ibid., 154, (emphasis added).

5   See McMaster, "Contributions to Canadian Art." See also Marie Battiste, "Maintaining Aboriginal Identity, Language, and Culture in Modern Society," in *Reclaiming Indigenous Voice and Vision*, ed. Marie Battiste (Vancouver: University of British Columbia Press, 2000), 202. One of Battiste's main points here is that "Western education has much to gain by viewing the world through the eyes and languages of Aboriginal peoples." She discusses the importance of respecting and protecting Aboriginal rituals, ceremonies, and tribal knowledge in this endeavour—all of which are issues engaged, operationalized, and shared through contemporary Canadian Aboriginal art, as we shall see.

6　These two points are especially evident through such significant markers of Canadian identity as Northwest Coast carving, woodland painting, and inuksuit (as in the logo for the Vancouver 2010 Winter Olympics). See McMaster, "Contributions to Canadian Art," 158; and John Ralston Saul, *A Fair Country: Telling Truths About Canada* (Toronto: Viking Canada, 2008), 36, 52–53.

7　This point is contra McMaster, "Contributions to Canadian Art," 157, and reflects the art process involving Aboriginal art in Canada as discussed below.

8　Ralston Saul, *A Fair Country*, 36.

9　See Kateri Akiwenzie-Damm, "First Peoples Literature in Canada," in *Hidden in Plain Sight: Contributions of Aboriginal Peoples to Canadian Identity and Culture*, ed. David R. Newhouse, Cora J. Voyageur, and Dan Beavon (Toronto: University of Toronto Press, 2005), 1:175.

10　Ralston Saul, *A Fair Country*, 79.

11　Battiste, *Reclaiming Indigenous Voice*, 196.

12　See Jo-ann Archibald, *Indigenous Storywork: Educating the Heart, Mind, Body, and Spirit* (Vancouver: University of British Columbia Press, 2008). Archibald (Q'um Q'um Xiiem), currently associate dean of Indigenous Education at the University of British Columbia, is a member of the Stó:lō Nation.

13　Ibid, 2, 153. Even though Archibald does emphasize orality in storywork, she also acknowledges that "transforming the orally told stories to another language and another form of representation [such as painting] so that the power and integrity of the stories remains" is possible, as long as there are people involved in the process who "know the essential characteristics of stories" (25).

14　Gregory Cajete, *Look to the Mountain: An Ecology of Indigenous Education* (Skyland, NC: Kivaki Press, 1994), 40.

15　For more on Morrisseau, see Donald C. Robinson, *Norval Morrisseau* (Toronto: Key Porter Books, 1997); and Greg A. Hill, *Norval Morrisseau: Shaman Artist* (Ottawa: National Gallery of Canada, 2006). Note that there is a discrepancy regarding Morrisseau's year of birth; some sources state 1931; others, 1932.

16　This is implied in the concept of *inaendaugwut* and evoked by the pipe-smoking ceremony. See Basil Johnston, *Ojibway Heritage* (Toronto: McClelland and Stewart, 1976), 78–79, and 134–40, respectively.

17　See ibid., 69–70. The innate ability in fish to teach this important responsibility in education and life resides in their strong example of living unseen, in the dark depths, behind rocks (behind the scenes), and yet equally "steadfast in the swirling current" of physical reality (70). They have the ability to live and thrive in two worlds at once—the visible and invisible.

18　For the the renewal of Anishinaabe heritage and the personal life-experience stories, see Rick Garrick, "Heritage Society to Document Norval Morrisseau's Art," Wawatay News Online, April 30, 2009, http://www.wawataynews.ca/archive/all/2009/4/30/Heritage-society-to-document-Norval-Morrisseaus-art_16481.

19 For example, Aaron Paquette and Dale Auger, have both recently highlighted this intention in their own art. Métis artist Paquette, in his personal blog, states that he enjoys "sharing what [he's] gleaned after twenty years of art making" because, in his words, "we're all in this crazy experiment together." Aaron Paquette, "HBC—Half Breed Clothing," *The Art of Aaron Paquette* (blog), September 11, 2009, http://aaronpaquette.blogspot. com. Auger, a Sakaw Cree artist, invokes the traditional practice of people gathering to share knowledge through arts and ceremony, in order to contextualize his own book of paintings. This invocation is intended as his way of continuing in this same tradition of "sharing knowledge with many nations, multiple generations and diverse communities throughout the world." Dale Auger, *Medicine Paint: The Art of Dale Auger*, foreword by Mary-Beth Laviolette (Vancouver: Heritage House Publishing, 2009), 7. Commentators have also highlighted this aspect in contemporary Canadian Aboriginal art, especially through the exhibition context. Doris Stambrau's work with the Iroquois for her exhibition *Lifeworlds* guided her toward discussing Iroquoian art "within the framework of a shared process of social development in a specific geographic territory." Doris Stambrau, "Art as a Mirror of Iroquois Life," in *Lifeworlds—Artscapes: Contemporary Iroquois Art*, exhibition catalogue, ed. Sylvia Kasprycki and Doris I. Stambrau (Frankfurt am Main: Museum der Weltkulturen, 2003), 23. Similarly, Gerald Conaty's recent exhibition in Calgary's Glenbow Museum of Aboriginal work from the prairies involved a collaboration between him, Cree guest curator Frederick McDonald, and various regional elders, Aboriginal community leaders, and Aboriginal artists. He subsequently described the exhibition as a profound sharing demonstrating the "continuing coexistence with all the beings of this world— with the Other Beings as well as other cultures," and concluded by stating that "this art is about all of us." Gerald T. Conaty, "Connections and Complexity," *Honouring Tradition: Reframing Native Art*, exhibition catalogue, by Glenbow Museum Staff (Calgary: Glenbow Museum, 2008), 19.

20 See James (Sákéj) Youngblood Henderson, "*Ayukpachi*: Empowering Aboriginal Thought," in *Reclaiming Indigenous Voice and Vision*, ed. Marie Battiste (Vancouver: University of British Columbia Press, 2000), 264–70.

21 Auger, *Medicine Paint*, 7.

22 See Ann McCormack, "Interview with Joanne Bigcrane [Pend d'Oreilles], Quill and Bead Artist, [1992]," in *A Song to the Creator: Traditional Arts of Native American Women of the Plateau*, ed. Lillian A. Ackerman (Norman: University of Oklahoma Press, 1996), 132.

23 See Leslie McCartney, "Respecting First Nations Oral Histories: Copyright Complexities and Archiving Aboriginal Stories," in *First Nations, First Thoughts: The Impact of Indigenous Thought in Canada*, ed. Annis May Timpson (Vancouver: University of British Columbia Press, 2009), 89–90. McCartney concludes her study on the importance of recognizing the value of the different perspectives that Aboriginal stories bring to mainstream stories by stating that Aboriginal stories "may not only be locally grounded, culturally specific, and highly particular" but can also communicate "frames of reference, or ways of knowing, to further experience the world" (89).

24 For more on Yuxweluptun, see Ian M. Thom, "Lawrence Paul Yuxweluptun," *Art BC: Masterworks from British Columbia* (Vancouver/Toronto: Douglas and McIntyre with

Vancouver Art Gallery, 2000), 218–19; and Charlotte Townsend-Gault, Scott Watson, and Lawrence Paul Yuxweluptun, eds., *Lawrence Paul Yuxweluptun: Born to Live and Die on Your Colonialist Reservations: June 20–September 16, 1995*, exhibition catalogue (Vancouver: Morris and Helen Belkin Art Gallery, University of British Columbia, 1995).

25 Quoted in Charlotte Townsend-Gault, "Let X = Audience," in *Reservation X: The Power of Place in Aboriginal Contemporary Art*, ed. Gerald McMaster (Hull: Canadian Museum of Civilization and Goose Lane Editions, 1998), 45.

26 Loretta Todd, "Yuxweluptun: A Philosophy of History," in *Lawrence Paul Yuxweluptun: Born to Live and Die on Your Colonialist Reservations: June 20–September 16, 1995*, exhibition catalogue, ed. Charlotte Townsend-Gault, Scott Watson, and Lawrence Paul Yuxweluptun (Vancouver: Morris and Helen Belkin Art Gallery, University of British Columbia, 1995).

27 Joane Cardinal-Schubert, quoted in Jackie Bissley, "Joane Cardinal Schubert: An Artist Setting Traps," *Windspeaker* 17 (June 1999): 9–13.

28 For a discussion of this phenomenon of naming entities in the landscape, see, for example, Keith H. Basso, *Wisdom Sits in Places: Landscape and Language Among the Western Apache* (Albuquerque: University of New Mexico Press, 1996), 84–85.

29 See Allan J. Ryan, *The Trickster Shift: Humour and Irony in Contemporary Native Art* (Vancouver: University of British Columbia Press, 1999). The author discusses contemporary Canadian Aboriginal art within the long tradition of humour and Trickster stories in Aboriginal cultures.

30 See Bissley, "Joane Cardinal Schubert," 11–12.

31 Nancy J. Turner, Iain J. Davidson-Hunt, and Michael O'Flaherty, "Living on the Edge: Ecological and Cultural Edges as Sources of Diversity for Social-Ecological Resilience," *Human Ecology* 31 (September 2003): 440.

32 See, for example, Marie Wadden, *Where the Pavement Ends: Canada's Aboriginal Recovery Movement and the Urgent Need for Reconciliation* (Vancouver/Toronto: Douglas and McIntyre, 2009), 226–29. Aboriginal peoples have made many important contributions to the dominant Canadian system, as demonstrated by the contributors to *Hidden in Plain Sight* (ed. David R. Newhouse, Cora J. Voyageur, and Dan Beavon). However, as many Aboriginal writers have argued, Canada's colonial structure is still deeply entrenched within educational, political, and judiciary systems that are characterized less by a possibility for an equal partnership and more by an emphasis on a one-way, top-down flow of knowledge.

33 The comment about treaty making is from Wanipigow's administrator of social development programs, Marcel Hardisty, quoted in Wadden, *Where the Pavement Ends*, 226. It relates to Hardisty's statement to Wadden about the importance and intensity of "sharing" to Aboriginal peoples in this historical context. The treaties, he notes, originally involved a level of intercultural sharing that holistically included the actual raw resources of water, minerals, land, and air, but that has often been concealed or neglected in mainstream Canada today. For more about "sharing" as it relates to the reconciliation process in Canada, see Michael Murphy, "Civilization, Self-Determination, and Reconciliation," in *First Nations, First Thoughts: The Impact of Indigenous Thought*

in Canada, ed. Annis May Timpson (Vancouver: University of British Columbia Press, 2009), 251. Murphy argues, contra Tom Flanagan, *First Nations? Second Thoughts* (Montreal and Kingston: McGill-Queens University Press, 2000), that reconciliation is indeed bound up with Aboriginal nationalism and "encompasses a forward-looking relationship among equals who will seek to establish bonds of trust and mutual respect." This kind of sharing, however, is, according to Murphy, often thwarted by civilizationist policies and paradigms, such as Flanagan's, which predict the inevitability of assimilation. For "sharing" and sustainable development, see David A. Lertzman and Harrie Vredenburg, "Indigenous Peoples, Resource Extraction and Sustainable Development: An Ethical Approach," *Journal of Business Ethics* 56 (2005): 239–54. The authors argue that a substantive intercultural sharing through dialogue between Aboriginal peoples and the resource extraction industries is key to sustainable development in Canada.

34 Saul, *A Fair Country*, 79.

35 Murphy, "Civilization," 267.

36 Archibald, *Indigenous Storywork*, 27. To be sure, there is a very important component in many stories, including Aboriginal ones, whose main purpose is simply to entertain: see, for example, Keith H. Basso, Wisdom Sits in Places (Albuquerque: University of New Mexico Press, 1996), 50. I am not belittling this equally crucial role of art in people's lives but only pointing out, as I also take Archibald to be doing, that this is just a small part of "stories" and is all too often, and detrimentally so, the only part ever acknowledged or considered.

37 Archibald, *Indigenous Storywork*, 139.

38 "Lily," interview with Troy Patenaude, March 20, 2010, Edmonton. For the purposes of confidentiality and anonymity, I have used pseudonyms for all interviewees.

39 For more about these stages of learning as they build into storywork, see Archibald, *Indigenous Storywork*, 47.

40 For more about the paradigm shift being effected by Indigenous peoples in general in order to move back toward a "natural context" from a strictly Euro-centric "artificial context," see James (Sákéj) Youngblood Henderson, "The Context of the State of Nature," in *Reclaiming Indigenous Voice and Vision*, ed. Marie Battiste (Vancouver: University of British Columbia Press, 2000), 11–38. Youngblood Henderson argues that the basis of the modern state shifted to an "artificial context" (15), privileging a Euro-centric, cognitive, or "interpretive monopoly of human nature" (30) with the ideas of Thomas Hobbes and subsequently expanded on in the colonialist ideas of John Locke. Youngblood Henderson sees a recovering of the "historical and legal legacy of the treaty commonwealth" (33) contra these colonialist ideas, to be of paramount importance to the rebalancing and reuniting of the "best of Indigenous and European traditions" in Canada today (33).

41 See Frances W. Kaye, *Hiding the Audience: Viewing Arts and Arts Institutions on the Prairies* (Edmonton: University of Alberta Press, 2003).

42 "The Artist's Eye: Modernist and Postmodernist Visualizations of the Prairie West," in *The Prairie West as Promised Land*, ed. R. Douglas Francis and Chris Kitzan (Calgary: University of Calgary Press, 2007), 375.

43 For more on Reid, see Doris Shadbolt, *Bill Reid* (Vancouver: Douglas and McIntyre, 1998); and Robert Bringhurst, ed., *Solitary Raven: The Essential Writings of Bill Reid* (Vancouver/Toronto: Douglas and McIntyre, 2009).

44 Bill Reid, "The Spirit of Haida Gwaii," in *Solitary Raven: The Essential Writings of Bill Reid*, ed. Robert Bringhurst (Vancouver/Toronto: Douglas and McIntyre, 2009), 244.

45 Ibid., 246.

46 Lertzman and Vredenburg, "Indigenous Peoples," 251.

47 See, for example, Ralston Saul's discussion of the "elite failure" of Canadian politicians and the fisheries industry in regards to West Coast shrimp trawling (*A Fair Country*, 189–91). See also Lertzman and Vredenburg, "Indigenous Peoples," 241–42, for a more general discussion regarding the unsustainability of current industrial trends. This discussion helps introduce their proposed model for sustainability within the context of a case from the West Coast logging industry. To be sure, there are people within governments and industries in Canada who are working to change unsustainable trends. And change has been happening, however slowly, especially as more and more Aboriginal people, with their knowledge and cultural teachings, are included as equal and respected consultants and contributors in the courtroom and on scientific panels. However, much of this particular life-experience story has yet to unfold.

48 "Mark," interview with Troy Patenaude, Calgary, March 25, 2010.

49 Bill Reid, "Haida Means Human Being," in *Solitary Raven: The Essential Writings of Bill Reid*, ed. Robert Bringhurst (Vancouver/Toronto: Douglas and McIntyre, 2009), 147, 150, 161. The essay was published in full for the first time posthumously in 2000.

50 Reid, "The Spirit of Haida Gwaii," 246.

51 During another interview with a private collector in Calgary, who wished to be referred to only as "Crow," he brought me into his dining room where a massive 6⊠ x 5⊠ cityscape painting—with many overt references to nature and the city's relationship to the land—hung over the dinner table, creating an intense effect. Crow described to me how it very frequently became the centre of dinner party conversations, which sometimes included very wealthy executives of Alberta's oil industry, of which Crow was also a part.

52 "Leo," telephone interview with Troy Patenaude, Calgary, April 19, 2010.

53 For more on this process, see the work of ecopsychologist Bill Plotkin, especially *Soulcraft: Crossing into the Mysteries of Nature and Psyche*, foreword by Thomas Berry (Novato: New World Library, 2003).

54 *Contemporary Aboriginal Arts in Canada* (Ottawa: Canada Council for the Arts, 2008), 5. This number is based on the findings of a 2004 Ipsos Reid public opinion poll.

55 A recent proliferation in books discussing Canada in a new, more holistic way and from a diverse range of fields—including language arts, anthropology, history, landscape painting, and politics—demonstrates that many Canadians *are* seeking a more meaningful relationship with their own geophysical and social-ecological realities than is currently being provided through mainstream political and social structures. See, for example, J. Edward Chamberlin, *If This Is Your Land, Where Are Your Stories? Finding Common Ground* (Toronto: Vintage Canada, 2004); Robert Bringhurst, *The Tree of Meaning:*

Language, Mind and Ecology (Berkeley: Counterpoint, 2008); Victor Suthren, *The Island of Canada: How Three Oceans Shaped Our Nation* (Toronto: Thomas Allen, 2009); Petra Halkes, *Aspiring to the Landscape: On Painting and the Subject of Nature* (Toronto: University of Toronto Press, 2006); Ralston Saul, *A Fair Country*; Kaye, *Hiding the Audience*; Annis May Timpson, ed., *First Nations, First Thoughts: The Impact of Indigenous Thought in Canada* (Vancouver: University of British Columbia Press, 2009). The latter three works further discuss this trend as being directly related to or influenced by Indigenous ways of knowing and the contributions of Aboriginal peoples to Canada.

Richard Sutherland

Intimate Strangers: The Formal Distance Between Music and Politics in Canada

On October 3, 2009, Prime Minister Stephen Harper appeared unannounced at a gala fundraising event at Ottawa's National Arts Centre, where—with a little help from cellist Yo-Yo Ma, among others—he gave a performance of the Beatles tune "With a Little Help from My Friends." Generally, this performance seems to have gone down well, at least with the audience and the press. The prime minister's piano playing was adequate, the quality of his singing just about right—neither so good nor so bad as to occasion suspicion about prodigious competence or a lack thereof.

The choice of material was also clever on a number of fronts. If the song was not a Canadian one, it was, as a Beatles song, a suitably ecumenical choice. This particular Beatles tune was especially well chosen, not least for its self-deprecatory opening ("What would you do if I sang out of tune? Would you stand up and walk out on me?"), which disarms potential critics of the performance at the outset. It is also worth remembering that Lennon and McCartney wrote this song for Ringo Starr, bearing in mind his limited range. Thus, the song does not demand vocal pyrotechnics from its performer. The context also helped: it was a singular event and it took place as part of a performing arts gala, a plausible setting for a prime minister to engage in public music making.

These are all prudent strategies for reducing risk through very careful deployment of music in what is incontestably a political and potentially risky situation. If Stephen Harper were a politician given to bursting into song or sitting down at the piano on the slightest pretext, his performances might simply have been tiresome. Here, the prime minister earned points for being willing to depart from his buttoned-down image, showing a more relaxed side of himself. It was a moment where he could be seen as uncharacteristically, albeit briefly, apolitical, convincing at least some Canadians that he has a life outside of partisan politics. And while it is unlikely that we will see a sudden unveiling of political leaders' hitherto unsuspected musicianship in any widespread fashion, in December 2010, Liberal MP Bob Rae did challenge Harper to a piano play-off.[1] Unfortunately, the dueling pianos scenario did not materialize. Shortly after issuing the challenge, Rae slipped on ice and broke his wrist—in any case, the prime minister had not responded.[2]

At first glance, many of the characteristics of the Arts Centre event may serve to reinforce the notion that in Canada, music and politics have little to do with one another: it is certainly one of the few examples of such an encounter. But Harper's performance was in fact rife with politics. The presence of Yo-Yo Ma, who earlier in the year had played at the US presidential inauguration of Barack Obama, may have had some political resonance. Harper's performance was vaguely reminiscent of Bill Clinton's saxophone playing on MTV during the 1992 presidential campaign. (Jean Chrétien also took a turn with the trombone at a National Arts Centre gala in the 1990s). Much more than this, the background of Stephen Harper's relationship with the Canadian arts community adds a great deal to the political dimension of this event. A year earlier, during the fall 2008 election campaign, the prime minister referred to precisely this sort of arts gala in less than complimentary terms: "I think when ordinary working people come home, turn on the TV and see a gala of a bunch of people at, you know, a rich gala all subsidized by the taxpayers—claiming their subsidies aren't high enough, when they know those subsidies have actually gone up—I'm not sure that's something that resonates with ordinary people."[3] These remarks were made in response to criticism from the Québec arts community of his government's decision to cut two arts programs aimed at promoting Canadian culture abroad—Trade Routes and PromArt. The examples rolled out as alleged evidence of their wastefulness were primarily music related—an African tour by guitarist Tal

Bachman, a European Tour by a punk band with a suitably confrontational name (Fucked Up), and a visit to a Swedish conference on digital music by music business entrepreneur Al Mair. Some pundits and pollsters viewed the decision to cut these programs (and Harper's response to criticism for this) as at least partially responsible for a collapse in Conservative support in Québec, a development that may have cost the party a majority government.[4]

So Harper's appearance might be viewed as a way of mending fences with the Canadian arts community. Above all, his performance was unavoidably political because he is the prime minister and almost anything he does in public has a political dimension. Moreover, in performing this way, he possibly achieved some political goals precisely by appearing apolitical. This was immediately apparent in the mostly positive comments from political pundits.[5] Some pollsters opined that his performance played a role in a sudden spike in the party's popularity.[6] This is not to say that the entire episode was cynically constructed in every detail but merely to point out the difficulty of separating music and politics in such a situation.

MUSIC IN POLITICS

This event is interesting because it provides one example of how music can figure in political communication in Canada. There are, however, many other ways of framing the subject. To better understand the possible variations on this theme, we might pose the following questions:

How do Canadian politicians and political parties use music in their communication with the public?
How do Canadians comment on politics or express political opinions through music?

In addressing the first question, we could examine the use of music in campaigns at public events or in political advertisements. This would also include the rare instances in which our political figures have used music, as in our above example. What role does music play in shaping the messages communicated in these situations? In answering the second question, we might examine instances of politically motivated music making in Canada. With regard to both questions, it seems that Canadians do not very often deploy music for political ends, and it is worth asking why this is the case.

If music has not played a prominent role in political communication, one reason may be wariness about aestheticizing our politics. For most of us, music serves primarily as entertainment and, as such, is distinct from politics.[7] Framing political messages musically might seem to trivialize their content. This hasn't prevented Canadian politicians altogether from engaging in the odd performance, as in our above example, or from associating themselves with musicians—for instance, Paul Martin's friendship with Bono of U2, which had all sorts of political ramifications for both parties. Such associations are ways in which politicians and political figures convey something of their personalities. For both Harper and Martin, this was music (and politics) as performance inasmuch as it consisted of particular events and the taking on of certain personas in the course of these events. Such events seldom entail much in the way of content, or the content is so diffuse as to be difficult to articulate. Music has often been acknowledged as the least referential of art forms, which limits its use for political messaging.[8] In any case, such performances are directed more at how we feel about these politicians than at what we think of their performances.

It is in its relation to our feelings and emotions that music features in political events and campaigns. Its aim is to excite the audience, to cue certain moments such as the arrival of a candidate or applause at the end of a speech. It is a signal for emotion, attaching itself to rather than forming the content of what may have been said at such events. So, too, with campaign songs, which are frequently well-known pop songs with recognizable and vaguely suitable titles, frequently repeated throughout the song: for instance, "Takin' Care of Business" or "Let's Work Together," the latter, a Canned Heat song, used by both Barack Obama in his presidential campaign and New Brunswick PC MLA David Alward.[9] The song's content probably does not matter very much: indeed, there have been cases where closer examination of the lyrics could potentially have undermined the candidate or her message.[10]

The music in campaign ads is generally unremarkable—chosen to align with the message. Two fairly recent examples from the Canadian political ads illustrate this approach. The Conservative Party's attack ad that questioned Liberal leader Michael Ignatieff's motives as a politician featured a minor key and a vaguely agitated, unresolved melody that might prompt in listeners a certain uneasiness, which they might attach to Ignatieff himself.[11] A Liberal Party ad attacking the Harper government's economic policies does so to a sprightly rhythm, with the melody arriving just as the ad switches to laying out the Liberals' own policies, thus subtly underscoring the difference in approach while providing continuity within the ad.[12] But it is difficult to see these uses of popular music as central to the conduct of Canadian politics. Certainly, nobody has ever suggested that a campaign has been won or lost on its choice of music or that musical talent is crucial to a career in politics.

Although Canadians are not unique in this respect, there are perhaps some particular aspects of Canadian politics that further limit music's deployment. Music may not generally be representational, but it can be, and much of its political relevance derives from this ability.[13] Music may serve as a marker of identity for many different kinds of communities, including entire nations. In Canada, we do not have an identifiable national musical style: we have no musical genre that represents the country as a whole in the way that, for instance, flamenco does for Spain or samba for Brazil. This limits, to some degree, the ability of politicians to use music to invoke a national identity (apart from singing the national anthem). Thus, it is worth asking just how and what music represents in Canada. Certainly, we can point to music as a marker of differences among regions across the country, especially in Québec. Other regions—for instance, Newfoundland or Cape Breton—can also lay claim to regionally distinctive styles of folk music. But for English Canada, at least, this does not amount to a national music. The enormous range of music produced by Canadians militates against any definition that would adequately sum up its national character. It is, therefore, not an easy task to point to a particular style of music that we ourselves, or others, would identify as essentially or distinctively Canadian. In fact, Canada's problem (if indeed it is a problem) may not be a lack of musical identities around which to form but rather a plethora of them that stubbornly resist any attempt to reduce them to a unified character. Testa and Shedden argue persuasively against a number of attempts to define a Canadian national style in rock music, characterizing such views as based only on the thinnest evidence and as being overly selective, not only in the artists they consider but also in which career phases of those artists they examine.[14] Likewise, Elaine Keillor, faced with the diversity of Canadian musical expression, questions whether it is possible to identify a singular, distinctive Canadian music style.[15]

This state of affairs is in no way essential. In Brazil, samba, which also began as a local style, may act as an index of music's "Brazilianness," but this is only as a result of decades of deliberate appropriation by government through control over broadcast programming.[16] Closer to home, Line Grenier similarly suggests that Québec's national identification with the musical tradition of *chanson* has been produced by "historically contingent linkages of discourses and institutions."[17] In English Canada, the linkages necessary to knit together national identity and musical style have simply not been made. This lack of an identifiable national musical style limits the degree to which music can be used in Canada to represent the country on a national level. There may be styles or songs with which segments of the population might identify closely in Canada, but these would probably be meaningless to a much larger number of Canadians. This does not mean that Canadian music has no elements of nationalism, but that sentiment plays itself out in a different fashion. Rather than being able to hear *how* music is Canadian, we depend, as Will Straw suggests, on the knowledge *that* an artist or a song is Canadian to produce the "excess of affect" of national identification.[18]

The prominent use of music throughout the opening ceremonies at the Vancouver Olympics in February 2010 illustrates both forms of Canadian musical nationalism and some of the challenges. First, there were performances by a number of distinguished Canadian musical artists: Nelly Furtado, Bryan Adams, Sarah McLachlan, Measha Bruggergosman, k.d. lang, Garou. Some of these were renditions of classic Canadian songs (Joni Mitchell's "Both Sides Now," Leonard Cohen's "Hallelujah," and Jean-Pierre Ferland's "Un peu plus haut, un peu plus loin," among others). Both the performers and the songs register as Canadian (at least with Canadians)—not because they offer a distinctively Canadian musical style or contain lyrical references to Canadian places or people but because we know that they are Canadian. The drawback with this form of nationalism is that one does indeed have to know in order for identification to take place, and such knowledge can be unevenly distributed across regions, communities, and even generations.

The segment comprising fiddle music was different—indeed, one could see it as an attempt to promote a particular Canadian musical style, but there are difficulties with an easy identification here. First, the styles were still primarily regional rather than national markers—even if the differences are inaudible to all but aficionados—and its internal diversity notwithstanding, it did not appear to encompass any region of the country west of Ontario. Nor is it evident to most listeners how these regional styles are distinctive from those of other countries. If Canadians identify strongly with this music, it is not reflected in our overall listening habits. For many Canadians, this music is in no way a part of their national identity. The point is not that this music is not Canadian but that it has no particular priority over any number of other styles of music. No Canadian musician would or could be accused of not working in a Canadian idiom, musically speaking. We have made ourselves at home in any number of styles and, indeed, have participated in their development as musical genres. Again, we suffer not from a shortage of national identities here but from an overabundance such that none takes priority nor acts as a particular marker of "Canadianness."

The fiddle music at the Olympic opening ceremonies could be read as an attempt to develop such a national music, but the style may not yet have acquired sufficient weight or cohesion to play this role effectively. The other notable Canadian musical presence in the opening ceremonies was that of Canada's First Nations. Here again, we are presented with diversity, as well as identities that may be vital to a complete sense of Canada but that are in no sense reducible to it. Once again, the attempt to portray Canadian identity musically results in putting more diversity into play, further complicating any attempt at representing Canada in musical terms.

In the Canadian context, then, nationalism in music faces a number of challenges. It must address a plethora of identities—regional, ethnic, and others. It depends upon the audience knowing that artists and/or their songs are Canadian—knowledge that is by no means guaranteed. The Vancouver Olympic opening ceremonies took years of planning and millions of dollars to create and, more to the point, had several hours over which to deploy various strategies in an attempt to meet these challenges. Such diversity bedevils political communication with music inasmuch as any single musical gesture is probably insufficiently representative—a particular problem when musical events in politics are relatively few in number.

Canadians can and do identify with music in any number of ways as members of subcultures, fan groups, or scenes, but it is likely that relatively few of these are accessible to conventional politics. Stephen Harper's performance demonstrates some of the constraints as well. The fact that our musical identity remains fragmented and multiple—and is becoming increasingly so—makes the use of music risky since it can potentially be more divisive than unifying. Even our most popular musical figures such as Celine Dion have a polarizing effect.[19] The risk, then, with using musical style to address Canadians politically is that in the context of a broad audience, it is more likely to be divisive than unifying, if it signifies at all.

Of course, musical style is not the only way in which the content of songs could be said to be Canadian. In the very brief discussion over proposed changes to our national anthem in March 2010, the focus remained on the words: there was no suggestion to alter the music. Lyrics can be explicit in a way that musical style cannot, and they are perhaps a more straightforward means of referencing Canada.[20] For political scientist David J. Jackson, it is in the practice of naming and referring to Canadian places, people, and events that Canadian popular music has most clearly cultivated a national consciousness among listeners. As he points out, assessing the extent of this is difficult, to say the least. One could also suggest that his argument has some of the flaws that Testa and Shedden identify in attempts to define English Canadian popular music stylistically.[21] Jackson bases his analysis on a fairly narrow selection of Canadian popular music. While acts such as The Guess Who, Blue Rodeo, The Tragically Hip, or Rheostatics may offer frequent and obvious Canadian references in their work, such references remain relatively infrequent or altogether absent in the work of many Canadian artists and, again, their specificity may make them more local and regional than national in their appeal.

POLITICS IN MUSIC

Given these limitations, Canadian references in lyrics may still act as reference points for nationalist sentiment. This is surely an important element in politics, but we might also reasonably expect political songs to be more specific and direct in addressing particular issues. We might also expect that, given this specificity, the effect of these songs might be more easily detected, but this does not seem to be the case. Political scientist David J. Jackson argues that popular music should have some role in shaping politics in English Canada but admits that there is no study showing that musical communication has played a major role in shaping Canadian attitudes toward an issue or has affected our basic political disposition.[22] Jackson's suggestion that empirical research be done in this area has not yet been taken up. All he can offer in support of his claim for popular music's political influence in Canadian politics is the brute fact of fifty million recordings sold in Canada in 2003, and the assumption that the messages embedded in those recordings must have some effect.[23] That may be so, but this figure includes several thousand different recordings (the majority of them not Canadian) containing a wide variety of messages, most of which are not political except in the very loosest sense of the word. Moreover, British popular music scholar Simon Frith suggests that in general popular music, lyrics are not the most effective way to convey political messages. Whatever messages such songs contain are frequently lost as audiences misunderstand, reappropriate, or fail to identify the message, as occurred with Bruce Springsteen's "Born in the USA," an anti-war song, adopted as a patriotic campaign song by Republicans.[24] Frith's point is that it is difficult to identify specifically what effects political songs might have on the attitudes of listeners. This contradicts any claims that might be made about the efficacy of song lyrics in intervening in Canadian politics, as elsewhere.

Canada does not have a particularly strong tradition of political song. Just as we have been reluctant to aestheticize our politics, so too have we been disinclined to politicize our music. Here again, we encounter the distinction between entertainment and politics, but on slightly different grounds. *The Encyclopedia of Music in Canada* suggests that "for much of the 20th-century songwriters in Canada have remained of the persuasion that music and politics inhabit separate spheres of life."[25] Nonetheless, political songs have always been a feature of popular music, even if we cannot be sure what effect such songs have had. It is easy to identify any number of well-known musical artists (for instance, Bruce Springsteen and U2) who voice their political concerns both in their music and in their public pronouncements. Some of the most iconic figures of twentieth-century popular music, such as John Lennon and Bob Dylan, made overtly political music at various stages of their careers. It would also be inaccurate to suggest that Canada has no tradition of political song whatsoever. One can find political songs scattered throughout the catalogues of our best-known artists, including Joni Mitchell ("Big Yellow Taxi"), Neil Young ("Ohio," "Let's Impeach the President"), and Stars ("He Lied About Death"). This may not amount to an enormous number of songs, but it is enough to suggest that Canadian musical artists do, at least occasionally, engage with politics directly.

But what is perhaps more interesting is the degree to which all of the above songs concern issues and political situations taking place outside of Canada. Other Canadian songs as well—such as The Guess Who's "American Woman" or Bruce Cockburn's "If I Had a Rocket Launcher," for example—are certainly political but contain critiques of other governments, not ours. Neil Young has a fair number of overtly political numbers in his songbook, but these are primarily addressed to the Americans by an American citizen. Yet the fact that these songs are aimed at governments and issues located outside of Canada does not, by any means, negate their meaningfulness to Canadians. It might be more accurate to say that such concerns reflect our awareness of our connection with other parts of the world and of the fact that decisions, conflicts, and movements in these places, particularly the United States, may have a profound effect on us. This is consistent with Canada's economic and political reality, not only in the promulgation of the view that we are "a trading nation" but also in our aspirations to see ourselves, if not as a major power, then at least as a participant in international affairs.

Nonetheless, whatever our attitude to or level of involvement in Canadian politics, this does not generally find expression in musical terms. This state of affairs may say less about the political indifference of Canadian musicians than it does about political and historical circumstance. Our politics does not often provide the kinds of issues that might move songwriters to voice their protest. We did not participate in the Vietnam War or in the recent Iraq War, nor did we go through the struggle for civil rights. These are the issues that have been the focus for political songs in the United States over the past fifty years. Our involvement in the War in Afghanistan has not resulted in much songwriting. A number of Canadian artists have been more than happy to voice support for the military by visiting bases in Afghanistan but have remained largely silent on matters concerning the conduct or aims of the war. Nor do other political issues—such as trade, taxation, social programs, or health care—seem to inspire much in the way of musical comment or involvement. Here, again, we have to make an exception for Québec, which does have an identifiable and long-standing tradition of political comment through song. *Chanson*—in the hands of writers and performers such as Félix Leclerc and Raymond Lévesque, for instance—has proved an instrument capable of voicing the political commentary. It may be that the issue of Québec sovereignty is relatively unique in providing the suitable conditions in Canada for political musical expression.

In the rest of Canada, however, political songs that deal with domestic concerns are relatively few and far between. David Jackson's examination of the political content of Blue Rodeo's oeuvre manages to raise a few examples.[26] Of these, "Fools Like You" seems to offer a rare case of explicit political commentary. The song celebrates the defeat of the Meech Lake Accord, with reference to its inadequate recognition of First Nations. Even more unusual is "You Have a Choice," a song released by a group of Canadian musicians—including K-Os, Sara Harmer, and members of Barenaked Ladies and Broken Social Scene—during the 2008 federal election. The song enjoined the populace to get out and vote against the Harper Conservatives in the election.

POLITICS OVER MUSIC

Although these may be significant and interesting examples of political music in Canada, they do not cumulatively amount to an expansive or cohesive body of work. If they are all that we have to work with, then we must conclude that, in general, music and politics have little to do with one another in Canada. Music appears to have little calculable effect on our politics and has been used relatively sparingly in this context. However, there are other ways of examining the relationship between the two. To do so requires us to reorder the terms of our examination somewhat, giving us two new questions to consider:

> To what extent is music itself a political issue in Canada (in terms of access to music or control over its creation)?
> How, and to what extent, has government policy shaped the production, circulation, and consumption of music in Canada?

This moves us into the terrain of cultural policy. From the suite of policies that deal with the music industry in Canada, several not only have profound implications for what John Street calls "the power *over* music";[27] they have also, in some cases, occasioned political debate. There is nothing particularly novel in such a suggestion. Street suggests that any discussion of popular music and politics must concern itself with such questions. Many discussions of the relationship between Canadian politics and music reference the centrality of cultural policy.[28] To do this, we have to shift our focus from music as such to encompass the elements that contribute to its production, circulation, and consumption.

Yet even as we shift the terms of the discussion, there are some interesting continuities to explore. One of these is found in Canadian content regulation for radio, which provides us with a standard for determining what constitutes a Canadian musical recording. To do this, the CRTC uses the patriotically named MAPL system, devised by journalist and producer Stan Klees.

Music—The music is composed by a Canadian.
Artist—The principal performer is a Canadian.
Production—The selection is performed or recorded in Canada.
Lyrics—The lyrics are written by a Canadian.[29]

Any selection meeting two of the four criteria qualifies as Canadian content (which means that Stephen Harper's performance qualifies on the basis of Artist and Production). This kind of system is entirely in keeping with a musical nationalism that relies on simple identification of the performer or song as Canadian. Canadian content regulations label material "Canadian" based on the nationality of the creator. Matters such as lyrical references or musical style play no role in this classification system.

The introduction of Canadian content on radio in 1971 marks, in many ways, the entrance of music into cultural policy. The intention of the policy was to ensure a Canadian presence on radio, and this has itself been a political matter. Canadian content regulation—although solidly enshrined in Canada's cultural policy and, in many quarters, viewed as successful—has at times generated controversy, as well as considerable opposition, especially from broadcasters who must abide by the regulations. A Fraser Institute study suggests that the policy is inherently "anti-American" and a restraint on freedom of expression.[30] Bryan Adams and his manager, Bruce Allen, in a dispute with the CRTC over the non-qualification of his hit single "Everything I Do (I Do It for You)," suggested that the policy simply fostered mediocrity by protecting Canadian artists from real competition.[31]

Yet the policy has generally thrived, albeit in the increasingly limited world of radio broadcasting. Even broadcasters wishing to limit its application have not suggested abandoning it, as it has become a potent symbol of Canadian cultural nationalism. Musicians, record companies, and others involved in the music industry have had varied attitudes to the regulations. Adams is perhaps one of the few who have been actively hostile to the policy, but other musicians, including Anne Murray, Gordon Lightfoot, and Bruce Cockburn, have at times expressed ambivalence about the regulations and the way in which they seem to privilege nationality over individual artistic identity.[32] Here we see music in relation to politics not so much as a means of expression but as an issue in its own right, subject to political deliberations and the policies that they generate. In this case, it is the tacit assumption that music is an important means of national expression that must be fostered.

Political disputes over music's production have also emerged relatively recently in the attempt to revise Canadian copyright laws. The issue here has been less one of nationalism (although it has been invoked by some involved in the debate) than of access to music and control over its circulation. In December 2007, just as the Conservative government was about to introduce legislation to amend the *Copyright Act* and to substantially restrict Canadians' ability to download and upload music on the Internet, public protests at Industry Minister Jim Prentice's constituency office and the growth of a substantial online protest through Facebook alerted the public and the government to the level of opposition to these measures.[33]

The bill was shelved for six months and the controversy was renewed with its reintroduction in June 2008.[34] Many perceived the bill as the government's attempt to appease US-based copyright holders at the expense of Canadian Internet users.[35] Again, music was at issue in this dispute. Musicians and listeners involved themselves in the debate through various means, motivated not by any particular piece of music but by music more generally. The debate was also inflected by nationalism. Both Jim Prentice and Canadian Heritage Minister Josée Verner appeared at the 2008 Juno Awards ceremony (the Canadian music industry's major gala) to affirm their support for copyright and, by implication, the music industry.

This was hardly the first time politicians had done so but it was an unusual gesture for a government not noted at the time for reaching out to Canadian cultural industries. Some Canadian recording artists called for a "Made in Canada" solution, as opposed to the measures in the bill supported by major multinational labels.[36] Evidence of Canadians' involvement in the issue was also apparent during the government's consultations with the public on copyright during the summer of 2009. From July 20 to September 13, the government accepted letters from any and all who wished to express their opinions on copyright. In addition, the government held a series of nine public round tables on the issue across the country, as well as three town hall meetings (in Vancouver, Montreal, and Toronto) with simultaneous electronic forums. All this was announced and reported through a government website.[37] Participation seems to have been relatively high. During six weeks of what is generally a quiet season for politics, the site received several thousand letters, the round-table discussions were generally well attended, and the town halls seem to have attracted a large number of participants.

Canadians had to wait until June 2010 to see the resulting legislation, Bill C-32. In most respects, it was substantially the same as its predecessors. Unauthorized downloading and uploading of cultural goods such as music would be rendered definitively illegal. The only sign of any concession toward consumers was that it was somewhat clearer in spelling out consumers' rights with respect to intellectual property. As the bill moved toward its second reading, all of the opposition parties announced their misgivings about it. The Liberal Party felt that the bill remained too ambiguous in terms of its language.[38] The NDP was more critical, suggesting that the bill did little to address the needs of individual artists and creators, and was aimed primarily at satisfying the requirements of "major media corporations."[39] This was also the view of a number of arts organizations.[40]

Nonetheless, all parties voted to keep the bill alive as it went to committee hearings. This is the furthest that any attempt at Canadian copyright revision has progressed in the last decade, but like its two predecessors, the bill died on the order paper as the government fell in the spring of 2011. While it remains to be seen when the new Harper majority will introduce the legislation again, their majority government makes it quite likely that we will finally see an updated *Copyright Act* in the next couple of years.

Criticism of the government's plans for copyright reform may not constitute one of the top priorities for any of the opposition parties, but for at least one new political party in Canada, it is absolutely central—a sign perhaps that access to music and other cultural goods is, for at least some Canadians, a key political issue. The Pirate Party of Canada was founded over the summer of 2009 with the goal of rebalancing Canada's intellectual property and information laws away from what they see as the bias toward corporate interests; it received official party status in the spring of 2010.[41] The relative youth of the

Pirate Party's leadership should perhaps encourage those who bemoan the lack of political engagement by the young.

That said, the party's platform is remarkably narrow by any standard, dealing exclusively such issues as copyright, patents, privacy, and net neutrality. This in itself may suggest the degree to which online activity has emerged as a species of citizenship. Clearly, this goes beyond concern with ready access to cheap (or free) music. But in the media's coverage of the party, and indeed, of the copyright issue in general, reporters most often turn to the music industry for responses to such assertions of consumer rights.[42] It seems as though music is the field in which the divergent interests of creators, owners, and consumers can be most clearly delineated and where spokespersons for each are most readily located.

The Conservative government's decision to cut programs such as PromArt and Trade Routes is yet another instance in which music, among other arts, became an object of politics. The reasons offered by sympathetic journalists for the cutting of these programs, such as the leftist or vaguely subversive character of some of the recipients, suggested that the government might be playing partisan politics with arts funding.[43] This accusation seemed credible in light of its 2007 attempt to control tax credits for film and television projects based on their conforming to government policy.[44] Whatever the government's intentions for a certain portion of the population, support for Canadian culture, including music, was deemed an important element of government policy, and it put Harper's Conservatives into direct conflict with many members of Canada's musical community, both artists and others involved in the industry. Harper's comments on the issue, which we quoted near the beginning of this chapter, did nothing to dispel the impression that his government did not value music or other culture very highly.

The suggestion that this perception actually had consequences for his electoral fortunes is yet more evidence that music can, on occasion, constitute an important political issue in its own right. But even in these cases, we can still see some distance maintained between music and politics. Interestingly, the resulting protest has taken a number of forms—op-ed pieces, press releases, Facebook pages, media interviews, and letters to the editor. In the case of the funding cuts, a YouTube video released during the 2008 federal election by a Québec musician discussing his grant rejection also served to focus attention on the Conservative government's lack of understanding of the community.

Likewise, in the federal election of spring 2011, political comment on the part of musicians came most often in non-musical form. Arcade Fire's somewhat oblique criticism of the Harper government and exhortation to vote was issued as a communiqué on their website, not as a song. Broken Social Scene guitarist Andrew White painted "Vote Harper Out Now" on his guitar for the band's performance at the 2011 Juno Awards but there were no political songs as such from the band.[45] In Canada, most political activities on the part of musicians came mainly in such prosaic forms rather than as music. Even they, it seems, might believe that putting their case in terms of music might diminish its effectiveness.

CONCLUSIONS

Music follows a complex relationship with politics in Canada. Although it remains a relatively minor element of political communication, an examination of the manner in which it appears may nonetheless be informative about certain aspects of Canadian politics. Music's role as a marker of identity, both to unite and to divide, may be particularly problematic for politics in a country that not only has profound regional divisions but also has embraced official multiculturalism.[46] In the Canadian context, what political power music does possess appears, paradoxically, to derive from seeming to exist outside politics. It is not that music and politics have nothing to do with one another, but in Canada, but they maintain a formal distance. This is so for Stephen Harper's performance, for music's use in national events such as the Olympic opening ceremonies, or for complaints over cuts to funding programs.

Music remains largely an accoutrement in the communication of Canadian politics, not a focus. Stephen Harper's performance at the National Arts Centre Gala, in its rarity, its diffidence, and, indeed, its peculiar effectiveness, but also in its ultimate triviality, remains emblematic of music's involvement in Canadian politics. Does his performance signal a newfound support for music's importance? Probably not. Although he seems to enjoy music, it is hard to see it making much of an impact on his politics. This incident will likely not go down in history as a political event of tremendous importance. Given the concern over youth disaffection with mainstream politics, it might seem that music may offer a venue for their involvement. Campaigns such as Rock the Vote in the United States have attempted to use music stars as a means to interest youth in the political process through events and commercials, with varying results.[47] Similar programs in Canada, such as Rush the Vote, have had a much more limited profile and little, if any, discernible impact on youth participation in politics.[48] It is difficult to assess the precise reasons for this lack of success, but it may be that the distance between politics and music applies here too. It is too easy to dissociate the music from the message, and there is no particular reason why youth would be more willing to take the advice of musicians over that of anybody else on this matter.

Politics' encounters with music in Canada occur more frequently *around* music than in music. Music as an object of political expression—from the government side, in terms of policy, or from the side of the populace or artists, such as the activism around copyright issues—tells us that music can be the focus of political activity. This issue is also political and divisive: it creates new identities and groups oriented toward positions within music's cycle of production, distribution, and consumption. This is a way in which the distance between the two is maintained. We may bemoan musicians' marginality, but we are equally anxious to preserve music from what we perceive as political interference, as the above policy examples suggest. We acknowledge that government policies affect the means by which music is produced and consumed in this country, but our concerns over limits on our capacity to make or consume music can be political issues for us. In this way, the two spheres may have a great deal to do with one another in Canada, even while our music is seldom political and our politics almost never musical.

NOTES

1   Scott Stinson, "Two Pianos, Four Hands, One Early Morning Duel," *National Post*, December 14, 2010.
2   Jane Taber, "Bob Rae's Tumble Buys PM Time Before Piano Showdown," *Globe and Mail*, December 16, 2010.
3   Andrew Mayeda and David Akin, "PM Slams Quebec Arts Community; Protests Over Cuts Fail to 'Resonate with Ordinary People,'" *National Post*, September 24, 2008.
4   Lysiane Gagnon, "Insensitivity Sinks Tories in Quebec," *Globe and Mail*, October 13, 2008; Janice Tibbetts, "Arts Cuts May Have Cost Tories Quebec; 'Culture Stopped the Conservative Majority in Its Tracks,'" *National Post*, October 15, 2008; Konrad Yakabuski, "Quebeckers Poised to Support Duceppe's Vision of French Power," *Globe and Mail*, October 14, 2008.

5   John Ibbitson, "Harper's Harmony, Ignatieff's Discord," *Globe and Mail*, October 5, 2009; John Ivison, "PM Picks 'Rich Gala' to Change His Tune; And Now for Something Completely Different," *National Post*, October 5, 2009.

6   Andrew Mayeda, "Tories' Lead Still Shy of Majority; Ipsos Reid Poll; 'They're Still Challenged in Quebec,'" *National Post*, October 13, 2009.

7   Linda Trimble and Joanna Everitt, "Belinda Stronach and the Gender Politics of Celebrity," in *Mediating Canadian Politics*, ed. Shannon Sampert and Linda Trimble (Toronto: Pearson Canada, 2010), 50–74.

8   Richard Dyer, "Entertainment and Utopia," in *The Cultural Studies Reader*, ed. Simon During (New York: Routledge, 1999), 373.

9   "PC Candidate Turns Up the Heat with 'Let's Work Together,'" *The Northern Light*, August 26, 2008.

10 Nick Lewis, "Campaign Songs Can Be Powerful—or Perturbing—Political Tools," *National Post*, February 14, 2008.

11 The ad, titled "Arrogance," has been removed from the Internet.

12 "Turn the Page," Liberal Party ad, September 15, 2008, http://www.youtube.com/ watch?v=2TRpNo75qPU.

13 John Street, "Rock, Pop and Politics," in *The Cambridge Companion to Pop and Rock*, ed. Simon Frith, Will Straw, and John Street (Cambridge: Cambridge University Press, 2001).

14 Bart Testa and Jim Shedden, "In the Great Midwestern Hardware Store: The Seventies Triumph in English-Canadian Rock Music," in *Slippery Pastimes: Reading the Popular in Canadian Culture*, ed. Joan Nicks and Jeannette Sloniowski (Waterloo: Wilfrid Laurier University Press, 2002), 177–216.

15 Elaine Keillor, *Music in Canada: Capturing Landscape and Diversity* (Montreal and Kingston: McGill-Queen's University Press, 2006).

16 Bryan McCann, Hello, *Hello Brazil: Popular Music in the Making of Modern Brazil* (Durham, NC: Duke University Press, 2008).

17 Line Grenier, "Governing 'National' Memories Through Popular Music in Quebec," *Topia* 6 (2001): 11–19.

18 Will Straw, "In and Around Canadian Music," *Journal of Canadian Studies* 35 (September 2000): 173–83.

19 "Song Opposes PM," Trail Times, October 7, 2008.

20 Ryan Edwardson, "Of 'War Machines and Ghetto Scenes': English-Canadian Nationalism and The Guess Who's 'American Woman.'" *American Review of Canadian Studies* 33 (Autumn 2003): 339–56; David J. Jackson, "Peace, Order and Good Songs: Popular Music and English-Canadian Culture," *American Review of Canadian Studies* 35 (Spring 2005): 25–44.

21 Testa and Shedden, "In the Great Midwestern Hardware Store."

22 Jackson, "Peace, Order and Good Songs," 29.

23 Ibid., 25.

24 Simon Frith, *Performing Rites: On the Value of Popular Music* (Cambridge: Harvard University Press, 1996), 165–66.

25 "Political Songs" in *The Canadian Encyclopedia/The Encyclopedia of Music in Canada*, 2011, http://www.thecanadianencyclopedia.com/index.cfm?PgNm=TCE&Params=U1ARTU0002830.

26 Jackson, "Peace, Order and Good Songs," 29–35.

27 Street, "Rock, Pop and Politics," 252.

28 See also Robert A. Wright, "Dream, Comfort, Memory, Despair: Canadian Popular Musicians and the Dilemma of Nationalism, 1968–1972," in *Communication History in Canada*, ed. Daniel J. Robinson (Don Mills: Oxford University Press, 1988), 253–63; Edwardson, "Of 'War Machines and Ghetto Scenes'"; Straw, "In and Around Canadian Music."

29 "The MAPL System: Defining a Canadian Song," Canadian Radio-Television and Telecommunications Commission, 2009, http://www.crtc.gc.ca/eng/info_sht/r1.htm.

30 William Stanbury, "Canadian Content Regulations: The Intrusive State at Work," special issue, *Fraser Forum* (August 1998), 6–7.

31 Larry LeBlanc, "Bryan Adams to Government: 'Get Out of the Music Biz,'" *Billboard*, January 25, 1992, 44.

32 Wright, "Dream, Comfort, Memory, Despair."

33 Matthew Ingram, "In Your Facebook," *Globe and Mail*, December 20, 2007.

34 Ivor Tossell, "Copyright Cock-Up," *Globe and Mail*, June 19, 2008; Steve Lambert, "Copyright Bill Stirs Debate About Privacy, Consumer Rights," *Globe and Mail*, July 9, 2008.

35 Carly Weeks, "Anti-Piracy Strategy Will Undermine Privacy, Critic Says," *Globe and Mail*, May 25, 2008.

36 "A New Voice: Policy Positions of the Canadian Music Creators Coalition," Canadian Music Creators Coalition, April 26, 2006, http://www.musiccreators.ca/docs/A_New_Voice-Policy_Paper.pdf.

37 "Copyright Consultations," Government of Canada, last modified November 19, 2010, http://www.ic.gc.ca/eic/site/008.nsf/eng/home.

38 Kate Taylor, "Can Copyright Bill Survive with All Its Kinks?" *Globe and Mail*, October 7, 2010.

39 Jennifer Ditchburn, "Tories Aim to Get MPs Working on Copyright Bill During Summer," *Globe and Mail*, May 28, 2010.

40 Kate Taylor, "Ottawa Pushes Ahead with Copyright Bill amid Opposition," *Globe and Mail*, November 1, 2010.

41 "Copyright-Fighting Pirate Party Coming to Canada," *CBC News*, June 30, 2009, http://www.cbc.ca/technology/story/2009/06/30/tech-pirate-party-canada.html.

42 Pirate Party of Canada, accessed October 9, 2010, http://www.pirateparty.ca; Taylor, "Can Copyright Bill Survive with All Its Kinks?"

43 "Ending PromArt's Gravy Train," *National Post*, August 9, 2008.

44 Jane Taber and Gayle MacDonald, "Minister Snubs Genies amid Film Flap," *Globe and Mail*, March 3, 2010.

45 Frank Appleyard, "Celebrities Put In Their Two Cents: Canada's Politicians Face the Music," *Calgary Herald*, April 9, 2011.

46 Straw, "In and Around Canadian Music."

47 Martin Cloonan and John Street, "Rock the Vote: Popular Culture and Politics," *Politics* 18 (1998): 33–38; Lucas Mann, "Noted: Tune In, Turn Out," *The Nation*, November 10, 2008, 5.

48 Rush the Vote, accessed October 9, 2010, http://www.vengeance9.com/websites/ rushthevote2/rush_ourstory_more.html.

Christopher Waddell

Final Thoughts: How Will Canadians Communicate About Politics and the Media in 2015?

The start of the second decade of the twenty-first century feels like the end of an era in political communication in Canada. As noted in chapter 4, the 2011 federal election and the series of provincial elections that autumn were the last gasp of an old system that remained stubbornly oblivious to the digital revolution seething around it. That digital world is transforming how Canadians communicate about politics, but much of the electoral apparatus remained stuck in the past, doing things the way it had long done them while the world was changing around it.

By 2015, when Canadians next vote in another federal election, communications and the political environment will have changed yet again. If politicians, parties, and the electoral system haven't moved forward by then, the extent of public indifference that already greets politics and elections in Canada may reach levels that will undermine the credibility and continuing authority of both the system itself and its players.

The classic 1988 campaign is a benchmark against which all subsequent federal elections have been compared; it was fought over fifty-seven days with passion about free trade with the United States, an issue that all sides agreed would change the nature of Canada. It may be more than a coincidence that the 1988 campaign was also the last federal election before the arrival of all-news television in Canada, with its minuscule attention span and its reduction of every issue to the lowest common denominator.

If 1988 was a high point, then 2011 may in future be looked upon as a low one. It was a campaign in which everyone talked about new technology, the digital revolution, social media, and interactivity, but virtually no one used it to communicate with voters. Parties and politicians remained stuck in their ways, adopting new technology but using it for the same old purposes—to broadcast their messages to the public, not to engage in debate that could lead them or their views to be challenged.

Despite all the noise, made chiefly by the media, about the power of social media to engage voters (and particularly young people) in discussion and debate about issues affecting their communities and country, social media had virtually no impact on voter turnout. The number of people voting in almost every election held in 2011 continued an apparently inexorable decline. In some provincial campaigns, such as Ontario, turnout fell below 50 percent for the first time. The all-time low came in Alberta in 2008, when barely 40 percent went to the polls.

Yet outside of Canada, communication largely led by young people using the tools of the digital revolution is contributing to a substantial revolution. It helped overthrow autocratic and dictatorial regimes in the Middle East. In the United States in the fall of 2011, the same tools and strategy were used in the Occupy Wall Street campaign, which spread around the world to protest economic inequities, corporate greed, and the lack of criminal and financial accountability borne by the financial services sector for the economic collapse that began in 2008. Regardless of the long-term success of this movement, it produced a new form of protest that is likely to become more popular, thanks to the tools of digital communication. It remains impossible to predict, though, around which issues such digital activism might emerge, what form such future digital involvement will take, what impact it will have, and which, if any, of the existing political actors will be the beneficiaries and the victims.

Certainly, both the digital revolutionaries of the Arab Spring and the regimes they were organizing to overthrow recognize that information—even as simple as cell phone numbers to call out protestors—is the lifeblood of communication. Who controls information and how it is controlled usually determines the winner in any struggle for public support and legitimacy. The irony is that digitization means that a tsunami of general, and often worthless, information now at the fingertips of Canadians threatens to drown them. At the same time, information that should be publicly gathered and available, and that the public needs for national political communication and debate as citizens is increasingly being restricted and denied to them.

Examples of such denial and restriction are easy to find. They go far beyond those noted in chapter 10, Robert Bergen's essay on the Department of National Defence's widespread use of "operational security" to prevent the release to Canadians of information about the activities of their military in Afghanistan or Libya. The Conservative government, in 2010, eliminated the mandatory long-form census, claiming it was too intrusive and thereby interrupting all longitudinal statistical databases on economic, social, and cultural issues upon which policy debate and decisions rely. That database of information is also essential to ensure that government responds most efficiently to public requests for action on a broad range of social and economic concerns. As two more examples, scientists working for the federal government now cannot speak publicly about their research and discoveries even after they are published, and the broader civil service is constrained from providing factual information or explaining government policies in response to requests from the public or the media.

The centrally mandated sclerosis that is rapidly consigning the federal access-to-information process to irrelevance is a prime example of the challenges facing informed political communication in the years ahead. As the Information Commissioner of Canada, Suzanne Legault, noted in her 2010–11 annual report:

> Over the past decade, there has been a steady decline in two important measures of access to government information. In terms of timeliness, slightly more than half of all access requests made to federal institutions are now completed within the 30-day limit set by the *Access to Information Act*. In terms of disclosure, fewer than one fifth of all requests currently result in all information being released. Far from reflecting the presumption of disclosure inherent in the *Access to Information Act*, the exercise of discretion in determining which information to disclose has been skewed toward greater protection of information. For example, the percentage of exemptions claimed for national security has increased threefold since 2002–2003.[1]

Newspapers Canada, the group representing Canada's daily newspapers, reached a similar conclusion in its 2011 annual audit of federal, provincial, and municipal compliance with freedom-of-information legislation.[2] The federal government performed the worst in terms of releasing documents in response to access requests. The audit found that 55 percent of requests for release of specific federal information were denied in whole or in part.

Even such promising developments for the expansion of political communication as the move to open data—releasing information collected by governments to allow for independent analysis and assessment that can assess the quality of decisions made by government using that data—risks being undermined in its infancy at the federal level. As the 2011 Newspapers Canada study also noted: "The federal government recently launched an open data initiative to give citizens access to federal databases online. But the word appears not to have reached access coordinators in federal departments and agencies, who continue to respond to requests for electronic records by releasing unreadable image files [or paper printouts]. As data becomes increasingly important as a way of holding governments accountable, Ottawa seems stuck in the 20th century."[3] Fortunately, the situation is much better at the provincial and municipal levels, where more information is generally available more quickly and where there is much more enthusiasm and support for open data releases to those interested in designing applications to analyze it. This raises the prospect that political communication in Canada will increasingly focus around issues at the provincial and municipal levels. National debates and discussions about policy options will be replaced by more local ones, further breaking down the ability to confront issues nationally and, by resolving them, develop and strengthen national identity.

In his essay, David Marshall notes the important role that political biography has played in the development of that Canadian identity. Yet such biographies are also under threat, thanks to governments' conscious failure to create or retain records that have been the lifeblood of historians' work. The digital revolution is in part to blame, as is the desire to avoid access-to-information rules. From the point of view of politicians and bureaucrats, if it doesn't exist, it can't be released.

As Robert Marleau, then the Information Commissioner of Canada, warned in a 2008 report:

It is of particular concern that standards for information management seem to be poorly applied across the federal government. Outmoded, inconsistent or inefficient records management practices and systems tend to slow down the process of finding and retrieving records. This year's process also uncovered irregularities and inconsistencies between the information that institutions provided the OIC [Office of the Information Commissioner of Canada] and data collected by TBS [Treasury Board Secretariat].

Clearly, the federal government has not succeeded in addressing the challenge that the modern digital information environment presents. There is now an urgent need for leadership and government-wide action in this area, including developing and maintaining state of the art information management practices and resources.[4]

Despite that admonition and similar ones from previous information commissioners, there has been little action. The situation continues to deteriorate. Poor records management, coupled with the widespread and deliberate refusal to maintain records, thereby ensuring that they cannot be retrieved under access to information laws, risks crippling the archival process. If the trend continues, documents that should be available to future generations will not be, which will fundamentally undermines the ability of scholars to reconstruct events. As an issue, this lacks the drama and immediacy of a revolution or an election, and its impact may not even be noticed by 2015. However, it produces a slow but steady deterioration in the long-term quality of information available to Canadians, their ability to understand how and why decisions were made, and the government's awareness of the impact of the options it considers before choosing a course of action.

It is hard to escape the conclusion that, at the federal level at least, a government hopelessly enamoured with "talking points" as the anodyne response to every question really isn't interested in talking at all, in the hope that government will be neither talked to nor talked about. That poses its own risks for the future.

In the end, the success of the tactic of message management and control may be determined by the news media, the institutions that are supposed to hold governments and political actors to account. Here, though, the prospects are also mixed. The news media, the conduits through which much of Canadian political communication has traditionally coursed, and the journalists who work for those news organizations face an equally trying future looking beyond 2011. Both are only slowly coming to grips with three concurrent pressures that are fundamentally reshaping their perceptions of themselves, their roles and responsibilities, and those of Canadians, as well as their understanding of what the media are and should do.

First, news organizations have spent a decade trying to adapt to the speed and interactivity of the Internet as former barriers between print, radio, and television have broken down. Supplementing these traditional media is a new online medium that combines text, audio, video, and still photography and that requires new skills in storytelling. Television, radio, newspapers, and magazines are all changing and adapting as they simultaneously face demands to accelerate their news gathering and reporting to the speed of newswires. The old days of once-a-day deadlines are long gone, and with them a loss of accuracy, reflection, and perspective.

Second, the participatory component of the Internet has also overrun the traditional media's longtime role as gatekeeper and filter in determining what news Canadians will receive and when they will get it. It has been difficult for them to adjust to that loss of status and influence and to figure out how and if to compete in the world of rumours and opinion spawned by blogs and a world where anyone can instantly spread information to a broad audience through social media such as Twitter and Facebook.

These two challenges are complicated by a third: the impact of recession and a stumbling economy since late 2008 that has steadily reduced revenue from advertising in newspapers and over-the-air television. Hopes that advertising could be profitably shifted to the Internet have been largely dashed. While advertising has gravitated online, it produces much less revenue for the media than it did in print or on the air.

These three forces will continue to shape the media for years to come. Rather than succumbing, some organizations are starting to respond. Past attempts to charge readers and viewers for access to news websites have failed completely, but the arrival of new technology in the form of tablets such as the iPad offer the media the potential to finally start generating income from digital subscriptions. The *Globe and Mail*—as well as international publications such as the *Wall Street Journal*, *New York Times*, and *Financial Times*— are now doing this successfully with tablet editions of their newspapers. The *Montreal Gazette* and *Victoria Times-Colonist* (members of the Postmedia newspaper chain) were also experimenting with charging readers for access to online content in the fall of 2011. In some cases, intermediaries such as

Apple, Facebook, Amazon, and so on may take a cut: how much revenue will ultimately go to the news organization remains to be seen.

No one yet knows what combination of price and access over what period of time will work with consumers. It is highly likely that one size won't fit all. Each news organization will have to adopt its own pay model based on the characteristics of its audience. Although it is early to make predictions, a likely result is continuing pressure to move away from mass readership and mass audiences. Theme-based television may have pointed the way, with its narrow focus in content and audience. The former print media seems likely to emulate this approach through the push toward pay models and pay walls for access to online information from traditional news sources. It is too early to tell whether this stratification will be organized around an audience's income level (targeting wealthy consumers who can afford the hardware and the subscriptions); its narrow interests in specific content; the age of prospective readers, listeners, and viewers; or on the geographic location of consumers of news.

All of this rapid and ongoing change suggests a continued fracturing of mass discussion about political issues and public policies into piecemeal debates among smaller groups concerned about their own issues, receiving political messages tailored specifically for them and relying on the narrowly targeted media designed with their interests in mind. The outcome driven by the digital revolution may be a further decline in the breadth and extent of national debate and discussion that engages Canadians across all socio-economic and geographic levels, in contrast to the free trade debate in 1988.

Other developments seem likely to reinforce such trends. The so-called cord-cutting movement is growing—that is, subscribers deciding to abandon their cable or satellite TV service and replace it with the Internet. This trend is already well established among young people and students, many of whom simply find it too expensive to pay a monthly fee for both cable and Internet. Having only Internet still allows them to watch TV when they want to, not when broadcasters deliver it to them. It also allows them to maintain what is most valuable to them—their ability to communicate with their friends using social media sites, which, in turn, further fracture publics into smaller and smaller groups.

Another trend worth watching is the growing use of satire to inform young audiences about political issues and to encourage them to participate in the political process. Jon Stewart and Stephen Colbert in the United States are matched by Rick Mercer and *This Hour Has 22 Minutes* in Canada. The satirists have all recently moved beyond television to become faces of larger movements such as Stewart and Colbert's "Rally to Restore Sanity" in Washington in the fall of 2010. Mercer's campaign in 2011 to persuade young people to vote in the federal election included appearances at various university campuses, although his efforts had limited effect.

In fact, the links between young people and political satire are becoming stronger as the *Toronto Star* began a partnership in 2011 to print, market, and distribute a Canadian version of the US satirical newspaper *The Onion* in southern Ontario, with a goal of distributing 50,000 copies a week aimed at those eighteen to thirty-four years of age. *The Onion* already distributes 450,000 copies a week in fourteen cities in the United States.[5] Although this may further fracture mass audiences for politics, it might paradoxically engage an age group that currently pays little or no attention to public policy, political debate, and participation.

Into this mix comes social media, with all of its as-yet unrealized potential in Canada as a catalyst for political communication and involvement. Will today's popular social networking sites and those of the future be used by increasingly smaller groups of people with narrowing interests to talk among themselves, primarily to reinforce their preconceived notions or prejudices? Or might social media be the way in which Canadians cross the self-imposed boundaries of their interests to engage in broader communication and organization around political, cultural, social, and economic causes that span the spectrum of political partisanship.

In simple terms, can social media become the political organizers and organizations of the future by bringing together different pieces to create wholes? That would certainly pose a threat to the continuation of the current political parties and to those who derive power and influence from their roles therein as gatekeepers that restrict the entry of both people and ideas into the political and public policy process. Just as the public no longer accepts the media playing that role and instead has created its own media, ignoring and undermining the institutional media along the way, the digital revolution creates the conditions and provides the tools for encouraging the same revolution in political communication. How quickly that occurs and how fundamentally it changes Canada's political system, the participants in that system, and the engagement of the broader public in political communication will be the story of the decade just beginning.

NOTES

1   Office of the Information Commissioner of Canada, "Paving the Access Ramp to Transparency: Annual Report, 2010–2011" (Ottawa: Minister of Public Works and Government Services Canada, 2011), 2.

2   See "2011 Freedom of Information Audit Released," Newspapers Canada, September 26, 2011, http://www.newspaperscanada.ca/news/public-affairs/2011-freedom-information-audit-released.

3   Newspapers Canada, "National Freedom of Information Audit 2011," 6. Available at http://www.newspaperscanada.ca/sites/default/files/FOIAudit%202011%20ReportFINAL%20.pdf.

4   Office of the Information Commissioner of Canada, "Report Cards 2007–2008: Systemic Issues Affecting Access to Information in Canada," (Ottawa: Minister of Public Works and Government Services Canada, 2009), 3.

5   Vanessa Lu, "The Onion to Hit Toronto Newsstands," Toronto Star, September 27, 2011.

Contributors

Elly Alboim works on strategic communications for the Earnscliffe Strategy Group. He is associate professor of journalism at Carleton University and a former Parliamentary Bureau Chief for CBC Television News.

Robert Bergen was a journalist for twenty-five years. He has a doctorate in strategic studies and has written extensively on media coverage of war. He teaches and is a research fellow at the Centre for Military and Strategic Studies at the University of Calgary.

Richard Davis is professor of political science at Brigham Young University and past chair of the political communication section of the American Political Science Association. He is the author, most recently, of *Typing Politics: The Role of Blogs in American Politics* and *Justices* and *Journalists: The U.S. Supreme Court and the Media*.

Roger Epp is professor of political science at the University of Alberta, former dean of the university's Augustana Campus, in Canmore, and the author of *We Are All Treaty People: Prairie Essays*, among other works.

Alvin Finkel is professor of history at Athabasca University and the author of numerous books, including *The Social Credit Phenomenon in Alberta* and *Social Policy and Practice in Canada: A History*.

Tom Flanagan is professor of political science at the University of Calgary and holds the title of University Professor. He served as chief of staff to Stephen

Harper when he was leader of the opposition and managed the Conservative Party national campaign during the 2004 federal election. He is the author of *Harper's Team: Behind the Scenes in the Conservative Rise to Power*, among other works, and is a frequent media columnist and commentator.

David Marshall is associate professor in the Department of History at the University of Calgary. He specializes in religious history and the history of Canadian popular culture and is the author of *Secularizing the Faith: Canadian Protestant Clergy and the Crisis of Belief, 1850–1940*, among other works. He is writing a biography of Charles W. Gordon.

Troy Patenaude is completing a doctorate in the culture and society program at the University of Calgary. He is of Métis heritage and works as a wilderness guide. He is also a songwriter and facilitates nature-based education and intercultural sharing programs with First Nations Elders that include traditional living skills, traditional stories and music, and experiential learning opportunities in the natural world.

Dominique Perron is associate professor in the Department of French, Italian and Spanish at the University of Calgary and has written books on both Hydro-Québec and the Alberta oil sands as symbols of state and society.

Jonathan Rose is associate professor in the Department of Political Studies at Queen's University and has been a visiting professor at Victoria University in New Zealand and at Kwansei Gakuin University in Japan. In 2006–7, he was academic director of the Ontario Citizens' Assembly on Electoral Reform. He has written extensively about government and political advertising.

Shannon Sampert is associate professor in the Department of Politics at the University of Winnipeg. She is co-editor, with Linda Trimble, of *Mediating Canadian Politics* and the author of "Let Me Tell You a Story: Sexual Assault Myths in English Canadian Newspapers."

Florian Sauvageau is professor emeritus at Université Laval and chairman of the Centre d'études sur les médias. He has been the managing editor of *Le Soleil* and the host of a number of public affairs programs on Radio-Canada.

He was co-chair of the Federal Task Force on Broadcasting Policy and is the author, with David Schneiderman and David Taras, of *The Last Word: Media Coverage of the Supreme Court of Canada*, among many other works.

Tamara Small is associate professor in the Department of Political Science at the University of Guelph. She has published widely on the influence of web-based media on Canadian politics.

Richard Sutherland is assistant professor in the Department of Policy Studies at Mount Royal University. He specializes in cultural industries and cultural policy in Canada.

David Taras holds the Ralph Klein Chair in Media Studies at Mount Royal University. He served as an expert advisor to the House of Commons Standing Committee on Canadian Heritage and co-edited the first two volumes in the How Canadians Communicate series. He is a co-author most recently of *The Last Word: Media Coverage of the Supreme Court of Canada*.

Christopher Waddell is director of the School of Journalism and Communication at Carleton University and holds the Carty Chair in Business and Financial Journalism. He is a former national editor for the *Globe and Mail* and Parliamentary Bureau Chief for CBC Television News.

Index

Aberhart, William, 190–91, 192, 265
Aboriginal art: political consciousness of, 20–21, 317–18; and *The Spirit of Haida Gwaii* (Reid), (20, 334, 335, 336–37, 339–40; and storytelling, 20, 318–29; synergy with non-Aboriginals, 329–34, 338, 340–42. *See also* Cardinal-Schubert, Joane; Morrisseau, Norval; Reid, Bill; Shillinglaw, Heather; Yuxweluptun, Lawrence Paul
Abrioux, Dominique, 201
access to information, 21–22, 370–73
Adams, Bryan, 360
Adler, Charles: analysis of, 311–12; methods of, 304–8; political guests of, 308–11; popularity of, 19, 295–96, 297; on Senate, 306; targets of his attacks, 19, 302–3
Afghanistan war, 219–23, 227, 228–29
Akin, David, 97
Alberta Growth Summit, 203
Alberta Surface Rights Federation, 268
Alberta Treasury Branch, 192–93
Allen, Bruce, 360
Alpac mill, 267
Alward, David, 352
Androgyny (Morrisseau), 324
Anglin, Joe, 270
Ansolabehere, Stephen, 173
Arcade Fire, 364
Archibald, Jo-ann, 319, 320
Athabasca University: and plagiarism by Ralph Klein, 201
Atkinson, Michael, 296
Atkinson, Peter, 222–23
attack ads: analysis of, 158–63, 178–83; in Canadian elections, 12–13, 76, 153, 156, 163–65; Canadian websites for, 14, 175–78; effectiveness of, 12–13, 134–36, 164–65; on Facebook, 182–83; on Internet during US elections, 174–75; against Michael Ignatieff, 12–13, 131, 133, 134, 135, 162, 163, 176–77, 179, 252–53; and music, 352–53; and NDP, 132, 135, 175; news media view of, 131, 135, 159, 164, 166; and permanent campaign, 14, 183–84; in pre-writ period, 12, 71, 129–34;

positive effect of, 13–14, 161–62, 173; public view of, 23, 130, 133, 159; against Stéphane Dion, 130–31, 164–65, 169, 175; against Stephen Harper, 130, 135–36, 154, 156, 164, 177, 353; on social media, 154, 182–83, 185; techniques of, 172–73

Baran, Yaroslav, 154
Barbier, Christophe, 40
Barney, Darin, 171
Barrie, Doreen, 203
Barton, Rosemary, 97
Basen, Ira, 176
Bear's Delight (Shillinglaw), 327
The Beaver: Canada's History Magazine, 234–35
Bechtold, Lisa, 269
Beck, Glenn, 300
Bell Canada Enterprises (BCE), 116
Bell Globemedia, 116
Bennett, Lance, 15
Bentivegna, Sarah, 172
Berton, Pierre, 301
bilingualism, 286–87
Bill C-24, 129, 140–44, 154
Binamé, Charles, 286
biography: and access to information, 372–73; dictionaries of, 236–37, 242; "extraordinary Canadians" series, 249–51; heroic tradition of, 237–40; historical progress of, 16–17; and national history, 233–36; private becomes public in, 243–48; as reflection of when they were written, 240–41, 244, 248; for understanding Canadian identity, 249–53; and understanding human condition, 241–42, 248
BlackBerry, 11, 97, 121–24
Blevis, Mark, 96, 98–99, 125
Bloc Québécois, 79, 101, 139, 175
blogs/bloggers: in Canadian elections, 92, 123; and closed-loop networks, 9, 63; commercialization of, 65–66; connection with traditional media, 31, 66–67; effect on politics, 55–57; influence of, 8–9, 64–66; profile of readers of, 8–9, 57–61; reasons

Herle, David, 92–93, 94, 95
Hesketh, Bob, 193
Higgins, Christine, 304
Hill, Tom, 317
Hindman, Matthew, 59
Hobson, Sharon, 221
Hoeppner, Candice, 133
Holtz-Bacha, Christina, 174
Houston, Stan, 211n62
Huard, Patrick, 287
Huckabee, Mike, 56
Huffington, Arianna, 169
Huffington Post, 65, 67

Ignatieff, George, 247
Ignatieff, Michael: and Charles Adler, 306, 309, 310–11; and coalition with NDP, 73; focus of attack ads, 12–13, 131, 133, 134, 135, 162, 163, 176–77, 179, 352–53; as Opposition leader, 109, 133, 134; and 2011 election campaign, 75, 76, 77, 78, 87–88, 99, 100, 126
Ignatieff Me! website, 170, 176–77, 179, 180, 182–83
I Have a Vision That Some Day All Indigenous People Will Have Freedom and Self-Government (Yuxweluptun), 325, 326
image making: of Alberta dynasties, 189–90; for Conservatives under Lougheed, 194–96, 206–7; and Ed Stelmach, 206; and Ralph Klein, 203–4, 206, 207; for Social Credit, 190–92, 206, 265. *See also* communication strategy/strategists
immigrant Canadians, 283
Internet: and alternative party websites, 153–54; attack ads during US elections, 174–75; and *Canada Election Act*, 181–82; Canadian attack sites on, 14, 170, 175–83; impact on journalism, 119, 123, 374; and media ghettos, 51–52; as medium of protest, 271, 361, 363; newspapers and, 5–6, 35–37, 38, 374–75; and opinion polling, 90, 91; and permanent campaign, 14, 184; and sense of connectedness, 7–8, 11, 22, 375; and talk radio, 297; and 2011 federal election, 364; used by Canadian political parties, 170–72. *See also* blogs/bloggers
Inuit, 287–88
Iraq war, 219
Iyengar, Shanto, 173

Jackson, David J., 356–57; 359
Jamieson, Kathleen Hall, 8, 85–86, 157
Jansen, Harold J., 182, 184
Janzen, Jay, 219–20, 221
Jean, Michaëlle, 324
Jones, Alex S., 29
Journal de Montréal, 30
journalism: commoditization of, 46; impact of BlackBerry on, 11, 121–24; impact of convergence on, 117–20, 121; impact of Internet on, 119, 123, 374; who will pay for, 37–39. *See also* news media; newspapers
Jurkowski, David, 217

Kaid, Lynda, 172, 174, 180
Keddy, Gerald, 177
Keillor, Elaine, 353
Kemmis, Daniel, 274
Kent Commission, 41–42
Kernaghan, Kenneth, 171
Kerry, John, 145, 174, 184
King, Mackenzie, 172, 243–45
Kiss, Simon, 191, 194, 195, 200, 276n19
Klees, Stan, 360
Klein, Ralph, 153, 198–205, 207, 260, 268, 276n19
Klotz, Robert, 174
Konrad, George, 278n42
Koring, Paul, 226
Kosovo air war, 216–18, 224
Kozlowska, Tamara, 196
Kozolanka, Kirsten, 153
Kratochvil, Andre, 226
Krauthammer, Charles, 55
Kyoto agreement, 204–5

Lady Chatterley's Lover (Lawrence), 242–43
Lament for a Nation (Grant), 247
Lampe, Cliff, 8
land-use conflict groups, 18, 266–74, 278n42
Lang, Michelle, 228
Laporte, Pierre, 250, 291
Lawson, Tom, 213
Layton, Jack: and Charles Adler, 310; and 2008 election campaign, 165; and 2011 election campaign, 73, 74, 75, 76, 77, 78, 87, 100
leaders' debates: importance of, 85–86, 88, 103–104; setting up of, 84–85; suggested reforms for, 89; in 2011 federal election, 76, 87–89, 104

leaders' tours: in 1997 election, 115, 116; permanent readiness for, 138; in 2011 federal election, 75, 77–81, 82–83, 103
Leclerc, Félix, 358
Legault, Suzanne, 371
Lertzman, David, 335
The Lesson (Cardinal-Schubert), 328–29
LeSueur, William Dawson, 238–39
Létourneau, Jocelyn, 290–91, 293
Lévesque, Raymond, 358
Lévesque, René, 250–51
Levin, Murray, 305
Lewis, John L., 239
Liberal Party: in attack ads, 132, 133, 175–77; attack websites of, 175, 176, 177–78, 179–81, 182; attempt to force 2009 election, 109, 110; and Bill C-32, 362; fundraising of, 142–44, 155; and media convergence, 116; near coalition of with NDP, 73, 75, 98, 132, 134, 151, 162; non-attack websites of, 179, 181; and permanent campaign, 138; and political advertising, 135–36, 158–59, 160, 163–65; and talk radio, 306; and 2011 election, 72–73, 79, 87–88; use of attack ads, 12, 130, 135–36, 156, 161, 175, 177–78; use of social media by, 100, 154
Liberal Party (Alberta), 192, 198, 199, 205
Libya mission, 213–14, 223–26, 229
Limbaugh, Rush, 300
Lisac, Mark, 197
Little Savage (Shillinglaw), 328, 330–31
Livingstone Group, 266, 271–72
long-form census, 371
Losing the News: The Future of the News That Feeds Democracy (Jones), 29
Lougheed, Peter: as critic, 205, 262; image of, 206–7; in Opposition, 190; as premier, 153, 194–96, 270
Ludwig, Wiebo, 276n21

Ma, Yo-Yo, 349, 350
Macdonald, John A., 235, 239–40, 241, 251–52
MacKay, Peter, 223
Mackenzie, William Lyon, 238–39
Macqueen, Ken, 300
Mair, Rafe, 300–301
Mann, Thomas, 11
Manning, Ernest, 191–93
Manning, Preston, 262–63

Mansbridge, Peter, 303
Mark, David, 172, 174
Marleau, Robert, 372–73
Martin, Don, 276n19
Martin, Paul, 130, 152, 352
May, Elizabeth, 79, 85, 98
McLuhan, Marshall, 35
Meech Lake Accord, 283, 359
Meisel, John, 152
Melnyk, George, 334
Ménard, Sylvain, 224
Menzies, David, 304
Mercer, Rick, 101, 376
Milner, Henry, 31
minority government, 136–38, 150–51
Mitchell, Joni, 357
Moore, James, 99
Morang, George, 238–39
Morin, Robert. *See* Le Nèg'
Morrisseau, Norval, 320–24
Morrissey, Ed, 56
Morton, W. L., 265
Moss, Peter, 304
multiculturalism, 306–7, 364
Murphy, Michael, 331–32
music: and Canadian national identity, 21, 353–56; as political issue, 359–64, 365; and political messages, 21, 356–59, 364–65; and politicians, 349–51, 352, 364; use of, in politics, 352–53, 364

National Post, 30, 114, 120
NDP: and advertising, 158, 160, 163–65; in attack ads, 132; and Bill C-32, 362; fundraising of, 142–44, 155; near coalition of with Liberal Party, 73, 75, 98, 132, 134, 151, 162; non-attack websites of, 179; and 2011 election, 73–74, 77, 79, 100, 126; use of attack ads by, 135, 175; use of third-party surrogates by, 145–146
Needham, Ed, 301–2
Le Nèg' (Morin), 288–89, 293
negative ads. *See* attack ads
Nelles, H. V., 251
Newman, Peter C., 243
news media: and Afghanistan war, 219–23, 228–29; blog readers' view of, 61–64; and by-election analysis, 139; and Canadian Forces, 16, 214, 226–29; converging with blogosphere, 31, 66–67; correcting